Servitude in Modern Times

Themes in History

Published

Servitude
in
Modern Times

M. L. BUSH

Polity

The right of Michael Bush to be identified as author of this work has been asserted in accordance with the Copyright, Designs and Patents Act 1988.

First published in 2000 by Polity Press in association with Blackwell Publishers Ltd

Editorial office:
Polity Press
65 Bridge Street
Cambridge CB2 1UR, UK

Marketing and production:
Blackwell Publishers Ltd
108 Cowley Road
Oxford OX4 1JF, UK

Published in the USA by
Blackwell Publishers Inc.
Commerce Place
350 Main Street
Malden, MA 02148, USA

ISBN 0-7456-1729-8
ISBN 0-7456-1730-1 (pbk)

A catalogue record for this book is available from the British Library.

Library of Congress Cataloging-in-Publication Data
Bush, M. L.
    Servitude in modern times / by M. L. Bush.
        p. cm. – (Themes in history)
    Includes index.
    ISBN 0-7456-1729-8 (alk. paper) – ISBN 0-7456-1730-1 (pbk. : alk. paper)
        1. Slavery – History.   2. Forced labor – History.   3. Serfdom – History.
    4. Indentured servants – History.   5. Progress.   I. Title.   II. Series.

HT867.B87 2000
331.11′73′09 – dc21   00-035645

Typeset in 10.5 on 12 pt Ehrhardt
by Best-set Typesetter Ltd., Hong Kong
Printed in Great Britain by T.J. International Limited, Padstow, Cornwall

This book is printed on acid-free paper.

Contents

In order that I might inquire better into the matter of this science with the same freedom of mind with which we are wont to treat lines and surfaces in mathematics, I determined not to laugh or weep over the actions of men but simply to understand them, and to contemplate their affections and passions such as love, hate, anger, envy, arrogance, pity . . . not as vices of human nature, but as properties pertaining to it in the same way as heat, cold, storm, thunder pertain to the nature of the atmosphere.

Spinoza, *Tractatus Politicus*

Preface

Servitude was widely found, not only in antiquity and throughout the middle ages but also in modern times: that is, from 1500 onwards. In fact, between 1450 and 1750, it underwent a massive extension, as slavery came to prevail in the Americas, as serfdom was adopted throughout eastern Europe, and as the Ottoman Empire – a dynamic regime run by a slave elite – achieved a spectacular aggrandizement. Emancipation in the late eighteenth and early nineteenth centuries brought much of this to an end; but servitude continued, with the widespread practice of indentured labour in the French, German, Dutch and British colonial empires, of debt bondage in Latin America, Africa and Asia, and of slavery in Africa, China, Southeast Asia and the Middle East. In the twentieth century the imposition of servitude proceeded a stage further when forced labour became a central part of the totalitarian state.

Characteristically, the servitude imposed in modern times sought to solve a vital labour problem, at the root of which was the transient inability of commercial systems of agriculture to operate in the normal capitalist manner: that is, by enlisting sufficient free labour through the offer of a wage. Responsible for the failure of this basic recruitment mechanism was either the absence of a native work-force, or the presence of one that was unsuited to wage labour because it was hunter-gatherer or peasant. Thus, instead of providing an alternative to capitalism, servitude became a device upon which capitalist systems short of labour were compelled to rely.

The pervasiveness of servitude in modern times is a measure of the degree to which economic production was a skewed form of capitalism. It also expresses the extent to which modern societies remained structured by something other than class. The two obvious alternatives to class were a society stratified by servitude or a society stratified by juridically defined orders (i.e. nobility, clergy, commons). In eastern Europe the two went together, whereas in the Americas slavery provided the non-class element in the absence of orders. The social implications of servitude were no different in principle from those associated with the society of orders. Proposed in both cases was an inequality defined in the law rather than simply determined by wealth. In this respect, modern servitude helped to preserve traditional social beliefs and thus to limit the impact of capitalism in transforming social attitudes and relationships.

The extensive use of servitude in modern times also reflected upon the failure of the modern state to enable governments to secure enough support for their policies, and sufficient resources for their implementation, without having to employ primitive methods such as force or subjection. This applied especially to the prevalence of serfdom in early modern eastern Europe and the modern state's frequent resort to penal servitude, either to uphold the law or to impress the government's will. Although the modern state, with its centralizing apparatus of bureaucratic professionalism and military power, along with its centralizing ethos of king-worship and nationalism, tends to be appreciated as a marked improvement upon the medieval state in terms of governmental effectiveness, the durability of servitude would suggest that its reputation, in this respect, has been grossly exaggerated.

Until recently, the scholarly treatment of modern servitude has been dominated by an abiding point of view inherited from the anti-slavery movement of the early nineteenth century. Essentially, it proposed that the powerlessness to which the servile were reduced rendered them, inevitably, the victims of gross maltreatment. This neo-abolitionist view has been upheld in recent years by a number of highly influential books: notably Orlando Patterson's *Slavery and Social Death* (1982), a comparative overview of slavery; Hugh Tinker's *A New System of Slavery* (1976), a study of indentured service in the late nineteenth-century British Empire; Jerome Blum's *The End of the Old Order in Rural Europe* (1978), a picture of serfdom in eastern Europe; and Robert Hughes's *The Fatal Shore* (1987), a vivid account of convict transportation to Australia. Swayed by the grim scenario that these books depict, some historians have come to doubt the authenticity of certain familiar expressions of servitude simply because they tell a different story: thus, William Hagen now regards serfdom as a misnomer when applied to the peasantry of early modern Brandenburg-Prussia (M. L. Bush, ed., *Serfdom and Slavery*, London, 1996 , pp. 308–9); while some historians think it inappropriate to regard as true slaves the servile elites that ran the Ottoman Empire (see Daniel Pipes, *Slave Soldiers and Islam*, London, 1981, pp. 12–23).

But what was the essence of servitude? No one would doubt that it was a legal institution; and no one would doubt that it represented a lack of freedom, in the sense that the servile were bound to obey whoever owned their time and labour. Yet it is clearly evident that servitude came in a number of quite different forms, some of them far more exploitative than others; it is also clear that one particular form of servitude could contain

differing degrees of harshness or leniency. For these reasons, it does not do
to regard all forms of servitude, say, as variants of slavery, or all forms of
slavery as basically alike. In other words, what the servile have in common
– that is, a legally sanctioned subjection to the will of another – does not
determine their character or condition. Instead of simply accepting servitude as a legal institution, historians and social scientists need to discover
what it meant in practice, essentially by establishing, comparatively, the
factors responsible for the way the servile were treated and the extent to
which they could make a nonsense of the system. To uncover the real
nature of servitude, then, not only a pragmatic approach is required but also
a willingness to regard the servile as something other than the passive
victims of their lord or master.

In recent years certain key works have challenged the neo-abolitionist
position. For USA slavery there is the pioneering research of Eugene
Genovese, notably his *Roll, Jordan, Roll* (1974), and of Herbert Gutman in
his *The Black Family in Slavery and Freedom* (1976). For indentured service,
there is the Canberra school, founded in the 1960s by J. W. Davidson to
study the plantation labour enlisted from the Pacific islands, and, latterly,
David Northrup's *Indentured Labour in the Age of Imperialism* (1995). For
debt bondage in Spanish America, there is the overview provided by Arnold
Bauer in his article 'Rural workers in Spanish America: problems of peonage
and oppression', in the *Hispanic American Historical Review*, 59 (1979).
For serfdom, there is William Hagen's article 'How mighty the Junkers',
in *Past and Present*, 108 (1985) and Steven Hoch's *Serfdom and Social
Control in Russia* (1986). For penal servitude, there is J. B. Hirst's study of
convict labour in early nineteenth-century Australia, *Convict Society and its
Enemies* (1983).

If a great deal has changed in the approach to the subject, a problem
remains which was present from the start: that is, how to handle objectively
a clearly loaded issue. A sense of responsibility for imposing the more
virulent forms of servitude – and thus of sanctioning the terrible crimes
against humanity that they represent – has left an indelible stain on
the reputation of a broad spectrum of nations – not only because of the
involvement of Nazi Germany and Soviet Russia with concentration camps
but also because of the slave regimes historically associated with the USA,
Great Britain, France, Spain, Portugal, Holland and Denmark. Objectivity
is difficult to attain, as scholars in their work on modern servitude – it is
a different matter with ancient slavery or medieval serfdom – are inclined
to be either apologists or prosecutors for the crimes of their forebears.

This book's particular concern is not so much the complete range of
servitude found in the modern world, but rather its role in determining the
process of modernization. It therefore largely ignores the sedimentary servitude that, having survived from earlier times, endured as a passive, imma-
nent social fact. Instead, it concentrates on the white bonded service used
to settle the British Caribbean and North America; on the slave practices of
the Americas and the Ottoman Empire; and on the serf regimes of central

and eastern Europe: essentially because, between the sixteenth and early nineteenth centuries, each played a major part in shaping the way societies, economies and states developed, especially through acting as a dynamic means of generating commercial wealth or as a dynamic source of state power. Furthermore, the repudiation of serfdom and slavery in the early nineteenth century did not bring servitude to an end or even reduce it to insignificance. The book therefore examines the extensive use made of indentured service and debt bondage to man the plantations of the Third World in the late nineteenth century, as well as the reliance placed upon penal servitude by colonial regimes in the nineteenth century, and by totalitarian regimes in the twentieth century: the one for cheap plantation labour, the other for hard labour and political control.

Generally, the book offers a counterview to the progressiveness with which the process of modernization is normally represented, showing how the forms of bondage that have featured prominently in the history of the world over the last five hundred years were not merely a legacy of primitiveness – a leftover from earlier times which societies sloughed off as they became modernized – but rather a positive, creative force. The book also reverses the normal approach to servitude, which is to take slavery as the standard by which the other forms of bondage are measured. Having begun as a comparison of slavery and serfdom, initially the work was based on preconceptions of servitude drawn from an extensive familiarity with serfdom. Applied to the subject of slavery, these serf-based premises helped to convince me that, rather than simply imposed in accordance with the master's interest, slavery was shaped by a process of negotiation between master and slave. In the course of time the study broadened to accommodate the whole range of servitude. This enlargement of scope created another bench-mark for assessing slavery, through permitting its comparison with the forced labour of totalitarian regimes: one that reinforced the view reached by relating slavery to serfdom. The outcome is to make slavery appear, in reality, less harsh than it was once presented, and slaves less victimized than was once thought. In this respect, comparative study has not served simply to provide a convenient means of studying the subject comprehensively but has offered a means of revision, since, with slavery comparatively reconceived, the whole subject of servitude, along with its component parts, can now be seen in a new light.

The seeds of this study were first sown in 1954 when H. E. Howard (alias R. Philmore or George Passant) opened a school exercise book with a faded mulberry cover and, from half a page of notes neatly and minutely written with the fine nib of his Parker 51, confidently, but with an unnecessary air of conspiracy, delivered an inspiring talk on comparative world history to a group of sixth-formers who, at the time, were more interested in the *Goon Show* and existentialism. Needless to say, the talk had nothing to do with the A-level syllabus. The ideas sown lay dormant for many years, buried under the refuse of more conventional history. Responsible for their eventual germination was a conference held at Manchester in September 1994.

This book is a contentious thank-you to the scholars from the USA, the UK, France, Germany, Norway and Russia who took part. Thanks are also due to Doug Munro of the University of the South Pacific who, after establishing contact through an enquiry about G. R. Elton, discreetly impressed upon me the subject of servile labour in the Pacific; to Bertrand Taithe of Huddersfield University who allowed me to give a talk on 'social death' to his seminar; to Tony Taylor of Hallam University who offered reading lists, books and a receptive ear; to Brian Turner of the Manchester Metropolitan University who generously read a final draft and gave me access to his considerable knowledge of slavery; and to Sarah Bush who set about getting rid of the long sentences.

M. L. Bush
Didsbury
Manchester

Part I

The Forms of Legal Bondage

1

Servitude Comparatively Considered

Modern servitude came in five basic forms: slavery, serfdom, indentured service, debt bondage and penal servitude. All shared a special state of personal unfreedom that was quite distinct from the constraints political systems normally placed upon their inhabitants or societies normally expected of their members. No matter the form, the effect was to impose upon the servile a legally authorized domination which denied them choice as to work, residence or remuneration, and assumed that their labour lay in the ownership of some lord, master, employer or custodian.

Nonetheless, while these basic forms had certain characteristics in common, they also possessed considerable differences. Generally, the bondage involved was either temporary or permanent. In the temporary category belonged indentured service, debt bondage and penal servitude; in the permanent category belonged serfdom and slavery. Temporary servitude ended automatically when the indenture expired or the debt was paid off or the sentence had been served. In contrast, permanent servitude lasted for ever, unless terminated by a grant of manumission. Central to it was the principle of inheritance, resting on the belief that bondage was in the blood. Slavery and serfdom thus shared a servile condition that was not only for life but also passed to the descendants, whereas the bondage of the other forms usually lasted for less than a lifetime, often for less than a decade, and was rarely passed on.

Some forms of servile labour were typically unwaged, as with slavery, serfdom and penal servitude. This, however, was not true of nineteenth-century indentured service; nor was it true of a great deal of debt bondage. Furthermore, slavery and serfdom were not, characteristically, systems of consent, although instances can be found of voluntary submissions made to the one or the other in search of protection. People were usually slaves or serfs through the accident of birth; or a financial transaction in which they had no say; or because of a forceful act of subjugation and possession which they had failed to stop. In complete contrast, indentured labourers and those in debt bondage usually became servile by agreement. What is more, debt bondage and indentured service had essentially an economic purpose, whereas certain types of slavery (notably military slavery), along with serfdom and penal servitude, were political devices that provided governments with a means of rule or repression. All this would suggest that, in general terms, slavery and serfdom not only resembled each other but, in being unpaid, hereditary, permanent and without consent as well as in having a political function, they also differed from indentured service and debt bondage, with penal servitude lying in a category all of its own.

Other distinctive features, however, propose a different demarcation. Servitude was found in public or private forms. Since slavery could come in both, it differed, on the one hand, from serfdom, debt bondage and indentured service, which were exclusively expressions of private ownership, and, on the other, from penal servitude which, in making the victim the property of the state, was inevitably a form of public ownership. Commercially, slavery and indentured service resulted from the democratization of luxury. They provided the labour to meet a mass demand for sugar, tobacco, cotton, tea and coffee. Serf and penal labour had a different provenance, with serfdom providing basic agricultural produce such as corn, and with penal labour providing basic constructional services on the building of roads, harbours and railways. Furthermore, slavery, indentured service and penal servitude often involved an extremely painful rite of passage, the new recruits suffering a long, arduous journey to an alien world. In contrast, serfs and debt bondsmen tended to remain attached to their native place. This meant that slaves, servants and convicts were often part of a trade in labour, whereas serfs and debt bondsmen were usually not. It also meant that serfdom and debt bondage – both of them devices whereby members of the same community placed each other in subjection – escaped much of the horror associated with the other forms of servitude, which lay principally in the frightful journey out and the psychological problems caused by abduction to a strange and distant land.

Other identifiable differences separated out the forms of servitude. Distinguishing serfdom was the essentially peasant nature of serfs: the fact that they possessed their own farms which they worked for a subsistence purpose with family labour. Distinguishing slavery was the manner in which slaves were seen as permanent social outsiders. Distinguishing indentured service was the fact that those subjected to it enjoyed the benefit of a terminal contract as well as payment for their work, either through a fixed wage or the freedom dues paid when the service ended. Distinguishing debt bondsmen was their automatic right of liberation once they could clear the debt, although this was usually more easily said than done. Distinguishing penal servitude was a preceding verdict of guilty passed at some form of trial and the fact that it represented an act of condemnation by the state.

Setting terrible problems of definition and characterization for all five forms of servitude is the variety of bondage each in practice contained. The demands made by any one form could be light as well as heavy. The tendency to regard servitude as intrinsically harsh – a natural assumption to make in the light of the gross imbalance of rights and obligations that normally existed between the servile and their masters – has imposed a simplification that was often not borne out in reality. Partly at fault has been, on the one hand, the inclination to use slavery as a representative image for all forms of modern servitude and, on the other, to take as typical of modern slavery one of its most exacting labour commitments: plantation field work. The mixture of leniency and harshness found in all five forms makes it pointless to regard servitude as inevitably exploitative or to grade them according to their oppressiveness.

At the heart of any discussion of servitude is how it compared with free waged labour. What is clear is that the latter was not necessarily more protective of the work-force than the former. To the task of defining servitude, the issue of exploitation is therefore irrelevant. Central to servitude was a system of bondage authorized by law which could, but did not necessarily, permit gross exploitation of the work-force. In addition, a general consideration of servitude has to take into account that it possessed a variety of non-economic purposes. Rather than simply to maximize profit, its aim was often to maximize control, denote status and signal dishonour. For these reasons, servitude cannot be presented simply as an expression of class. For the servile the quintessential concern was freedom, not poverty; for the masters the quintessential aim was to possess, not to exploit.

2

Modern Slavery

The overriding difficulty in studying modern slavery is the adoption of a dispassionate approach. This arises from the guilt engendered by the slave systems of the New World. Scholars are inclined to condemn or to extenuate. On the one hand, they present a horrendous picture of slavery, one heavily dependent on the prejudiced evidence and conclusions of the abolitionists who in the early nineteenth century mounted a massive and effective propaganda campaign to secure its termination. On the other, scholars seek some excuse for slavery: on the grounds that, no matter how bad, it was an economically efficient system of labour, for which there was no workable alternative; or by arguing that, although a crime against humanity, its practice was less extreme in the USA than in the Caribbean and Brazil (partly because the field work required of slaves was less severe there, and partly because North American slavery was less dependent upon the transatlantic slave trade); or – in subscription to a cold war discourse – by reasoning that American slavery was at least more lenient than Russian serfdom. In other words, the work of extenuation is as riddled with special pleading as the work of condemnation. The emotiveness present is graphically declared in the Hollywood-style titles of several outstanding studies: *Slavery and Social Death*; *Time on the Cross*; *Roll, Jordan, Roll*; *Way of Death*.[1] At the root of the difficulty is the sense of a nation on trial.

A second major difficulty is the reconciliation of what slavery meant in law with what it actually meant in practice. The slave was formally the disposable possession of his master, the latter's domination stopping only short of the right to maim and kill. Slaves, therefore, had some recognition in the law as persons, but the rights it assigned to them were minimal. Usually lacking were autonomous legal rights to family or property, since both were subjected to the master's superior claim. Moreover, the law awarded the slave neither a social nor a political identity. Politically, he was represented by his master; socially, he was part and parcel of his master's effects. Rather than protecting the slave, then, the law appeared to set him or her up as the eternal victim.

In reality, however, slaves acquired a very different persona from the one assigned to them by law, since customs and accepted practices awarded them a social identity in their own right, rather than recognizing them simply as an appendage of the master. This makes it quite inappropriate to regard them, in the law-given manner, as existing in a state of social death that started with enslavement and only ended with manumission.[2] Establishing the slave as a social being was partly the *peculium* – that is, the wealth a slave was allowed to acquire and possess; partly the family relationships slaves were able to sustain; partly the right slaves were awarded to share their master's religion; partly the slaves' ability to create an independent culture; partly the traditional practices and liberties established as customs that masters were obliged to respect.

Unless forfeited in punishment for a crime, the *peculium* was usually regarded as the slave's possession for life. As a right of property, it clearly differed from what freemen were entitled to enjoy, since it was not sanctioned in law as a personal possession of the slave and, upon the slave's death, was legally assigned to the master. Yet the usage and provenance of the *peculium* offered recognition of the slave's membership of society. In the first place, it could be used to purchase manumission, thus demonstrating society's willingness to accept that it belonged rightfully to the slave. In the second place, it was accepted as a means by which a slave could acquit himself of a conviction: that is, through the payment of a fine. This applied to offences committed not only against the master but also against other free persons. That the slave was held publicly responsible for the latter offences – rather than having them simply charged to the master's account – suggests that, in spite of being legal defined as a chattel, he or she was accepted by society at large as a social being.

Sustaining the *peculium* in modern times was the customary right slaves enjoyed to make money: through selling, for example, produce collected in the wild and grown on their own plots of land; or by exploiting their own special skills as craftsmen or traders; or from selling their physical labour and personal services. The practice of allowing slaves free time, during which they could work for themselves, was widespread. In this way, the *peculium* provided for slaves, within the framework of servitude, a degree of economic independence, the basis of a moral economy and a recognized social identity that transcended the confines of the master's household and plantation.

Slaves also attained social identity through their own family relationships. Often uprooted from their homeland and planted in an alien world, the slave tended to be seen as an individual unit of labour freed from the complications of kinship. He has been labelled 'a genealogical isolate'.[3] Legally in the British Caribbean and the USA, and in practice in Latin America

and the French and Spanish Caribbean, for example, masters could separate partners or take away their children. But how often did this happen?
In reality, kinship among slaves was often respected and, even when their
sexual unions were denied the formal sanction of marriage, partnership
between slaves tended to receive customary recognition. What is more,
their offspring were often recognized, as rightful heirs to their parents'
possessions. In this respect, slave families acquired a dynastic dimension
that rendered them little different from the families of the free. Furthermore, in Africa, India and Southeast Asia slaves could be, in the peasant
manner, awarded a plot of land which they had to work for the benefit of
the master with the labour provided by their own families. Here, the slave's
family was integral to the system. The same could be said of those peasant
communities in parts of modern India that at some point had been enslaved
by their conquerors and remained in bondage thereafter. When slavery
shaded into a form of serfdom, it inevitably operated through the medium
of the family.[4]

Slaves also gained social recognition by adopting the religion of their
masters. Enslavement frequently presupposed alien religious beliefs. The
most extensive enslavements of modern times involved Christians subjugating non-Christians, and Muslims subjugating non-Muslims. However,
in both cases, enslavement did not rule out religious conversion but rather
promoted it. Slavery acted as an instrument of evangelization second only
to missionary work. The Muslims and Pagans shipped as slaves to the New
World were admitted to the Christian faith through baptism. Although this
removed the justification for their original enslavement, they remained in
bondage, as did their children. Likewise, the Christians and Pagans enslaved
by Islamic regimes were not denied admission to the Muslim religion
but encouraged to convert. As a result, an anomalous distinction existed
between enslavement, which was exclusively imposed upon Pagans and
infidels, and the practice of slavery, which allowed slaves and masters to
share the same faith. In acknowledging the slave's humanity and moral
responsibility, the willingness of masters to allow slaves to share their
religion represented a major admission that they all belonged to the same
society. Systems of indigenous slavery – such as existed in Africa and
Asia – where members of the same faith were allowed to enslave each other,
had the same effect.

Ideally, the slave was the automaton, programmed to do no more than
efficiently fulfil the master's wishes. But this ideal was thwarted by the
counter-culture slaves were able to develop: a private world, often shrouded
in secrecy, to which the master had no access and over which he held no
sway. Central to this other world was a culture resting upon alien kinship
patterns and practices derived from the free homeland. In the New World,
for example, masters found themselves with a slave work-force deeply
moved by customs derived from Africa which, in the course of time, inter-
mixed with European ways to achieve a culture distinct from both. Impart-

ing a social identity to the slaves, then, was possession of an independent culture that masters resented but could not deny. The ideal of the slaves as automata was also upset by the traditional practices and liberties that slave communities established and that masters had to accept: in the form of free time, the length of the working day, feasts provided by the master, and the rations of food and clothing slaves were entitled to receive. Little of this was upheld in the law but custom made up for that.

Slave rights – to *peculium*, to families, to the religion of the free, to an alternative culture, to customary liberties – were conceded essentially because, as a means of control, the whip was not enough. Incentives had to be offered to make slaves work well and loyally; in the same cause, respect had to be shown for the ways and customs they valued; while the social controls exerted over freemen, through religions that emphasized the virtue of obedience, had also to be employed for the ordering of slaves. In the same manipulative cause, differential privileges were granted, enabling the lower slaves to be controlled by hope of promotion and the upper slaves to be controlled by fear of demotion.

Obliging the masters to rule by other means than force was the slaves' reputation for resistance. Slaves could and did flee; they worked badly in response to maltreatment; they stole excessively to get their own back. In response, fantasies easily developed in the minds of the masters and their families of imminent violence and constant subterfuge, leading them readily to believe that slaves were plotting revolt or committing covert acts of arson and poison. The application of force, it was felt, might be counterproductive and lead to further resistance, calling for repression on a prohibitively expensive scale. Also shaping the attitude of the masters was the intrinsic nature of slavery. After all, slaves could not be won over by lowering rents or raising wages, since neither payment constituted a normal part of the slave–master relationship. Therefore ameliorative steps had to be taken which recognized the slaves' humanity and showed respect for their material and cultural needs.

Nonetheless, force was undoubtedly an integral part of slavery. Most slaves, after all, did not choose to be unfree; nor did they wish to remain in bondage. But, rather than simply imposed, the actual condition of slavery was something conceded: the result of the master's inability to control his slaves as a work-force simply by exercising the rights of domination conferred upon him by law. In this respect, to describe slavery, in the Marxist manner, as quintessentially 'a relation of domination' or, in the adapted Patterson manner, as 'a state of powerlessness', conceals what slavery meant in practice.[5] The law on slavery expressed the master's view of the slave. Prejudiciously, it defined what slaves did not have, thus treating them in a diametrically opposite way to the freeman. Yet the slave was never, in practice, the nullity laid down by law. Within the shell of dependence and subjection sat a kernel of autonomy, resting upon customary rights and liberties which the masters had to tolerate in order to make the system work. In this respect, the rigours of slavery were effectively warded off by generations of slaves who, operating effectively within the regime, ensured that the slave condition was the product not of the master's will but of a process of reciprocity between him and them.

Making slavery tolerable was not simply the liberties the slaves gained as slaves but also a tangible prospect of becoming assimilated into the free community. All the terrible drawbacks of slavery became bearable when it appeared as no more than a temporary state. Within most modern slave systems, slaves could expect that either they, or at least their children, would be freed. Although there were glaring exceptions – notably in the USA South, the British Caribbean and much of Hindu India – slavery tended to be a tunnel of servitude lit from one end by the memory of freedom not so long ago enjoyed, and from the other by the prospect of its reclamation. Slave masters liberated individual slaves for several reasons: to make money from the manumission price; to escape the obligation of maintaining workers whose age placed them beyond useful service; to earn virtue, even salvation; and to encourage good work.

That slavery was not in practice just a legal construct is also evident in the variety of conditions under which it operated. Apart from the master's meanness or benevolence, much depended upon function. Generally, those slaves employed as servants or servitors were better treated than those employed as labourers. The same could be said for skilled craftsmen. Not surprisingly, public slaves were better treated than private slaves, simply because they tended to be engaged as servitors, many of them as elite soldiers, administrators or household officials, whereas private slaves were mostly engaged in some form of manual labour.

Quite apart from having to perform less back-breaking tasks, slaves in service and skilled craftsmen had the opportunity to secure favours through their work. This was especially the case with slaves who served their masters as sexual partners, or who tended the persons and households of the master, mistress and their children. In addition, the bonds of familiarity that developed between household servants and the master's family qualified them to earn not only lenient treatment but also manumission. The prospects of liberation and reward provided them, in return, with a strong incentive to work well, even more so because the individual nature of their duties gave them a good chance of receiving the credit for what they did. Furthermore, slaves in managerial positions, or who were skilled craftsmen, could often relieve their lot by acquiring slaves of their own; or they could amass sufficient *peculium* to purchase their own freedom.

Opportunities to secure individual credit were less available to slave labourers who, as a result of working *en masse* down mines or on plantations, tended to obtain personal recognition from the master only when singled out for punishment. Moreover, their chances of accumulating wealth were minimal; their health easily broke down under the weight of the work; they could suffer from malnutrition because of the master's inefficiency or meanness; their accommodation could be primitive in the extreme; their dependence upon a supply of clothing issued from the master meant wearing a uniform of coarse cloth that, as well as humiliating to wear, was often an inadequate protection against the summer heat and the winter cold. Yet, compared with domestic slaves, labouring slaves enjoyed a greater freedom to create and practise their own culture, especially if they worked on large plantations. Some labouring slaves, moreover, were better off than others. Much depended upon whether or not they were engaged in large-scale commercial operations geared to the export market: supplying the domestic market or the master's household meant far less onerous work. Much depended upon the nature of the crop, sugar involving heavier work than cotton or tobacco or growing food; and much depended upon the way slaves could exploit their free time. Plantation slaves, for example, could receive plots of land for growing their own produce, or were allowed to scavenge nearby wasteland or waters. Likewise, some mining slaves were well placed to escape their lot, especially if they were engaged in extracting precious metals: thus, in parts of Latin America (e.g. the Colombian Chocó and Minas Gerais in Brazil) slaves were allowed to mine in their free time, on condition that they sold what they produced to the mine owners. Their keenness to exploit this moneymaking opportunity was reflected in a high rate of enfranchisement, as they used their earnings to purchase manumission.[6] Since so much depended upon the opportunity to put free time to profitable use, slaves living in or near large towns enjoyed a decisive material advantage over slaves lodged in the depths of the countryside. Favouring service slaves was their inclination to live in towns and to benefit from the trading and wage-earning opportunities found there.

Among the slaves in service, easily the best treated were the military servitors of the Ottoman Empire, Safavid Persia and a number of Islamic states situated in North and West Africa. These slaves comprised a ruling elite, in possession of power as well as wealth. Their essential purpose was to give the ruler a means of action independent of his leading subjects and one that he could fully control, although, in reality, he tended to fall under the sway of his slaves. Their existence gives a whole new meaning to the term 'slave', so much so that some scholars argue that servitors of this nature were really freemen, likened to slaves simply to emphasize their humility in relation to the ruler. Yet, in reality, many were genuine, not metaphorical, slaves. Some were purchased from the slave market; others were enslaved as a result of capture in battle; the rest were readily donated as slave tribute by subject peoples; and all remained slaves until formally freed.[7]

Although virtually unknown in the modern West, enslavement by consent occurred frequently in other parts of the modern world, notably in Africa, India, Southeast Asia and China, where men sold themselves or their kin into slavery to clear debts or avoid starvation, and chose slavery to escape the death sentence or to secure assimilation into an alien community. Enslavement of this nature produced a somewhat different type of slavery from enslavement by compulsion, although strong similarities existed between the two in that both entailed a bondage that was at least for life and involved the slave's ownership by his master. On the other hand, central to enslavement by consent was the issue of protection, and normally absent was the racial distinction common to Western slavery. In fact, enslavement by consent was usually indigenous, with individuals becoming subjected to other members of the same society. The absence of religious objection encouraged the practice. The prohibition of enslavement within the faith was a feature of Islam and Western Christianity, but not of the Greek Orthodox Church, Hinduism, Confucianism and Buddhism.[8] As a result, fresh slaves in India, Southeast Asia, Russia and China could be recruited from the native population, notably in times of famine.

Slaves by consent had a great deal to gain from forsaking their free status: life, in the case of criminals who thus escaped the death penalty; survival, in the case of families who escaped starvation by acquiring a master; social acceptance, in certain African societies where slavery was the price of admission; wealth and power, in the Muslim regimes where enslavement was the entry qualification to a political elite from which the ruler selected his leading officials and officers. Yet consent could give way to compulsion, especially when the bondage agreed to by the parents was transmitted to the children. Moreover, enslavement in the modern period typically involved an act of compulsion determined, if not by birth, then by capture or sale. Of those subjected to involuntary enslavement – the majority of slaves in modern times and probably at any other time – those receiving the worst deal were the ones designated for human sacrifice. By the late modern period this practice was on the decline. It was a device for appeasing the gods that European colonists, content with the sacrifice of Christ, sought eagerly to stamp out, both in the Americas and in Africa. Nonetheless, in its place the same colonists often substituted something almost as inhumane: plantation slavery. In Brazil and the Caribbean, slavery took on an added dimension of oppressiveness, through the development of the sugar plantation manned by slaves and geared to the export trade, although, in the course of time, its harshness was alleviated by the customary rights slaves were conceded in order to secure their cooperation.

Defining the essentials of slavery is difficult because of the variety of conditions it could assume. If there were rich as well as poor slaves, it is not possible to regard all slaves as the victims of economic exploitation; if there were powerful as well as downtrodden slaves, all slaves cannot be regarded as intrinsically powerless. And in view of the discrepancies that normally existed between slavery in law and slavery in practice, it does not help to dwell upon the slaves' chattel status; nor even upon the slave's subjection to the will of his master. Combating the law was the buffer of custom. Whereas the law catered for the master, custom served the slave, with the slave–master relationship resting upon a conjunction of the two.

At the root of slavery was the distinction societies made between the free and the unfree, or between the good and the debased, or between the pure and the polluted. Typically, those located in the unfree/debased/polluted category were definably slaves. Slavery was usually taken as a mark of dishonour. This sprang from the nature of enslavement and the degrading way it made one person the possession of another, thanks to capture or donation. The stain of this humiliation, moreover, unless erased by manumission, seeped down from one generation to the next. For all these reasons, the condition of slavery was never relished by its victims, no matter how beneficial. No one could take pride in being a slave.

Slavery was not alone in being deeply dishonourable. Penal servitude and serfdom shared the same fate, although not to the same degree. The shame of serfdom was diluted when, as was often the case, the bulk of society consisted of peasants and the majority of them were serfs. Furthermore, the dishonour attached to convicts was not something intrinsic to their human nature: simply a consequence of their conviction, it was extinguished by their release. The same could be said for debt bondage and indentured service. In fact, there was nothing to match the dishonour of the slave.

Besides an automatic lack of honour, the second basic attribute of slavery was a frail right to inherit wealth. Because the offspring of slaves usually acquired their parents' status, the disposable wealth they stood to inherit tended to remain the proprietorial right of the master. This was not true of other forms of servitude. In contrast to slaves, serfs possessed inheritable property rights which guaranteed a fixed rent, access to the common and permanent tenancy, rights vividly declared in a saying of the Polish and Russian peasantry: 'We are yours but the land is ours.'

A third attribute of slavery lay in the limited control slaves exercised over their own labour. Quintessentially, this labour was the property of the master. The main work performed by slaves was normally decided for them. Tied to their employer, their means of lawful objection to what was demanded of, or done to, them was limited in the extreme. What is more, the payment they received for their main work was not renegotiable. Much of their labour had no value for them. Withdrawing it by flight rendered them fugitives from the law; withdrawing it by refusal to work easily led to a flogging. Their limited labour rights left slaves less well off than serfs, whose services tended to be arranged by negotiation and defined in custumals, and who mostly worked for themselves on their own farms. Slaves were also less well off than indentured servants, whose terms of work were set out in a contract. On the other hand, their lot bore no comparison with the victims of the forced-labour systems developed in the twentieth century by totalitarian regimes where, in contrast to slavery, the acquisition of labour involved no capital outlay and the absence of replacement costs removed all restraint on its maltreatment. In these circumstances, it did not matter much if labour was worked to death. To treat slaves in that manner made no economic sense since it simply destroyed a capital asset.

Slavery was by no means free of brutality. Its distinctive punishment was a flogging. This resulted from the priority placed on the extraction of labour. Ruled out therefore were counter-productive punishments such as long-term imprisonment or starvation. For this reason the imprisonments imposed in Christian societies tended to be confined to Sundays, the slave's day of rest. Moreover, with no wages to reduce or rents to increase, the master's repertoire of punishment was necessarily very limited. The principal forms of punishment had to be those that did not remove the slaves from work. One was the practice of hobbling with chains, a device to prevent flight; another was the use of the whip, the pain intensified by rubbing salt, or dripping hot fat, on to the lash marks; yet another was assignment to more oppressive work. As a punishment, whipping was probably used more extensively on slaves than upon any other form of servitude, largely because serfs, indentured servants, debt bondsmen and convicts could be called to order in other ways: notably by increasing the rents and services extracted from serfs, by reducing or docking the wages of indentured servants or debt bondsmen, and by extending the sentences, increasing the workload and reducing the food allowances of convicts.

A final distinctive attribute of modern slavery lay in its immigrant nature. Compulsory enslavement typically involved a journey to a strange land, not for a fixed period, as with indentured service, but for ever. Through enslavement, men and women found themselves forcibly attached to societies far removed, both geographically and culturally, from those into which they had been born. This demand for immigrant slaves was preserved by the high rates of manumission practised in Islamic regimes, which rendered slavery a form of assimilation (with outsiders continually introduced as slaves and their children freed as natives). Demand was also maintained by the low fertility and high mortality associated with Caribbean and Brazilian slavery. By continually calling for fresh supplies of slaves, these factors ensured a high proportion of first-generation immigrants within the slave population. Working against the importation of slaves were the practices of enslavement by consent found in Africa, India, Southeast Asia and China. Working to the same effect was the capacity of slave communities to reproduce themselves in societies that permitted little manumission. This created in the southern states of the USA a slave system in which large numbers of slaves resided in the country of their birth. On the other hand, many did not live in, or close to, their birthplace thanks to the latter-day profitability of cotton in the Deep South which created an internal traffic in slaves that could be as disturbing as the external one from Africa.[9]

Slaves tended not to be as indigenous as serfs or debt bondsmen. Moreover, those whose bondage often began with a journey to a strange land – notably convicts dispatched to distant labour camps or the indentured servants sent overseas to distant colonies (from India to the Caribbean, for example) – often left with the hope of returning. Indentured servants even consented to the journey outward and selected its destination. In contrast, transported slaves had no say in the matter and virtually no prospect of returning to their ancestral home.

As in antiquity, modern slavery came in both public and private forms. Gone by 1500 was the equivalent of the *servi publici* who, in the manner of ancient Greece and republican Rome, had belonged to the community. Still in existence, however, was the equivalent of the *familia Caesaris*, public slaves belonging to the ruler and used for running the political system. Although absent from the modern West, they were frequently found in the Islamic world. In addition, public slaves were created in the modern period, notably in modern Russia and China, through the humane practice of allowing criminals sentenced to death to have their penalty commuted to enslavement for life.[10]

The spectacular eastern and western aggrandizement of the Ottoman Empire in the fifteenth and sixteenth centuries, and the regime's reliance upon the sultan's slaves for military and administrative purposes, brought public slavery to world prominence as a system of government; while the importance the Americas acquired in the early modern period, as a supplier of cash crops grown on slave-operated plantations, brought private slavery to the fore as a system of economic production.

The European powers of the Atlantic seaboard actively promoted slavery in the New World through the medium of colonial rule, but gave it no encouragement at home. Not that it failed to exist in Europe. In countries with access to Africa, especially those engaged in transporting slaves to the New World (i.e. Portugal, the Dutch Republic, England, France and Spain), slaves were to be found, notably employed in domestic service and usually confined to the big cities.[11] In Europe slave labour had been a mode of agri-culture once upon a time, a legacy of the Roman Empire. It was phased out – in the empire's declining years, and following its fall – as the great estates came to be worked by serfs. In modern Europe, especially in the region to the east of a line drawn from Hamburg to Trieste, a system of commercial agriculture emerged also based on compulsory labour, but this was again provided by a native peasantry subjected to serfdom. Otherwise in modern Europe, agricultural labour was supplied by non-servile means, notably through sharecropping and waged hire. The former was the work of peasants who paid rent in the form of a fixed proportion of their annual crop; the latter was the work of poor peasants, whose holdings were too small to provide self-subsistence, and ex-peasants, both surviving in the countryside through the paid employment they found on commercial farms. With sufficient labour recruited in this manner, little scope existed for a revival of field slavery. When the latter resurfaced in the fifteenth and six-teenth centuries, it did so on certain offshore islands in the Mediterranean and Atlantic, significantly in connection with the commercial cultivation of sugar, thus creating the prototype for the slave plantation which, in the next two to three centuries, dominated the commercial agriculture of the New World.

Domestic slavery prevailed throughout the modern world. But this caused slavery to feature only peripherally in any one society simply because, with its economy dependent upon other forms of labour, the proportion of the population that was definably slave remained small. Societies therefore, according to the Hopkins's distinction, were 'societies with slaves' rather than 'slave societies' in the antique manner.[12] The rise of the slave regimes of the Ottoman Empire, Safavid Persia and the Mughal Empire in the fifteenth and sixteenth centuries failed to alter this general picture since their slaves, although enjoying great political power, played little part in production and constituted only a very small proportion of society.

Within the history of slavery, the slave economies of the New World had a much greater impact. In fact, their emergence revived the phenomenon of 'the slave society', notably in the islands of the Caribbean, Brazil and the US South. But it was a slave society with a difference. In the first place the distinction between slave and master was closely associated with race, the slaves being black and the masters white. Furthermore, the slave regimes of the New World were relatively harsh: a conjunction of the labour demands made by plantation agriculture and the inhumane attitudes generated by racism. In striking contrast, the slave regimes of the Middle East were comparatively lenient, thanks to their heavy reliance on a slavery of service. The same could be said for those of Africa and Asia, thanks to the use made of slaves as household servants and peasant labourers.

The modern period undoubtedly saw a huge increase in the practice of slavery, much of it extracted from Africa, with something like 11 million slaves transported to the New World and another 9 million transported to the Middle East.[13] After Africa, the highest recruitment area was provided by the Slavic societies of the Balkans and southern Russia, which were continually milked for slaves by the Ottoman Empire. Was this extensive practice of slavery explicable in terms of its usefulness?

The possession of slaves had value as a status symbol, or as an instrument of government, or as a means of production. Socially, the existence of slaves upheld the honour of the free, no matter how poor. For the slave owners, slavery was either a qualitative expression of conspicuous consumption or an honourable means of avoiding work. In keeping with the values of the time, it thus conferred social status on the possessors while taking it away from the possessed. Politically, slavery was useful, as a means whereby rulers could liberate themselves, militarily and administratively, from a dependence upon aristocracy or tribalism. But how useful were slaves in the production of wealth? Much depended upon the efficiency of their work and the scarcity of free labour. A commonsensical response proposes that, given their work to be unpaid and compulsory, slave labour conferred an advantage over free labour, even more so when, as in much of the New World, slaves were in plentiful supply and therefore cheap to buy, and free labourers were scarce and therefore highly waged. Yet a pervasive school of thought – fathered by Adam Smith, favoured by the abolitionists and furthered by Karl Marx – proposed that slave labour was 'dear' rather than 'cheap'. This was, they argued, because the slaves lacked an incentive to work well, since their remuneration (typically coming in the form of food, clothing and accommodation) remained constant, irrespective of the work they accomplished. Consequently, it was thought, their labour would fail to compensate for the price of their purchase and the cost of their upkeep. In contrast, the free worker would provide a much better return, simply because his remuneration would relate to the work done and inspire a positive attitude to work. Smith thought that the only means of obtaining from slaves any commitment to work was 'by violence' (i.e. by flogging them), but suggested that, even then, the motivation would be less than if, like the free worker, the slave had 'any interest of his own' in what he was doing.[14] This theory is reason gone mad. It overlooks the hired labourer's controlling fear of dismissal and the slave's controlling fear of being sold. Both of them, in this respect, were similarly motivated to work. It also overlooks something else. Without a doubt, slaves had their own devices for remedying the gross imbalance of advantage created by the slave–master relationship, notably feigned stupidity, working within limits and only to order, abiding by custom, malingering, petty theft, and so on. But masters could combat this array of negativity by dispensing rewards in the form of customary rights, recognized liberties, additional treats and the prospect of promotion to lighter work, all of which could encourage slaves to work well. In this respect, the role of the whip was not to motivate work but to curb disobedience and to display power. Finally, the Smith thesis overlooks the obvious advantage slavery enjoyed over free labour: generally, it cost less.

For the production of sugar and cotton with a minimum of mechanization, slavery proved to be a highly efficient source of labour. Yet how did it compare with other forms of compulsory labour? Slaves appeared to work better for their masters than serfs, since the latter's basic interest lay in their own farms. Moreover, the serf's capacity for foot-dragging, malingering and stealing produce was difficult to counter, given the security of tenure he enjoyed on his own holding and the restrictive customs that normally limited what the lord could demand of him. The white bonded labour used in North America in the early stages of settlement was likewise comparatively inefficient, simply because, without wages, there was nothing to work for, and poor work could not be punished by dismissal. For this reason, it came to be replaced by black slavery. Indentured service eventually replaced black slavery on the plantations, not because it was more efficient but because slave labour had been outlawed. On the other hand, slave labour was probably not as efficient as the work done by the inmates of twentieth-century prison camps where powerful punitive pressures could be brought to bear, either by lowering the food ration to starvation levels or by extending the sentence: measures which were much more effective in maximizing the return on labour than any of those available to the masters of slaves.

3

Modern Serfdom

The distinctive feature of serfdom was its location within a peasant society: that is, a community of farmers who worked their smallholdings with family labour for a subsistence purpose. This is not to say that the other forms of servitude lacked peasant associations. In Asia and Latin America there were slaves and debt bondsmen operating as peasants. Moreover, the indentured servants and debt bondsmen employed in the nineteenth century to work colonial plantations were chiefly recruited from the peasantries of China and India; while most of the slaves transported to the New World were taken from the peasant communities of western Africa. In fact, until the twentieth century, those held in servitude mostly came from peasant backgrounds, with many aspiring to regain their peasant status through the acquisition of a smallholding. Nonetheless, whereas serfs were typically of the peasantry, slaves, indentured labourers and debt bondsmen were mostly ex-peasants who, having been drawn to work on plantations, down mines or in cities, had been transferred to a world dominated by non-peasant values.

Serfs, then, were usually peasants; but what made a peasant a serf? As with slaves, serfs were the property of someone else, and often disposable through sale, either separately or along with the estate to which they were bound. In this respect, they were definably unfree. Conceived in the law as being 'at the will of the lord', serfs were either tied to the lord's estate or to the lord's person. Compared with the free peasantry, they were subjected to a greater range of obligations, many of which were payments to secure their lords' permission – for example, to marry, to adopt a new occupation, to live away from the estate and to inherit, sublet or sell property – and therefore explicit recognition of the lord's overall control.[15]

Serfdom of this sort was commonly found in both medieval western and modern eastern Europe. Peasants in bondage were not an exclusively European phenomenon; yet, elsewhere in the world, they tended to belong to another category of servitude. Thus, in India and Africa, unfree families could be found holding land in return for unpaid services, very much in the serf manner. Similarly, on the haciendas of Latin America native Indians were to be found tied to the estate as tenants owing labour services. But these Indian and African landholders were technically slaves, while many, although by no means all, of these Latin American service tenants were technically debt bondsmen.[16]

The serfdom found in medieval and modern Europe was lodged within the manorial system; so much so that serf owners were invariably lords of the manor: some of them princes, others churchmen or nobles. Determining the serf way of life was the tripartite division of the manor, with its demesne land, its tenures and its waste. Whereas the demesne was fully owned by the lord and completely at his disposal, the tenures lay only in his final ownership, making them, in practice, the conditional property of the serfs. Usage of the waste was shared between lord and serf, although on different terms.[17]

When the lord chose to farm the demesne himself rather than to lease it out, he could call upon his serfs to provide the necessary labour and equipment. They performed these services not for a wage but as an obligation of their serf status. In return, they were normally allowed to hold within the same manor a tenure of the lord. For this reason, individual serfs were often engaged in two distinct farming operations: one for the lord, the other for themselves, the former a commercial enterprise geared to the market and profit, the latter modestly aimed at feeding the serf's family and paying its taxes and dues. In addition, serfs received commoning rights to the uncultivated parts of the manor. This included the parts temporarily free of cultivation – the land left fallow, the fields after the grain harvest, the meadows after the hay had been cut – and the parts that were never cultivated (i.e. the waste). Legally, the waste was regarded as an extension of the demesne, but, in managing it, the lord had to respect the serfs' right to enjoy its natural resources. This right of common – an integral and vital part of the serf's existence – appertained to the free grazing of his livestock and also to estovers: that is, the collection of fuel, fungi, bracken, timber, nuts, nettles and berries; while preserved for the lord's exclusive use, unless he gave the tenantry licensed access, were the fishing and hunting. The manor created for the serfs not only a corpus of rights but also a strong sense of community, both upheld institutionally through their membership of the village assembly and their access to the jurisdiction of the manorial court. It was something that slavery did not permit.

Unlike slaves, serfs owed an allegiance to the state which obliged them to pay government taxes and to serve in the royal army. Dependent on serfs in these two important respects, governments, especially in the modern period, acquired an irresistible need to protect them from seigneurial exploitation. They therefore passed laws awarding serfs a legal personality which was far more substantial than what was ever enacted for slaves. Required to pay taxes to governments and dues to lords, serfs differed vitally from slaves. Slaves were simply a source of labour and service. In contrast, enserfment occasionally had nothing to do with the provision of either. Its purpose was simply to prevent a contraction of revenue, partly through banning migration from the estate, partly by offering the lord a flexible means of revising rents and dues in accordance with the level of inflation.[18]

Although differing from typical slaves – through living as peasants and owing obligations to the state – serfs could sometimes resemble them closely, especially when subjected to personal bondage and labour services. Serfdom came in two basic forms. Some serfs were bound personally to their lord. They were termed *Erbuntertanen*, or *Leibeigenen*, or *nativi per corpore* or *hommes de corps*. Their bondage, in the slave manner, was of the blood, so much so that they inherited their servile status and transmitted it to their offspring. Other serfs were bound to the land. They were termed *Gutsun-tertanen*, or *Realleibeigenen*, or *servi terrae*, or *gens de mainmorte réelle*, or *serfs de la glèbe*. Rather than being of the blood, their bondage rested upon tenancy, and therefore was sharply distinguished from that of slaves. Vital to this type of serfdom was the existence of bondland: that is, a tenure recognized in the law as unfree.[19]

If servile tenures had been exclusively held by personal serfs, it would have been pointless to distinguish between these two types of serfdom. But this was not the case: many servile tenures were held by families who regarded themselves as personally free. Moreover, making a distinction between the two types of serfdom would not have mattered much if they had imparted the same degree of servility. However, tenurial serfs tended to enjoy more rights in the law than personal serfs; while, because of the greater range of exactions to which they were subjected, personal serfs were prone to suffer greater exploitation. When both types were found in the same society, personal serfs were regarded as the more base. Furthermore, the differences evident between the two led to different social consequences. Unlike tenurial serfs, personal serfs could be sold apart from the land, making them more likely to suffer family separation and deracination. Moreover, if the serf was in personal bondage, he could exist in a landless state, like the household serfs of eighteenth- and nineteenth-century Russia who subsisted on the estate as craftsmen in receipt of rations from the lord's store, not as peasants in possession of tenures; or like the serfs who, in return for the payment of a licence fee, were permitted to reside off the estate and work as artisans and traders in the towns; or like the collateral lines of serf families who, denied the right to family land by the rule of primogeniture, remained resident on the estate as cottagers and lodgers. This did not alter the general equation of serf to peasant, but it did produce a serf society that was more socially complex than the one associated with tenurial serfdom. In the latter case, landlessness imparted freedom whereas, for personal serfs, emancipation was much more difficult to achieve, requiring, in the slave manner, a grant of manumission. Personal serfs were more prone to flight. Tenurial serfs had too much to lose by leaving, and so were more inclined to stay put. Finally, where serfs were mainly tenurial, serfdom was inclined to be less socially dominant than where personal bondage prevailed, with a much smaller proportion of the rural population in the servile state. When serfdom was principally personal it created a serf society; when it was principally tenurial it created a society with serfs.

New serfs normally resulted from procreation rather than purchase. What is more, serfs were expected to provide, compulsorily and without payment, the basic agricultural equipment – the tools, the ploughs, the teams of oxen, the wagons – as well as the work-force. For these two reasons, they appeared to offer a very cheap source of labour. Absent was the need to pay wages or to invest in equipment, the major drawback of a free labour system; absent was the need to purchase, restock, feed and equip the work-force, the major drawback of slavery. Yet serfdom had its own limitations, for lord as well as peasant. In the first place, a considerable amount of land had to be set aside in smallholdings for the serfs' own private use. In this respect, only with the removal of serfdom could estates develop as enterprises totally devoted to commercial farming. Moreover, serf labour may not have involved capital outlay but it was far from efficient. Subjected to the competing demands of smallholding and demesne, the serf family was naturally more devoted to the former. In fact, services on the latter tended to be skimped and slackly performed, with ancient equipment and decrepit relatives allocated for the purpose.[20] Furthermore, since the same type of produce was grown on the demesne and the tenures, serfs could help themselves to the lord's produce with impunity. With no means of proving that the grain in their possession had not been grown on their own farms, pilfering by serfs was extremely difficult to detect. It was the basic inefficiency of serf labour that eventually caused direct demesne farming to be abandoned, both in the late medieval west and in the late modern east.

For lords, serfdom had a second serious drawback. This lay in the way their ownership of the manor, although sanctioned in the law, came to be countered by the customary rights of the serfs. Protective of the serf interest, these customary rights imparted tenancy by inheritance, fixed rents of assize, fixed services, sometimes fixed dues, commoning on the uncultivated parts of the manor, and a say in local affairs, thanks to membership of the manorial court or village council.[21] If not fixed by custom, serf obligations could be limited by a concept of reasonableness. Thus, although subjected to manorial demands that legally were at the lords' determination, serfs acquired rights similar to those enjoyed by free manorial tenants. They tended to retain possession of the family holding from generation to generation. Moreover, their rents and services to the lord tended to become carefully defined and normally alterable only by negotiation, so that, for example, the lord's wish to increase the labour services was only possible in return for a lowering of the rent.[22]

These serf rights were sustained by a number of practical considerations. As with slaves so with serfs, force was an inadequate means of persuasion. It was in the lord's interest to establish serf communities that were obedient and self-operating, so that estates could be run with minimal supervision and economy. Cooperation could best be secured by allowing the serfs certain freedoms, notably through granting them customary rights and leaving them to their own devices.[23]

The policies that lords adopted towards their estates were also influenced by the capacity of serfs to offer resistance. This could take a number of forms: petitioning lords to complain of bad officials, even petitioning rulers to complain of bad lords; acts of non-cooperation such as the slack performance of services, or refusals to pay rent and dues; acts of reprisal, some of it clandestine – such as pilfering, poaching, arson and houghing (i.e. mutilation of the lord's livestock) – some of it overt – such as rough music expressing displeasure for the lord, or anti-enclosure action to reclaim common rights, or acts of violence against lords and their agents, or even flight from the manor. Serfs found some of these forms of protest preferable to others. For serfs subjected to week-work, foot-dragging and theft enabled them to avoid serious reprisal. In contrast, the refusal to fulfil manorial obligations could result in eviction; flight meant the abandonment of ancestral land; rebellion was punishable by death; while litigation, when possible, tended to be expensive and ineffectual. Much of this serf resistance did not represent a struggle for survival, or a revolutionary attempt to destroy the system, but was aimed rather at preserving hallowed rights against arbitrarily imposed innovations. Its purpose, then, was a constitutional one. Yet when it took the form of large-scale rebellion, it could advocate the complete rejection of serfdom. Insurrections of this nature happened infrequently and unsuccessfully but, because of their size and duration, they became important historical events which were, ever after, fearfully recalled by lords and princes, and, in this respect, capable of exerting a long-term influence on the policies both pursued.[24]

The establishment of serf rights was due not only to the ability of unfree peasant communities to defend their interests but also to the way in which governments intruded upon the lord–serf relationship. The government's military and fiscal dependence upon serfs, which was just as considerable as the lord's reliance upon them for dues and services, meant that it could not afford to leave them completely at his disposal: in other words, it could not allow the serf–lord relationship to acquire the autonomy normally associated with master and slave. In the course of the seventeenth and eighteenth centuries, as rulers in central and eastern Europe sought to increase their political power by developing large, standing armies and extensive bureaucracies, they became increasingly attached to a policy of serf protection. This was designed partly to safeguard a vital resource and partly to avoid peasant rebellion. Restrictions were placed upon what lords could demand of their serfs in order to reserve a substantial part of the serf's resources for government taxation, as well as to ensure that serf families were, on the one hand, sufficiently prosperous to produce reasonably fit conscripts and, on the other, sufficiently obedient that they did not threaten the stability of the state.[25] Governments therefore sought to prevent the land occupied by serfs from becoming incorporated in the demesne, and thereby exempt from taxation, and to place limits on seigneurial exactions. Such policies were notably practised in the Habsburg Monarchy (the Austrian Territories, Bohemia, Hungary), where, reacting in the late eighteenth century to its defeat at the hands of Prussia and to the outbreak of large-scale peasant uprisings, the government sought to improve its international effectiveness; but these policies were also present in the Prussian and the Russian monarchies. Traditionally, the rights of the serfs were contained in custumals (*Weistümer, urbaria*): statements of manorial duties and privileges that were reached and revised by negotiation between the community of tenants and the lord's officers. But, by the late eighteenth century, serf rights were often contained in regulations drawn up by the government. This meant that long before the demise of serfdom, serfs acquired a legal personality actionable in the law and comprising a corpus of rights validated by governmental decree. By 1781 the Habsburgs took a further step and abolished serfdom in Bohemia and the Austrian Territories. In the same cause of strengthening the state and avoiding revolution, the Hohenzollerns and Romanovs followed suit, the one in 1807, the other in 1861.[26]

Like slavery, serfdom came in a great variety of forms, some mild, others harsh. The severity of individual serf regimes, moreover, could alter profoundly over time. Much depended upon whether serfs had to provide weekly labour services. This, in turn, depended upon whether the demesne was directly cultivated or leased out. Serfdom was rendered harsh in sixteenth-century Poland and Brandenburg-Prussia, seventeenth-century Bohemia and late eighteenth-century Russia when lords decided to operate their demesnes commercially with serf labour. As a result, serfs were subjected to labour services amounting to several days a week. These services, moreover, applied not only to work in the fields but also, in Russia and Bohemia, to the textile and brewing industries. The weight of the week-work depended partly on the nature of the enterprise, with agriculture requiring more labour than pastoral farming, and with industrial concerns, in contrast to farming, imposing a constant demand for labour. It also depended on the extent of the demesne. Where demesnes accounted for more than 40 per cent of the cultivated land – as in Schleswig-Holstein, Pomerania, Galicia and parts of Transylvania – labour services could exceed four days a week. Elsewhere, they rarely exceeded three days a week. Some serfs were sufficiently well off to hire labourers to fulfil these services, as in eighteenth-century Brandenburg; but this could mean a heavy wage bill.[27]

Nowhere in the servile lands did the labour obligation required of serfs become as onerous as the one demanded of field slaves, largely because, acknowledged to be peasants, serfs had to be awarded sufficient time to run their own farms. The free time granted to slaves for the cultivation of their provision plots (Sundays, sometimes Saturday afternoons) was usually much shorter than the amount of free time granted to serfs, just as the amount of land allocated to serfs was normally much larger than that allocated to slaves.[28] Because the serf holding was by nature an agricultural rather than a horticultural enterprise – the recognized function of which was not only to feed the family that worked it but also to meet its bill for state taxes and manorial dues – plenty of time had to be allowed for its cultivation. Nonetheless, in practice the obligation of week-work placed upon serfs a heavy burden, since it competed with the labour required to work the family farm. It was this double demand for labour – coincidental because of the seasonal nature of farm work – that proved oppressive, particularly when the lord tried to increase the services owed him, no matter how slightly. In periods of rapid population growth, as in the sixteenth and again in the late eighteenth and early nineteenth centuries, an excess of labour could persuade lords to relieve serfs of some of their services, usually in return for a regular money payment. In the same situation, well-off serfs could employ waged labourers to carry out their demesne services. But in times of extreme depopulation – the result, for example, of war and plague in central and eastern Europe in the mid- to late seventeenth century, especially in Bohemia, Brandenburg-Prussia and Poland – the lords' persistence with direct demesne cultivation, in conjunction with a diminished labour force, imposed heavy demands upon the serfs who survived. Without a doubt, the ending of labour services, or their conversion to boons (i.e. an annual service as opposed to a weekly service), rendered serfdom much less objectionable. Freed of week-work, for example, the serfdom that endured from the middle ages in the west was economically light.[29]

Protected by tenant rights, well-off serfs were found in both eastern and western Europe. Moreover, a greater threat to peasant societies than enserfment came with the extension of leasehold, which swept tenant rights – but not free status – away and substituted for the hereditary tenures short-term, rack-rented leases. Whereas enserfment was the preferred solution for the landowners of early modern eastern Europe, conversion to leasehold was the preferred solution for the landowners of early modern western Europe. Which solution was the more exploitative? The policy of leasing created two types of society, one in which the land was rented to commercial farmers, the other in which it was rented to peasants. In the former case, the tenant–lord relationship tended to be benign since the profits from farming allowed the tenants to cope with raised rents. Yet this regime – in which rentier capitalism interlocked with capitalist farming – created a class of downtrodden, if free, landless labourers, many of them former peasants evicted from ancestral lands by commercial farmers with landlord approval. Where leaseholders remained peasants, another type of exploitation surfaced, the result of the disparate conjunction of rentier capitalism with subsistence agriculture. Arguably the free farm labourers and free peasant lessees of the west were far more oppressed than many serfs in the east. Futhermore, in the east, where serfdom was tenurial not personal, the free element in the countryside tended to be landless labourers who suffered greater hardship than serfs, since the latter retained their peasant status and protective tenant rights while the former became an oppressed proletariat, exploited by serfs and seigneurs alike through low wages and the threat of dismissal.[30]

To equate serfdom with the extremes of landlord exploitation would therefore be somewhat misleading. For serfs, week-work was undoubtedly a bothersome imposition. But many serf societies were without it, not just the serf societies that survived in early modern western Europe but also several in eastern Europe, for example in Upper Austria, parts of Silesia, sixteenth-century Bohemia and pre-eighteenth-century Russia. In all these cases the labour services exacted amounted to but a few days a year. When subjected to weekly labour services, other serf societies (for example in sixteenth-century Brandenburg) could be granted a fixing or a lowering of the rent in exchange. For serfs, manorial dues could also be oppressive. If numerous and revisable, they could undermine the value of tenant right through offering the lord a means of compensating for the lowness of the fixed rent. When unpaid, they offered a pretext for eviction. However, like rents of assize, dues tended to become fixed by custom. Those fixed at a proportion of the crop held their value; but many became cash payments which, rendered certain (i.e. fixed) rather than arbitrary (i.e. revisable), suffered depreciation in the course of time as prices rose.[31]

Serfs were not necessarily poor. In fact dietary studies suggest that their living standard could be reasonably high.[32] Moreover, the hardship to which they were subjected usually stemmed from factors affecting the peasantry as a whole, such as lack of security against crop failure, vulnerability to rapid population growth – as the latter diminished holdings through subdivision and devalued commoning rights through over-use – and subjection to the triple yoke, represented in contemporary cartoons by monarch, noble and cleric riding on the peasant's bent back. The serf's liability, not only to the exactions of his lord but also to the tax and military service impositions of the government and to the tithe demands of the church, could impose, altogether, a trying burden. The weight of this burden, however, was largely due to the manner in which taxes and tithes were levied. In the early modern period, a heavy reliance upon taxes from which the rich were exempt by virtue of the privileges they enjoyed as nobles characterized the fiscal systems of eastern Europe. In addition, by the late eighteenth century, the peasantry of Prussia, Russia and the Habsburg Monarchy provided a substantial part of the standing army, thanks to conscription and, again, the exemptions enjoyed by the rest of society.[33] Furthermore, given the importance of family labour to serfs for working their own farms and carrying out their service obligations to the lord, government demands for military service made a major claim upon their basic resources. As for the tithe, it fell heavily upon serfs not because they were unfree but because they were peasants. Tithes were a tax on agriculture rather than industry. Moreover, when exacted as a tenth of farm produce, they were not liable to devaluation. If, like manorial payments in kind, tithes had undergone commutation to a fixed money payment, inflation would have eased the burden in the course of time; but they often remained a fixed proportion of the crop. The triple yoke fell more heavily on serfs than upon the free peasantry because they were less well protected from the demands of lordship; but, given the safeguards that serfs enjoyed against seigneurial exploitation, thanks to their tenant rights, its extreme weight owed much to the additional demands made by government and church.

In early modern Europe, then, two very different types of serfdom existed: the one lingering on from the middle ages on Germany's western border, the other establishing itself between 1480 and 1650 in most of central and eastern Europe; the one relatively mild, the other relatively harsh; the one a means of tapping the peasantry's surplus through dues and rent, the other a means of enlisting the peasantry's labour for commercial purposes; the one, the legal status of a minority of the population, the other, the legal status of the majority; the one an incidental feature of society, the other a dominant social characteristic. Yet in comparison with slavery both appear alike. Between lord and serf there existed a degree of reciprocity not normally found between master and slave. Serfs, moreover, differed from slaves in that they tended to be peasants with hereditary farms. Unlike slaves, they worked in family units, and remained in physical touch with their forebears whose very land they continued to farm. Moreover, cocooned within the family holding and the peasant community, they enjoyed an autonomy unknown to most slaves. Compared with slaves, they had more control over their own labour and less exposure to humiliation. Finally, serfs differed from slaves in having a direct relationship with the state. Dependent upon them for raising revenue and supplying troops, princes had a strong incentive to offer them protection. In contrast, slaves were totally obliged to their masters and beyond the government's reach. For these reasons, to regard serfdom and slavery as interchangeable terms, or even basically alike, creates more problems than it solves.[34]

4

Indentured Service

Indentured service came in two distinct phases, the first confined to the seventeenth and eighteenth centuries, the second to the late nineteenth and early twentieth centuries. In both phases men and women bound themselves for something like three to five years to serve in a distant land, usually thousands of miles from home. Their bondage was defined in a written contract (that is, an indenture). Originally placed in the ownership of whoever paid for their voyage out, they were, on arrival, usually sold to a master who was legally entitled to exploit their labour until the contract expired, or to sell them on. These servants were distinguished from serfs or slaves by their right of consent: this applied both to being placed in bondage and to where it was served. However, indentured servants had no choice of master or of the work to be done; and fierce public laws tied them to the master's service. In this sense, indentured service resembled serfdom and slavery. It was, without doubt, another form of servitude and another expression of unfree labour.[35]

In the phase confined to the seventeenth and eighteenth centuries, something like 300,000 indentured Europeans – mostly English, Irish and Scots, but also some Swiss, French and Germans – were transported to the Caribbean and North America; in the nineteenth/twentieth-century phase something like 2.5 million non-Europeans – mostly Indians and Chinese, but also substantial numbers of Africans, Japanese and Pacific islanders – were taken to Latin America, the Caribbean, the islands of Mauritius and Réunion in the Indian Ocean, southern Africa, Queensland and certain islands in the Pacific, notably New Guinea, Fiji, Hawaii, Samoa and Tahiti.[36]

Indentured service was closely associated with the commercial concerns of European colonialism. To the fore in both phases were the British, although, in the second phase, indentured service was extensively practised in the colonies of the French, the Dutch, the Germans, the Spanish and the Portuguese as well. The aim was to furnish a plentiful supply of well-controlled and cheap labour, initially for clearing the land and, from the mid-seventeenth century onwards, for working plantations. Tobacco, sugar and other export crops created the demand for this labour while colonial rule sanctioned its use; but responsible for the large numbers recruited was destitution at home and the prospect of a better life abroad. Escaping the one to achieve the other involved a very long and costly journey, typically a sea voyage of thousands of miles, to pay for which the poor, driven by desperation and determined to better their lot, were willing to contract a debt that could only be discharged through several years of unpaid, or lowly paid, work. Hence they became bonded servants, most of them going as individuals rather than in families.

Both phases were deeply affected by the presence of slavery, but in diametrically opposite ways. Whereas the indentured service of the first phase was made redundant by the adoption of slaves as the main source of plantation labour, the indentured service of the second phase followed upon the termination of slavery, and resulted from the unwillingness of ex-slaves to continue working the plantations.

Although very similar in character, the indentured service of the first phase was far from identical with that of the second. In the first phase, the trade in labour was privately organized by merchants; in the second, it was publicly organized by governments. North America was a major recipient in the first phase, but uninvolved with the second. Work in the first phase mostly concerned the cultivation of tobacco; in the second, sugar. In the first phase, servant and master were racially alike, whereas, in the second, the masters were of European extraction and the servants mostly came from Asia.

Furthermore, the two phases differed markedly in their historical development, the first phase simply petering out, as slaves or free wage-earners came to be appreciated as a more efficient and effective source of labour. The second phase, however, was stopped abruptly by government acts of abolition, notably the decision of the British Raj in 1916 to forbid further exports of servile labour from British India.

The two phases also differed in the terms of employment. The indentures of the second phase usually offered a wage; those of the first phase simply provided board and lodging. The indentures of the second phase could promise the return fare upon expiry of the contract; those of the first phase assumed that, having served their time in the New World, indentured servants would settle there. Instead of the return fare, they were offered freedom dues, in the form of a grant of money or land, to assist their survival as free persons in the colonies. Furthermore, in the second phase, to counter the repatriation clause, the practice of serial contracts developed, with labourers offered incentives to sign on for a further term; whereas, in the first phase, the indentured joined the pool of free labour once their original contract ran out.

Cultural assimilation was distinctly possible in the first phase, although virtually ruled out in the second. This was largely because, in the first, but not in the second, master and servant were from the same European background; and also because of the different expectations raised by the terms of the contract which, in the first, implied that the indentured would stay on, and, in the second, made provision for their return home.

Also distinguishing the one from the other was the nature of the work. During the first phase the indentured servants often worked within, or close to, families, serving as domestic servants, or providing the skills and labour required in artisan workshops, mercantile offices and on small farms. If they worked on plantations, it was often in a skilled, supervisory or managerial role. Characterizing the work in the first phase was its varied nature, with the indentured performing a wide range of functions, and also the intimacy that existed between servant and master, thanks to their working alongside and living in the same house, or close by. In sharp contrast, the indentured servants of the second phase usually served as the employees of big business. Essentially, they provided unskilled labour on plantations or down mines, and lived in barracks or servile villages on the estate. The master inhabited another cultural and residential world. Often he was a disembodied company, represented on the spot by managers and overseers.

Finally, the role of indentured labour differed between the two phases. In the first, indentured service was intended to provide labour where none existed, either because the natives were unsuitable nomads or because European diseases had wiped them out; whereas in the second, it usually offered alternative labour to that which already existed, whether it be indigenous or ex-slave. As a result, in the second phase, the use of indentured labour was much more prone to incite social conflict, not only because it was seen as a deliberate device to lower the price of labour but also because it presented an ethnic challenge.[37] On the other hand, indentured service in both phases was generically alike in being of finite duration; in having the terms of work set out in a legal document and in colonial laws; and in enabling labour to be bought and sold in such a way as to deny the workers any choice in the vital matter of whom they worked for or what work they did.

Indentured service has been designated a kind of slavery. It has been claimed that 'regardless of legal technicalities, slavery and indentured labour were synonymous'. Terms such as 'short-term slavery' or 'the new system of slavery' are used to capture its essence. Justifying such a claim is the fact that the labour of both slaves and indentured servants was a form of alienable property. In this respect both were chattels, the one permanent, the other temporary.[38] Yet slavery and indentured service were very different. Since indentured service was often employed in the nineteenth century to replace slave labour on colonial plantations, precautions were taken, especially by the British government, whose empire was its major provider and employer, to ensure that it was free of the evils of slavery and was not branded as the perpetuation of slavery by other means. Moreover, in the early seventeenth century – when the practice of indentured service was first used to convey white labour to the New World and shortly afterwards the importation of black slaves began – the view was held, and explicitly expressed in eyewitness accounts and legislative acts, that slavery and indentured service were not the same thing. In certain basic respects, this was undoubtedly the case. Slaves in the New World were not there by choice. Enslavement resulted from forcible abduction or birth. In contrast, most indentured servants gave up their freedom voluntarily. Although their submission to servitude, very much in the slave manner, disqualified them from choosing their own master, it did allow them to decide where in the world they should serve their time. The kidnapping of freemen in order to convert them into indentured servants was not unknown but, unlike forcible enslavement, it was illegal and rare. Moreover, the temporary nature of indentured servitude meant that it could not be regarded as in the blood. This not only rendered servants less base than slaves but it also led to their being valued differently. In the eighteenth century, the purchase price for a servant was three times less than that of a slave; and, where both were evaluated as taxable property, the same ratio applied.[39] Unlike slavery, indentured service depended upon a contract which declared that the master's proprietorial rights did not appertain to the servant's person but only to his labour, and then, for no more than a fraction of the servant's life. What is more, the relationship between master and servant was more prone to public regulation than that between master and slave. Colonial legislatures were more prepared to accept the servant as a person rather than a thing, allowing him greater public protection against maltreatment. Finally, for New World slaves the prospect of release from bondage was, until the closing stages of the system, often a forlorn hope, whereas for servants it was guaranteed by indenture. The freeing of individual slaves depended upon an act of benevolence by the master and frequently had to be purchased; whereas the freeing of servants was an automatic response to the expiry of the contract and was normally followed by some form of reward.

How different was indentured service from free labour? This can be answered first, by comparing the migrations of indentured servants with those of free workers; and secondly, by examining the affinities that existed between indentured service and the employment ties found in the free labour market – notably those connected with apprenticeship and service in husbandry. Indentured servants might bear some resemblance to free migrants in making, on their own initiative, enormous journeys in search of self-betterment, with the difference that the servants' passage was paid for not out of their own savings but by means of a loan secured, and eventually redeemed, through the unwaged or low-waged labour the servants contracted with the creditor to provide for a fixed period. Indentured service, then, gave those who were too poor to afford the fare the opportunity to improve their lot through migration. They therefore appeared, not as the victims of oppression, but as enjoying certain advantages over free migrants, since not only was their fare paid for them, but once out there, employment was guaranteed and, once the term of service had ended, they were rewarded with a parcel of land or a grant of money to set up in business.

Yet the disadvantages that indentured servants suffered were formidable. Upon reaching the New World, free labourers enjoyed various options: for example, to found their own businesses or to work for an employer whom they were entitled to leave if the conditions of work or pay proved unsatisfactory. Such choices – elemental to the world of free labour – were denied indentured servants. Essentially, they were bound to work for the master to whom they had been sold. Non-cooperation and flight could offer a means of resisting bad employers but, in resorting to these means of protest, they broke the law laid down in master-and-servant and vagrancy acts, thus making themselves vulnerable, in the slave manner, to extreme forms of punishment, such as flogging, imprisonment, the pillory, wearing irons, the docking of maintenance, even extensions of the term of service. The severity of these punishments reflected upon the fact that the master had to pay for the service in advance, leaving him with the problem of obtaining a good return from the labour he could extract. This need placed top priority on preventing servants from foot-dragging or taking flight; and the servants themselves, through receiving reward only at the beginning and the end of the service, were poorly motivated to cooperate in between. With free labourers, cooperation could be secured in other ways: by raising wages or by the threat of dismissal. Neither of these options was available to the owners of indentured labour; they could only sell on. They therefore had to rely on forcing work out of their employees through a regimen of punishment and penalty.

In some of its forms, free labour was not all that free. Apprenticeship bound adolescents to a seven-year service, often involving residence under the master's roof, through an indenture that set out the obligations of master and apprentice. Service in husbandry, moreover, bound men and women to work on a yearly contract. Apprenticeship clearly had little connection with indentured service, in that it was designed to impart a training in a trade that was paid for by an initial sum of money.[40] In contrast, the indentured servant had to pay nothing in advance, and the purpose was to enlist labour, not to confer skills upon the young. As for service in husbandry, it may have been the progenitor of indentured service, but the two were far removed in character and function.[41] In the seventeenth and eighteenth centuries, when they were equally important – with service in husbandry accounting for a great deal of labour in rural England, and indentured service providing much of the white labour deployed in the New World – they represented different systems of labour recruitment. The former involved the payment of a wage, and usually a verbal contract of not more than a year; the latter involved a written contract and, in the first phase, unwaged service of several years' duration. Furthermore, the legal status of the labour provided differed, simply because indentured servants could be sold whereas servants in husbandry could not. The purpose behind the two forms of labour was quite different. Service in husbandry was used to entice labourers from one village to another; whereas indentured service was designed to persuade labourers to make intercontinental migrations. Not surprisingly, the work experiences the two underwent were worlds apart. Indentured service, then, offered a system of work that was quite alien to that of free labour. In fact, indentured service bore a much closer resemblance to the other forms of servitude: not only slavery but also debt bondage and convict assignment.

Debt bondage was yet another device for shifting labour about the world.[42] Like indentured service, it centred upon a debt incurred as a result of the migrants' inability to pay the fare. This subjected them to bondage until it had been acquitted. The difference between the two was that debt bondage was not terminally fixed. Moreover, central to debt bondage was the payment of a wage, which provided the essential means of redeeming the debt; whereas central to indentured service was the principle of redemption through providing an appropriate amount of labour. Not surprisingly, in the nineteenth and twentieth centuries, large numbers of Chinese and Indians submitted to both debt bondage and indentured service, as they migrated in search of work. The conditions of employment were very similar, with no choice of employer, only of destination, and harsh penal laws that branded disobedience to the master a heinous offence. Occasionally the two became joined in a hybrid system of servitude. Thus, Germans came to eighteenth-century Pennsylvania as 'redemptioners'. On landing they were technically debt bondsmen, the ships' captains, who had given them passage to the New World, allowing them a fortnight to pay the fare. If they failed to do so, they were sold as indentured servants, contracting, in the normal manner, to pay off what they owed through providing several years of unwaged labour.[43] On occasions the close similarities between the two forms of servitude made it difficult to determine which one was in operation. The Chinese brought to Peru and Cuba in the late nineteenth century were bound by indenture and sold, but then had part of their wages docked to pay off the debt incurred from receiving a free passage to the Americas. Were they indentured servants, or were they debt bondsmen?[44]

Indentured service was also closely related to penal servitude. This was essentially because, from the late seventeenth century, convicted felons in England were transported to the colonies, first to the New World and later to Australia, not to be incarcerated in penal settlements but to be assigned to private employers as indentured servants.[45] For the convicts, however, no right of consent figured, apart from the procedure of allowing criminals condemned to death to opt for transportation instead.

Furthermore, their term of labour – at least seven years – was considerably longer than that of indentured service. And their transportation was designed not to acquit a debt but to make them serve a due sentence. Nonetheless, like indentured servants, the convicts transported to the New World were brought by merchant contractors, sold to a master, with the terms of the sale set out in a legal document, and put to work in farms and workshops, not for a wage but for free food, clothing and accommodation.

Like serfdom and slavery, indentured service cannot be assessed in general terms as either harsh or mild, simply because of the broad range of exploitation associated with it. Much depended upon the nature of the work: like slaves, servants engaged in artisan work were better off than those providing field labour on plantations; and the latter were better off than the servants employed in quarries or mines, especially the guano mines of Peru or the gold mines of French Guiana and the Transvaal. Much also depended upon the degree of prosperity the industry for which they worked was enjoying at the time. The personality of the master was another determining factor. Thanks to the gross imbalance of power in the master's favour – the result of the servant's inability to change employment until the indenture had expired – and because of the lowly rewards the servants received, especially during the first phase, when wages failed to figure in the labour contract, the system could degenerate into a vindictive struggle between employer and employee, in which the latter's attempts to preserve some independence and dignity could incite reprisal from the former – ostensibly to hold him or her to the contract but frequently to exercise domination.

Since indentured service was by consent, the persons who submitted to it must have perceived some advantage in the arrangement. Besides the fare to a distant land and the guarantee of work and sustenance upon arrival, there were other benefits. The first phase offered prospects of reward when the contract terminated. In the second phase, servants normally received wages as well as maintenance, even the return fare. Once the contract was signed, however, the wages were not negotiable. Moreover, they were often pitched much lower than the wages paid to free labour. Nonetheless, rewards or wages might justify the sacrifices the workers had made to escape the much greater poverty of living in freedom at home. Blighting the indenture system for the servants was the overreadiness of employers to punish absenteeism or slow work by extending the terms of the contract or by docking wages; blighting it for the masters was, in the first phase, the high incidence of flight as servants, having reached the New World at no cost to themselves, became runaways: something they could easily do because as whites they were not branded by the colour of their skin. In the second phase, the servants were marked as servile by their Asian extraction and therefore less able to flee, but were prone to resist, usually through feigned illness and foot-dragging, and, if they were Chinese, by revolt.[46]

The extent to which indentured service was open to exploitation depended upon circumstance. Masters could not respond to economic recession by laying off indentured employees; and so they reacted by with-holding wages or by reducing maintenance. In determining the conditions of work, much depended upon the proximity of slavery. Thus, in the New World of the seventeenth century, the work for unskilled indentured labour became much more oppressive as plantations manned by slaves were developed. However, for skilled or managerial indentured service in the same regions, the work remained amenable. Likewise, immediately after the abolition of slavery in the mid-nineteenth century, the indentured labourers imported to work on the plantations tended to be treated like slaves, with poor living quarters, wages left unpaid and frequent use of the whip. In time, however, the work ethos created by slavery gave way to regimes in which the indentured were viewed as little different from free workers. Assisting in this process was the willingness of the state to offer them protection against their masters. This was especially true of the British Empire in the nineteenth century as, moved by slave emancipation, the government not only abolished slavery but also sought to prevent indentured service from becoming 'the new slavery'.[47]

Finally, the treatment of indentured servants depended upon the scarcity of labour. In the absence of affordable free labour, or because of an insufficiency of slave labour, or where there was a shortage of bonded servants or debt bondsmen, indentured servants benefited from the leniency masters chose to extend, either to attract further servants from the homeland or, in the second phase, to persuade servants to sign on for a second term. For the above reasons, indentured service was extremely varied in its oppressiveness. This feature eventually became lost to view as groups bent on its abolition – for example, Indian nationalists or racist white colonists in South Africa and Australia – indulged in its disparagement, arguing that it offered nothing to the worker but hardship and humiliation.[48]

For the servants, however, indentured service offered the opportunity to escape destitution and to achieve at least a state of lesser poverty, enabling them to migrate from a homeland, where an excess of labour meant high unemployment, to worlds where labour was scarce and work was guaranteed. The small number who went home in the second phase, when a free return passage was on offer, suggests that something had been gained from the experience. Many, in fact, fulfilled a traditional ideal through acquiring smallholdings or small trading businesses when their service expired.[49]

What did indentured service offer the employer? The lack of labour in the New World before the extensive use of slavery – a scarcity resulting from a low rate of free migration, as well as a high rate of mortality among indigenous peoples – rendered indentured service of outstanding importance, especially in the early development of North America and the Caribbean. The skills and labour required in the initial clearances of the land and in the creation of the first plantations – the tobacco farms, for example, in Maryland, Virginia and the Caribbean – were largely provided by bonded servants who, it is reckoned, comprised at least one half and perhaps as much as two-thirds of all white immigrants between the 1630s and the 1770s.[50] Not only did they provide much of the white labour but also a majority of white settlers since, having served their term, they stayed on. By 1700, however, their importance had been overshadowed by the Africans imported as slaves, and eventually in the late nineteenth century by Europeans, many of them ex-serfs from eastern Europe who arrived as free men, their passage self-paid. Nonetheless, in the original settlement of British America, indentured labour was a vital force.

In the second phase of indentured service, its value for employers owed much to the termination of slavery and the need to find sufficient labour for the sugar plantations. Since ex-slaves were inclined to shun plantation work, the latter had to be maintained and expanded with indentured labour: in the British colonies of Mauritius, Trinidad and Guiana, in Dutch Surinam and in French Réunion. The employment of indentured labour also allowed the sugar plantation to extend to new regions, notably Fiji, Hawaii, Queensland and Natal.[51] And this was in a period when the price of sugar was falling continually, the result of overproduction as well as competition from the sugar beet industry in eastern Europe. Replacing one form of bonded labour by another thus gave an extension of life to a plantation system that could not have survived in a world of free labour.

As a system of labour, indentured service lacked the cost-efficiency of slavery. This was largely because, unlike slavery, indentured servitude was temporary not permanent. Moreover, since it was not bondage in the blood, it could not be sustained by procreation. In the first phase of indentured service, a fresh supply of servants had to be imported every four or five years while the old supply had to be given their freedom dues. In the second phase, measures had to be taken to dissuade servants from returning home when their contracts expired. This involved giving them land or money or an increase in wages. Although the price of an indentured servant was something like a third of that of a slave, the need to purchase at regular intervals a fresh consignment of servants placed a high cost on maintaining the system. Furthermore, in the second phase, indentured labour had to be waged, presumably to distinguish it clearly from slavery. Although initially wages were well below that of free labour, in the course of time the wage differential was eroded away as, on the one hand, the alternative labour provided by servants brought down the price of free labour and, on the other, the competition between colonies for indentured workers, plus the need to persuade those completing a contract to re-indenture themselves, raised the price of servile labour. As a result, in the course of time indentured labour became a costly proposition. If indentured service had been highly productive, this would not have mattered. However, in the seventeenth and eighteenth centuries, the greater productivity of slave labour over indentured service caused planters to prefer slaves, both in the Caribbean and the North American colonies. Then, with the abolition of slavery in the mid-nineteenth century, it was felt that, controlled by the indenture system, Asians might provide a more efficient labour force than that which could be recruited from indigenous peoples, since they would work not only for lower wages but also with greater commitment, less distraction and more compliance. This, it was believed, would justify the cost of importing them to the plantation colonies. But Indian workers, the bulk of the Asian labour recruited through indenture to serve on colonial plantations, were distinguished by their low productivity, lack of cooperation and obduracy. The Indians recruited for plantation work were smaller in physique, and less suited to heavy labour, than, say, the ex-slaves of African extraction who populated the Caribbean, or the native Fijians, or the Zulus of Natal. Furthermore, expectations of the work to be achieved – originally set with the example of slave labour in mind – were far too high to be satisfied: thus, the number of tasks expected per annum of each indentured servant in British Guiana in the 1850s was almost double the average number actually performed. Accompanying this low work rate was a level of absenteeism which, in practice, reduced the statutory six-day week to one of four days.[52] A high rate of punishment and an extension of the term to compensate for work time lost provided no effective remedy. The planters, then, were unable to make this indentured labour fulfil its potential. Consequently, faced by continually falling prices, they were driven to pursue other strategies. The first was to separate the processing from the production of cane sugar by establishing a centralized mill to service all the plantations of the region, instead of expecting each plantation to have its own crushing and curing machinery. The second was to morcellize production by renting out the plantations in small units so that, rather than being worked by servile labour, they operated through a system of peasant agriculture, the labour and enterprise provided by former indentured servants who now produced sugar with family labour on their own farms. This was happening, for example, in Mauritius, Fiji, Trinidad and British Guiana at the close of the nineteenth century.[53] Its effect was not only to dismantle the large plantations but also to dispense with the labour demands that had brought servile labour into being.

In contrast to serfdom or slavery, indentured service provided only short-term solutions to the problems of manning large-scale commercial production: during each of the two phases, its usefulness in any one society lasted for no more than half a century. In the seventeenth and early eighteenth centuries and in the nineteenth and early twentieth centuries, it was responsible for spectacular overseas migrations – across the Atlantic, across the Pacific, across the Indian Ocean, round the Cape and across the Atlantic to the Caribbean. On the other hand, the 2.8 million Europeans, Asians and Africans who travelled abroad under indenture in the modern period were but a very small fraction of the Africans transported as slaves. Furthermore, the 2 million or so Asians who migrated as indentured labourers in the late nineteenth century comprised only a minority of the Asians who, in that time, went abroad in search of work.[54] Of the rest, not all migrated as free men. Many did so under terms of debt bondage – yet another form of servitude.

5

Debt Bondage

Debt bondage and indentured service were closely related since both were essentially a pledge of service for the repayment of a debt; usually, both were entered into by agreement; and, normally, both represented a temporary form of servitude. The two, then, were very different from slavery and serfdom. Yet they were far from being alike. Whereas indentured service was for a fixed term, debt bondage, in flexibly depending upon the discharge of a debt, could be quickly terminated; alternatively, if the debt could not be repaid, it might well last a lifetime – even longer in societies where indebtedness was inheritable – and could become transmuted into slavery. Furthermore, debt bondage was much more inclined to be involuntary, largely because much of it concerned the pawning of children. Although this was carried out with parental consent, it was imposed upon the child.

Debt bondage was an integral part of the credit system of many traditional non-European societies; indentured service, in contrast, was created by European colonialism to furnish migrant labour. Not surprisingly, given its much longer history, debt bondage had a greater range of purpose, serving not merely to organize long-distance labour migrations but also to raise credit and enlist local labour. Finally, debt bondage came in a much greater variety of forms: while indentured service was intrinsically voluntary, short-term and not hereditary, debt bondage contained elements of compulsion, permanence, even inheritability.

Debt bondage originated in the practice of pawning persons, as opposed to property, for the discharge of a debt.[55] Occasionally, the servitude imparted was permanent and compulsory, and therefore tantamount to slavery; more frequently, it was semi-slave-like in being compulsory but temporary. Often, however, debt bondage was entered into voluntarily, and therefore bore some resemblance to free labour.

An example of slave-like debt bondage, present in parts of Southeast Asia, was the practice of dealing with chronic indebtedness by officially awarding the creditor possession of the debtor and his family. Resting upon a compulsory order and regarded as permanent, this form of debt bondage was undoubtedly akin to slavery. Thus, in traditional Indonesia, Burma and Malaya, a debt officially regarded as irredeemable allowed the creditor to subject the debtor and his family to perpetual bondage.[56] Another source of compulsory, long-term bondage lay in the practice of debt redemption through the pawning of relatives, usually children and often girls, a practice found not only in traditional Thailand and Burma but also in China, India and non-Islamic Africa.[57]

Less slave-like, but still far removed from free labour, was the Cambodian practice of compelling debtors to enter a form of temporary bondage. In the same country, prisoners of war or convicted criminals could escape slavery by providing labour services for a sufficient length of time. Compulsory debt bondage in Cambodia resulted from a very large personal debt, that is, one where the interest on it equalled or exceeded the original loan. In this situation, the creditor was entitled either to seize the debtor for his own use or to order his public sale. Submission to servitude favoured the debtor because it arrested the growth of interest on the debt. Thereafter, the relationship between debtor and creditor was regulated by mutual obligations, the debtor having the right to purchase his freedom by clearing the debt. Defending this system of debt bondage in response to criticism from the French, King Norodom of Cambodia in 1884 declared: 'This enslavement for debt is one of the foundations of the Cambodian state. Our subjects reduced to that servitude are the happiest of them all.'[58] Such compulsory forms of debt bondage often resulted from hereditary indebtedness. Thus, in the Spanish overseas empire, both in Latin America and the Philippines, children found themselves in bondage simply because their parents had submitted to it under a legal system that did not allow personal debt to be cancelled out by death. The same was true of India, where members of the family were obliged to take over if the debt bondsman died, or if illness or old age prevented him from fulfilling the obligations of his debt.[59]

Common in Southeast Asia – and this was also true of Africa, India, China and Latin America – was debt bondage by consent. This form was normally terminated by the repayment of the debt. It could be very short in term, resulting from an advance of wages made for seasonal work. Where lengthy journeys were needed to bring the workers in, the debt comprised a loan of money to cover their travelling costs as well as an advance of wages, leading to a longer term of bondage.

Traditional debt bondage sprang from the interaction – usually in a region of high population density – of extortionate interest rates on loans with an extreme degree of poverty that left personal labour as the one disposable asset of any creditable value. In contrast, responsible for the development of modern debt bondage was the high demand for unskilled labour created by the large-scale cultivation of cash crops in tropical or semi-tropical regions, following the abolition of slavery. Debt bondage became extremely common in the late nineteenth century as it was used to draw thousands of labourers from India to the tea plantations of Ceylon, the rice plantations of Burma and the rubber plantations of Malaya.[60] The same device was employed in colonial and republican Spanish America, first to attach the native Indian labour to the haciendas and, in the nineteenth century, to attract native Indian labour to the plantations and mines. Notably in India, Southeast Asia and Africa it expanded as a substitute for slavery as the latter came to be outlawed.[61]

Like indentured labour, debt bondage was used to send workers on long overseas voyages, conveying, for example, Chinese labour to the Americas and Australia, and Japanese labour to Peru, Hawaii and Mexico.[62] But unlike late nineteenth-century indentured service, which was directly organized by colonial officials and therefore carefully regulated by formal procedures, the labour recruited by debt bondage was managed informally by private brokers and agents. They employed, for example, a system of *kangani* to take Indians to Ceylon and Malaya; or *maistry* to take Indians to Burma; or credit-ticket to take Chinese to Malaya, Australia, the USA and Canada, and to take Japanese – at the close of the nineteenth century, when indentured service had become illegal – to Peru, Hawaii, Mexico, the USA and Brazil.[63]

These modern debt-bondage systems were not all alike. In the credit-ticket system, the broker recouped what he spent in transporting workers abroad by selling them to employers who, in turn, sold them on, or exacted an unpaid labour service for an appropriate period of time. The *maistry* and *kangani* systems, in contrast, involved no sale. The broker retained control, clawing back the money he had advanced by taking charge of the wages the workers received, allowing them only enough for maintenance until their return home. In Latin America, labour was recruited by two systems of debt bondage. One might be called the hacienda system and operated from at least the seventeenth century onwards; the other, the plantation system, emerged largely in the late nineteenth century when a buoyant international demand for sugar, cotton, timber, coffee, rubber and tobacco (along with the rapid improvement in communications brought about by steam trains and steamships) encouraged American and European companies to invest in the region. In the hacienda system, native Indians were attracted to reside on the hacienda by the distribution of grants of land in return for labour services or sharecropping rents. Binding them to the estate were the debts they contracted with the *hacendado*. In the plantation system, the planters sent agents to the Indian communities, offering advances of wages for seasonal work in return for obligatory labour over a fixed period.[64]

Debt bondage served two basic purposes: either to discharge a debt or to supply a sufficient amount of suitable labour, the need for which was largely due to the emergence of capitalist enterprises in the Third World, usually in the form of plantations, mines or manufacturing workshops. Whereas redemptive debt bondage was of immemorial provenance, labour-recruiting debt bondage came to the fore in the late nineteenth and early twentieth centuries, the result of an inability to use slave labour or to rely on local free labour for operating these new enterprises. Eventually, a free labour force would come to their aid, but, meanwhile, debt bondage stepped into the breach, recruiting workers from distant parts or from villages in the same region. It also attached them firmly to the place of work, acting, then, not only to enlist labour but also to impose discipline.

Frequently, debt bondage, in the manner of indentured service, helped to replace local with migrant labour. The use of debt bondage for this purpose sprang from the view that, caught up in village ways and sub-scribing to a peasant culture centred upon the ideals of self-employment and family obligation, local labour would be unreliable and expensive. Thus, to avoid dependence upon it, the plantations of Ceylon, Malaya or Burma imported workers under debt bondage from India. Alternatively, in late nineteenth-century California, thanks to the importation of large numbers of credit-ticket Chinese – 300,000 between 1850 and 1890 – debt bondage provided cheap labour in a world where free labour remained scarce and costly, and where other forms of servitude (i.e. slavery and indentured service) had become illegal.[65]

However, unlike indentured service, debt bondage was often a device for organizing local labour. Thus, in the highly competitive metal and batik industries of late nineteenth-century Java, debt bondage enabled employers to bind skilled labour to their businesses and to rule out the high wages that a free labour market would have created; while in Central and South America from the 1870s – at a time when the traditional haciendas were being transformed into plantations – debt bondage was the means whereby labour was extracted from the independent Indian villages and placed at the planters' disposal. Eventually, the labour problem faced by these planters was solved by the annexation of village lands and water rights, thereby oblig-ing the inhabitants, through the destruction of their economic autonomy, to work on the plantations full-time. In other words, the labour problems faced by emergent capitalism were eventually remedied by a process of pro-letarianization. But, until that could happen, debt bondage acted as an important stopgap, providing labour especially for the unpleasant work asso-ciated with cane-cutting in Guatemala, timbering in Chiapas, henequen cultivation in Yucatán, or collecting rubber in the Amazon jungle.[66]

How efficient was this labour? From the employer's point of view it was certainly cheap, and usefully obliged workers to pay the cost of their passage to the place of work, often a considerable sum. But the brokers and agents took their cut, at the expense of both employer and worker. As for the workers, they were frequently inexperienced and, if drawn from Asia, often malnourished. Moreover, having paid the wages in advance, employers were not strongly placed to ensure that the work was properly done. The lack of worker incentive, and the likelihood of worker flight, were further defects in the debt-bondage system, forcing employers to hire at considerable cost supervisors and security guards in order to keep the work-force to its contractual promises.

Assessing debt bondage from a humanitarian point of view is made difficult by the varying degrees of harshness it represented. The benefits conferred upon the debtor must also be taken into account. To assist the assessment, two formulatory questions have been put in recent years: the one, asking whether persons in debt bondage were surrogate slaves or a surrogate proletariat; the other, asking if it might be more appropriate to regard debt bondage as a form of credit.[67]

Debt bondage, like indentured service, allowed poor labourers to escape the destitution of overpopulated societies and enter worlds where work was plentiful and labour scarce, as with the migrations of Indians, Chinese and Japanese to Southeast Asia and the Americas in the course of the late nineteenth century. Furthermore, debt bondage allowed peasants to buttress their traditional way of life with waged labour, enabling them to 'raid' the capitalist world of the plantation and then return to the pre-capitalist village to enjoy their earnings.[68] This was true of Peruvian peasants travelling down from their communities in the sierra to the cotton and sugar plantations on the coast; of Mexican peasants travelling north to find work in the mines of Coahuila or Zacatecas, or on the cotton plantations of Laguna; of the inhabitants of southern India travelling to the plantations of Ceylon. For the landless, debt bondage found paid work, even supplying them with land, as on the haciendas of Mexico, Bolivia and Peru. For the landed, it supplied extra resources. Debt bondage, then, could grant the destitute the benefit of becoming a paid proletarian or even a peasant, and award native peasant communities, through extending the range of credit available to them, a better chance of preserving their ancestral ideals.

Unlike indentured service, which quintessentially required workers to embark on long sea voyages and to leave their homes for several years at a time, debt bondage catered for shorter journeys to work and briefer absences from home. Most labour recruited through debt bondage had the agreement of those subjected to it, thanks to the wages paid in advance, and came with the assurance that the assigned work would not last for more than a season.

Besides providing paid employment, debt bondage allowed families to cope with debt and to obtain credit. For example, it allowed families to take out loans when they had nothing to pawn but themselves and their children. In this manner, they found the means to pay for funerals and marriages, or to survive famine. The price was a loss of liberty; but even this could have its benefits. In Cambodia, Laos and Vietnam the perpetual slavery imposed upon criminals and political prisoners in lieu of execution could be escaped by subjection to debt bondage; and placing children in bondage could, in effect, transfer them from a poor to a rich background, if the creditor adopted them as part of his family.[69] And where the law ordered incorrigible debtors to become the permanent bondsmen of the creditor, as in Cambodia, it offered some protection from abuse: it safeguarded them from work that was debasing or unhealthy, and awarded the maltreated, if proven in court, an automatic right of liberation.[70] Generally, debt bondage lacked the degradation associated with serfdom or slavery. Those subjected to it were normally regarded as the victims of misfortune, or as party to a temporary labour arrangement, rather than as people who were naturally base or had become debased. Moreover, unlike serfdom and slavery, debt bondage tended not to be hereditary or even for life, and, unlike slaves or indentured servants, those in debt bondage did not usually become commodities for sale.

Yet, for various reasons, debt bondage could be a mixed blessing. The credit it raised easily degenerated into an inextricable debt that could tip the bonded person into slavery. Often debt bondage became a mean measure of exploitation because it placed one person totally under the control of another. Once recruited by an advance of wages, workers could be retained for much longer than was originally contracted, for example, by luring them, via the company store or the plantation shop, to fall deeper into debt. Since the wages were often received before the work was done, extra-economic means came to be deployed – in the form of physical punishment, criminal prosecution or arbitrary extensions of the term of work – to extract what was considered to be the appropriate labour return. Moreover, devices were concocted to compensate for desertion, illness and death. For example, a feature of the *kangani* system was to make a gang of workers liable for the debt of each member, so much so that any individual shortfall in the provision of labour had to be made up for by the rest of the gang.[71] When work was year-round, rather than seasonal – as with mining, timbering and rubber-collecting – and labour was in short supply (because the work was extremely arduous and unhealthy, or because local communities could independently subsist on their own land, and were therefore inclined to regard waged labour with contempt), employers resorted to trickery and force, partly to retain those who had offered their labour through binding them by accretions of debt, and partly to resist the attempts of debt bondsmen to withdraw their labour by flight, foot-dragging or absenteeism. At times, debt bondage could resemble the worst type of slavery.[72]

In the development of plantation economies, debt bondage had a special part to play in two parts of the world: in post-colonial Spanish America, especially Mexico, Guatemala and Peru, and in southern Asia, especially Ceylon, Burma and Malaya. Along with indentured labour, it allowed plantation agriculture not only to survive but also to extend itself in the difficult period that elapsed between the abolition of slavery and the emergence of a fully-fledged capitalist system operated by free workers. While indentured service provided migrant labour from overseas and projected it intercontinentally, debt bondage provided it overland and within the same continent. An exception to this distinction resulted from the refusal of the US legislature to countenance indentured service in the late nineteenth century, which caused large numbers of Chinese to enter the country under a covert system of debt bondage.[73] Indentured labour was more inclined to man plantations previously worked by slave labour, as in the Caribbean islands of Jamaica, Cuba, the Leeward Islands and Trinidad, and on the Caribbean mainland of British and Dutch Guiana; whereas debt bondage was more associated with plantation systems that had emerged since the abolition of slavery. The one thus complemented the other in supplying labour to the plantations of the world.

Debt bondage, along with indentured servitude, was responsible for massive movements of non-white labour, especially in the late nineteenth century. Although debt bondsmen frequently returned home, many did not. Those who returned provided the extra resources for further population growth in already overpopulated societies; whereas those who settled on or near the plantations promoted a proletarianization of society. By solving their labour problem, they enabled the plantations to thrive and expand at the expense of independent village land systems. Moreover, by depositing within indigenous societies a counter-society of different race, which not only represented a different culture but also an alternative labour supply, debt bondage, like indentured service, incited an extreme degree of racial prejudice and conflict in the regions to which it brought workers.

Branded as a latter-day variant of slavery, debt bondage was frequently outlawed from the late nineteenth century – by the Dutch in Java in 1860, for example, by the British in India in 1860 and in Malaya in 1883, by the French in Cambodia in 1897, and in most Latin American countries between 1915 and 1920. But, as the Temporary Slave Commission of the League of Nations recognized in 1926, debt bondage was difficult to uproot, even when legally prohibited.[74] It remained much more tenacious than indentured service or slavery. Independent of governmental agencies, and not all that different from some forms of free labour, debt bondage could survive illegally – that is, so long as it served a special purpose. What eventually excluded it as a source of labour for large-scale capitalist enterprises such as plantations and mines was the creation of a sufficient free labour market, the result of population growth and the collapse of peasant systems in the early twentieth century. But left intact was its function as a creator of credit and a discharger of debt in poor societies where, in the absence of property, personal labour remained an important source of collateral.

6

Penal Servitude

Penal servitude in the modern period was not just a matter of making convicts perform pointless tasks behind bars. It also furnished a labour force of vital economic significance, notably in the British colonies, the Asian empire of Tsarist Russia, and the totalitarian regimes of Nazi Germany and Stalinist Russia. For this reason, penal servitude bears comparison with the other forms of bonded labour. Moreover, along with debt bondage and indentured service, it reveals how extensively the Western world continued to operate unfree labour systems long after its repudiation of slavery and serfdom.

The fact that convicts were quintessentially state property ought to have distinguished penal servitude sharply from the other forms of bondage, which mostly fell into private ownership. Its distinctiveness was markedly evident in totalitarian regimes, with a compound of barbed wire, fierce dogs and armed guards to deploy and control the convict labour. Yet penal labour could also be placed in private hands. This was even true of Nazi Germany, where inmates of concentration camps and prisoners of war were allocated to work for private firms.[75] It was especially true of colonial regimes. Rather than being locked up, the convicts transported by the British to North America and the Caribbean in the seventeenth and eighteenth centuries were 'property in the service' of the merchants who contracted with the courts to convey them across the Atlantic. At the end of the voyage, the merchants conveyed the convicts to 'their assigns': that is, anyone in the New World prepared to purchase the use of their labour for the remainder of the sentence. These assigned convicts, then, were very much like the early modern indentured servants – even more so as neither was allowed a free return passage – yet with certain notable differences: the convicts were not volunteers; their term of service was longer (seven to fourteen years, rather than four to five); and they had no entitlement to freedom dues when their time was up.[76]

A similar system developed in Australia, once the revolt of the American colonies had ruled out transportation to the New World. Authorized in 1786, transportation to Australia lasted until the mid-nineteenth century, when the discovery of gold there in 1851 caused it to be regarded as an inappropriate place to send convicts. Once in Australia, however, the convicts were not sold to settlers but kept as the property of the colonial governor. Some were held in penal stations; others were employed in chain-gangs on public works. However, to reduce maintenance costs and supply badly needed private labour, convicts were frequently granted to settlers through an indenture of assignment that authorized the recipient to have possession until the sentence expired, in return for which they would provide the convict with rations and clothing to the value of at least £10 a year. If the convict gained a pardon, or received a ticket-of-leave (which released him from the obligation to provide compulsory labour), the settler could claim compensation. In the event of the convict's removal to a penal station, the result of reconviction, the settler was entitled to a replacement.[77]

The Australian system of convict assignment was condemned in the late 1830s as akin to slavery; as was the prison camp labour used in the 1930s and 1940s by the Nazi and Soviet authorities.[78] Equating penal servitude with slavery was a lack of consent over the duration, place and type of work, and the fact that the convict's labour had no market price. Yet in practice convict and slave labour were profoundly different. Normally, slavery was perpetual; penal servitude was finite. Penal servitude rested upon conviction; enslavement resulted from gratuitous capture or birth. What is more, a prominent feature of modern slavery was a racial distinction between master and slave, whereas, except in Nazi Germany, with its antipathy to Jews and Slavs, penal servitude was unaffected by racism: in the Soviet camps and the British colonies, for example, convicts and guardians were of the same race. Furthermore, the Nazi and Soviet prison camps achieved a level of brutality rarely experienced by slaves, largely because the labour they deployed was much more expendable. After all, it did not have to be bought and could be readily replaced without extra charge. In contrast to slaves – whose commodity value and replacement cost meant a loss of capital when lives were wasted – the inmates of the camps were frequently worked and starved to death. Associated with the camps was a rate of mortality never found among slaves: for example, the annual death rate in the Soviet camps was 25 per cent in 1942–3; and in the Nazi Central Works, situated underground in the Harz Mountains, it stood at 68.4 per cent in 1943.[79]

Unlike most forms of slavery, the nature of penal servitude was determined by its political, as well as its economic, role. Penal servitude was a punishment aimed at maintaining a law-abiding society, or at preserving the security of the state. For this reason, harsh treatment was more easily justified for prisoners than for slaves, whose normal treatment rested upon getting value for money and whose punishment, if not motivated by sadism, was usually a device to curtail disobedience. Furthermore, in applying punishment, the Nazi and Soviet camp guards were more of a law unto themselves than slave masters had ever been, especially in administering the death sentence. Also distinguishing the two forms of servitude from each other were the measures each employed to make labour fully operational. Although the work of both was encouraged by a mixture of physical force and incentive, for slaves the latter tended to be in the form of rewards, whereas for the inmates of prison camps it tended to be acts of deprivation. Thus, in addition to the basic maintenance of food and clothing, New World slaves were permitted degrees of independence which allowed them to establish, quite apart from the master, their own culture (derived from African traditions) and their own economy (through, for example, cultivating plots and marketing the produce). The inmates of the prison work camps, however, were chiefly spurred on to greater effort by the prospect of having their basic food rations cut, their privileges reduced and their sentence extended. Starvation and death was the penalty for failing to meet the work targets set by the camp guards.[80]

This was not the case with the convicts sold or assigned to private masters in the British colonies. Their condition of work was more akin to that of slavery, in the sense that it owed a great deal to the master's personality and the economic situation. Positive incentives could be offered in the form of extra treats. In Australia, wages, the grant of a pardon or a ticket-of-leave, a free passage out for the convicts' family, the promise of land when the sentence ended, were all on offer to induce good work. Moreover, colonial convicts, like slaves, secured rights, customary and official, to specified workloads, leisure time and rations.[81] As with slavery, the resistance integral to the system meant frequent resort to punishment, especially flogging, but also the use of iron collars and chains to curb flight. Moreover, helping to keep convicts up to the mark in Australia was the awful prospect of being switched from private employment to a penal station (at Moreton Bay, Norfolk Island, Port Arthur or Macquarie Harbour), or, for men, placement on a mobile gaol-gang. This meant days working in chains to repair roads and nights locked up in a prison box on wheels.[82] Disobedient female convicts in Australia faced imprisonment in penal factories, or, after being desexed through having their hair cut off and their heads shaved, hard labour in the prison grounds.[83] Notwithstanding the incentive system, then, punishment was frequently applied. In the American colonies, it was the master's prerogative subject to reason; and flogging and the use of shackles to prevent flight were probably as frequently employed for dealing with convicts as for dealing with slaves. In Australia, however, the punishment of convicts remained exclusively a public matter; and, for assigned convicts, it had to be authorized by a magistrate.[84] Notwithstanding this inconvenience, employers frequently applied for it. For example, in 1833 three-quarters of the convict population in Van Diemen's Land (now Tasmania) came before the courts for punishment while, in 1835, one half did so in New South Wales. In 1835, 18 per cent of 12,651 convicts were flogged in Tasmania, and 26 per cent of 27,340 convicts in New South Wales. The fact that they were flogged distinguished them from free servants, whose punishment for disobedience was limited to dismissal or fine. But it did not render them slaves. Added to the convicts' right to be punished only upon the authority of the crown was their possession, at least in theory, of an extensive right of access to the courts.[85] For this reason, the convicts transported to Australia enjoyed a legal status far superior to that of slaves.

In general terms, penal labour was recruited through systems of law that applied the following punishments for both political and criminal offences: oar service in the galleys; hard labour maintaining sea walls in major ports at home; transportation to the colonies; or incarceration in work camps situated in the home country. Galley service was practised in France and Spain until the late eighteenth century when it was replaced, first by hard labour in the metropolitan ports, and then by transportation to the colonies, a practice used in England since the seventeenth century. By the mid-twentieth century, the work camp had become a major means of organizing penal labour, because of its use by Nazi Germany, Stalinist Russia and Japan during the Second World War; but it had a much longer history, having been employed in Tsarist Russia for the development of Siberia, and in European overseas colonies to deal with convicts who, for various reasons, could not be assigned. Promoting the use of convict labour, before the twentieth century, was a policy of commuting the death penalty to imprisonment for life. Limiting its use was the emergence, in the course of the nineteenth century, of a state penitentiary system founded on a philosophy that attached more importance to restricting the prisoners' freedom than to commandeering their labour.[86]

Since condemnation to hard labour often resulted from a commutation of the death sentence, penal servitude bore some resemblance to the slavery that was conferred upon prisoners of war as an alternative to execution.[87] The offences, however, for which galley service, transportation or work-camp internment were imposed could be relatively minor. Much depended upon the ferocity of the law and its enforcement, coupled with the inadequacy of the country's prisons to cope with the consequence. For example, after 1718 in eighteenth and early nineteenth-century England, transportation became a penalty for petty theft and riot. A bibliophile barrister was transported to the American colonies in 1736, to serve a seven-year sentence, for stealing rare books from Cambridge University; while in 1827 the artist William Gould was banished to Australia for appropriating a coat, a silk handkerchief and three gloves.[88] Grand larceny, the offence most commonly punished by transportation in the English courts, could apply to very minor offences, starting with the theft of goods worth 1 shilling. As for other transportable offences, in 1831 the Captain Swing riots in Hampshire and Wiltshire caused 256 men to be sent to New South Wales, while the great majority of transports from Ireland to Australia were for vagabondage and peasant insurgency.[89] Legal ferocity was evident in the Soviet Union where the 'five stalks law' of 1932 condemned as an enemy of the people anyone caught stealing state property, and a citizen could be arrested by the man who came to read the electricity meter, according to Solzhenitsyn. It was also found in Nazi Germany, where absenteeism and late arrival at work were designated serious crimes against the state, and where Jews, gypsies and homosexuals came to be interned for no other crime than being themselves. Since the latter groups tended to be dispatched to extermination rather than work camps, however, they provided only a minor source of penal labour.[90]

Another factor in the recruitment of penal labour was the total warfare of the 1940s when, in the struggle between Nazi Germany and Soviet Russia, industrial and agricultural production on both sides – having been starved of free labour by the high level of military recruitment – became heavily dependent upon exacting forced labour from prisoners of war, defeated peoples and political internees.[91] The labour resources engaged in this manner were enormous. In late 1944 the Nazis employed 7.7 million forced labourers, of whom between 2.5 and 3 million were in prison camps (i.e. concentration and prisoner-of-war). The remainder were workers conscripted from conquered states and for the most part barracked in closed camps which were not very different from those that held the prisoners of war. Stalinist Russia employed 18 million prisoners, with not less than 1 million and not more than 2.6 million employed in any one year between 1936 and 1953.[92] Earlier, only Tsarist Russia had used penal labour on a large scale, with 1.3 million transported to Siberia between 1800 and 1916. In comparison, the number of convicts put to work in the British colonies was minute, with something like 60,000 transported to North America and the Caribbean between the 1660s and the 1770s, and 162,000 sent to Australia between 1788 and 1867, although this was a large amount compared with the number condemned to the colonies in France and Spain.[93] Convicts transported to the colonies provided an important source of labour and of settlers. Since 90 per cent of the British transports to the American colonies went to Maryland and Virginia, convicts in parts of the Chesapeake in the eighteenth century comprised 10–12 per cent of the white population. Likewise, in Australia, the small numbers of free immigrants before the 1840s meant that convicts in New South Wales and Van Diemen's Land furnished a high proportion of the early settlers.[94]

Whereas the majority of penal labourers in Nazi Germany or Tsarist and Soviet Russia were political prisoners, the convicts transported to the British colonies were mostly criminals: in fact, 'political' offences accounted for only 9 per cent of transports to the Caribbean and North America (most of them Irish and Scots rebels, or supporters of the Monmouth uprising of 1685); and for only 3 per cent of transports to Australia (almost two-thirds of them comprised of Irish peasants convicted for protesting against bad landlordship).[95]

Apart from its punitive function, penal servitude had the same purpose as the other forms of bondage: that is, to compensate for a chronic shortage of labour. Besides resulting from a situation of total war (as in Nazi Germany and Soviet Russia), the use of prisoners as labourers was associated with the early stages of colonization. In the foundation of overseas empires by the Spanish, the French, the Dutch and the British, small numbers of convicts were used both to man the ships on the original voyages of discovery and to establish the earliest settlements.[96] When the conditions were too remote or inhospitable to attract free labour, penal labour stepped into the breach. Initially in Maryland and Virginia, convicts as well as indentured servants provided the heavy labour for clearing the land and establishing the first plantations; while in early nineteenth-century New South Wales, the absence of slaves and indentured servants, and the small numbers of free settlers, gave the convicts a vital part to play in converting a military base-cum-penal station into a settled colony. They did so by providing the labour not just for the construction of harbours and roads but also for the development of cattle and sheep ranches.[97]

In addition, convicts played an essential part in the exploitation of timber and minerals where the terrain and climate were so hostile that compulsion remained the only viable means of obtaining the necessary labour. This was true of the far northern and far eastern tundra and *taiga* regions of Russia, where the long Arctic winter, the permafrost and the short, mosquito-ridden summer ruled out free settlements, and the work was therefore done by convicts in camps. Having first built the camp, the prisoners then constructed the communicating roads and railways, and finally provided the labour to exploit the local resources. In this way, the timber operations of Siberia, the coal mines of Vorkuta, the gold mines of Kolyma and the nickel mines of Novil'sk came to be first developed.[98]

Furthermore, during the early 1940s, the war effort in Nazi Germany and Soviet Russia relied heavily on penal labour to produce not only raw materials but also weapons and military equipment. Of the Soviet Union's output in the Second World War, it provided 100 per cent of gold, 60 per cent of tin, 13 per cent of nickel and 13 per cent of mortar shells. In 1944, it produced 17 per cent of munitions.[99] In Nazi Germany, almost half the miners in the Ruhr collieries by late 1943 were foreigners and 75 per cent of them were eastern workers who were mostly Soviet prisoners of war. Furthermore, the use of prison camp labour for the manufacture of armaments began in 1942, notably at Buchenwald, Auschwitz, and Ravensbrück. By October 1943, 60,000 internees were engaged in making armaments. By August 1944 the Central Works, manned by 12,000 prisoners, had been established in the Harz Mountains to build V2 rockets. As a result, the secret police of the two states – the NKVD in Russia and the SS in Germany – who had direct responsibility for this penal labour, became heavily involved in industrial production.[100]

In many of these cases, the efficiency of penal labour cannot be reasonably compared with free labour since, at the same time and place, the latter hardly existed. Penal labour, it could be said, was better than the only real alternative: a totally insufficient labour supply. As Chief Justice Forbes pronounced of New South Wales in 1826: 'Without labour, land in this colony is useless, and the only labourers are assigned prisoners.'[101] The same was true of Arctic Russia. The advantages of penal labour were as follows: it did not normally need to be purchased or paid. Moreover, since convict labour was often used in place of machinery or haulage animals, and since the guards would have been necessary anyway – even if the prisoners had served their sentences without labour obligations – the expense of employing prison labour was a fraction of what free or slave labour would have cost. Apart from requiring a minimal capital investment, penal labour, especially when interned, offered the advantage of a very firm control over the workforce. It could also be highly manoeuvrable: when used to provide heavy labour in remote regions, convicts in prison camps could be easily shifted from place to place and from project to project.[102]

In the British colonies convicts ran away frequently – for example, 9 per cent did so in Maryland between 1746 and 1775 – or rendered themselves incapable of work through persistent drunkenness. However, if provided with incentives, such as the prospect of a freedom payment at the end of the sentence, or the payment of wages during it, they were able to work sufficiently well.[103] Commenting on the labour situation of New South Wales in 1828, Alexander Harris rated convict labour at half the cost of free labour. As for its effectiveness relative to that of free workers, he thought: 'between the fear of being flogged and the hope of getting a little indulgence . . . their labour was nearly as equal'.[104] Colonial convict labour, from the employer's point of view, also enjoyed some advantage over other forms of bondage. While probably less responsive to work than indentured servants or slaves, and certainly more prone to take flight, especially when under assignment, these convict labourers compared well both with slaves, in being much cheaper to acquire, and also with indentured servants, in providing a longer service and in lacking any entitlement to freedom dues.[105] Moreover, by the nineteenth century – when convict labour could be acquired without a down payment, and indentured service was now 'privileged' to receive wages as well as maintenance, and even the return fare – penal servitude seemed financially more efficient.

In the Nazi and Soviet prison camps, where the inmates were driven on by the threat of reduced rations – in fact, by the very real prospect of being starved to death – they understandably worked as hard as their strength allowed. However, physical weakness caused by malnutrition, coupled with the sheer inability of large numbers to work because of savage treatment, severely reduced their productivity, as did the corruption practised by camp officials. Albert Speer felt that a prison labourer in armaments produced only one-sixth of what a normal worker could produce, and emphasized that the Nazi rocket programme at Central Works, which relied on prison labour, was prone to fall way behind schedule. In making these points, however, he was driven to rubbish the forced labour plans of his rival, Heinrich Himmler. In Soviet Russia, prison labour was thought to possess less than half the capacity of free labour, although, in the first months of the war, the penal labour employed to produce mortars and grenades managed to exceed the set target by a remarkable 38 per cent.[106]

For British convicts, transportation was frequently regarded as a very soft option, a means whereby men and women received, instead of the extreme punishment they deserved, the handsome reward of a free passage to, and guaranteed employment in, a world rich with opportunity. Thus, a poem in *The Whitehall Evening Post* of December 1786 went:

> They go to an island to take special charge,
> Much warmer than Britain, and ten times as large;
> No custom-house duty, no freightage to pay,
> And tax-free they'll live when at Botany Bay.[107]

Pity the lot of the freeman, then, obliged to pay his passage, to search for work on arrival, and to pay taxes if he found it. Nonetheless, the convicts themselves, and the families they left behind, had good reason to think otherwise. After all, the convicts did not ask to be sent to Maryland or New South Wales; nor to be subjected to compulsory labour for seven years or more when they got there, often for a minor infraction of the law. Transportation to the Americas, moreover, in convict eyes, carried the ultimate degradation of having to work in the fields alongside black slaves.[108] Transportation to Australia – a journey of 15,000 miles with no return fare on offer – meant saying goodbye to the homeland for ever.

The convicts' antipathy to being transported to America was vividly expressed in the requests they made for alternative punishment: they preferred to be flogged, or to serve in the army, or to be used for medical research. It was also declared in the attempts runaway convicts frequently made in early modern America to return home, even though it was a capital offence to do so. However, transportation to the colonies was undoubtedly an improvement upon death, and so those convicts who were exiled rather than executed for major crimes arguably received not a bad deal. As for the many convicts transported to the colonies for petty offences, the punishment was clearly quite out of keeping with the crime; but the system of assignment, the freedom imparted by the nature of assigned work – especially when involved with ranching – the value placed upon their labour because labour was in such short supply, and the ticket-of-leave provision that licensed Australian convicts to work for themselves before the full sentence was served, were all facts that, combined, did not create a hell on earth, but rather offered convicts the opportunity to live in reasonable conditions and eventually to better their lot.[109] This was emphatically not the case in the Nazi or Soviet prison camps. There, the authorities might ironically congratulate the inmates on their good fortune in having escaped the death sentence, but the camp experience was so horrendous, dehumanizing and destructive that death could well seem a merciful release.[110] In fact, the extreme oppressiveness of these concentration camps made all other forms of modern servitude – slavery, serfdom, indentured service, debt bondage and convict labour in the colonies – appear almost benign: their victims able, by dint of perseverance, courage and guile, to secure in spite of their subjection a quality of life that was, at least, superior to mere survival.

Part II

Emergence and Development

7

White Servitude in the Americas

A distinctive feature of the British colonies, both in the Caribbean and North America, was their heavy reliance upon white bonded servants in the early stages of development.[1] Principally of English, Scottish, Irish, Swiss and German extraction, these servants had a vital part to play in clearing the waste, in establishing plantations and in bringing manufacturing and mechanical skills from the Old World to the New: so much so that the economy of these colonies, it could be said, was originally founded upon white servitude. A French equivalent, the *engagés à temps*, had a similar, if less important, role in the French Caribbean.[2]

Bonded service was also a major means of recruiting new settlers. Over half the new arrivals in the British colonies between 1640 and 1780 obtained passage to the Americas not by paying the fare but by binding themselves to provide labour for a number of years. As settlers, they played a vital part in frontier expansion. In 1717 Alexander Spottiswood reported: 'The inhabitants of our frontiers are composed generally of such as have been transported hither as servants and, being out of their time, settle themselves where land is to be taken up.'[3] The value of bonded service soon received official recognition: in 1664 a committee of the Council of Foreign Plantations in London, having stressed the need to populate the colonies in order to improve them, declared that 'people are increased principally by sending of servants'.[4]

Bonded servants came in several forms, although all were alike in being commodities for sale. Many reached the Americas as indentured servants who, before leaving the home country, had signed a legal document specifying the conditions and duration of service. Following their arrival and sale, a note was made to that effect on the back of the indenture. Others were simply bound by 'custom of the country' and the colonial laws appertaining. No legal document was signed. They were sometimes termed servants by statute. Thanks to a body of colonial legislation passed between 1661 and 1717, the transportation of servants, bonded by indenture and statute, was widely practised in the seventeenth century. In the eighteenth century, a third type of bonded servant came to the fore: the so-called redemptioners. After making the transatlantic passage without prior payment, they eventually signed an indenture of service in the New World and submitted themselves for sale. But this only happened after a fourteen-day period of grace in which they were given the chance to redeem themselves by somehow finding the fare. Succeeding, they settled as free persons; failing, they became bonded servants.

These three types of servant had two things in common: their bondage was by consent and due to transportation.[5] In addition, two other types of transported servant existed whose subjection to bondage was involuntary: the first were the servants whom unscrupulous merchants had 'spirited' away from the Old World against their will; the second were the convicts sent to serve their sentence in the colonies.[6]

There was yet one further type of servant: the settler who fell foul of colonial law. Settlers convicted of indebtedness could be sentenced to bondage until the debt was cleared. As an alternative means of redemption, they could sell their children into indentured service. Settlers convicted of crime could also be placed in bondage. In the absence of a penitentiary system, they were, initially, fined for a range of offences that included larceny, arson and forgery and then, if unable to pay the fine, subjected to bonded labour. Like indentured servants, all these convicts – metropolitan and colonial – were assigned for a given term to whomsoever was prepared to buy them.[7]

These various forms of bonded service had several characteristics in common. Besides being subject to sale, all bonded servants had to provide labour not in return for a wage but merely for maintenance. None of them had any choice of master: they simply went to the highest bidder. Yet bondage was not for ever. After a given period of service, it lapsed. Unlike the bondage of black slaves, then, it was not transmitted to the next generation. Nor was it often for life. For indentured and statutory servants, it lasted for four to seven years; for convicts, between seven and fourteen years.[8] This meant that, to survive as an important source of labour, fresh supplies of servants had to be found.

Bonded service originated in a device developed, between 1608 and 1619, by the Virginia Company to attract settlers to the New World. In return for loaning the fare out, the company required several years of contracted service. But unable to cope with runaways and foot-draggers, it escaped responsibility for organizing this labour first by renting, and then by selling, it to the free settlers. With the dissolution of the company in 1624, the system had become an important source of labour: in a Virginian white population of 1,227, 487 were bonded servants. And this was only the beginning. Something like three-quarters of whites who crossed the Atlantic in the seventeenth century to settle in Virginia arrived as bondsmen.[9]

In the transatlantic bonded servant trade, the Virginia Company was soon replaced by a host of English merchants. English regulations against 'spiriting' (a parliament ordinance of 1645, a privy council order of 1682, and an act of parliament of 1717) encouraged merchants to protect themselves against accusations of forcible abduction by requiring transports to sign indentures before embarkation.[10] However, throughout the seventeenth and eighteenth centuries, many servants still came to the New World unindentured. Upon arrival and faced with the debt incurred by the passage out, they consented to be sold into servitude. At the point of sale they either submitted to indenture, thereby becoming lapsed redemptioners, or agreed to abide by the custom of the country, thereby becoming servants by statute. Virtually all who had signed indentures in the home country were single persons; the same was true of the servants by statute. However, a fair number of lapsed redemptioners came as families – notably from Germany and Ireland – which, in the process of sale, were often broken up. Furthermore, a large number of those who consented to transportation as bonded servants eventually became victims of deception, when the promise of land at the end of the service went unfulfilled.[11] As former peasants, they were drawn to the New World by the prospect of regaining the landed status of their forebears. This was an ambition often denied by the spread of large-scale commercial farming which obliged them, once their term of service had expired, to make a living as landless labourers.

White bonded labour quickly became acceptable in all the British New World colonies. Yet in some, notably the New England colonies of Connecticut and Massachusetts – where enough free colonists existed to satisfy the need for labour – it remained unimportant. The greatest concentrations, in fact, lay in the Chesapeake colonies of Virginia and Maryland, and also in the Caribbean colonies of Barbados and Jamaica, the regions where black slavery first predominated.[12]

Well over half the men and women who came to the British American colonies as bonded servants went to Maryland and Virginia. Virginia was the major destination in the seventeenth century, Maryland in the eighteenth century. Pennsylvania emerged as an important destination in the early eighteenth century, but only in comparison with the mainland colonies above the Chesapeake. In the 1770s, when Pennsylvania took 18 per cent of imported bonded servants, 79 per cent went to Virginia and Maryland. By this time, very few were going to the West Indies. However, in the mid-seventeenth century Barbados was the major destination, taking 69 per cent against 28 per cent for the Chesapeake colonies, an intake that had declined to 3 per cent, against 85 per cent for the Chesapeake, in the 1690s. By the 1720s Jamaica had become the more important destination in the West Indies, with 21 per cent going there against 1 per cent to Barbados. Then, in the 1730s, it became the major destination for servants transported to the New World, taking 60 per cent of new arrivals against 24 per cent for the Chesapeake. Thereafter, however, it faded away as an employer of bonded service, taking no more than 1 per cent in the

1770s. By this time, most were going to the Chesapeake and the rest to Pennsylvania.[13]

A striking feature about the employment of white bonded servants in the Americas is that demand for them was not necessarily ruled out by the extensive use of black slaves. The experience of Barbados, where slaves quickly replaced servants, was not typical. Jamaica, for example, took its largest share of servants in the 1730s when 93 per cent of the island's population was black, most of them slaves; and in the 1770s – when the Chesapeake colonies were receiving most of the bonded servants sent to the New World – the proportion of blacks to the population as a whole stood at an all time high of 39 per cent.[14] Several factors allowed colonies to employ slaves and servants in large numbers at the same time. One was that, in societies dominated by plantations, a division of labour occurred, the unskilled work being provided by slaves, the skilled work and management by bonded servants.[15]

Furthermore, promoting a demand for white bonded servants – even where black slaves existed in profusion – was the scarcity and costliness of free labour. But bonded servants could also be difficult to find and therefore expensive to buy. Unlike slaves, bonded servants (other than transported convicts) had some choice of colony in which to serve. Since they made this decision before leaving their home country, it was heavily influenced by the relative reputation the various colonies had come to enjoy. Generally, the mainland colonies were preferable to those of the Caribbean. When selecting their destination, servants took into account the conditions and nature of the work, as well as the rewards on offer for good service. Barbados soon ruled itself out – between 1640 and 1660 – through becoming predominantly an island of large sugar plantations worked by slaves. This happened at the expense of the former system of small cotton and tobacco farms worked with white bonded labour and, in many cases, owned by ex-servants. The change was made evident in a petition from the council and assembly of Barbados to the king in 1675: 'In former times we were plentifully furnished with Christian servants from England . . . but now we can get few English, having no lands to give them at the end of their time, which formerly was their main allurement . . . Our whole dependence therefore is upon negroes.' With insufficient land left for distribution in freedom dues, and little likelihood of attracting white servants in competition with Jamaica or the American mainland, the Barbados planters were obliged to train slaves to carry out the skilled and supervisory work on the estate; otherwise, they were left dependent upon unreliable convicts or highly paid freemen. The Leeward Islands (Antigua, Montserrat, Nevis and St Christopher) underwent the same transformation between 1678 and 1713. Jamaica followed suit in the late eighteenth century. A crucial attraction for white bondsmen was the likelihood of finding employment once the term of service had finished. However, by 1739 a visitor to Jamaica, Charles Leslie, had to report: 'After the expiration of their four years, nobody is found to employ them and they generally remain in an abject state.'[16]

On the American mainland, the Chesapeake colonies enjoyed a decisive advantage over other British colonies in the recruitment of servants. This was because they grew a staple crop that was attractive to those merchants engaged in the white bonded labour trade. For these merchants it was highly convenient to arrive with a cargo of servants and return with a cargo of tobacco. In contrast to sugar, tobacco continued to be grown by small farmers, who preferred white bonded labour because the price of a servant remained much less than that of a slave. Bonded servants, then, continued to be used in the Chesapeake as unskilled as well as unskilled labourers: that is, while the price was held down by the existence of a surplus of workers in Europe, the absence of government restriction upon their emigration and the willingness of merchants to ship them under bondage to Baltimore.

Field work was carried out by bonded servants not only in the Chesapeake but also in the middle colonies of New York, New Jersey and Pennsylvania, where farming was largely for the American market. The intake of servants in these parts, however, was curtailed by the prevalence of farms worked with family labour, as well as an inability to compete with the Chesapeake in bidding for new arrivals. Promoting the employment of bonded servants as field workers in these parts above the Chesapeake was, on the one hand, the high cost of hired labour, which tended to gravitate to New England, and, on the other, the failure to purchase enough slaves. Indicating the continued importance of bonded white labour, the president of the council of Pennsylvania in 1756 declared: 'Every kind of business here, as well among the tradesmen and mechanics as the planters and farmers, is chiefly carried on and supported by the labour of indented servants.'[17]

The history of white bonded service stemmed naturally from its basic characteristics: notably, the principle of consent that enabled servants to decide their colonial destination; the relatively short-term nature of the service; the fact that, apart from basic maintenance, payment for service was received only at the very beginning and very end; and also the fact that those in bonded service were exclusively white, allowing them to benefit from the distinction that colonial society made between black and white servitude.

The principle of consent, in conjunction with the short term of the service, created a problem of supply; for the consent principle obliged the various colonies to compete for new recruits, while the shortness of the bond rendered recruitment a vital precondition of the system's survival. As a result, incentives had to be offered to attract bonded servants; and the less popular areas (such as the Caribbean relative to the American mainland, and, in the Caribbean, Barbados relative to Jamaica) were driven to legislate into existence a more benign system. This involved curtailing the punishment masters could administer; guaranteeing servants minimal limits on the provision of food, clothing and lodging; granting them immunity from gang work in the fields; promising generous freedom dues; even paying wages and shortening the service.[18] In addition, certain other factors encouraged leniency, notably the method of payment and the ingrained need of colonial society to distinguish between white and black bondage.

The service owed by white bonded servants was specifically in return for their free passage to the New World; then, at the end of the service, they received a freedom due to reward their good work and loyalty. In between, they were entitled to nothing but maintenance. This hiatus in remuneration presented the master with the problem of extracting from the servants diligent, committed and efficient work, even more so as his capacity to control them through a regimen of punishment was restricted by colonial law. Heavy-handedness by the master, moreover, could lead to further foot-dragging or more running away. After the early days, when the penalty for absconding was death, captured runaways were usually sentenced to an extension of their term of service; but this measure hardly benefited the master who had to pay the cost of capture only to regain a servant who was even less prepared to work.[19] A master wishing to secure willing work from white bondsmen and women needed to have some incentive to offer. As a result, fair treatment of servants by masters could exceed what contracts of indenture or colonial statute laid down.

Originally in the New World, Africans or Amerindians could be regarded as servants in temporary bondage, and therefore no different from white bondsmen. But based on an assumption of the elemental Christianity of whites and the elemental Paganism of the non-white, a distinction became entrenched in colonial and metropolitan law: one that subjected bonded blacks to perpetual servitude transmissible in the blood and binding upon future generations, while imposing upon bonded whites a servitude that simply suspended freedom for a specific period. This distinction lost its rigidity only in connection with the abolition of slavery when, for example, in Pennsylvania the Gradual Abolition Law of 1780 turned newborn slaves into indentured servants. The same happened to liberated slaves in the British Caribbean during the 1830s.[20] Furthermore, the bondage imposed on blacks presumed that they had no legal identity as persons, apart from what the law exceptionally conceded. In contrast, the bondage imposed on whites simply denied certain rights until the term of service was over, while presuming their retention of the remainder during the period of servitude.[21]

The clear distinction made between black and white servitude in the New World manifested itself in 1664 when an official registry office was established in London to keep a record of those transported. Its remit was to recognize two types of servant, one black, the other white. Defining the blacks as 'perpetual servants', it recommended their sale for £20. Defining the whites as temporary servants priced at £16, it specified that they were to be freed after a period of time and given a payment of £10.[22] Three years earlier, the same distinction had been firmly made in the Barbados Servant Code of 1661, a code imitated in Jamaica and the Leeward Islands.[23] Thus, servants received privileges relating to clothing allowances, food rations and working conditions. These privileges they were entitled to defend in court, having the right to sue their masters and to give testimony. Furthermore, when appearing as defendant, servants were allowed, in the manner of freemen, trial by jury. If found guilty, they were normally punished by having the term of sentence extended. If found to be victims of their master's brutality, servants could expect the law to be as retributive as if they were free. Apart from their colour, society's attitude towards them stemmed from the fact that their servitude was of short duration. For this reason, they were even allowed to own property, although not to marry or follow a trade without the master's permission. Regarded as potential settlers, they were given duties associated with free status (although they were not permitted to vote, hold office or serve on a jury), especially militia service – initially, to defend settlements against Indian incursions; later, to defend the white community from black dissidence.[24]

For blacks it was a different matter.[25] The Barbados code of 1661 failed to specify what rations slaves should receive or what work they should be required to do. Moreover, they had no rights of legal action, testimony, or trial by jury. The punishment of slaves, it was accepted, lay with the master rather than the courts; and, since they could not be punished by an extension of service, they tended to be whipped, branded and mutilated. If this led to the killing of a slave, the master stood liable to no more than a fine.[26]

In Virginia, Maryland and Pennsylvania, servants were awarded fewer legal rights than in Barbados. This was because servants preferred to go to North America, and so did not need additional perquisites to lure them there. Colonial law on the mainland, as it evolved in the seventeenth century, certainly distinguished between black and white servitude, to the benefit of white servants. But it also established similarities in legal status.[27] Both servants and slaves were considered as chattels for tax purposes, with the taxable wealth of masters assessed on their value. Both could be sold, or hired out for a wage. Both could be willed to another or attached to acquit debt. And the absconding of both was regarded as a major offence in the law: a peculiar form of theft in which the object stolen was held to have perpetrated the offence through walking away with itself. In this respect, bonded service was unequivocally a form of servitude.[28]

The presence of black slaves in substantial numbers not only promoted a more elevated view of white bonded servants but also lightened their burden of work. Originally, bonded servants were required to do whatever the master ordered. When this led to making artisans labour in the fields, the work must have seemed extremely arduous. However, the arrival of slaves narrowed down, and alleviated, the work expected of them. By the 1680s the field work on the plantations of Barbados and Jamaica was confined to blacks, with the possible exception of a few white convicts. Within the next hundred years, Maryland and Virginia went the same way. In fact, the employment of bonded servants as farm labourers only endured in the regions with a low concentration of slaves, notably the American middle colonies and New England. Where slave labour was extensively used in the fields, bonded servants came to be mainly employed as skilled artisans. This was reflected in the import figures for bonded servants. Thus, on the American mainland the proportion of skilled servants brought from England increased from 23 per cent in 1683–4 to 77.2 per cent in 1773–5;

while, in the Caribbean, it rose from 37.4 per cent in 1683–4 to 100 per cent in 1773–5. Eventually the black slaves took over the skilled positions on the plantations. This resulted from the increasing difficulty planters had in obtaining servants, and from the growing numbers of slaves born in the New World who, reared on the plantations, seized the chance to acquire artisanal skills in order to escape field work and to better themselves. Displaced by slaves as skilled and unskilled labourers, white servants continued to be employed in domestic service, as labour supervisors and as plantation managers. In this way, the range of work required of them became confined to relatively light and amenable tasks.[29]

Two serious drawbacks countered the legal and labour gains bonded servants derived from the presence of slavery. In the first place, the process that lightened their work reduced them to economic insignificance. In the second place, their entitlement to freedom dues suffered. In the early days of settlement, colonial laws frequently specified that servants should receive a grant of land once their term was over: 30 acres was specified in a Jamaican statute of 1661; 50 acres by a Maryland statute of 1640. A Barbados statute of 1647 awarded ex-servants land in Nevis or Antigua. And, when Pennsylvania was founded in 1682, each servant was promised 50 acres by William Penn. Virginia was most unusual in having no such statute, but even there the crown instructed the governor in 1679 to set land aside for freed servants. In these early days grants of land were awarded to ex-servants either out of waste or out of headright land, that is, the 50-acre plots awarded settlers for each white person they brought to America at their own expense.[30]

But the regions to which bonded service was drawn soon became dominated by slave plantations, which tended to accumulate whatever land became available for cultivation. To appease the planters' acquisitiveness, colonial laws were changed to convert the former freedom due in land to a grant of sugar (as in Barbados by 1661), or a payment of money (40 shillings in Jamaica by 1681; £3 in North Carolina by 1741), or an outfit of clothes (as in South Carolina by 1717, or in Pennsylvania by 1682). Even when the law remained unchanged, as in Maryland, the land tended to adhere to the planters, so much so that, in the 1670s, only one quarter of freed servants were able to prove their right to a freedom due in land; and most of them quickly sold it. In Virginia, it was reported in 1696 that 'there has not for many years been any waste land to be taken up . . . by servants who have served their time', and consequently 'they are forced to . . . go to the utmost bounds of the colony for land, exposed to danger and often times . . . the occasion of war with the Indians'. Working against the chance of bonded servants becoming landholders was the planters' need not only for more land but also for hired labour. The freedom due, initially a device for establishing the freed servant as a small family farmer, very quickly became a device for obliging him, if he stayed put, to sell his labour. If the land system in the New World had followed that of the Old – with the landowners inclined to rent out their estates rather than to keep them in hand – the outcome would have been different. But the profitability of the slave-operated plantation dictated otherwise. No matter what landed promises were made in the Old World to attract white labour to the New, those who came as bonded servants mostly finished up without land, or were obliged to trek into Indian country to acquire it.[31]

Bonded service, with the exception of convict assignment, never aroused much colonial objection. Even in Pennsylvania, where plans were made to end slavery in 1780, bonded service remained perfectly acceptable and continued in use until the 1830s.[32] The termination of the practice was due partly to metropolitan restrictions placed upon the export of servant labour – the work of governments in Germany, Switzerland and Britain between 1764 and 1819 – and partly to the introduction of a cheap passage to the Americas, the result of the spare stowage that ships carrying cotton from New York and timber from Quebec possessed on the westward passage. From the 1820s, with the fare reduced to half of what it had been two centuries before, a flood of free workers and their families could afford to sail to America.[33] A traditional justification for the employment of bonded labour, slave and servant, had been the scarcity, costliness and unreliability of free labour. The latter point was made by Benjamin Franklin of Philadelphia in 1751. Comparing free labour with slavery, he wrote: 'Slaves may be kept as long as a man pleases, or has occasion for their labour, while hired men are continually leaving their master (often in the midst of his business) and setting up for themselves.'[34] The first part of the remark also indicated the advantage of slave over servant labour, but the second part highlighted the advantage of bonded servants over free employees. What it failed to reveal was the Smithian point (applicable to servants as well as slaves) that the motivation of workers, who were paid merely in maintenance, was poor relative to workers who received a wage.

In the early nineteenth century a massive influx of free workers transformed the labour situation on the American mainland, thus removing at a stroke the traditional problem to which bonded service had been addressed. The flow of white workers, however, did not go to the British Caribbean. There, a labour problem reappeared with the abolition of slavery, leading to another phase of short-term bonded labour, this time of ex-slaves required to serve for a time as a condition of their emancipation, and of Asians brought to work the plantations, partly in order to depress the wages of the ex-slaves, partly in order to compensate for the latters' unwillingness to continue working on them.

Long before its demise in the New World, white bonded service was fading away, largely because European countries placed restrictions on the export of servants, and slaves made it redundant by providing the plantations with skilled work and management. Thanks to the European export restrictions, bonded service had slipped into insignificance in America by 1800; and with slaves taking on the skilled and supervisory work, the same had happened in the Caribbean by the 1780s.[35] However, the history of bonded service in the New World was not simply a story that told of its great importance in the early stages of colonial settlement, its steady decline due to the rise of the slave plantation, and an end brought about by an influx of the free. A statistical snapshot of the migrant situation in 1773–6 vividly reveals the durability of bonded service and its latter-day importance in peopling the New World. In that period, 6,000 persons – a figure that probably included Thomas Paine – were recorded as leaving the old country to settle in the new. Against the 34 per cent who paid their passage and settled as free persons, 66 per cent arrived in bonded service, with 55 per cent crossing the Atlantic as indentured servants, 6 per cent as redemptioners and 5 per cent as convicts. Of these bondspersons 95 per cent went straight to the mainland, mostly to Maryland and Pennsylvania; the remainder went to the West Indies.[36]

Sustaining bonded service in early eighteenth-century North America was the willingness of large numbers of impoverished or persecuted Europeans to forfeit temporarily their freedom in order to cross the Atlantic. They were predominantly Irish and West Germans. For the most part, they travelled out as redemptioners with the forlorn hope of paying their passage once they had reached the Americas, presumably by selling the goods and chattels they had brought with them, since many came as 'sold-up' families who settled for indentured servitude after failing to raise the money to meet the fare. The impact made by the arrival of the Irish was reflected in the startling difference between those working as indentured servants in Pennsylvania between 1682–7 (when 86 per cent were English against 12 per cent Irish) and 1741–6 (when 93.6 per cent were Irish against 4 per cent English). The Irish flood followed the repeated famines of 1725, 1726 and 1727. It was further stimulated by the decline of the Ulster linen industry. As a result, something like 31,000 came from Northern Ireland alone between 1725 and 1775.[37] In the same period over 40,000 entered Pennsylvania from western Europe. The flow started between 1685 and 1715, caused by a flight of Protestants from France, Germany and Switzerland to escape religious persecution, and by an exodus of peasants from a Rhineland and Palatinate ravaged by the armies of Louis XIV. It continued in the early nineteenth century, the result of the damage committed by the armies of Napoleon.[38] The high proportion of white settlers who came to the New World to work as bondspersons – normally calculated at over half of those who settled between the mid-seventeenth century and the revolt of the American colonies – was due to the considerable numbers that came in the early eighteenth century.

A final important source of white bonded labour in the Americas stemmed from the British practice of sending convicts there, a practice abruptly ended by the revolt of the American colonies. Transportation was first authorized by an order in council of 1615, specifically for convicts reprieved from the death sentence, and briefly extended to non-capital offences in 1662, when transportation 'to any of the English plantations beyond the seas' became the penalty for incorrigible vagabonds.[39] In the seventeenth century, however, transportation was not extensively used, other than for rebellion. By 1700 only about 10,000 convicts had been dispatched to the New World, mainly since the late 1640s. Roughly one-third of them were rebels, mostly Scottish or Irish – in fact, all but the 840 convicted for Monmouth's Rebellion of 1685.[40] In spite of the small numbers of criminals transported in this period, colonial protests were made against the practice; and in the 1670s, following disturbances allegedly stirred up by convicts, both Virginia and Maryland sought to ban further entry.[41]

The bulk of the convicts Britain transported to the New World – 50,000 of them – were sent between 1700 and 1775. The objecting colonies of Virginia, Maryland and Pennsylvania received 90 per cent or more of them. The rest went to Jamaica, the Leeward Islands, Barbados and New Jersey.[42] This resulted from the Transportation Act of 1717. Citing the 'great want of servants' in the colonies, it overrode the prohibition that the colonies had placed upon entry, authorizing transportation for fourteen years in lieu of the death sentence, and for seven years to punish a range of non–capital crimes, such as grand and petty larceny. Transportation was extended to other non–capital offences by a spate of legislation enacted between 1720 and 1765.[43] In keeping with seventeenth-century practice, the act of 1717 did not establish overseas penal settlements. In fact, the whole measure was aimed at avoiding the cost of incarceration, both at home and in the colonies. Modelled on bonded service, but with the vital difference that the parties to the initial contract were the merchant and the British prison authorities, not the bondsperson, the transportation system awarded the merchant 'property and interest' in the convicts' service in return for shipping them to the colonies. The merchant was also awarded the right to confer his interest to an 'assign'. This he did by selling the contract to a colonial settler who thereby was entitled to possess the convicts' labour until the sentence expired.[44]

Thus, transported convicts, as well as indentured and statutory servants, provided the colonies with bonded white labour. Adding marginally to this labour pool were colonial convicts placed in bondage for indebtedness, or crimes such as larceny, arson and forgery. This practice was found, by the mid–eighteenth century, throughout British America. Like bonded servants, all of these assigned convicts lived attached to private households, farms and plantations. As for their rights, they had fewer than the bonded servant, but more than the slave. Unlike the slave, for example, they could sue their master for abuse, but, unlike the servant, their testimony was not admissible in court.[45] Since the convict's bondage was temporary, some thought had to be given to his or her inevitable liberation – even more so in view of his proclivity to flee from service and to foot-drag. Paying the passage home for transported convicts was out of the question – just as it was for transported servants – but what about giving them freedom dues at the end of the sentence? Virginia legislated in favour of this in 1749, but repealed the measure in 1753. Maryland left the matter to the master.[46] His inclination was to keep payment to a minimum in order to justify the original purchase price. Moreover, the buyers of transported convict labour tended to be the small tobacco planters of the Chesapeake. They opted for convicts because they were much cheaper than slaves to buy and, with a longer term to serve, offered better value than bonded servants.[47]

Employers of this sort were unlikely to grant freedom dues, simply because their limited resources did not easily stretch that far. Instead they were inclined to flog. A punitive regime, with little reward and considerable scope for escape, led to a high rate of absconsion, which in turn raised the level of punishment.[48] The nature of the work was another source of convict discontent. The labour of indentured service became much lighter as the heavy field work fell to black slaves, but this was not the case with convicts since the smaller planters, who could not afford many slaves, continued to use them as field workers. Although unskilled work in the field was not overwhelmingly arduous, at least for seasoned labourers, in a society where it had become closely associated with slavery, it was increasingly seen as a mark of degradation.[49]

By 1800, white bonded labour was no longer important in the Americas. The former British colonies banned the import of convicts in 1788, while the British government turned against exporting servants from its own shores, regarding the practice as a means whereby the rebel American states gained skilled labour at British expense. Moreover, by this time the American practice of assigning convicted debtors and criminals to private employers was being replaced by imprisonment, or chain-gang labour on public works: a change of procedure initiated by Pennsylvania in 1776.[50] But, for at least another century, bonded labour – slave or by indenture or by debt – continued to be extensively employed in the New World. In the nineteenth century, however, the bondspersons were predominantly of African, Asian or Amerindian descent. By the 1830s, white labour in the Americas had become almost completely free.

8

New World Slavery

Slavery was practised in the Americas long before the Europeans arrived. It was primarily appreciated as a source of honour and a form of disposable wealth, since its main purpose was to provide sacrificial victims for the propitiation of gods, the articulation of grief, and the performance of potlatch. Rather than being transmitted by birth, enslavement resulted from the postponement of the death sentence on prisoners of war. Masters and slaves, moreover, were distinguished from each other by no more than nation or tribe.[1] In sharp contrast, the slave system brought by the Europeans was hereditary, racist and designed to generate wealth, notably through the mining of precious metals and the cultivation of cash crops.

The new slavery depended upon a massive transportation of manpower from Africa: one principally funded by the profits the colonists made in the mines and on the plantations. As a result, it had become well established in Latin America by 1650, in much of the Caribbean by 1700, and in Virginia and Maryland by 1750. Certain distinctive features marked it out. First, masters and slaves were distinguished from each other by race: the slaves of the New World were predominantly of African descent and black, whereas their masters were mainly white and European. The almost total reliance on black slaves derived from a process of elimination that had ruled out other sources of labour. No attempt was made to convert whites into slaves, largely because the masters were drawn from a culture that associated whiteness with Christianity and strongly opposed the enslavement of fellow believers. The masters were also – as western rather than eastern Europeans – drawn from a culture that had largely abandoned the practice of serfdom, and no longer considered it proper to attach whites to the land in return for a labour service. Since it was associated with indentured servants and convicts, the servitude imposed upon whites in the New World remained of temporary duration. It was therefore hardly a form of enslavement.

Although white bondsmen were employed extensively in the New World before 1750, they failed to satisfy the long-term labour needs of colonial society. True, they proved extremely useful in the early stages of settlement, notably in the British and French colonies; but, by the mid-eighteenth century, the supply was drying up and the reduced price differential between white bondsmen and black slaves had created a strong preference for the latter, largely because, although more expensive to buy, they were held in perpetual possession. What is more, for a long time the supply of white hired labour failed to compensate for the decline in white bonded labour. This was due partly to the prohibitively high transatlantic fare which, before the 1820s, severely restricted the number of free migrants to the New World, and partly to the abiding peasant nature of western European society which, aided by the growth of great cities, proved mostly capable – at least before the population explosion of the nineteenth century – of absorbing the demographic surplus.[2]

What of the aboriginal labour in the Americas? In much of the New World the Indians were nomadic hunter-gatherers. Accustomed to living off the natural resources of the land – the abundance of which made it easy to achieve – they were totally unsuited for settled agricultural work. Attached to territory rather than land, moreover, they were very difficult to pin down and train in the ways of cultivation. The first colonists made initial attempts to domesticate this labour by enslaving it; but in the Spanish and Portuguese empires the church stepped in as the Indians' protector. In response, Indian enslavement was outlawed in the late sixteenth century and rooted out by 1650.

Exceptionally, Mexico and Peru had large Indian populations long familiar with agriculture. They were attached to one settled place by communal landownership, and, conditioned by their former Aztec and Inca overlords, they were accustomed to providing a regular tribute of labour. Since the Spaniards were able to make use of this labour, partly by hire and partly through compulsory service, enslavement was unnecessary. However, this labour supply was severely reduced in the first century of colonial rule by a massive depopulation, the result of its vulnerability to European diseases. Consequently, from the late sixteenth century, large numbers of slaves had to be brought from abroad, not only to those parts where extensive agriculture had failed to develop and the Indian presence was transient, but also to regions where a dense, settled population had traditionally existed. Enslaved Africans offered the best solution to the labour problem for a variety of reasons: they were experienced in agriculture, epidemiologically sturdy, familiar with slavery, unaccustomed to the New World terrain and therefore less capable than the Indians of effective flight, easy to identify by race and therefore to keep under surveillance, and supplied in profusion, the result of a well-founded slave trade in Africa.

A second distinctive feature of the new slavery in the Americas was its close association with plantation agriculture. The majority of slaves came to be employed in commercial agriculture, producing mostly for the European market. Whereas in European societies, agricultural labour was largely the work of peasants, either producing for the market themselves, or providing their lords with marketable produce in rent, or cultivating the demesne under a system of labour service, in the Americas commercial farming was achieved through a system in which the landowners did not rent out the land but farmed it directly. In the absence of sufficient hired labour, this non-peasant New World system had to use a mixed bag of servitude which included state tribute, convict labour, indentured service and debt peonage, while relying principally upon slavery.

The slave plantations of the New World came in a variety of forms, the differences between them determined by the nature of the crop, the extent to which production was geared to the export trade, plantation size, and whether or not the master was resident. Yet all these plantations tended to impose a similar discipline, largely because of the slave condition of the work-force and the inherent commercialism of the operation. As a mode of production, the slave plantation was undoubtedly primitive, the reliance upon slavery providing a disincentive to search for labour-saving devices in the field, leaving the hoe rather than the plough as the primary implement of cultivation. But it was far from inefficient, for the capital investment and high maintenance costs obliged masters to squeeze the maximum out of the work-force, while the powers slavery conferred over this labour helped masters to succeed in this aim. To the fore was the use of the whip for punishing disobedience and driving the workers on; but no slave plantation was operated simply by brute force. The degree of efficiency achieved depended upon slave cooperation. This, in turn, relied upon the masters' offer of rewards and rights, the former dispensed to selected slaves and featuring special treats or promotion to less arduous tasks, the latter granted to the slave community through the recognition of customs, cultural differences and degrees of autonomy.

The most rigorous form of plantation to emerge in the Americas was the one devoted to sugar production. In this particular industry, production costs were high because of the capital outlay on the processing machinery; but the high work rate achieved, principally through the system of slavery, enabled huge profits to be made where the climate was right, that is, in tropical and semi-tropical regions – hence, its spectacular expansion. By the mid-eighteenth century, 40 per cent of slaves in the Americas – 1.4 out of 3.5 million – worked on sugar plantations.[3] These were largely situated in the Caribbean, especially on the islands of Barbados, Jamaica, St Domingue, Guadeloupe and Martinique; but they were also extensively found in Brazil, where the slave sugar plantation originated, and, on a much smaller yet still considerable scale, in the lowlands of Mexico and Peru. Nonetheless, the 'classic' plantation was only confined to part of this sugar-producing world; and even where the system was most fully developed, no more than 60 per cent of the slaves were engaged in the onerous, driven, gang-organized field work.[4]

Sugar plantations in the Caribbean reached considerable size, typically worked by hundreds of slaves. But elsewhere this was not the case. In Brazil, where the businesses that milled the cane were not necessarily those that grew it, cultivation occurred in much smaller units. In Mexico and Peru, moreover, the labour force employed in growing sugar was often a mixed one, consisting of Indians working for wages as well as black slaves. The plantation regime in these sugar-producing parts of Latin America, in fact, bore strong similarities to the agrarian systems associated with the production of tobacco or cotton – that is, on the tobacco plantations of the Caribbean in the early seventeenth century and those of eighteenth-century Maryland, Virginia and North Carolina, and on the cotton planta-tions of the US South in the early nineteenth century. There, the slave plantations tended to be much smaller than those in the Caribbean sugar colonies, the planters were more likely to be resident and directly involved in supervising a handful of slaves, the work of the slaves was less onerous, and a much closer relationship existed between the slaves, the master and his family.

The work experience of the plantation slaves, then, could differ greatly, even when it involved growing the same crop. What the plantation imposed uniformly was the rural way of life, with the slaves confined to country estates in societies where urban settlements were few and far between. Yet, in the Americas, large numbers of slaves worked away from plantations, often in towns and frequently on small farms. For this reason, to stress the connection between slaves and plantation work in any overview of New World slavery is as misleading as to stress its involvement with sugar. In Mexico, Peru and Brazil, there were large numbers of urban slaves, working as liveried retainers, domestic servants, porters, messengers, artisans and labourers. The same was true of the north and middle colonies of British North America. Each urban master tended to own but a few slaves and therefore to know them well. Quite often, the slaves were hired out for paid work, a proportion of their wages accruing to the master in recognition of his or her proprietorial right. Whereas plantation slaves usually had little hope of escaping the condition of bondage, urban slaves were better placed to receive manumission, either through an act of benevolence on the master's part or through the slave's ability to acquire sufficient cash to purchase his own freedom.

A third distinctive feature of American slavery was its close association with long-distance, international trade. This applied both to human beings and products. By the eighteenth century, the flow of slave-produced goods to the Old World was spectacular. From the British mainland colonies alone, tobacco exports rose from 20,000 lbs in 1619 to 38 million lbs in 1700, while rice exports from the slave plantations of South Carolina and Georgia rose from 12,000 lbs in 1698 to 83 million lbs in 1770. In the USA, exported cotton rose from a mere 189,000 lbs in 1790 to 204.5 million lbs in 1826; and from 854,000 bales in 1827 to 3,127,000 bales in 1861.[5] Brazil and the French Caribbean colonies were also great exporters of slave-produced goods; in contrast Mexico and Peru tended to cater for the internal market created by their own colonial cities.

Even more spectacular was the long-distance flow of slaves. Between 1502 and the 1860s 10–11 million Africans were transported to the Americas, of whom 85 per cent went to Brazil and the Caribbean, 8–9 per cent, to the Spanish mainland colonies, and 6–7 per cent to North America. Over half (5.7 million) made the crossing in the eighteenth century alone.[6] Another 3.3 million followed in the nineteenth century, notwithstanding the embargoes that the British and US governments had placed on the slave trade in 1807 and 1808.[7]

Besides the journey to the African ports of embarkation and then the transatlantic passage, slaves were subjected to spectacular trans-American journeys. This began with the Spanish conquests on the mainland, when, after disembarking at Vera Cruz, they had to make the arduous journey overland to Mexico City or the plantations of Central America. The slaves transported to Peru had to cross the Isthmus, after landing at Cartagena, and then travel by sea to Callao. Some had to make long overland journeys from Trujillo to Lima and from Lima to Cuzco, or from Peru down into Chile. These American transportations reached epic proportions in the USA when, between 1790 and 1860, 1 million (i.e. one quarter of the country's slave population as it stood in 1860) were moved westwards from the old slave regions of Maryland, Virginia and the Carolinas to the cotton states (Kentucky, Tennessee, Alabama, Mississippi, Louisiana, Texas): a deracination as disturbing as the transatlantic passage.[8] By acts of sale, which broke up families, and through long-distance transportation, which ruled out family reunions, they were abruptly, forcibly and for ever removed to an alien world. Similar internal transportations occurred between the 1790s and 1820s, when slaves were moved to Peru from Chile and Argentina, and in late nineteenth-century Brazil when 300,000 slaves were moved from the old sugar region in the north-east to the coffee plantations of the south-central provinces.[9]

The huge extent of the transatlantic flow of slaves, then, resulted from the rapid development of a plantation economy in the Americas; but it also stemmed from the failure of slave populations to reproduce themselves. The slavery Europeans established in the New World was hereditary but, para-doxically, needed further enslavement for its maintenance. Transportation remained a key element in the New World slave system. The low pro-creativity of slaves was not simply due to a high rate of manumission. Where manumission was low, as in the British Caribbean, slave populations were also prone to contraction, through a combination of low fertility and high mortality. The great exception was the North American British colonies where the right balance between the sexes, the nature of the work, the way masters provided slaves with rations instead of expecting them to grow their own food, the tendency of slaves, although of African descent, not to be African-born, the lack of opportunity for male slaves to produce free off-spring from mating with free women: all this created a slave society capable not only of reproducing itself but also of considerable natural growth. Virtually unaided by fresh imports of slave labour, the slave population of the USA grew from 697,897 in 1790 to 3,953,760 in 1860.[10] On the other hand, a good deal of internal transportation was required to get it to the right workplace.

Black slavery in the Americas was finally distinguished by its over-whelming economic and social importance. For the Americas, it was a major source not only of wealth but also of immigration. Without it, the peopling of the New World, before the nineteenth century, would have proved an extremely difficult task. In fact, not until 1840 did migration from Europe regularly exceed that from Africa.[11] Faced by the unwillingness of Euro-peans to settle in the Americas, and following the near decimation of the Indian populations in the sixteenth and early seventeenth centuries – the result of the transference of diseases from one epidemiological zone to another – the immigration of Africans played a vital part in populating the Americas. Moreover, since black slaves were employed not just to serve wealth but to generate it, they played a vital economic role in establishing a buoyant commercial economy.

The economic and demographic importance of Africans in the New World produced not simply societies in which slavery was a marginal and inessential feature, but also societies in which it was a central and integral part. This was clearly the case in the Caribbean where the population was principally slave. It was also true of the plantation regions on the North American mainland and of the plantations and urban centres of Brazil, where the slaves were not normally in the majority but, nonetheless, a sub-stantial minority and vital to the economy. It was not the case in Mexico where the Indians remained a valuable labour resource and the slave popu-lation was, from the mid-seventeenth century, prone to serious contraction because of the low rate of slave imports and the high rate of manumission. Peru, in contrast, was arguably a slave society, because of the importance slave labour retained in the plantation economy of the coastal lowlands and in the capital city of Lima.

How novel was New World slavery? From the slave point of view, it was undoubtedly a new experience. The servile practices of the societies from which the Indian and African slaves were recruited bore no relationship to those the Europeans imposed upon the New World. In both pre-Columbian America and pre-colonial Africa, the plantation was virtually unknown. The masters, however, must have found New World slavery quite familiar. The urban slavery introduced by the Spanish conquistadors to Lima and Mexico City, or developed by the Portuguese in the cities of Rio de Janeiro or Salvador, was identical with the slavery present in contemporary Lisbon or Seville. The slaves were blacks from Africa, working as domestic servants and artisans. They were expected to become Christians. Manumission was not out of the question. Sugar and slavery were first united, moreover, in the fifteenth century, as the Spanish and Portuguese cultivated it on plantations in the Atlantic, notably in the Canaries, Madeira, São Tomé and Principe. From these islands, the slave plantation spread to Brazil, parts of the Caribbean, Mexico and Peru during the late sixteenth and early seventeenth centuries. As for the French, the Dutch and the British, they all lacked prior, firsthand experience, but they could reach back into history for guidance and inspiration. The historical precedent for the slave plantation was the familiar one of ancient Rome, which offered not only the convenient legal definition of the slave as a thing but also an instructive example of how to use slaves productively, both in large-scale, commercial farming and in urban crafts. No matter how badly the slave masters of the New World treated their slaves, no matter how different the ethical codes were that they applied to slaves and to themselves, they could find comfort in the knowledge that the slavery they practised belonged to a fine classical tradition which the Western world regarded not as a sump of barbarism but as the acme of civilization.

Spanish America

Black slavery was first implanted in the Americas by the Spanish. Having conquered the Aztecs, the Mayas and the Incas between 1519 and 1535, they converted their empires into the huge colonies of Mexico (New Spain) and Peru. The outcome was to replace one slave system by another. Sustained by large imports of Africans, the new system underwent rapid consolidation. By 1600, 70,000 black slaves had been transported to Mexico and another 40–50,000 to Peru. The silver deposits of these colonies provided the means of purchase, while the union of the Spanish and Portuguese crowns in 1580 facilitated the flow, for the Portuguese at the time were the world's major supplier of African slaves. By 1650 a further 100,000 had been shipped to Mexico, and a further 50,000 to the much less accessible Peru.[12]

Black slaves quickly became a prominent part of the Spanish colonial presence. By 1570, they easily outnumbered the Spaniards in Mexico: 18,500 against 14,700. By 1646, their number had doubled to 35,000. Peru had 3,000 African slaves by 1555 and 30,000 by 1640.[13] By the mid-seventeenth century, a time when the slave plantations of the Caribbean were only just emerging, and the North American colonies mostly used white labour, black slavery in the New World was principally to be found in Mexico, Peru and the Portuguese colony of Brazil.[14]

In the Spanish Empire, black slaves were typically used for a variety of purposes. Reflecting Iberian practice, the Spanish settlers and officials appreciated them as attendants and servants. But reflecting the peculiar conditions of the New World, where skilled labour was originally in short supply, they were also valued as craftsmen.[15] As artisans, slaves had a high

market value as well as a special usefulness.[16] Through being hired out for
a wage, part of which was paid to the master, they could serve as a regular
source of income.[17] For these reasons, it was important for settlers to
have their slaves trained in crafts, as well as to import specially skilled
slaves.[18] The role slaves fulfilled as servitors and artisans led to a considerable slave presence in the colonial cities and towns. In this respect, the
society that developed in Lima and Mexico City resembled that of
Seville. In 1570 almost half the black slaves of Mexico resided in Mexico
City, where they equalled the number of whites. The same proportion of
blacks to whites was found in Lima in the 1590s.[19] Slaves, were also
employed extensively in the countryside, basically to feed the urban settlements. They were employed, for example, to operate small farms on the out-
skirts of towns, growing a range of food for the urban inhabitants, as well
as to labour on plantations in the coastal lowlands for the production of
sugar and grapes. Slaves also did ranching work.[20] In both Mexico and Peru
the primary purpose of the plantations and ranches was, like that of the
small farms, to feed the colonial towns rather than to produce exports. For
this reason, the demand for slave labour and the demands made of it were
less extreme than, say, on the plantations of coastal Brazil, in the Caribbean
and in British North America, where the slave regime was sustained,
enlarged and intensified by the market in Europe for tobacco, sugar, rice
and cotton.

Another restraint on the employment of slaves in Mexico and Peru was
the presence of an extensive Indian population whose labour could be
recruited by waged hire or governmental compulsion. In Mexico through
the *repartimiento*, and in Peru through the *mita*, Indians were obliged to work
for white settlers on a fixed wage.[21] Problems arose in the late sixteenth
century when, in both Mexico and Peru, the Indian population was ravaged
by smallpox and measles: diseases the Spaniards brought with them and
against which the Indians had no immunity. As a result, by 1600 the Indian
population of central Mexico was reduced from 25 to 1.25 million, and that
of Peru from 9 million to 600,000.[22] These problems, moreover, were intensified by the policies the Spanish government adopted to protect the Indians
from exploitation. By 1550, it had forbidden the enslavement of the Indian
population and, by the early seventeenth century, it had placed restrictions
on the compulsory labour services exacted of Indian communities.[23] By 1600
repartimiento labour was not permitted on Mexican sugar plantations; and
in 1632 its use in the colony was banned for all economic enterprises apart
from mining.[24] Similar restrictions were attempted in Peru, with the *mita*
abolished in 1601 but restored in 1609. Another restriction on the *mita*,
however, remained in force – one that prevented Indians from being made
to travel long distances in order to fulfil their labour obligation.[25] The
restrictions placed upon compulsory Indian labour meant that certain parts
of the economy could only be manned by enticing Indians to work for wages,
or by introducing an alternative form of labour. In Peru the mining of silver

took place in the Andean uplands, a region where the Indian population was less in contact with the Europeans and therefore better able to survive their diseases.[26] For this reason, the silver mines could be worked with Indian labour, mostly supplied through the *mita*. In contrast, the coastal plantations had run out of sufficient Indian labour by the 1580s and were unable to recruit it easily from the uplands because of the official restrictions placed upon long-distance *mita* service.[27] In these circumstances, the choice for the planters was either to lure Indians down from the uplands by offering them wages or to import slaves. The first choice was rendered impracticable by the self-sufficiency of the upland communities which, equipped with their own land, were able to follow a peasant way of life that met most of their needs, as well as having the opportunity to supplement their basic resources by earning wages in the upland mines.[28] Reliance on slave labour in Peru, then, was forced upon the settlers by the absence of a satisfactory alternative.

In Mexico the labour situation likewise led to slavery, though not in exactly the same way or to the same extent. There, the major silver deposits were located in the north, a region where Indians tended to be nomadic, not settled, and therefore less employable as miners.[29] In compensation, slaves were used: in 1570 the labour force engaged in the Mexican silver mines comprised 3,690 slaves as well as 4,450 Indians. But this was a short-term expedient. By 1597, the slaves working in the mines had contracted to 1,022, while the number of Indians employed in them had increased to 6,229. Significantly, 4,610 of the latter had not been recruited by the *repartimiento* but were free labourers.[30] Limiting the number of slaves employed in mining – the same was true of farming and textile manufacture – was the readiness of the Indian population to seek waged work.[31] This did not rule out completely the use of slave labour which, in the sixteenth and early seventeenth centuries, was already found on sugar plantations, in the textile workshops of the larger towns, as well as down the mines; but its gradual effect was to marginalize slavery, rendering it a form of domestic service rather than of productive labour, and turning it into something of social rather than economic significance.

As a result of this key difference, the history of slavery in Mexico and Peru followed divergent courses. In Mexico, slaves never comprised more than 2 per cent of the population; and, from the mid-seventeenth century, the institution of slavery faded away. Dissociated from production, the slave population had fallen to less than 10,000 by 1800.[32] In contrast, slaves in mid-seventeenth-century Peru comprised at least 10 per cent of the population; and, since they were largely concentrated in the coastal lowlands, the proportion there must have been a great deal higher: in Lima, for example, it accounted for 28.4 per cent of the population in 1796.[33] Whereas the slave population of Mexico fell steadily from the mid-seventeenth century, that of Peru continued to rise. By 1800 it amounted to 40,000 and was still increasing, thanks to a massive importation of 65,700 slaves between 1790 and 1802. Yet, with the increase in white settlers and the recovery of the Indian population, it comprised only 3.8 per cent of the population in 1821.[34] What had determined the extent of slavery in Peru was not only the insufficiency of Indian labour to meet colonial needs but also its isolation from the world market. For this latter reason, the slave labour force in Peru was but a fraction of that found in Brazil's plantation provinces of Bahía, Pernambuco and Rio de Janeiro.[35]

From the very early days of the Spanish-American Empire, a body of slave rights had existed in the law. It partly rested on the *Siete Partidas*, a code for the regulation of slavery that was originally issued in 1263. It had been applied specifically to the New World in the royal ordinances of 1545.[36] The granting of legal rights to slaves rested on the ingrained belief that enslavement was an integral part of the crusading mission: in fact, a device for converting infidels and Pagans to Christianity. The corollary of this belief was the entitlement of slaves to baptism and the other Catholic sacraments, which included marriage. In this way slave rights became ensconced in colonial and canon law, and slaves in Mexico and Peru were officially recognized as having a legal and moral personality.[37] Legally, they could take action against their masters, both in royal and ecclesiastical courts.[38] Morally, their masters were obliged to see to their Christian instruction. Slavery itself had been presented in the *Siete Partidas* as 'the most evil and the most despicable thing which can be found among men', and therefore as something that could be virtuously terminated.[39] But whether the recognition of slave rights in the law made much difference to the slave condition is debatable. Slave owners had strong incentives to prevent slaves from marrying, undergoing baptism and receiving Christian instruction. By legitimizing sexual partnerships and their offspring through marriage, masters were tying their own hands when it came to selling their slaves. Without marriage, slaves could be sold separately; with marriage, they could only be sold in family groups. Instruction in the Christian faith was seen as making slaves less obedient, because it raised their expectations of emancipation and reduced the time that they could be put to work.[40] In practice, few marriages took place between slaves, and little provision was made for turning slaves into informed Christians, with slave owners antipathetic to the matter, and the church keener on ministering to Indians. However, some of the religious orders, notably the Jesuits, Dominicans and Augustinians, sought to convert slaves.[41]

The lot of the slaves was relieved not so much by the possession of rights as by the nature of the work and the opportunities they acquired to develop their own culture and secure manumission. Employed as retainers and domestic servants, many slaves in Mexico and Peru were removed from the hard labour of field work, enjoying with their masters a companionship not found on the plantations. Furthermore, as artisans, many slaves were lightly worked and valued for their skills. The prevalence of urban slavery was a major source of relief – especially because of the occupations, relationships and freedoms associated with town life – but so was the nature of rural labour.[42] Absent were the oppressive, impersonal, intensely commercial, highly regimented plantation systems that by 1700 had emerged in the Caribbean; instead, the plantations of Mexico and Peru were inclined to be small in size and geared merely to the home market.[43] Also in the country-side were self-operating truck gardens (*chácaras*), worked by slaves for the purpose of providing the local town with produce.[44] Agricultural slaves of this type enjoyed a freedom and self-motivation approaching that of free peasant farmers. Even on large-scale commercial farms, slaves could escape the closely supervised and whip-driven work of the classical plantation, for slaves were engaged in ranching: both in caring for great herds of cattle and in looking after pigs and goats.[45] Even where production was export-led in Spanish America – as, for example, with the chocolate industry in late eighteenth-century Venezuela – slaves could be protected from the rigours of plantation work by sharecropping systems which left them to organize their own work and allowed them to acquit their obligations to the master in produce rather than labour.[46]

The most onerous labour in Spanish America was connected with mining. However, the production of silver was largely the work of Indians. The slaves engaged in mining principally worked to extract gold, notably in the Chocó region of New Granada where, in the early eighteenth century, the Spanish government had banned the use of Indian labour. By 1782 over 7,000 slaves were panning its rivers and streams.[47] Like the slaves operating the truck gardens of Peru, or the slave sharecroppers of Venezuela, or the slave artisans of Lima, Mexico City and Buenos Aires, these Chocó slaves were able to work on their own account and in this way to accumu-late *peculium*, for in their free time they were allowed to continue panning for gold on condition that they sold what they found to their master. By making a down payment on manumission to the master, they could even liberate themselves to work for whomsoever they liked, if, by instalments, they eventually paid him the agreed manumission price.[48] Furthermore, within Spanish America, large numbers of slaves worked for wages, the result of the common practice of hiring out slave labour, the wages earned being shared between master and slave.[49] Rather than being concentrated in a few hands, the possession of slaves was spread throughout society, thanks to their employment as servants and the practice of slave-hire. This meant that large numbers of slaves had personal relationships with their masters which permitted favours to be earned by creditable service or personal attraction.

Also relieving the condition of slavery in Spanish America was the cultural independence the slave communities managed to achieve. Colonial pressures were applied to break the African connection, through the imposition of Christianity and through municipal and inquisitional bans on non-Christian ceremonies, festivities and practices. But these regula-tions failed to achieve their purpose, partly because the church concen-trated on the conversion of Indians; partly because slave owners had material reasons for disobeying government orders to provide slaves with

Christian instruction; and partly because the colonial authorities, and even the Inquisition, were incapable of enforcing the laws banning African practices.[50]

Since the essential burden of slavery lay not in the hard work it imposed but in the freedom it denied, the major source of relief for slaves was the opportunity to escape from bondage. As in Brazil and parts of the Caribbean, they could withdraw into the jungle or to the mountains and establish free regimes that effectively existed outside the law.[51] But the major means of escape in Spanish America occurred within the law, and was achieved by grants of manumission or right of birth. Manumission was authorized either by *carta de libertad* (licence of emancipation) or by final testament. In each case the master made a formal grant of freedom to individual slaves, either as a gift to reward loyal service or in return for an appropriate payment.[52] The process of manumission was promoted, on the one hand, by the master's gratitude and desire for virtue, and, on the other, by the slaves' ability to accumulate sufficient wealth and spend it on emancipation. Relief for slaves lay not only in manumission but also in the expectation that it might well be granted. In this respect, the presence of large numbers of free people of African descent helped to alleviate the lot of those who remained enslaved. By the early seventeenth century, a quarter of the African–descent group were free in Mexico and one-tenth in Peru.[53] With large numbers of free blacks in society – the result of earlier manumissions – it became easier for slaves to expect and plan their own liberation.

The freeing of people of African descent was also promoted by the law of inheritance.[54] Slave status in Spanish America was transmitted on the female side. This meant that, through cohabiting with free women, slaves produced children who were legally free. Racial taboos minimized open relationships between slaves and white women, but not between slaves and Indian women. The fact that Indians had been immunized against enslavement by 1550 provided a major means whereby the sons and daughters of male slaves could be born free. Another liberating sexual relationship occurred between masters and their female slaves. In law the offspring of these relationships were born slaves, but their free paternity increased the chances of manumission, both for them and the mother. Miscegenation, therefore, offered a major source of escape. Another escape lay in the capability of slaves to pay the manumission price – the result of being able to earn money on their own account, thanks to the practice of hiring themselves out for wages, and because of the high proportion of slaves who were skilled craftsmen. In certain regions, even slaves who were no more than labourers could earn the necessary surplus, whether they panned for gold in the Chocó or share-cropped cocoa in Venezuela. Given the chance to earn money, slaves eagerly seized it to fund their freedom. And by the late eighteenth century they were aided by *coartación*: a system of manumission which allowed them to agree a price with the master, fix it with a deposit, and pay it off by instalments.[55]

With such a high wastage rate, and because the slave population was unable to sustain itself by procreation, slavery in Spanish America depended heavily on the import of fresh slaves.[56] Until the mid-seventeenth century, the slaves brought from Africa to the New World mostly went to the mainland empires of Spain and Portugal. Between 1600 and 1650 they received over 400,000, roughly half to each, while only 40,000 had gone to the Caribbean islands, and no more than a handful to North America.[57] From 1650 onwards, however, strong competition for African slaves from the Caribbean and, by the eighteenth century, from the British colonies in North America as well, severely reduced the numbers brought to the Spanish mainland.[58] In these circumstances, the extent to which slaves served as a means of production, rather than of service, was vital in determining their numbers. In Mexico, the recovery of the Indian population and the willingness of Indians to sell their labour, coupled with the high prices fetched by new slaves, caused slave numbers to contract sharply during the seventeenth and eighteenth centuries.[59]

It was a different story in Peru, even though slavery there was likewise affected by a high rate of manumission and by a competing demand for slaves from the Caribbean and North America. In fact, the Peruvian slave population grew from 30,000 slaves in 1640 to about 37,000 by 1790, achieving a maximum of 50,000 slaves in 1821. Thereafter, it tailed off, influenced by the enactment in that year of a free-womb law which liberated automatically the newborn offspring of slaves. In 1855, the year of abolition, it amounted to 19,000; but even then it remained two to three times as large as the Mexican slave population in 1800.[60] In Peru the durability of the slave system clearly stemmed from the importance of the coastal sugar plantations and their reliance on slave labour, the latter stemming from the difficulty planters had in enticing Indians down from the highlands. By the late sixteenth century, Peru had divided into two zones: the one for the coastal towns and plantations that remained heavily dependent upon slave labour; the other for the uplands where the Indians' villages were situated, along with the silver mines that were worked with their labour.[61]

It would therefore be wrong to regard Mexico, with its reduced dependency upon slavery, as typical of the rest of Spanish America. In fact, by the late eighteenth century slavery was acquiring an increased importance, not only in Peru and the adjacent regions of Chile and Venezuela, but also in Cuba and Puerto Rico, especially to produce cash crops for export to Europe.[62] It would also be wrong to regard slavery in Spanish America as a peripheral matter on the grounds that the proportion of slaves was low relative to the rest of the population. This was due, at least in Mexico and Peru, to the overwhelming size of the Indian population. Only when the latter could be recruited on a scale sufficient to meet the settler demand for labour was slavery marginalized. In this respect, Mexico was the exception, not the rule, in the Spanish–American world.

Brazil

The black slave population of Portuguese Brazil easily dwarfed that of Spanish America. In the latter, it never exceeded 250,000, whereas, by the 1790s, in the former, it stood at 1,582,000. By 1817 it had grown to 2 million, peaking at 2,500,000 in 1850. In 1817, black slaves comprised half the total population of Brazil. In contrast, in any one Spanish colony on the American mainland, it never exceeded 10 per cent.[63]

Brazil's plethora of black slaves was no latter-day phenomenon. It was evident even in the early seventeenth century: by 1630 the colony already contained 50–60,000. By 1700 the figure had risen to 120,000 and to 500,000 in 1750.[64] These numbers were exceptionally large by any contemporary standard. In fact, in comparison with the rest of the Americas, Brazil possessed easily the largest slave population at any point in time before the early nineteenth century, when it came second to the USA. For this reason, any attempt to characterize the system of slavery in the Americas without giving due weight to the slave regime the Portuguese established in Brazil must be grossly deficient.

The demand for black slaves in Brazil stemmed partly from the development of a vigorous export economy; partly from the inadequacy of Indian labour to meet the colony's economic needs; partly from the suitability and cheapness of imported African slaves and the high mortality they suffered when taken to Brazil. Brazil's development as an export economy went through three distinct phases: the first connected with sugar, the second with gold and diamonds, the third with coffee.

Failing initially to find precious metals, and not content with exporting brazilwood, the Portuguese, by the second decade of the sixteenth century, had come to appreciate Brazil as a place to grow sugar, a crop that was already familiar to them, since they had cultivated it in the Algarve and on the Atlantic islands of Madeira and São Tomé.[65] The sugar industry, moreover, was ripe for expansion because the processing of sugar had been recently transformed by the invention of a milling system of rollers for crushing the cane, and also because its product was in great demand in Europe. As early as 1519, Brazilian sugar had become a commodity on the Antwerp market. By 1570 the industry was well established in the colony, its mills and plantations mostly concentrated in the north-eastern coastal provinces of Pernambuco and Bahía.[66] By 1580, Brazil had become the leading supplier of sugar to Europe. Thereafter, it remained a major supplier: even in the late eighteenth century its sugar exports were only exceeded by those of St Domingue and Jamaica.[67]

In the meantime, gold had been discovered in Minas Gerais. This happened in the 1690s. Brazil became a major exporter of the metal, its production reaching a peak in the 1750s.[68] Finally, in the early nineteenth century Brazil acquired a second major export crop, when coffee came to be extensively cultivated in the south-central provinces of Minas Gerais, Rio de Janeiro and São Paulo.[69] All three exports relied on black slave labour. In contrast, black slavery in Mexico and Peru principally served the internal economy. For this reason, in Brazil the pressure of demand for slaves and upon slave labour was that much greater.

The problem was how to man these commercial operations. The initial solution was to enlist the native Indians, but their primitiveness raised difficulties. Many were hunter-gatherers and, for this reason, necessarily nomadic, while those engaged in agriculture and settled tended to allocate cultivation to the women. The menfolk were prepared to clear the land for cultivation, and therefore to engage in logging, but, apart from hunting, fishing and war, to do no more than that.[70] Brazilian Indians, moreover, had not been trained to respect the demands of imperial overlordship, like the Indians under Aztec or Inca rule. In this respect, the Indians the Portuguese encountered were much less amenable to plantation or mining work than those the Spaniards ruled. Nothing in their previous experience had obliged the Brazilian Indians to provide labour services, or to produce a surplus for paying taxes or rent. Barter was a means of securing their cooperation in supplying brazilwood, but not to man the plantations.[71] Attempts to subject them to a wage system by debt peonage were thwarted by regulations the government introduced in 1596 to prevent wages from being paid in advance and to disallow Indians from being bound to a labour contract of more than two months' duration.[72]

In view of the unreliability of Indian labour, enslavement appeared to be the best means of preparing it for the work in hand.[73] Yet, as in the Spanish Empire, crown and church intervened to protect the Indian. In 1570 the enslavement of Indians was banned, although, for a time, exceptions to the ban were permitted: Indians taken as captives by other Indians and ransomed to the Portuguese could be worked as slaves, as could Indians taken in just wars or found practising cannibalism. Thus, in 1589, the labour force on the plantations of Bahía comprised 14–15,000 Indian slaves and 3–4,000 African slaves.[74] But then another problem arose: the vulnerability to smallpox and measles of all Indians entering the Portuguese domain.[75] In Bahía and Pernambuco, the Jesuits had established protected Indian villages (*aldeias*), in order to safeguard the Indians from enslavement, as well as to turn them into a waged plantation work-force. The inhabitants of these villages, however, along with the Indians who worked as plantation slaves, were dramatically wiped out in the late sixteenth century by a succession of epidemics.[76] As a result, the labour problem remained unsolved. Immigration from the homeland provided no answer. In the sixteenth century Portugal had a minute population of 1 million; and those who came to Brazil removed themselves from the labour market by settling as small farmers.[77] In fact, it was not until after 1850, when most agricultural land had been taken, that white labour could be extensively recruited.[78]

The Portuguese had first exported slaves from Africa in 1441; and, in the late fifteenth century, they were brought in largish numbers to Lisbon.[79] They were employed mainly as servants and craftsmen, although some were used to provide labour in the sugar mills and plantations of the Algarve and the Atlantic islands. This meant that, when the Portuguese first considered the establishment of sugar plantations in Brazil, they already had a tested alternative to Indian labour. What is more, transferring Africans to Brazil was a much easier operation than to any other part of the Americas, simply because the transatlantic journey was shorter and because the Portuguese controlled the slave supply by means of trading agreements with powerful African states and forts strategically placed along Africa's western coastline. Consequently, slaves were cheaper to buy in Brazil than anywhere else in the New World.[80] Moreover, thanks to the profits made first from sugar, then from gold, and finally from coffee, the Portuguese were never short of resources to purchase them. Indian labour continued to be employed into the early seventeenth century, although from the 1580s Brazil contained a large contingent of enslaved Africans. The transition from Indian to African labour had occurred by 1620.[81]

The outcome was a massive transportation of Africans to Brazil, without equal in any other New World colony: 31 per cent of the total of those transported from Africa to the Americas went there, against 23 per cent to the English Caribbean, 22 per cent to the French Caribbean, 9.6 per cent to the Spanish colonies, and 6 per cent to English North America.[82] In the period 1500–1850, the slaves imported by Brazil amounted to between 3.5 and 5.5 million: the number ranged from 50,000 to 100,000 in the sixteenth century; from 0.5 million to 2 million in the seventeenth century; from 1.5 million to 2 million in the eighteenth century; and from 1,350,000 to 1.5 million in the nineteenth century.[83] Without this continual injection of fresh blood, slavery in Brazil would have faded away naturally, just as it did in eighteenth-century Mexico.[84] The extent of Brazil's dependence upon the transatlantic slave trade is vividly illustrated by what happened when the traffic was effectively stopped. This followed the government's decision in 1850 to enforce its 1831 legislation banning slave imports. Within the next twenty years the Brazilian slave population fell from 2.5 to 1.5 million.[85] Then, aided by the free-womb policy enacted in 1871, the contraction continued apace, reaching a figure of 723,419 on the eve of abolition in 1887.[86]

Brazilian slavery was regularly subjected to two potent erosive agents: negative reproductivity (that is, the incapacity of the slave population to maintain its size through procreation) and a high manumission rate.[87] Accounting for the former was the relative scarcity of female as compared to male slaves – the result of the slave trade's preference for men – coupled with the high mortality Brazilian slaves naturally suffered because, as new-comers to the country, they were highly susceptible to its diseases, and because of the general unhealthiness of the climate, which also took its toll on the rest of the population. A high death-rate was also due to the rigours of working on the sugar and coffee plantations, in the mines and as porters, and to the poor housing, clothing, diet and medical care that many slaves had to suffer.[88] Average life expectancy for Brazilian slaves in 1872 was as low as 18.3 years, against 35.5 for slaves in the USA, while for the white population it stood at 27.4 for Brazilians against 39.9 for Americans.[89] Several factors accounted for the high level of manumission: the opportunities slaves had to buy their own freedom or, if they were women, to receive it – either for themselves or their children – from masters with whom they had mated; the practice of freeing the aged and the ill to avoid the responsibility of caring for them; and the willingness to call upon slaves for military service and to grant them freedom in exchange – the result of the colony's vulnerability to attack and the free population's inability to provide a sufficient defence.[90]

In reducing slave numbers so effectively, these factors placed an onus on transportation to maintain the slave system in a flourishing state. Its reliance on transportation meant that, at any one point, the slave population of Brazil contained a high proportion of men and women who were Africans born and bred. In Bahía, for example, it amounted to 70 per cent, both in 1600 and 1820; in Pernambuco, to 35 per cent in 1838; and in São Paulo, to 44 per cent in 1836. This undoubtedly contributed to the degree of resistance slaves showed to their masters, not only through displays of counter-culture, lethargic melancholy and alternative religious beliefs, but also through acts of rebelliousness which featured open revolt, the establishment of independent kingdoms in the jungle, and a high rate of suicide (as slaves willed themselves back to Africa by putting themselves to death).[91]

The slave society of Brazil was also shaped by the existence of large numbers of men and women who, although of African descent, had managed to shed their slave status. At the start of the nineteenth century this accounted for 40 per cent of the total population in Bahía, and 12.5 per cent for the whole of Brazil – figures similar to those found in the Spanish colonies about 1800, but totally different from those of the US South, which stood at 4.5 per cent, or for Jamaica, which stood at 3 per cent. All this meant that, for Brazilian slaves, bondage was not something ingrained and eternal but a temporary lapse: a condition to which many had not been born and from which they, or at least their children, stood a fair chance of escape. For the masters, manumission provided a means of slave control and a growing alternative to slave labour. It was largely freed men who served the masters as overseers of slaves and as slave-catchers, and who supplied them with skilled and managerial work, acting, especially on the plantations, as a third force. They were clearly a vital element in the maintenance of the slave regime, especially in view of the absence of white hired labour.[92]

Brazil was a plantation economy geared to export and chiefly worked by slaves. Its slave regime therefore resembled those of the Caribbean and

North America. Yet several factors rendered the experience of the Brazilian slaves somewhat different. The first was the peculiar nature of the country's sugar industry; the second, the short-lived but influential development of its mining industry; the third, the prominence of urban slavery, thanks to the importance of such cities as Salvador, Recife and Rio de Janeiro; the fourth, the very broad basis of slave ownership in Brazil; and the fifth, the many opportunities Brazilian slaves had to accumulate *peculium* by working on their own account.

In contrast to the British and French Caribbean, where the cultivation of sugar created massive plantations manned by very large numbers of slaves, in Brazil the smaller farmers were integrated into, rather than expunged from, the system of sugar production.[93] On the one hand, there were the *senhores de engenho* who were authorized to operate mills for processing the sugar cane. Involved in some sugar cultivation as well, they resembled the planters of the Caribbean. But, besides them, there were the *lavradores de cana* who, lacking mills of their own, supplied the mill owners with much of their sugar, either as proprietors who paid for the milling service by conceding half the cane they produced, or as tenants of the mill owners who paid a share of the sugar crop in rent and another share for the milling service. The existence of these cane farmers meant that large numbers of field slaves worked on small farms. In fact, relatively few slaves in Brazil worked on plantations with over 100 slaves: for example, in 1800 no more than 15 per cent did so in Bahía against 61.5 per cent in Jamaica.[94] On the mill owners' estates in Bahía, the average number of slaves was a substantial sixty-two.[95] However, the Bahía cane farmers possessed on average no more than ten slaves each.[96] Altogether, these small cane farmers owned one-third of the Bahía slave force that was engaged in sugar production in 1817.[97] This meant that, even in the sugar-growing regions, slaves operated in very small units and also on farms where their owners were resident and directly involved. Whether this worked in the slaves' favour is not entirely clear. Lacking was the cultural freedom of the large estates. As a slave commented in 1821: 'The more the master is removed from us in place and work, the greater the liberty we enjoy.'[98] Coupled with the greater likelihood of paternalistic supervision and interference was yet another drawback: the greater chance of isolation, with slaves on small farms lacking the varied company found on a large plantation. Slaves on small farms were, arguably, more strongly placed than those on the larger plantations to ease their lot by earning the master's favour, but the workload placed upon them was not necessarily any lighter. The burden of work depended upon the amount of available labour and how it related to the needs of the enterprise. In the cities, the slaves most susceptible to exploitation were those attached to poor households, simply because so much was expected of them; it was likewise in the countryside for slaves attached to poor farms.

A prominent feature of Brazilian slavery was its association, from the late seventeenth century, with the mining of gold. Thanks to gold, the inland province of Minas Gerais had acquired by 1800 a larger number of slaves than any of the sugar plantation provinces: 163,543, against 97,633 for Pernambuco and 147,263 for Bahía. The Minas Gerais slaves were engaged not only in mining but also in growing food to support the mining communities.[99] As the mining industry went into decline in the late eighteenth century, the agricultural system created to sustain it endured, partly to provide food for the surviving Minas Gerais townships and partly to feed the plantation regions of Bahía, Pernambuco and Rio de Janeiro. In conjunction with some coffee production, this kept the slave regime of Minas Gerais very much alive, so much so that it continued to grow, even in the nineteenth century. By 1872 it possessed 381,893 slaves, against 167,824 in Bahía and 89,028 in Pernambuco. Its only rival was the coffee-planting province of Rio de Janeiro, but this fell far short of Minas Gerais with a slave population of 306,425.[100]

Only a small percentage of this Minas Gerais slave force ever worked on coffee plantations, for not until after 1850 were they extensively developed in the province; and even then they engaged the labour of no more than 15 per cent of its slaves in 1873, rising to 24 per cent on the eve of abolition in 1887.[101] This meant that, in Minas Gerais, less than one quarter of the slave population was ever directly involved in an export-led, monocultural plantation economy.[102] Other cash crops with an export potential were grown there – such as sugar, tobacco and cotton – but mainly on small farms to meet local needs.[103] Large numbers of slaves worked on huge, self-subsistent estates (*fazendas*), but they were feudal rather than commercial operations which developed to meet the internal needs of a world cut off by poor communications. These *fazenda* slaves performed a broad range of work – agricultural, manufacturing, domestic – in the absence of free labour, which tended to be siphoned off by the availability of land.[104] But many slaves also worked on small farms that practised a general agriculture.[105]

With the collapse of the mining industry in the late eighteenth century, agriculture became the major source of slave employment in Minas Gerais. Yet even then it accounted for no more than 45.4 per cent of the slave population.[106] Another 32.5 per cent were in domestic service, and 10.6 per cent were in some form of manufacturing which, by the early nineteenth century, included not only the range of artisan work but also labouring in cotton mills and iron foundries.[107] Complicating the picture further was the fact that the coffee plantations that sprang up in late nineteenth-century Minas Gerais were relatively small, employing in 1883 an average of 36.4 slaves per plantation; while the hundred plus slave estates lay outside the export economy and were engaged in producing food and raw materials for the needs of the region or of adjacent provinces.[108] Of this huge slave force in Minas Gerais, only a small minority (5.2 per cent in 1887) lived in towns or villages.[109] The rest inhabited the estates of their masters. Minas Gerais therefore differed from the other regions closely associated with slavery not only in having such a small proportion of slaves linked, by the export trade, to the world economy, but also in lacking the urban slavery that the coastal cities of Rio, Recife and Salvador possessed in profusion.

Living in Salvador in 1724 were as many slaves as free people; and, as late as 1849, the city of Rio was inhabited by 78,855 slaves (against 116,318 free).[110] Their dependence upon slavery left each of these coastal cities resembling Lima or Mexico City. In this respect, the nature of slavery in Brazil can be likened to that found in the Spanish Empire. It meant that many slaves enjoyed the freedoms of town life, possessing opportunities for social contact and commercial gain that life on the plantation tended to lack. Urban residence also opened up for slaves a much greater range of service occupations than was to be found in the countryside. Undoubtedly, as attendants and servants attached to rich urban households, slaves could be well off. Many urban slaves, however, were engaged in the hard or unpleasant labour of porterage and waste disposal. Large numbers, moreover, were onerously obliged not only to serve their master's basic domestic needs but also to support him and his family in a lifestyle of aristocratic ease: that is, through waged work or by street peddling and prostitution.[111]

Slave ownership in Brazil undoubtedly rested on a very broad social basis. This resulted from the low price at which slaves could be bought. No section of the economy was independent of slavery; and Brazilian society generally had a vested interest in its preservation because so many families owned slaves, with something like one in two urban households relying upon slave labour and well over 50 per cent of rural households doing likewise. As a source of income, slaves were important to a very wide spectrum of society: those with farming, mining or manufacturing businesses, and private persons who, to avoid working themselves, hired out their slaves. Slaves, then, were useful not only to the well-off but also to the relatively poor, even to smallholders who were no more than peasants.[112] Underpinning Brazilian society and economy in this comprehensive manner, the slave institution, not surprisingly, lasted until 1888.

Slaves received little effective protection from the Portuguese government. Although they were awarded human rights in the manner of the slaves of Spanish America – for Portugal, like Castile, had been moved by a crusading mission which involved the use of slavery as a means of converting Pagans to Christianity – there was little chance of enforcement.[113] In the treatment of slaves, Brazilian masters could get away with murder, although normally they settled for a high-handed paternalism. Provoked by maltreatment, Brazilian slaves took part in conspiracies and, compared with slaves in North America, a large number of open revolts. They also fled into the forest or to the cities. The terrain, moreover, allowed here and there the establishment of *quilombos*: communities of fugitive blacks who formed outlaw bands in inaccessible regions.[114] Such protests and acts of resistance helped to curb the misbehaviour of masters by instilling a climate of fear, while justifying in their eyes a tightly disciplined system of slavery, through revealing how vicious slaves could become if their disobedience was tolerated.

However, chiefly responsible for making slavery bearable were the customary rights slaves established, maintained and enlarged not by revolt or flight but by trade–off negotiations with their masters, backed up by acts of non–cooperation.[115] Some of these rights related to distinctive cultural expressions originating in Africa, notably the use of African languages, African religious practices, African musical instruments such as the drum, the marimba and the oricongo, and African dances such as the *lundú* and the *batuque* (which eventually became the samba).[116] Familiarity with them was sustained by the constant inflow of newly enslaved Africans and the large numbers of slaves inhabiting the coastal cities, although the isolation many slaves suffered through having to live on small farms in the depths of the countryside could lead to their dilution and loss.[117]

Other customary rights resided in the opportunities slaves had to earn money on their own account. In contrast to Mexico and Peru, slaves in Brazil were frequently provided with garden plots and time off to work them. This practice was authorized by a government order of 1606, requiring masters to grant slaves one day per week to tend their plots.[118] By the close of the seventeenth century it was normal to allow slaves the free use of Saturdays specifically for that purpose. The original function of these plots was to give the slaves the chance to feed themselves, usually by growing manioc and rearing ducks or chickens. From the master's point of view, it provided the simplest and most convenient way of ensuring that the slaves were properly fed. But, in the course of time, the plots became commercial operations, a means by which slaves obtained cash by selling produce either to their masters, or in local markets, or by peddling it in the streets of a local town.[119] Slaves also became profitably involved with *petite culture*, thanks to the truck farms that developed around the large cities. Operated by slaves, they produced fruit and vegetables which the slaves themselves had the responsibility of selling in the city. Although obliged to return an agreed sum to their master, they could, nonetheless, profit from what was sold.[120]

Another moneymaking right stemmed from the limits placed on the amount of work required of slaves. The free time this created – on Sundays, holidays and in the evenings – was used by urban slaves to sell goods in the street.[121] On the plantations, moreover, payment was made for work over the limit. The purpose of this system of limitation was to provide the slaves with an incentive to work efficiently. It took the form of quotas. The slaves were required to perform so many a day and upon their completion were given 'free time'. Payments for work done in this time arose out of respect for the customarily fixed quotas. They were made usually at harvest time, when the labour needs of the plantation exceeded what the quota system could provide. These payments for extra work were found both in the sugar and coffee industries, and also in gold mining.[122] In addition, there were skilled slaves or managerial slaves, in both town and country, who were offered wages to secure their cooperation, often in produce that they could sell on their own account.[123]

Another profitable slave right was to receive part of the wage when hired out. In the cities *negros de ganho* were frequently found, either working for someone other than their owner or self-employed, and paying part of their income to the master. Especially well paid were the stevedores in the ports and the craftsmen and skilled women of the large cities.[124] By virtue of these various moneymaking devices, slaves were able not only to contradict their servile condition by assuming the characteristics of freemen, but also to accumulate the means to purchase their emancipation. The extensive opportunities slaves had in Brazil to work on their own account were reflected in the large amount of manumission that occurred: with a rate, for example, of 1 per cent per annum in Bahía.[125] However, the ability of individual slaves to use their rights as bridges to freedom ensured, paradoxically, the survival of slavery, partly by making slaves tolerant of the system, partly by obliging slaves to work well, and partly by providing masters with a means of slave control through the services the freed were prepared to offer in managing the slave work-force and in hunting down runaways.[126]

Brazilian slavery, then, had its own distinctive character. It differed from Peruvian and Mexican slavery because of its involvement with an extensive export trade. The profits to be made from slave labour thanks to this connection ensured that slavery was found on a much larger scale than anywhere else in Latin America. It also differed from Caribbean slavery in that it was not so dominated by the plantation, with many slaves living on small farms and in large cities. Finally, it differed from North American slavery in the degree of manumission that occurred, as well as in the extent of its dependence on the transatlantic slave trade. But all these distinctions occurred within the common framework that embraced the Americas: a slave regime that was essentially racist, commercial and colonial.

The Caribbean

Slavery in the Caribbean was shaped first by the transference, in the seventeenth century, of certain islands from Spanish to English and French rule; second, by the development upon these islands of a sugar industry geared to the export trade with North America and Europe; and third, by a policy of amelioration resulting from the revolt of the American colonies in the 1770s, the Haitian Revolution of 1791, the British government's decision in 1807 to terminate the transatlantic slave trade, and the long-term attempt of slave communities to acquire customary rights and liberties. Such was the impact of amelioration that, when terminated in the nineteenth century, the Caribbean slave system differed fundamentally from the one first established in the late seventeenth century, even though it still retained a close connection with the sugar industry.[127]

In the early seventeenth century a number of out-of-the-way islands in the Lesser Antilles were seized from Spain, the French taking Martinique and Guadeloupe; the English taking Barbados, St Kitts, Nevis and Antigua. In the late seventeenth century Spain also lost possession of key islands in the Greater Antilles, notably Jamaica to the English in 1655, and the western part of Hispaniola to the French in 1697. Following their transfer, all these islands quickly became sugar-exporting colonies. In contrast, the islands that remained Spanish – Cuba, Trinidad and Puerto Rico, for example – failed before the nineteenth century to acquire a sugar industry.

The Dutch were initially crucial to the establishment of the Caribbean sugar industry. Evicted from Brazil in the 1650s, they brought plants, machinery and expertise to Barbados, Martinique, Guadeloupe and Jamaica. They also took charge of the slave trade from Africa to the Caribbean, as well as the sugar trade from the Caribbean to Europe.[128] Thanks to the Dutch, then, Caribbean sugar had Brazilian origins; yet its development followed a somewhat different course, for in Brazil the sugar industry remained dependent upon the small cane farmer; whereas, following the example set in Barbados, the Caribbean sugar industry operated mainly through large-scale plantations, each with its own grinding mill and pro-cessing equipment.

The sugar plantations on Barbados, however, quickly followed the Brazilian example in employing imported slave labour. Tobacco, the staple that sugar replaced in Barbados, had mainly relied upon white bonded labour, supported by a few Indians and a few African slaves.[129] But the labour demands of the sugar industry and its profitability, coupled with an inadequate supply of white or native labour, led to an exclusive dependence upon African slaves for the field work, with white bondsmen employed as craftsmen and managers. The system first established on Barbados in the 1650s was adopted on the English Leeward Islands (i.e. Nevis, St Kitts, Antigua, Montserrat) between 1678 and 1713, on the French islands of Martinique, Guadeloupe and St Domingue between 1680 and 1740, and in Jamaica between 1700 and 1774. In each case the economy was trans-formed as sugar excluded other crops, to the extent that basic provisions had to be imported to feed the inhabitants.[130] In addition, colonial society was transmogrified. Originally the colonies had survived by attracting settlers and serving as bases for adventurers and pirates. Society had been a collec-tion of Europeans, some free, others bonded, who aspired to root them-selves as small farmers. Now it became black and African, with the whites strongly inclined to leave, partly because engrossment thwarted the farming ambitions of the poorer element, and partly because the large planters pre-ferred residence in the old country. The blacks had no choice but to stay. By 1700 the ratio of blacks to whites was 2:1 in the French sugar colonies and 4:1 in the English sugar colonies.[131] Unlike the white bondsmen, the blacks were subjected to a servitude that was permanent and inheritable. Also unlike the white bondsmen, black slaves were subjected to an extremely rigorous labour regime, since most were made to work as field hands on the sugar plantations.

The labour required to cultivate sugar was intrinsically heavier than for cotton, rice or tobacco; but, adding to the burden of work, was the large-scale nature of the typical Caribbean sugar plantation, the debts the owners contracted in purchasing the machinery and slave labour, and the power the absentee owners necessarily delegated to overseers. Paternalism gave way to short-term commercialism, from which only the planters, their creditors and their agents benefited.[132] As oppressive for the slaves as the nature of the work was the inadequate sustenance they received. The need to maximize the amount of land planted with cane, the large numbers of slaves employed upon each plantation, the urgent desire to maximize immediate profits, the absence of long-term planning: all this created a series of basic logistical difficulties. Since they were unwaged, slaves could at least expect to be given sufficient food, but, at certain times of the year in the sugar colonies, this was not the case. Rations were meagre and the opportunities slaves had to grow their own food were limited, either by the smallness of the plots assigned to them or by the little time they were granted for their cultivation. June to September was designated the 'hard time' or 'hungry time'. During it, slaves driven by starvation ate unripe or bad food and died, at double the normal rate, from diseases associated with malnutrition. No matter how efficiently the plantations were run as labour regimes, they tended to be badly organized from a victualling point of view. Accounting for the hardship suffered by the slaves on the sugar plantations, then, was not only the intensity of the work but also the inability of the planters, for much of the seventeenth and eighteenth centuries, to ensure that the work-force was adequately fed.[133]

Yet the history of Caribbean slavery was not simply a story of rampant profit-taking. It was also one of effective slave resistance. Spectacular instances involved the establishment of independent communities, notably in Jamaica, Cuba, St Vincent and St Domingue.[134] This type of resistance, however, depended for its success upon an extensive terrain of mountain and forest, something that few of the islands possessed. For most slaves, the sugar plantation was as inescapable as their bondage. For this reason, their strategy of resistance was not to reject the plantation regime but to construct within it a protective counter-culture. This was possible because of several exploitable weaknesses in the system.[135] The size of the plantations, and the large number of slaves on each, gave Caribbean blacks an unusual degree of freedom to develop their own beliefs and ways, while the system's dependence upon the transatlantic slave trade maintained the linkage with Africa, the basic source for an alternative culture. It quickly became evident that, in order to function properly, plantations had to be downwardly answerable, with overseers dependent on the cooperation of slave-drivers and the slave-drivers dependent upon commanding the respect of the slave workforce.[136] Furthermore, the monocultural tendencies of the sugar plantation meant that, having little land to grow foodstuffs, coupled with the expense and inconvenience of buying it elsewhere, and needing to have the workforce employed full-time in the production of sugar, planters were prepared to allow slaves, in their own time, to grow their own food and rear their own livestock. In this way, the plantations became heavily dependent upon the basic provisions produced on slave-holdings, and therefore more amenable to the idea of allowing slaves some free time to cultivate them. Connected with these slave-holdings were Sunday markets where slaves traded their surplus and acquired in return a fund of cash, or goods they could not make or grow themselves. Within the framework of the plantation economy there thus developed an independent slave economy which the masters had no choice but to tolerate.[137]

A central flaw in the plantation system of the British Caribbean was exposed in the 1770s by the revolt of the American colonies: the heavy reliance upon provisions imported from abroad. With this supply interrupted, planters were left in the lurch and the provisions produced by slaves became doubly important.[138] In the circumstances, it made sense to grant slaves more free time to produce what was now a vital resource for whites and blacks alike; and from then onwards slaves successfully negotiated additional time to cultivate their plots. With two days guaranteed, three days became the goal; so much so that, by the 1830s, Caribbean slaves were assuming the appearance of serfs: having secured their own land to cultivate they now resented the labour demands required of them for working the lord's demesne.[139]

Another major flaw in the Caribbean slave system was exposed in the closing years of the eighteenth century. This happened when the horrors of the slave trade led to demands for its abolition, in an attempt to undermine slavery without challenging the sanctity of property. If the Caribbean slave populations had been naturally reproductive, this campaign would not have mattered much. For the most part, however, they suffered continual depletion, the result of very low birth-rates and very high mortality, making fresh supplies of slaves essential just to maintain the present labour force. Highly dependent upon the slave trade, then, planters had to take the movement for abolition very seriously. In response, they sought to raise the birth-rate by requiring less field work of pregnant slaves, by allowing maternity leave, and by offering mothers cash rewards for rearing large families. Through colonial assemblies, they enacted slave rights – often rights already established as customs by the slave communities – to demonstrate that plantation slavery was something other than the brutal regime depicted by abolitionist propaganda.[140] The actual abolition of the slave trade after 1807 drove planters to try even harder to raise the slave birth-rate and to demonstrate their paternalism. Needless to say, easing the system made it more objectionable to the slaves as it suggested that the door of concession was now wide open. Then there was the Haitian Revolution of 1791 which revealed to the masters the capacity of Caribbean slaves to destroy the system. True, by removing the strongest competitor in the industry, the same event made it easier for the planters on the British islands to continue, but it impressed upon them the need for reform in order to ward off revolution.

It would be wrong to think, however, that by this time the planters were in retreat. In the late eighteenth and early nineteenth centuries the slave–sugar regime underwent a massive extension. Immediately following the Seven Years War, four islands (Dominica, Grenada, St Vincent and Tobago) passed from the French to the British. They were quickly turned into sugar colonies, with 70,000 slaves imported in a decade to man the new plantations.[141] Between 1739 and 1800, sugar production was extended to the north side of Jamaica, more than doubling the number of sugar planta-tions and the colony's stock of slaves.[142] Towards the close of the eighteenth century Cuba woke up to the profitability of sugar. Given its size and fecun-dity, it quickly became the major producer, as well as the major importer of slaves. The social and economic effect upon the island was profound. Cuba had employed slaves for centuries. In the typical Spanish-American manner, they had served a settlement, rather than plantation, colony, with large numbers working in a diversity of occupations: for example, as domestics, on small tobacco farms, on ranches and in urban workshops. In 1774 they had formed no more than one quarter of the population. Yet by 1846, they comprised almost half. By this time, sugar accounted for 84 per cent of the colony's exports; 47 per cent of Cuba's slaves worked as field hands on sugar plantations; and, in the typical Caribbean manner, 79 per cent of the slaves lived in the countryside. Vital to this transformation was first the example of nearby St Domingue, and then the Haitian Revolution, which wrecked its sugar industry, causing a flight of planter refugees, along with slaves, capital and experience, to the larger island next door.[143]

The sugar industry in the Caribbean, then, created a distinctive slave regime. Yet on several Caribbean islands it failed to gain a hold. Instead, they grew a variety of crops, including tobacco and cotton as well as provi-sions to supply the home demand, passing ships and nearby sugar colonies. The Bahamas, Puerto Rico and Trinidad remained in a pre-plantation state, at least until the end of slavery. All these islands possessed a fair number of slaves whose functions resembled those of Cuba before its sugar revolution, or of Mexico and Peru; and, when compared with the colonies founded on sugar, their societies – comprised of small farmers, slave minorities and relatively relaxed work regimes geared to subsistence rather than the realization of massive profits – possessed a slave regime that was much more benign.

Most slaves in the Caribbean lived in conditions that differed markedly from those found in the rest of the New World. Distinguishing the Caribbean was the very high proportion of slaves to non-slaves. In addition, it was, more so than anywhere else, a world of large-scale, monocultural plantations. Apart from Brazil, it was more dependent upon the slave trade.

Not surprisingly, in view of these three basic differences, slaves in the Caribbean were more imbued with African culture than elsewhere in the New World.

Already by 1700 three-quarters of the Caribbean population was of slave status; whereas, in the rest of the New World at that time, slaves comprised either a small minority, as in the Spanish mainland empire and the British North American colonies, or a substantial minority as in Brazil.[144] This basic distinction remained a century or so later, in spite of the massive growth of slavery in the US South where, by 1860, the overall proportion of slaves was 32 per cent and 44.8 per cent in the Deep South. Slaves in South Carolina and Mississippi now formed a majority of the population, but the proportion – 57.2 per cent for the one and 55.2 per cent for the other – was low compared with the Caribbean.[145] For example, the Leeward Islands in 1800 contained 81,000 slaves against 3,200 non-slaves: amounting to 95 per cent. At the same time Jamaica had 337,000 slaves against 37,000 non-slaves: amounting to 89 per cent. The outstanding exception in the Caribbean was Cuba, whose slave population grew spectacularly from 38,900 in 1775 to 323,759 in 1846, but never exceeded 43 per cent. However, this is to be explained by the late development there of a sugar plantation economy, which meant that it had to be superimposed upon a populous settler society of long standing, one that was well established and very much on the increase, rising from 96,400 in 1775 to 426,000 in 1846.[146] In sharp contrast, the other plantation regimes in the Caribbean had been imposed upon societies that were in the very early stages of settlement and therefore more susceptible to transformation.

A startling characteristic of the Caribbean islands was the rapid disappearance of their indigenous population. Under Spanish rule they were annihilated, mainly by imported diseases from which they had no immunity; whereas in Spanish and Portuguese America, the Indians, although initially decimated by disease, survived to form, by the mid-seventeenth century, a substantial proportion of the free population.[147] The Caribs were replaced by free white settlers and white bonded servants, the former working small farms with the assistance of the latter who, having served their time in bondage, tended to acquire small farms themselves. Export crops such as tobacco and cotton provided these farmers with the means to purchase bonded servants, usually from the British Isles. Probably the majority of white immigrants to the Caribbean arrived in bondage, but upholding the free element in society was the temporary nature of the servitude. After five years or so, it expired.[148]

The obliteration of the Caribs was followed by the exclusion of the small farmers. Having emigrated to escape the engrossment of farms in the Old World, they now found themselves threatened by it in the New, not in the form of the capitalist farmer amalgamating smallholdings and, in the process, converting a peasantry into a rural proletariat, but in the form of the large sugar planter who, in swallowing up land, not only dispossessed the small farmers but also offered whites little employment, confining the available work opportunities to a few managerial positions and the skilled crafts associated with processing the cane into sugar, molasses and rum. The planters created a huge demand for field work but met it with slave labour.[149] Having few natives to enslave, they fell back upon Africa, a labour resource already well tried and tested for growing sugar – first on the Atlantic islands and then in Brazil – with a supply system that, by the mid-seventeenth century, had already dispatched to the New World over 400,000 slaves, and, in the late seventeenth century, sent 264,000 slaves to the British Caribbean colonies alone.[150]

Characteristic of Caribbean slavery was the relative lack of opportunity for emancipation, especially in the sugar islands under British rule. In the USA, freedom was virtually unattainable for slaves in the South, but liberation lay in fleeing to the free states of the North. In the Spanish- and Portuguese-American empires, moreover, liberation could be achieved without flight: through miscegenation, donation or self-purchase.[151] Such opportunities for emancipation were much less available in the British Caribbean where there was a lack of free Indian women with whom slaves could mate and produce free children. Planter absenteeism, moreover, not only reduced the number of resident whites but also limited the number of sexual relationships that might lead to manumission by gift. Furthermore, the confinement of most slaves to field work on the plantations left them with few opportunities to accumulate the cash necessary for purchasing their freedom. Flights to freedom became possible where maroon communities were established, but, apart from St Vincent, this only happened on the large islands. On the smaller islands, bereft of the cover of forest by the planta-tion regime, such flights became acts of heroism verging on the impossible. Moreover, in 1739 the Jamaican maroons, in return for the government's recognition of their freedom, agreed to return runaway slaves to the plan-tations. The productive value of slaves on the plantations – as field labour, as artisans, or as skilled processors – ruled out freedom by donation, although slaves in the last two occupations might eventually find the money to purchase their manumission. In Mexico, Peru and Brazil, the rate of manumission was raised by the large numbers of slaves employed in the service of urban households. Having no productive value, they could be released without incurring the expense of replacement, and, working close to the master and his family, they were well-placed to earn favours. In the Caribbean, this was much less of a likelihood, simply because the planta-tions absorbed much of the slave labour. Nonetheless, in the course of time, the distinction between slave and free ceased to be one between black and white, as large numbers of free blacks emerged, even in the British colonies. For example, by 1800 there were 10,000 free blacks in Jamaica, comprising 27 per cent of the free population, but only 2.9 per cent of all blacks on the island. By the same date there were 2,600 free blacks in the Leeward Islands, comprising 83 per cent of the free community, but only 3.1 per cent of their total black population. In contrast, even in the US South, where liberation was achievable by flight from the region rather than by manumission, the proportion of free to unfree blacks was higher, amounting to 4.7 per cent in 1790 and 8.5 per cent in 1810. Countering the limited enfranchisement possible in the British colonies was the degree of emancipation possible in the French and Spanish Caribbean, especially the latter. In Cuba, for example the chances of securing manumission were probably no different from those on the Spanish-American mainland.[152]

Another distinctive feature of Caribbean slavery – the harsh labour regime to which it was subjected – was yet another consequence of the sugar plantation and its prevalence.[153] The sugar industry, as it developed in the Caribbean – export-driven, highly commercial, single-mindedly bent on maximum profit, operating in large units – oppressed the slave work-force in two senses: first, in the heavy labour demands it made, especially at crop time when slaves were required to work night shifts in the processing plant as well as day shifts in the field, but also earlier in the growing season, when holes had to be dug and manured in preparation for the new cane, and when intensive weeding was necessary. This contrasted with the sugar industry in Brazil where the processing was separated from much of the cultivation and slaves found themselves – as a result of being engaged in either the one or the other – less oppressed by the work.[154] In the Caribbean, moreover, the scale of the operation called for the careful and rigorous organization of labour. The adopted solution was a gang system under threat of the whip. In contrast, in Brazil and North America, a great deal of plantation work was much less severe, partly because it was organized in smaller units and under the personal and paternalistic direction of the master, partly because it involved the cultivation of less demanding crops such as cotton, tobacco, coffee and rice.

The Caribbean sugar plantations also gave slaves a raw deal through failing to ensure that they were properly fed. Elsewhere in the New World malnutrition was not part of the slave condition. In Brazil the sugar provinces were fed with supplies from other parts of the country; the US slave states received supplies produced elsewhere in the Union; in Mexico and Peru, the mixed nature of agriculture and the internal trade in produce, as well as the relatively smaller numbers of slaves, also avoided the provisioning problem. Only in the island colonies of the Caribbean, densely populated with slaves and intensely concentrated on the production of one cash crop, did the problem of malnutrition become an annual feature of slave life.[155]

Another distinctive feature of Caribbean slavery lay in its heavy dependence upon the transatlantic slave trade. Of the 10–11 million slaves transported to the New World, easily the largest share went to the Caribbean: something like 42–47 per cent – 4–7 per cent more than were taken even to Brazil, the second largest importer of slaves and reliant upon the trade for at least a century longer.[156] At the root of this dependence was the failure of Caribbean slave communities to counter mortality with a sufficient number of births. As a result, the slave population was prone to a rapid contraction – unless sustained by fresh recruitment from abroad. The depletion rate, for example, in the British Caribbean sugar colonies was over 30 per thousand per annum in the early eighteenth century. In spite of the amelioration policy applied from the 1780s in the British colonies, and notwithstanding the ending of the slave trade in 1807 – which made it vitally necessary to encourage the slave population to reproduce itself naturally – a depletion rate of 3 per thousand per annum existed for the period 1817–32.[157] This contrasted not so much with Latin America, where depletion also occurred, but with North America, which took only 6 per cent of the slaves transported to the New World from Africa, yet, by dint of natural growth (following its prohibition of slave imports in 1808), raised its slave population from 1 to 4 million in the space of half a century.[158]

In Latin America, a major erosive agent was manumission: thanks to it slavery in Mexico faded away in the course of the seventeenth and eighteenth centuries.[159] Depletion in the Caribbean stemmed from other causes – principally the interaction of a very low slave birth-rate with a very high slave mortality. Helping to determine both rates was the high degree to which the slave population was African-born. In this sense, the slave trade created the conditions that justified its existence. Reliance on the slave trade led to a gender imbalance in the slave population, with an excess of men over women, simply because, intent on securing the best labour return, planters preferred to buy males. This, coupled with the low fertility of African-born female slaves, led to a very low birth-rate. Slaves brought from Africa, moreover, were less likely to cope with the diseases of the Caribbean, having been reared in a different epidemiological zone. Slaves born in the Caribbean achieved a better balance between the sexes, as well as having a greater immunity to its diseases. Creolization therefore offered a solution to the problem, but only a partial one, for the fertility of Caribbean slave women remained low until the final emancipation.[160] Low fertility, in conjunction with a high infant mortality, prevented the slave population from achieving a natural increase. For most of the Caribbean colonies, the problem was to prevent a population contraction. To achieve this end, a relaxation of the severe work regime on the sugar plantations was required, along with the banishment of seasonal malnutrition. That depletion could be overcome in this manner was shown in Barbados and the Leeward Islands by 1800.[161] Yet the natural demographic growth achieved was slight, largely because, although mortality was much reduced, slave fertility remained low. By the 1830s, and in response to the ending of the slave trade, the slave populations of the British and French colonies had succeeded in sustaining their numbers naturally but, in contrast to the slave population of the USA, they still lacked much capacity for natural growth. A price therefore had to be paid by the masters for what was achieved. To prevent depletion, they had to allow a reduction in the available slave work-force, simply because the increase in slaves who were excused field work (childbearing women, young children, the elderly) was not compensated for by natural growth. The only parts of the Caribbean to possess a natural growth in the slave population that approached USA levels were islands such as Barbuda and the Bahamas, where the sugar plantation failed to gain a hold.[162]

The long dependence on the slave trade in the Caribbean ensured a continually high proportion of slaves who were familiar with Africa: for example, 66 per cent in the French colonies for 1780 and 37 per cent in Jamaica for 1817. As a result, the European ways of the colonists were countered by a constant infusion of African beliefs and practices. Allowing the latter relatively free scope to flourish was the very high ratio of blacks to whites, and also the fact that, in the sugar colonies, most slaves inhabited plantations and therefore lived apart from the colonists who mainly lived in town. The plantation system, then, may have deprived the slaves of a great deal, but it also permitted a highly distinctive culture to survive.[163] In this respect, slavery in the Caribbean stood a world apart from slavery on the mainland, where urban influences, the white majority, the tendency for slaves to live and work in small units (such as farms, households, workshops), and the pressures of Christianity worked against the preservation of Africa in the Americas.

To complicate matters further, obvious differences existed not only between the slavery found on the sugar islands and in the rest of the Caribbean but also between the slave regimes of the various sugar colonies: between the British Caribbean and the islands owned by France and Spain; between the French and Spanish possessions; even between the British sugar colonies themselves.

The British colonies were distinguished by the degree of autonomy they enjoyed. They were plantocracies, the planters ruling not only by virtue of owning the bulk of the population but also through controlling colonial legislative assemblies which were largely free of interference from the metropolitan government.[164] In contrast, the French and Spanish colonies were by nature overseas provinces, their regulations determined for them by governments based in Paris and Madrid and enforced by centrally appointed professional officials. Eventually all these Caribbean colonies acquired regulations protective of slaves and respectful of their interests; but, not surprisingly, they had existed in the French and Spanish possessions long before they were found in the British. Laws of slave protection were only introduced to the British colonies in the late eighteenth century, in response to abolitionist pressures; whereas slaves in the French colonies had received protection in the *Code Noir* of 1685, and those in the Spanish Caribbean owed much to the medieval *Siete Partidas* and the ordinances that, in the sixteenth century, had applied them to the Americas.[165] Both sets of regulations emphasized the legal personality of the slave and the duties of the master. Both asserted the need to regard the slave as a prospective Christian, awarding him a right to baptism and even marriage. Both countenanced the possibility of manumission, encouraging masters to grant it as a means of earning virtue. Yet whether all this made much difference in practice is a debatable point. Where laws existed to restrain the masters in their treatment of slaves they were difficult to enforce. This was because of the limited means available to slaves for making legal complaint against their masters, coupled with the extensive resources the masters possessed to control officials through bribery and corruption.[166] Furthermore, where protective laws did not exist – as in the British colonies before the 1780s – custom, in accordance with a long English tradition, developed to fill the breach. The Reverend Robert Robertson commented in 1729 on his experiences in the British island of Antigua: 'The slaves have (or, which is the same, think they have) some rights and privileges, of which they are as tenacious as any freeman upon earth can be of theirs, and which no master of common sense will once attempt to violate.'[167] The ability of slaves to create, extend and defend customary rights, usually through a process of negotiation with plantation managers backed up by threats of non-cooperation, meant that, in practice, they stood a better chance of protection than when laws were imposed upon a colony by the metropolitan government and consequently met with unwillingness, intransigence and contempt from the planters.

Nonetheless, some vital differences distinguished the French and Spanish colonies from those of the British. One related to manumission. That it was much easier for slaves to secure their freedom in the French and Spanish colonies was evident in the larger proportion of free blacks. In the late eighteenth century it amounted to 5 per cent of the population in the French colonies, against 2.5 per cent in the British colonies. In mid-nineteenth-century Cuba it stood at 16.6 per cent of the population in spite of a massive importation of new slaves in the preceding years and a large increase in the number of white settlers.[168] Helping to create this difference was the larger number of small resident planters in the French and Spanish colonies: the result of the late establishment of the sugar industry in Cuba and the fact that the French sugar islands never became as monocultural as the British sugar colonies. They continued to grow crops such as coffee, cocoa, cotton and indigo that were associated with small-scale production. The presence of these small farmers increased the amount of sexual intercourse between masters and slaves and raised the number of mulattos. Mulatto slaves stood a better chance than black slaves of manumission, partly because of the favours masters granted to relatives, partly because of the greater opportunities enjoyed by mulattos to buy their freedom. In this respect manumission and miscegenation were closely connected.[169]

In all probability, differences in legal definition had little effect upon how the slaves were treated in the Caribbean colonies. What did make a difference, however, was the extent to which the sugar industry dominated the colonial economy, and also the extent to which this industry was dominated by the large plantation. In both the French and Spanish colonies the survival of other export crops meant that large numbers of slave field hands were involved in relatively light work, in contrast to the British sugar colonies where sugar tended to annex a much greater share of the cultivated land and squeeze out other forms of commercial farming. Furthermore, in the French and Spanish colonies – again as a result of the lesser dominance of sugar – more land was set aside for growing food, enabling them to avoid the subsistence crises that seasonally affected the slaves of the British Caribbean.[170]

Plantations, moreover, in the French and Spanish Caribbean tended to be smaller than those found in the British sugar colonies.[171] This made a difference in several respects: the smaller the enterprise, the less likely the owner to be absentee and the more likely the slave to experience paternalistic favour and interference. The larger the typical plantation the greater the chance that slaves would fall victim to exploitative overseers but also the greater their freedom when not at work. The prevalence of the large plantation in the British Caribbean, along with the autonomy the planters gained thanks to the constitution granted to most of the British colonies, meant that little was spent on creating a public infrastructure. In contrast, the French island of St Domingue and the Spanish island of Cuba were distinguished by the amount spent there on public works, either to establish irrigation schemes or good communications. Cuba benefited from the coincidence of the consolidation of its sugar industry with the application of steam, both as a means of communication through the laying down of railroads, and as a source of power through the use of steam engines to crush the grain.[172] But of crucial importance in both cases was intervention by the metropolitan government, its way eased by the colonial constitution and by the fact that individual plantations were quite small and therefore more amenable to public assistance.

The sugar colony in the French Caribbean was essentially an eighteenth-century development; whereas in the Spanish Caribbean it emerged only in the early nineteenth century. In the French colonies settlement and plantation had grown together, the former serving the latter; while in the Spanish colonies a plantation system had been imposed, late in the day, upon a mature settler society. As a result, the sugar regime was much less dominant in Cuba than it was in the French and the British Caribbean. Although the construction of the Cuban sugar industry involved a massive import of slave labour, the result was not demographically overwhelming. In fact, by the mid-nineteenth century, slaves in Cuba still formed a minority of the population, having increased from 23 per cent in 1775 to no more than 36 per cent in 1846.[173] A second vital difference with the French colonies lay in Cuba's much larger proportion of ex-slaves, a result not only of miscegenation and the slave's ability to accumulate wealth, but also of the greater degree of manumission practised in the Spanish-American Empire. In Cuba this was promoted by the system of *coartación*, which was given legal sanction in the 1760s and eventually incorporated in the slave code of 1842. By means of it a slave gained an automatic right of emancipation if he could afford to buy himself back. Whereas manumission was twice as likely in the French colonies as in the English, in the Spanish it was at least three times as likely as in the French.[174]

In the British Caribbean differences in the nature of the slave regime stemmed from not only the extent of its association with the sugar industry, but also island size, climate and terrain. Slavery in the non-plantational Bahamas was very different from that of the sugar colonies; while, among the sugar colonies, the largish island of Jamaica possessed a slave system that differed a great deal from what was found on the small islands of Barbados and the Leewards. These small islands tended to be more sugar-dominated, with a greater share of the cultivated land and the slave population engaged in sugar production: so much so that 80 per cent of their slaves worked on sugar plantations, whereas in Jamaica not more than 60 per cent did so.[175] In addition, on the small islands much less land was devoted to the growing of food than in Jamaica, where the existence of land not conducive to sugar cultivation and the low population density – 75 persons per square mile in 1800 compared with 600 in Barbados and 236 in Antigua – allowed slaves to receive not only garden plots but also provision grounds of several acres.[176] The slave ambition of attaining 'freedom' by means of peasant self-subsistence reached its peak in Jamaica, where the development of an alternative to the plantation economy caused the latter to founder once slavery was abolished. In contrast, on Barbados, St Kitts and Nevis the plantations outlived slavery because, having no other livelihood, the ex-slaves had to remain tied to them as a hired proletariat.

Barbados, the first of the sugar colonies to be established, was, by the late seventeenth century, an intensely cultivated island. Thanks to its healthy climate and relative safety from foreign attack, it quickly attracted a largish number of white settlers. Comprising 20 per cent of the population, their presence distinguished the island from the other British Caribbean colonies, where the ratio of white to black was something like 1:10.[177] A second notable distinction lay in its relatively limited dependence upon the slave trade. By the mid-eighteenth century the slave population of Barbados was entering a self-reproductive state, the result of a good balance achieved between the sexes and also of a plantation regime that was less severe than elsewhere in the sugar world. This was because of the problem of soil exhaustion, and its effect on plantation management. Unable to extend cultivation to new land, the planters were driven to reduce the acreage devoted to sugar. The existing slave labour therefore became quite sufficient, if maintainable in a steady state. Since this could be achieved by reproduction rather than by the purchase of new slaves, the African-born proportion of the slave population inevitably declined. By 1817 it stood at 7.1 per cent, whereas in Jamaica it stood at 37 per cent. The outcome of creolization – coupled with the presence of large numbers of white settlers capable of defending themselves with a well-armed militia – was the infrequency of slave revolt.[178] In this peaceful situation, masters operated a liberal regime and slaves sought, successfully, to secure better conditions within the system. The slaves of Barbados lacked the provision grounds of the Jamaican slaves. But they were allowed garden plots while retaining the right to receive rations from the master; and, indomitably, they established trading rights – in spite of attempts to stop them with legislation to protect the commercial activities of the island's small white farmers.[179]

Also influencing the slaves of Barbados and the strategies they adopted to cope with servitude was the smallness of the island, its distance from other islands and its unprotective terrain. Lacking the mountains of Jamaica, and stripped of its forests by the sugar plantations, Barbados offered its slaves little means of escape. For slaves, improving the system – rather than overthrowing it by force or escaping it by flight – became the only viable policy.[180] In contrast, Jamaican slaves resisted their masters both by force and flight.[181] They were enabled to do so both by the small numbers of white residents, and also by the protection the mountainous and wooded terrain offered to runaways. Until 1739, rebellious slaves in Jamaica were inclined to establish enclaves of freedom on the island. The same enclaves served as retreats where runaway slaves could take permanent refuge. Their success was such that, following the First Maroon War (1725–40), the enclaves that were prepared to treat with the government were recognized officially as free zones, in return for agreeing to live in peace and to return all future runaways. The agreement of 1739 was both a victory and a defeat for the slaves. It meant liberation for some but a curtailment of the chance to escape for the rest. Thereafter, slave rebellion in Jamaica principally took the form of attacks on whites as in 1760, 1766, 1776, 1798 and 1808. The culmination of this tradition was the Baptist War of 1831 in the western part of the island, a major influence on the British government's decision to end slavery in 1834.

In all the Caribbean colonies slave societies continually struggled to extend their rights. Occasionally the struggle would erupt in violence, often with crushing counter-reprisals from the planters, occasionally with spectacular success for the slaves, as in 1739 and 1831 in Jamaica, and in 1791 in St Domingue. However, emancipation was only the ultimate achievement. Preceding it was the establishment of liberties within the slave regime: an achievement that was just as creditable, and mainly the result of the slaves' non-violent and awkward capacity to create and preserve customary rights.

A final difficulty in characterizing Caribbean slavery lies in the changes it underwent over time: first, as the large sugar plantation became dominant, and second, as slave life on the sugar plantations underwent amelioration. A vital ingredient in the latter process was the slaves' insistence that culturally and economically they should enjoy some degree of independence. This basic desire eventually acquired legislative sanction when external threats, notably the black revolution in Haiti, drove the planters to make concessions in an attempt to shore up the slave regime; but it first established itself as a set of customs that the planters tolerated because they could not stamp them out and because, for the sake of economic efficiency, they needed to preserve a good rapport with the work-force.

A remarkable feature of the Caribbean slave regimes was the ineffectiveness of the official regulations applying to them. On the one hand, there were the protective laws made by the metropolitan government for the Spanish and French colonies. These the planters ignored.[182] On the other, there were the restrictive laws made by the legislative assemblies of the British Caribbean. These the slaves ignored. In the British colonies, for example, a permit system was enacted in the late seventeenth century which deprived slaves of the right to absent themselves from their master's estate without his formal, written licence. In practice, this regulation fell by the board, aided by the administrative problems it created for the master's staff.[183] On Barbados and Jamaica, legislative restrictions were placed in the early eighteenth century upon the petty trading activities of slaves, especially peddling, but without effect.[184] In 1688 a law was enacted in Barbados banning slaves from playing drums and horns, again to no avail.[185] In Jamaica, a law of 1696 ruled out the slave's right to own property; yet, except in relation to goods that might pose a military threat – such as firearms and horses – it was allowed to lapse.[186] The law was countered by the force of custom, the two reconciled by the non-enforcement of the one and the eventual legalization of the other.[187]

The customs slaves created and imposed on the slave regime were as follows: the right openly to practise their beliefs in festivals and ceremonies; the right to develop their own commercial economy, essentially through the opportunity to grow, collect or make produce and products for sale; and the right to establish family relationships reinforced, in the manner of the free, by the possession of inheritable property. Responsible for their establishment were the persistent initiative of slave communities, and the complaints and non-cooperation that attempts to reduce or remove custom inevitably encountered.[188] In this respect, the contribution eventually made by planters towards improving the system was built upon what the slaves had already achieved. Faced by the prospect of an end to the slave trade, and, in the light of Haiti, moved by the fear of revolution, planters concentrated upon improving the capacity of slave populations to reproduce themselves naturally. They did so by seeking to reduce mortality and raise the birth-rate, chiefly by ensuring that the slaves were better fed, immunized against smallpox and less overworked, with night shifts removed and the field work required of women lightened. This policy undoubtedly had an effect in the early nineteenth century, dramatically lowering the slave depletion rate and rendering slaves more compliant and cooperative, with not so much running away and less theft.[189] Working to the same effect was the creolization that occurred as the proportion of African-born slaves fell, thanks to the abolition of the slave trade. In addition, there were the gains the slaves made from securing freedoms to follow their own beliefs, to control their own lives, to make money, and to establish

propertied lineages: an achievement that mocked the slave system while
allowing it to continue.

North America

The large-scale employment of black slaves in North America was a relatively late development, mainly because of the reliance placed by the first
settlers on white bonded labour. While the slave systems of the Caribbean
and Latin America were well established by 1680, the one brought to North
America remained in its infancy, its slave population amounting to less than
7,000. Only in the next 100 years did it reach maturity. By 1790 the number
of slaves approached 700,000. In the next 70 years it rose to 4 million.[190]

What distinguished the North American slave system from that found
elsewhere in the New World was the limited part sugar played in its creation. Only in Louisiana and Texas were slaves and sugar associated.[191] Yet,
in a typical New World manner, its development was due to the cultivation
of export staples. They were tobacco, rice and cotton. Tobacco first established the slave system, at the close of the seventeenth century and principally in the Chesapeake colonies of Virginia, Maryland and North Carolina;
then, in the early to mid-eighteenth century, rice extended it to the lowcountry of South Carolina and Georgia. So far, the slave regime had been
confined to the eastern seaboard; but, from the 1790s, and thanks to cotton,
it came to cover much of the South: Kentucky, Tennessee, Missouri,
Alabama, Mississippi, Arkansas, Florida, Louisiana north of the Red River,
and Texas.[192]

North American slavery was further distinguished by its limited dependence upon the African slave trade. Elsewhere in the New World, slave
regimes tended to flourish in accordance with their capacity to import
Africans. With fresh supplies interrupted, a shortage of slave labour quickly
followed. Yet the USA's huge slave population in the early nineteenth
century derived from the import of no more than 400,000 slaves.[193] By 1700
this slave population was self-reproducing, as surviving births equalled
deaths; and thirty years later positive growth was occurring in the tobacco
zone and, forty years after that, in the rice zone as well.[194] In the eighteenth
century, then, the massive growth of this population rested upon the fertility of slaves, as well as their importation; while, following the stoppage of
the transatlantic slave trade in 1808, its great increase in the early nineteenth
century was due entirely to their reproductiveness. This capacity for natural
growth – a sharp contrast to the chronic depletions suffered by most New
World slave populations – reflected the distinctiveness of North American
slavery. Absent in most of North America were the vicious tropical diseases
that, in the Caribbean and Latin America, cut down whites and blacks
alike.[195] Furthermore, tobacco, rice and cotton made less exacting demands
of field hands than sugar.[196] Adding to the burden of work in the Caribbean

and Brazil was the practice of obliging slaves to be self–subsistent. In their spare time they had to cultivate individual plots to grow their own food. In North America, slaves tended to be relieved of this chore and were provided instead with rations.[197] Also absent in North America was the seasonal malnutrition that slaves had suffered in the Caribbean.[198] As a result, a relatively low slave mortality occurred. Encouraged by a more temperate climate, fertility in North America was generally higher than in the Caribbean, Brazil and Spanish America: this was true for whites as well as blacks. Furthermore, the inability of many eighteenth-century planters in North America to compete in the slave market with the wealthier planters of the Caribbean and Brazil obliged them to attach greater importance to reproduction as a means of replenishing the slave stock and consequently to encourage their slaves to have children. Natural population growth helped to redress the excess of males to females that resulted from the transatlantic slave trade, promoting a further increase in the number of slaves. The rapidly decreasing proportion of Africans to Americans in the slave population reduced the numbers of women who, distressed by enslavement and deracination, failed to have children. With large numbers of women acclimatized to the New World and the slave condition – largely because they had known nothing else – and ready to start families while still in their teens, a high rate of fertility was guaranteed.[199]

The consequences of natural population growth left a distinctive mark on North American slavery. Creolization, a process undergone by all the slave regimes of the New World, happened more decisively in North America than elsewhere. Even by 1750, only one in three black adults were African-born; a century later all slaves were American-born. Disconnected from Africa, the beliefs and ways of the slaves became less alien to the European-based culture of settler society. This is evident in the differences between the slavery of the Chesapeake and that of lowcountry South Carolina, the culture more obviously African in the latter than the former. In 1700 the slave population of both was 50 per cent African, but whereas in the Chesapeake the African-born element had fallen to 21 per cent of the slaves in 1750 and 9 per cent in 1770, in South Carolina it still comprised 42 per cent by 1750 and 35 per cent by 1770.[200]

A second consequence of natural growth in the slave population, however, was a great increase in the likelihood of sale. In creating an excess of workers on individual plantations, the reproductivity of the North American slaves tempted masters to exploit them, not simply by making demands of their labour but also by selling off the surplus. The abolition of the slave trade between Africa and the USA in 1808, coupled with a coincident demand for slaves from the newly emerging cotton plantations, created in the course of the early nineteenth century a flourishing internal slave trade between the Old and New South which, in the manner of the transatlantic slave trade, broke up families and uprooted slaves from their birthplace, leaving them with no hope of return.[201] Yet the development of this interregional trade only increased the likelihood of sale. The prospect of being sold – along with the fears it engendered and the control that these fears allowed masters to exert over their slaves – had existed long before, especially in the Chesapeake. There the slave population had achieved a natural growth from the 1730s. In this region, the prevalence of small planters increased the chances of slave family disruption through the sale of individual members. Moreover, the settlement of piedmont Virginia had involved the movement of 60,000 slaves from the tidewater region between 1730 and 1780.[202] In the Caribbean and Latin America, a high rate of slave mortality and a continual influx of Africans made masters less inclined to sell.

Associated with the greater prospect of sale was another distinctive feature of North American slavery: the greater willingness of slaves to accept what masters chose to allow. In much of the New World, slaves made a mockery of slavery by annexing freedoms and establishing money-making opportunities. Alternatively, they threw off their bondage, by creating maroon settlements or obtaining manumission. In North America, however, the rights slaves attained were extremely limited, not only in the law but also in custom; and slavery was less easily repudiated by flight or emancipation. Occasional revolts occurred, but they were small-scale and infrequent – especially in comparison with the slave uprisings of the Caribbean or Brazil – and often no more than the fantasy of fearful settlers.[203]

The relative docility of North American slaves sprang from a number of causes: the overbearing size of the white settler population; the tendency of the slaves to be dispersed in small groupings under a resident master; the latter's paternalism, which served to protect slaves against the malevolence of a racist society; the presence of hostile Indian nations, which ruled out maroon settlements on the frontier; as well as the relatively small proportion of slaves who had been transported from Africa and remained deeply alienated by the memory of that horrendous experience.[204] But looming large in this set of conformist pressures was the fear of sale, especially between 1790 and 1860 when, in response to the rise of the cotton industry, 1 million slaves were transferred from one state to another.[205] Some slaves simply accompanied their masters, but 60–70 per cent made the journey because their masters had put them on the market.[206] Half of them, predominantly teenagers and young adults, were the victims of family separation: either children sold apart from their parents, or husbands and wives sold apart from each other.[207] For slaves as a whole, there was a 30 per cent chance of sale.[208] Intensifying the fear of sale were the family relationships slaves had managed to establish, notwithstanding the fact that slave marriages went unrecognized in the law and the children of slaves were legally regarded as the possession not of their parents but of the master. What the internal slave trade did was brutally to sweep away family custom and reassert the law's definition of the slave as a disposable chattel. It also awarded the master a means of reprisal that conveniently served as a source of profit as well as of slave control. For masters, most sales were a matter of choice. Rather than enforced by death or debt, they resulted from a desire for profit or power.[209]

The threat of sale was a major weapon in the armoury of slave control.[210] Its general effect was to counter another factor that, otherwise, might have strongly favoured the slave. Emerging late in the day, North American slavery came to fruition in a world beset by movements critical of slavery. By the 1770s the racial solidarity so far achieved by whites, through sharing the belief that slavery was acceptable on condition that it was confined to blacks, was decomposing. In North America itself, the overthrow of British rule in the 1770s and 1780s, accompanied by the revolutionary declaration that 'all men were created equal' with an inalienable right to 'life, liberty and the pursuit of happiness', established a glaring discrepancy between theory and practice. In response, every northern state in the Union had, by 1804, passed laws for the complete, if often gradual, eradication of slavery. Furthermore, legislative attempts were made to prevent the extension of slavery into unsettled parts. Thus, in 1787 the North-West Ordinance banned slavery in the North-West Territories. Unfortunately, a similar measure for the Western Territories was defeated three years earlier by one vote, permitting the employment of slavery in what became the cotton belt.[211] Nonetheless, as a result of its revolution, the United States acquired a split polity, with one part prohibiting slavery and the other allowing it to remain. In this peculiar situation, the masters of the South might have made concessions to their slaves in order to prevent them from fleeing to freedom in the North. But little was conceded, and there was no equivalent of the ameliorative policies applied in the British Caribbean. Deterring southern masters from following suit was the control they could exert through the threat of sale, which 'for all slaves in the selling states' was, according to Michael Tadman, a 'fundamental fact of life'.[212] The impact upon the surviving slave regime of prospective flights to the North was therefore nullified by the terrible fear slaves reasonably had of being 'sold south' or sent 'down river'.

It would be completely misleading, however, to regard the slaves of North America as totally dependent upon their master's instruction; or automatically responsive to his wishes; or constantly lodged in a state of social limbo that only death or manumission could obliterate. What was laid down in the law was often repudiated in practice, as contrary customs came to be established, the result of the insistence of slaves and the concessions of masters. In this respect, North America was similar to the rest of the New World.

North American slaves were notably unsuccessful in developing an independent economy. A major handicap lay in the method by which they were provisioned. Although gardens were often granted to them, along with permission to keep chickens and pigs, even horses, their purpose was to supplement rather than replace the rations directly supplied by the master. Therefore the gardens were normally very small and no extra time was permitted for their cultivation. North American slaves were consequently less well placed to acquire marketable produce than those of the Caribbean or Brazil.[213] And they were less able to demand more free time. A second major handicap lay in the restrictions placed upon their trading activities. In parts of the Caribbean, the petty, local trading carried out by slaves or ex-slaves did not compete with anything provided by white society, but flourished in a commercial vacuum. The same was true of Brazil. In North America, however, a settler society serviced its own commercial needs, leaving little scope for slaves. As an additional deterrent, laws were enacted in North America reserving trading activities for the free. Limiting the independent commercial opportunities of slaves was a mass of poor whites, operating both as small producers and petty traders. The commercial activities of slaves were further limited by the dispersed nature of settlement, the deeply rural nature of society and the scarcity of large towns. Where the latter existed, so did extensive petty trading by slaves. This was evident in New Orleans and Charleston, in whose streets slaves peddled eggs, milk, coffee and gumbo.

Yet, generally in North America, slaves did trade in produce: some of it grown on the family plot, some of it extracted from the master's rations or stolen from his store; some of it caught or collected in the cornucopia of the wild; some of it home-made. The restrictions under which slaves had to operate simply meant that, but for the hucksters operating in the few large towns, they tended to trade on a much smaller scale than in the Caribbean or Latin America. Much of their trading, moreover, involved selling to the master and his family, or bartering with other slaves. Absent, for the most part, was the Sunday marketing system found in the Caribbean.[214] Although North American slaves could also make money through using their free time to earn wages, they were, overall, much less able than slaves in other parts of the New World to acquire *peculium*.[215] What was earned tended to be spent on consumption. Arguably, however, this was not because money was hard to come by but because of the barriers erected against manumission – the primary incentive elsewhere in the Americas for slaves to put money aside.

Compared with slaves in other parts of the New World, those of North America were less capable of establishing an independent culture. The strong African influences sustained elsewhere – either by frequent imports of Africans, or by the large plantation with its absentee owner and a slave population undisturbed by paternalistic interference and left to its own cultural devices – were severely diluted in much of North America not only because its slaves soon became predominantly American-born, but also because they mostly lived within societies of settlers and on relatively small plantations where, sugared by frequent benevolence and enforced by the threat of sale, the regulatory intrusiveness of the master was difficult to resist. Quite exceptional was slavery in lowcountry South Carolina and Georgia, where a combination of African imports, relatively large plantations and a high degree of non-residence imparted a cultural autonomy of Caribbean proportions.[216] Nonetheless, the lack of cultural independence in North America did not render the habits, values and beliefs of slaves a simple replication of those to which the settler society subscribed, as was demonstrated by the manner in which they adopted and adapted the Christian religion.

In the earliest blanket justifications offered for enslavement in North America, Paganism was given a great deal of prominence, so much so that colonial law was obliged to pronounce that, when administered to slaves, the sacrament of baptism admitted them only to the Christian Church, not to the free society.[217] As a result, little attempt was initially made to convert slaves to Christianity. However, from the mid-eighteenth century, in recognition of the slaves' humanity, as well as the part religion might play in preserving their obedience, a massive evangelical crusade was waged which, by 1850, had succeeded in converting most slaves to some form of Protestantism, chiefly Baptism and Methodism.[218] Although initiated by whites, slaves in the process of conversion created their own Christianity. This had some African roots, but its basic nature was shaped by the slave experience and the colonial ban on slave literacy.[219] Black Christianity emphasized man's equality – 'before God, we are [as] white as he is' a slave said of some preacher – but not the need for obedience or man's intrinsic wickedness. It dwelt on Moses and overlooked Ham, appreciating the Christian message of betterment as a promise of deliverance from oppression and hardship rather than as a means of redemption from original sin.[220]

Slaves also formed their own congregations, created their own procedures and appointed their own black preachers. Their funeral services, mostly conducted at night, were designed to give the dead a good send-off, so that they would not linger to haunt the living – a residue of African religion – and featured processions, running with the corpse and graveside music. Their church services were characterized by emotional fervour and rhythmic body movement. In place of the solemn and 'taught by the Book' practices of the whites, they expressed joy rather than contrition, and relied upon memorizing, improvisation, inspiration of the spirit and congregational call-and-response participation.[221] No matter what the original intent, black Christianity undoubtedly served the slave interest, creating, through congregational affiliation, communities that were independent of the master–slave relationship, especially as the religious denomination they joined was often different from the master's, with a membership that was exclusively black, drawn from different plantations, and subscribing to an alien collective culture whose heterodoxy masters found repugnant but had to accept.[222]

Working to the same independent effect was the slave family. Although the marriages of slaves in North America were never sanctioned in the law, they nonetheless occurred, warranted by special ceremonies such as jumping over the broomstick. Moreover, these marriages conformed to clearly defined codes of family conduct which masters were obliged to recognize. As a result, the slave quarters were transformed from a barrack or dormitory into separate dwellings for each family.[223] Marital relations came to exist between slaves which – characterized by their appreciation of the nuclear family, their durability, and the emphasis they placed upon child care and lineal attachment – reflected those of the white settlers, although distinctive characteristics derived from African memory and the constraints of slavery were also present.[224] Slave families could be broken up with impunity by acts of individual sale. They were frequently complicated by the fact that husband and wife had to live apart: either because they belonged to different owners or because the master decided to hire out a slave for work in a factory, on a railroad or with another plantation, the hiring-out arrangement usually taking place on an annual basis and removing slaves far from home.[225] Nonetheless, the slave family established social ties binding together different generations with obligations of care, customs of inheritance and naming practices.[226] They also interconnected (rather in the manner of church congregations) the slave inhabitants of different plantations. In this way, slaves developed a social organization that was somewhat removed from the master–slave relationship. This disengagement was preserved by the ability of slaves to conceal their real lives and feelings from the master and his solicitously interfering family, both in the privacy of the quarters and behind the masks they adopted when dealing with whites. The same policy of concealment even applied to the use of surnames. These remained unknown to their masters who assumed either that slaves had no more than first names, or that they sported, in recognition of their bondage, the surname of their current master.[227]

North American slaves, then, attained various degrees of economic, cultural and social independence. Another source of independence lay in the establishment of plantation rights. This was in keeping with what had happened elsewhere in the New World. Again, the rights obtained in North America were, for the most part, less extensive than those of the Caribbean and Latin America. Their effect, however, was to curtail the master's powers. None of these rights was ensconced in the law, but rested solely upon custom. Some related to free time; others to private possession, off-plantation activity, self-management, and the treats that masters were seasonally expected to offer the slave community. Although North American slaves were unable to claim free time for growing their own provisions – through reasoning that otherwise they would starve (a case undone by the regular, if monotonous, rations supplied to them by their masters) – they managed to extend it beyond the basic amount. This had been confined to the evenings of the week, Sundays, the two to three days off at Christmas, and the one day off to celebrate harvest home. Instead, it came to include part of Saturday afternoon, an extended midday break (2–3 hours in Louisiana), the afternoons of each weekday if the work could be finished in the morning (in the lowcountry of South Carolina), as well as additional days off, notably the period between Christmas and New Year, Thanksgiving Day and Easter Monday, and days when rain stopped work in the fields.[228] Slaves acquired such rights by inventing custom, by acts of

non-cooperation – notably slow work, feigned illness, deliberate misunder-
standing, the misplacement of goods and equipment, and temporary flight
– and by making formal complaint to the master when their rights were
breached.[229] Slaves secured confirmation of these rights by persuading
masters to pay them wages when they worked for them in their own
free time.[230]

In addition, slaves acquired rights of possession to the gardens and
livestock attached to their quarters, even a right of inheritance vested in
the next of kin.[231] Their right of possession also applied to what they
found in the wild. Associated with the latter were hunting, fishing and collecting rights, along with the freedom to leave the bounds of the estate
to exercise them, and the keeping of dogs for hunting rabbits, racoons and
opossums.[232] Their right of absence also derived from the smallness of individual plantations, which drove slaves to seek as mates the slaves of other
masters. A feature of the North American slave regime was extensive
visiting – usually at night or on Sundays – which masters tolerated because
they were powerless to stop it and also needed to maintain the goodwill of
their slaves.[233]

North American slaves acquired some right of self-management: through
systems of task work in which the slaves were assigned daily work quotas,
often fixed by custom, which enabled them to enlarge their free time by
speedily completing the assignment; or through systems of gang work, in
which a customary work rate – decided by negotiation between master
and slaves – was respected; or through establishing opportunities to sell
their own labour. The latter resulted partly from the free time granted
to slaves, during which they were entitled to work for a wage, and partly
from the existence of off-plantation specialists – artisans, servants, porters,
boatmen – who, apart from having to hand the master a portion of their
pay, hired themselves out in the manner of free workers. Task work, along
with its free-time opportunities, however, was confined to the rice zone
(South Carolina and Georgia); and self-hire was curtailed by limited urbanization, the severe restrictions placed upon free time, and competition
from landless whites. Yet, within the gang system, slaves could determine
the pace of work: on large plantations by reporting disrespectful overseers
to the master, and on small plantations by temporarily hiding in the
woods.[234]

Finally, it became customary for masters to dispense food and drink to
their slaves on festive occasions.[235] Thanks to these rights, and the restraints
they placed on the arbitrariness of the master, the practice of slavery was
somewhat different from what was laid down by law. The existence of these
rights also meant that the quality of life that slaves were able to enjoy did
not simply stem from the paternalism the master chose to dispense, but
derived from their own ability to exact what they wanted.

North American slavery was the victim of an oppressive plantocracy. It
therefore resembled what was found in the British Caribbean. From the very

early days, colonial assemblies existed dominated by the planter interest. Virtually uncontrolled by the metropolitan power, they passed laws to uphold the master's authority over the slave. In the law the slave was left with virtually nothing since, defined as a chattel or freehold property, he or she was excluded from seeking redress in the courts. In this respect, the master's tyranny over the slave was not usurped but quite legitimate.[236] Roads to freedom came up against prohibitive laws. These were aimed as much against enlightened planters as the slaves. They banned the education of slaves, even in the basics of literacy; petty trading by slaves; the assembly of slaves for church and funeral services; the freeing of slaves from bondage.[237] Such laws were not without effect, but, as in the British Caribbean, they failed to determine actual practice, as the slave interest fought back through persistent disobedience, and because individual masters needed to reach a *modus vivendi* with their slaves. As a result, laws went unenforced or suffered suspension. In practice, the master–slave relationship became not one between owner and thing but between person and person.[238] The most effective laws, in fact, were not those that constrained slaves from doing this or that – as slaves with no cause whatsoever to respect the legal system had no qualms in disobeying it – but rather those laws that forbade masters from providing their slaves with certain important benefits: notably a formal education and manumission.

The Spanish and French colonies of the New World experienced considerably more manumission than the British possessions. They acquired, as a result, a sizeable second caste, interposed between the free and the slave. Its members provided the planters with a means of slave control, as well as supplying services and skills which might otherwise have fallen to slaves.[239] For example, when joined to the USA in 1803, Louisiana, with its Spanish and French past, contained a sizeable element of free blacks (amounting to 7.3 per cent of all blacks): something the other states of the Union, all of them former British colonies, had traditionally lacked, thanks to a policy of banning manumission.[240] Virginia, for example, in 1691 had only allowed masters to free slaves if they took responsibility for transporting them, once emancipated, out of the colony; then, in 1723, masters lost the right to manumit completely.[241] The North American slave states held the free black in horror, partly because, if a society were to develop in which enslavement was not simply equated with colour, the chances of capturing fugitive slaves would be much reduced; partly because it was feared that free blacks would spearhead an overthrow of the slave system; and partly because the useful services free blacks provided in the Caribbean and Latin America were already provided by poor whites.[242] This horror remained until the end. As slavery spread to new states in the Union, these states passed laws to discourage the presence of the free black, either by banning entry, or by compelling departure, or by denying masters the right of manumission. As a result, only 11 per cent of blacks were free in 1860, 2.5 per cent less than the figure for 1810.[243] Nonetheless, this antipathy to free blacks failed to stop them from emerging. Certain events quickened the process, notably the American War of Independence. At that time, the offers of manumission the British government made in 1775 and 1779 to enlist the slaves' loyalty, and then, the positive response to these offers by 20,000 slaves, led the Americans to repeal their laws against manumission, and to dispense it generously for the rest of the war.[244] Moreover, inspired by the message of the revolution, the emancipation process continued after the war. In the North it became a public matter as states legislated slavery out of existence.[245] The numbers of free blacks in North America were also increased by those who fled from St Domingue in the early 1790s, as the black revolution on that large island created the Republic of Haiti.[246]

By 1790 the free blacks formed 7.9 per cent of all North American blacks; by 1810, 13.5 per cent.[247] This was not just the work of the North. Virginia, for example, in 1782 had but 1,800 free blacks, who comprised less than 1 per cent of the black population. By 1790 this had risen to 4.2 per cent, and, in 1810, to 7.2 per cent, reaching 10 per cent in 1840.[248] Similar patterns of increase were evident in the rest of the Upper South: so much so that the proportion of free blacks to the black population rose from 5.5 per cent in 1790 to 10.4 per cent in 1810 and 12.5 per cent in 1840. The Deep South offered a different picture, with 1.6 per cent rising to 3.9 per cent in 1810 and contracting to 3.1 per cent in 1840 and back to 1.5 per cent in 1860.[249]

Making generalization difficult is the coexistence in North America of two slave systems, the one confined to the North, the other to the South; the one phased out in the late eighteenth century, the other destroyed by war in the 1860s; the one existing within a slave-owning society, the other in a slave society; the one highly diversified with a substantial service sector, the other principally geared to plantation field work; the one mainly involved with the domestic economy, the other engaged in the export trade. To avoid the difficulty of incorporating them in one general picture, the tendency is to dismiss the former as unimportant – usually on the grounds that it involved far fewer slaves.

But the slave system of the North appears inconsiderable only when compared with that of the South. Thus in 1700 the North possessed only 5,206 slaves against 23,750 in the South. By 1770 the slave population in the North had risen to 47,735, and, in the South, to 422,132.[250] Whereas in 1700 the slaves of the South formed 21.1 per cent of its population, those of the North formed a mere 3.6 per cent.[251] Seventy years later, the figure for the South was 39.7 per cent; that of the North, 4.4 per cent. By 1860 there were but 64 slaves in the North against 3,953,696 in the South. Nonetheless, a mid-eighteenth-century slave population of 48,000 cannot be overlooked. Moreover, at the time, slaves comprised 14 per cent of the population in New York state; 7 per cent in New Jersey; 10 per cent in Rhode Island.[252] Where large-scale commercial farming developed in the North, slaves replaced white bondsmen as the work-force. The only factor that

restricted their use as field labourers was the prevalence of small-scale commercial farming, in which the labour was mainly provided by the farmer's
family. Otherwise, slaves were frequently found as domestic servants, artisans, petty traders and porters, performing, in fact, the multiplicity of functions associated with the slave regimes of Spanish America, where the
absence of a dominant export trade in agricultural produce had prevented
the development of an all-absorbing plantation system.[253]

In spite of all their differences, the slavery of the North and South
had in common the fact that they were both for the most part lodged within
what was essentially a white society with blacks, rather than a black society
with whites.[254] In this respect, the context in which slavery operated in both
the North and the South was very different from that of the Caribbean
sugar colonies where, with the exception of Cuba, slaves formed the great
majority.[255] Parts of the North American South, it is true, had slave majorities: by 1775 the population of the tidewater region in Virginia, which
held half the colony's slaves, was over 50 per cent slave; while by 1760
in lowcountry South Carolina fifteen of its eighteen rural parishes were
more than 70 per cent slave. Moreover, by 1860 slave majorities existed
in two states of the Union: South Carolina and Mississippi. The former
had come into existence a century before. It had prevailed ever since, apart
from a period in the late eighteenth century when, between 1770 and
1790, it fell from 60 per cent to 43 per cent, the result of flights from
slavery during the War of Independence and a temporarily high incidence
of manumission.[256] However, in each case the majority (57.2 and 55.2 per
cent) was a small one, and, in the South as a whole, slaves comprised no
more than 39.7 per cent of the population in 1770 and 32.1 per cent in
1860.[257] This made a considerable difference to the world the slaves
inhabited. Whereas in the Caribbean the scarcity of whites left the slaves
free to develop their own culture, in North America the substantial settler
populations pressured them strongly to undergo cultural conformity. If
the slave system of the North resembled that of the Spanish colonies of
Mexico and Peru, that of the South was like Brazil's, which also engaged
large numbers of slaves on smallish plantations with resident owners,
and where whites were slightly in excess of the slave population.[258] Nonetheless, between the North American and Brazilian slave systems notable differences existed, especially the latter's greater reliance on Africa to supply
fresh slave labour. In Brazil the high mortality rate of a tropical climate
coupled with a high incidence of manumission created a slave depletion
rate that did not exist in North America. Whereas the slaves of the latter
simply regenerated themselves, the slaves of the former had to be continually replaced by imported Africans. This meant, first, that slave culture
in Brazil was much more African than that of North America; and second,
that Brazilian slavery, although lasting twice as long, tended to be much
shorter in term for its individual victims. Brazilian slavery lacked the
generational dimension achieved in North America: its slaves tended to
be the offspring of non-slaves and their children stood a good chance of

regaining the freedom enjoyed by their grandparents.[259] In contrast, in North America by 1800 the majority of slaves represented a chain of inherited bondage, with origins that were too distant to recall and a prospect of termination that appeared too distant to contemplate. A crucial element in Brazilian society was the large numbers of blacks who had thrown off slavery. In the American South, the absence of this phenomenon meant that its slaves inhabited a very different world.

9

European Serfdom

Although by 1450 the serfdom that had once prevailed over much of western Europe was disappearing fast, a rebirth was imminent. During the next three centuries, a new serfdom emerged, not in the west, however, but over much of central and eastern Europe. In spite of the differences in period and place, strong similarities existed between the old and new systems.[1] Both were part of a peasant world subjected to a manorial/seigneurial regime. Both featured two basic types of servitude, one tenurial, the other personal.[2] Both legally prohibited the serf's right of migration in order to supply lords with sufficient labour or revenue. While each regime was founded upon denying serfs certain legal rights, in both of them manorial custom often compensated for the shortcomings of the law. Modern, like medieval, serfdom had an economic and political importance. In the first place, it acted as an agent of commercialization, the labour services of serfs enabling lords to pursue large-scale agricultural enterprises geared to external markets. In the second place, it helped to make government more effective. On the one hand, the political authority serfdom conferred upon lords could compensate for the government's inability to rule directly at the local level. On the other hand, the control over the rural population that it licensed them to exercise could persuade the nobility to accept a more centralized polity.[3]

Yet medieval and modern serfdom were far from alike. Medieval serfdom initially developed as an expression of lordly benevolence: for enserfment elevated field slaves into peasants through allowing them to hold land, while freehold peasants obtained, through voluntary submission to serfdom, either protection and patronage or virtue and piety. The one resulted from giving themselves to powerful lords, the other from giving themselves to the church. In sharp contrast, modern serfdom began as an act of seigneurial aggression, with lords imposing control on peasants who, in reward for settling uncultivated frontier regions, had been free and lightly burdened with services and rent. What is more, whereas in the medieval west serfdom had spread gradually and in a piecemeal manner, the result of the estate or territorial management that individual lords chose to pursue, in the modern east it was established suddenly by parliamentary acts or royal decrees, which defined the inhabitants of private estates as the subjects of the land-lord, with no right of departure unless he licensed it, and with little redress against him. The outcome was to make serfdom in the modern east much more certain, complete and uncomplicated than in the medieval west. Whereas in the medieval west individual societies were a mixture of per-sonal and tenurial serfs, in the modern east, with serfdom defined by government order, either the one or the other system is to be found. Thus, serfdom was tenurial in Bohemia, Brandenburg and the Austrian Territories, and personal in Poland, Prussia, Mecklenburg, Pomerania, Livonia, Estonia, Hungary and Russia.

The imposition of serfdom by government order usually left a majority of the peasantry definably serf – well over 70 per cent in Hungary, Poland, Bohemia and the Baltic provinces of Livonia and Estonia. Russia had one of the smallest proportions of serfs in eastern Europe, but, even there, over 50 per cent of the peasantry was serf in 1811. In contrast, in the medieval west the proportion of the peasantry that was indubitably unfree usually comprised no more than a minority (with notable exceptions in Old Catalonia and parts of fifteenth-century Swabia).[4] Again, because it was legally defined by government edict and parliamentary statute, serfdom in the modern east was more cut and dried. There was little doubt as to who was serf and who was free, no matter whether serfs were personal or tenurial. In the medieval west the issue was more open to dispute. Although the unfree status of the personal serf was a certainty, the unfree status of those with bondland was open to question: in fact, many families in possession of servile tenures in the medieval west believed themselves to be free.[5]

Although serfdom in both medieval and modern Europe was associated with commercial farming, the relationship was not exactly alike. In the early middle ages, commercial farming had preceded the establishment of serfdom, thanks to the use of slave labour for working the demesne. More-over, medieval serfdom long outlived the practice of direct demesne farming as lords, in the high and late middle ages, chose to rent out all their land. In contrast, in the modern east the imposition of serfdom often preceded the commercial cultivation of the demesne, as in Brandenburg, Bohemia, Little Poland and Russia. Once interconnected, however, serfdom and demesne farming remained together until the very end. Initially, serfdom in eastern Europe was imposed to prevent peasants from exploiting their scarcity value by migrating either to newly colonized territories or to the estates of more lenient lords. It then came to be appreciated as the best solution to a labour problem created by the decision to operate demesnes for a commercial purpose, a decision influenced by the sixteenth-century development of the Baltic grain trade – largely the work of the Dutch – which conveniently connected the northern plains with the markets of the west. But, given the inadequacy of long-distance transport overland, access to this profitable trade relied upon the rivers flowing into the Baltic. The link between serfdom and commercial farming was therefore more quickly established in Poland and Brandenburg-Prussia than in the empires of the Austrian Habsburgs and the Romanovs.[6] Nonetheless, by the late eighteenth century, demesne farming with serf labour had become typical of eastern Europe, the result of a strong urban demand for grain in both the east and the west. However, the low wages created by rapid population growth, along with the proven inefficiency of serf labour, was by now encouraging lords to hire their work-force, just as it also enabled well-off serfs to pay proxies to perform their service obligations for them.

In the modern east, lords used their control of legislative assemblies – as in Poland, Bohemia, Hungary and Brandenburg – to make serfdom law, first by denying a right to emigrate from the estate, second by requiring week-work, and third by taking jurisdictional control. The basic aim was to uphold the value of their landed income, as it came to be threatened, in the late middle ages, by high mortality and migration, in the sixteenth century by inflation, and in the seventeenth century by depopulations resulting from war.

Most of the early modern European nobilities suffered, at some point, from depreciating land revenues. The problem stemmed partly from the fact that, protected by custom, revenues drawn from manorial rents and dues tended to become fixed, so much so that, in periods of high inflation, as in the early sixteenth century, they suffered severe devaluation. But the problem of depreciating revenues also stemmed from rural depopulation, as peasants fled to towns or other estates and regions, in search of a better life. The lords' remedy was to develop the demesne, either by renting it out (the western solution) or by working it directly (the eastern solution). The western solution centred upon the leasehold. It involved the conversion of the manorial tenures with their fixed rents and inheritable rights into leases, essentially by incorporating them into the demesne. The mode of exploitation was rent, not labour. The eastern solution centred upon serfdom and a farming nobility. In one form, it allowed the tenures to remain while making them more open to exploitation. This was accomplished by defining their holders as serfs subject to a range of dues and labour services. In another form, one especially associated with the Baltic littoral, the western policy of incorporating tenures into the demesne was combined with the eastern policy of a demesne directly cultivated with serf labour, in this case provided by landless workers – a bonded proletariat rather than a bonded peasantry. Why the west should have responded to the problem of depopulation with a policy of emancipation, while the east resorted to a policy of enserfment, is open to speculation.[7] In deciding to lease out the demesne and to stay clear of enserfment, western lords were acting in the wake of a disgraced and dismantled serfdom. The chronic inefficiency of serf labour

had in fact already caused them to abandon direct demesne farming. Moreover, they were unable to forget that, in the period of high mortality following the Black Death, serfs had fled rather than stayed put. They also
knew they faced massive resistance if they sought the reintroduction of
serfdom. In contrast, in the east medieval serfdom had originated in the
enslavement of conquered peoples. It was closely associated with defeat in
war. By the late middle ages, a process of colonization and settlement had
largely wiped it out, creating peasant societies free in status and lightly burdened with dues, services and taxes. At the start of the modern period, then,
serfdom was largely unexperienced in the east, its drawbacks unknown.
Moreover, given the control lords possessed over the legislature, and in view
of the profitability of direct demesne farming, they easily appreciated
serfdom as a feasible device, not only for tying the peasantry down but also
for enlisting its labour.

Both solutions caused lords to expand their demesnes, but each produced
a different attitude towards the manor. Having to rely upon a serf peasantry
gave the eastern lords less incentive to destroy the tenures. In fact, their
dependence upon serfs to provide not only labour but also plough teams
and freightage, caused them to maintain tenures of sufficient size, so as to
leave their holders prosperous enough to own horses and oxen. This consideration was evident in the standard sizes of full serf-holdings: usually at
least 20 acres and frequently over 40.[8] In the east, then, progressive lords
were more inclined to uphold the manorial system, whereas those in the
west tended to phase it out.

None of these reform programmes, however, was easily accomplished or
totally successful. In both east and west, tenant rights of the traditional sort
endured: in the west, thanks to the survival of customary tenures – or their
replacement by beneficial leases (which were hybrids of the two forms of
tenancy) – and commoning rights; in the east, because the legal powers
imparted to lords by serfdom were unable to stop customs from placing
restrictions upon their demands. Moreover, what was first established
in eastern Europe by custom tended, in the course of time, to become
legalized, as princes with an extensive and expensive machinery of state
to run needed to annex a greater share of the serf's surplus in order to
pay for it. Furthermore, along the Baltic littoral, where lords eventually
sought to establish a system of demesne farming dependent upon landless
serfs, they encountered the problem of large-scale migration as the serf
work-force, with no incentive to stay, migrated to Brandenburg-Prussia
or Poland to work as free, paid labourers.

Originally in the modern east the direct government of the serfs was
presumed, in the slave manner, to be their lords' responsibility. This process
of political privatization was at its most extreme in regimes of personal
serfdom – for example, in Poland from 1518, in Hungary from 1608, in
Russia from 1649 – where the crown ceded its right to receive appeals
from serfs, leaving their jurisdiction completely with the seigneurial courts.

Generally, through the process of enserfment, lords acquired an extensive political authority over the inhabitants of their estates. By means of it, they became the basic link between the state and the bulk of the rural population.[9] Lords had to fulfil this political role because the peasantry, having been turned into serfs rather than slaves, owed obligations to the state as well as to the manor. The direct taxes that serfs paid the prince were assessed, collected and handed over by their lords. Likewise, with the introduction of conscription to man the huge royal armies of the eighteenth century, the lords received the right to decide which of their serfs should be called up.

This delegation of authority was not necessarily due to an imbalance of power between crown and nobility, for, although serfdom acquired a firm grip in the east during periods of royal weakness, it developed and thrived under royal absolutism, which further increased the lords' powers, essentially by enlarging their repertoire of reprisal for punishing serf intransigence.[10] However, long before the demise of serfdom, and especially in the late eighteenth century, governments infringed upon the relationship between lords and serfs, by issuing urbarial regulations which subjected it to legal limitation.[11] With the serfs now protected from lordly exploitation in the law rather than simply through custom, serf regimes, at the point of abolition, were very different from what they had been when first created about 1500.

The development of modern serfdom was finally influenced by serf resistance. The terminal decline of serfdom in the medieval west had been accompanied and promoted by five spectacular peasant rebellions, all objecting explicitly to its existence: the French Jacquerie of 1358, the English Peasants' Revolt of 1381, the Remença uprisings in Catalonia between 1380 and 1480, the German Peasants' War of 1524–5, and the East Anglian Ket's Rebellion of 1549. The creation of another serfdom in the modern east led to a further spate of large peasant uprisings: the Austrian uprisings of 1525, 1594–7 and 1626; the Brandenburg revolts of 1646–8; the Bohemian uprisings of 1679–80, 1775 and 1780; the Polish uprisings of 1768 and 1846; the Silesian revolts of 1766, 1784, 1793, 1798 and 1811; the Russian uprisings of 1670–1, 1707 and 1773–5 (along with a mass of local riots in the early nineteenth century); and the Hungarian uprisings of 1735, 1753, 1755, 1763–4, 1784 (in Transylvania) and 1790.[12] In demanding abolition, these peasant movements showed that serfdom was an alien principle in both the medieval west and the modern east, even though kings, the church and the nobility found it perfectly acceptable.

Yet, while peasant rebellions were clearly responsible for the demise of medieval serfdom, this was not so obviously the case in the modern east, where serf regimes endured and expanded in spite of, and sometimes because of, them. Nonetheless, the relief of serfdom in the modern east was not simply the work of governments legalizing custom. No matter how they came to be first established, serf regimes were intrinsically 'a world the serfs made'. Although the modern revolts failed in their basic aim of eliminating serfdom, their capacity for radicalism, violence and large-scale organization caused lords to proceed with care; and the urbarial regulations passed by governments were often a response to serf uprisings, for which the government blamed the lords so as to conceal the part its tax policies had played in provoking them. However, serfs also made their mark by other means than insurrection; and the parameters that the serf–lord relationship acquired reflected the wide range of resistance serf communities could employ. Especially effective was the memory of what rebellious serfs might do if driven to the limit, but also influential was their capacity for non-cooperation. For example, what drove lords to dispense with labour services in the modern east, as well as in the medieval west, was the refusal of serfs to perform them efficiently.

As a result of these pressures, serfs acquired compensatory rights that were especially attractive to the peasant interest (such as hereditary entitlement to land, rents and dues fixed by custom, commuted services and commoning). These rights were essentially conceded by lords seeking a *modus vivendi* with the serfs. In this respect, the legal regulations that governments eventually introduced did not so much create serf rights as make them uniform and legitimate.

Western Europe

Originally rooted in the slave-operated latifundia of the declining Roman Empire, serfdom in the west had first emerged as slavery faded away. Awarded their own lands to farm as an incentive against flight or disorder, slaves became serfs bound to the person of their master and obliged to provide him with labour services. In the course of time, some of their farms became detached from bondage in the blood as freemen chose to occupy them. In order to retain control over these farms, however, lords sought to preserve the restraints that had attached to them when the tenants were personal bondsmen. In this way, serfdom came to comprise the servile tenure as well as the servile person, and to include within its membership the descendants of freemen as well as of slaves.[13]

Serfdom was further extended by commendation, a process whereby freeholders donated their land to lords in return for protection, receiving it back as servile tenure.[14] Extending it yet again was the fragmentation of bannal lordship that followed the collapse of the Carolingian Empire. As bannal authority (i.e. independent rule) was alienated to castellans – a process underway from the tenth to the twelfth centuries – even more freemen became subjected to serfdom, especially as the castellans, by virtue of the ban, claimed that the inhabitants of their territories were personally tied to them. This was done to stop them from emigrating and to subject them to regular direct taxation. The practice echoed the Roman law of AD 332 which, for tax purposes, had attached the free colonate to the soil.[15]

Fiscal serfdom reappeared in the late middle ages, in the politically frag-
mented world of south-west Germany where, for example, the counts of
Württemberg – faced by an extreme depopulation in the late fourteenth and
early fifteenth centuries, caused by high mortality and extensive migration
– assumed their subjects to be personally dependent upon them and proceeded to require of them an annual oath of subjection. The purpose was
to impose heavy penalties on those who sought to settle abroad, and to tax
at will those who loyally remained at home.[16] Lords also sought, in the late
middle ages, to control and exploit peasantries through the medium of the
servile tenure. In doing so, they followed a policy founded in the twelfth and
thirteenth centuries by major princes, who sought to consolidate their
realms not only by imposing royal upon private justice but also by attempting to pacify powerful subjects through sanctioning the rights they claimed
over the peasantry. This involved refusing servile tenures cognizance in the
royal courts and permitting lords to regard their holders as unfree. The
French legist Beaumanoir, for example, laid down in the thirteenth century
that, if held for a year and a day, a servile tenure automatically enserfed the
occupant.[17] In this way, government policy permitted lords to run their
manorial estates as servile regimes.

Serfdom in the west, then, was not created at one point of time, but
experienced – over something like a thousand years – several stages of re-
generation. Likewise, it was not abolished suddenly, but underwent a long
phasing-out. Like slaves, personal serfs could be freed by manumission.
This happened extensively in the thirteenth century when economic prosperity provided them with the means to purchase their liberty. At the time,
lords were keen to make money from selling manumissions, simply because
inflation was devaluing the dues, rents and taxes that they extracted from
serfdom, all of which had become fixed by custom.[18] In the same period
lords had also sold exemptions from servile dues to individual families or
whole communities. Unlike manumissions, these exemptions did not completely expunge serfdom, which continued to reside in tenures legally
defined as servile; but, by restricting the lord's powers, they relieved its
oppressiveness.[19] The same processes of elimination and alleviation proceeded a stage further when, following the great depopulation of the
fourteenth century – the result of spectacular famines and then the Black
Death – a competition for tenants led lords to abandon the policy of using
enserfment to tie tenants to the estate. Instead, they sought to retain or
attract them through favourable terms of tenancy. The outcome was either
complete emancipation or sufficient freedom to render the servile taint
meaningless.[20]

Working to the same effect was the abandonment of demesne farming.
Central to serfdom in the medieval west had been the conjunction of
large-scale with small-scale farming, the former carried out on the demesne
with slave or serf labour, the latter carried out on the tenures by free and
unfree peasants. Commonly found in the Carolingian Empire, the system
gradually disappeared as lords leased out the demesne and commuted the

serfs' weekly labour services to a payment in cash. This had happened extensively in northern Italy and parts of France by the end of the thirteenth century. Demesne leasing became general in late medieval western Europe as depopulation and economic recession made commercial farming unprofitable, and the flight or non-cooperation of serfs, coupled with the high cost of wage labour, rendered it impracticable. In this medieval phasing-out process, governments had a very limited part to play.[21] Essentially, it was a private affair, the work of lords seeking to keep their manors well populated. Exceptionally in Old Catalonia, the government intervened in 1486, mainly to end a history of disruptive peasant revolt, prohibiting serfdom entirely.[22] Elsewhere in the west, this failed to happen until the late eighteenth century when, moved by fiscal considerations, the fear of disorder, the Enlightenment and the French Revolution, governments, conservative and radical, followed suit.[23] Long before that, however, serfdom was losing much of its meaning as customary tenant rights received recognition in the law.

This, then, was the situation in the early modern west. Serfdom survived there for another three centuries, notably, in the eastern provinces of what became the Dutch Republic, that is, Gelderland, Overijsel and Drente; in certain easterly provinces of France, especially Burgundy, Franche-Comté and Alsace-Lorraine; in certain regions of western Germany, notably Westphalia, Franconia and Swabia; and in the north Italian state of Savoy.[24] In parts, it constituted a community obligation, with all inhabitants in certain states, towns or villages defined as personal serfs; elsewhere, it was conferred upon individual families as a result of choosing to occupy a servile tenure. In none of these regions could it be called an oppressive regime; and, after 1525, no further attempts were made to enserf the free or to exploit grossly the unfree. A critical event in the history of western European serfdom was the Peasants' War of 1524–5 which affected most of the servile regions in Germany. It demanded an end to serfdom. Although this was not granted, the rebellion had a profound effect in restraining the way lords treated serfs, so that, when pressured by inflation to raise their landed incomes – as in the sixteenth and late eighteenth centuries – or by depopulation – as in the aftermath of the Thirty Years War and the Northern Wars of 1655–60 and 1700–21 – they proceeded with circumspection.

A critical factor in alleviating the condition of serfdom in the west was the general decision made by lords to lease out, rather than directly operate, the demesne. This favoured the serfs in two respects. It meant the complete disappearance of weekly labour services; it also meant that lords were under less pressure to breach the customs protecting the servile tenures. Having sources of revenue that could be raised in accordance with the rate of inflation – from taxation or from demesne leases on revisable rents – lords could afford to respect the land rights of the serfs, allowing them, in the manner of free tenants, to enjoy hereditary possession and to pay fixed rents and dues.[25] Furthermore, as the rural population changed its character in the early modern period – largely because of proto-industrialization and the emergence of families who subsisted not as peasants but as artisans and waged labourers – the landholding serfs became part of a rural elite, in bitter conflict with the landless over wages as employers, and over commoning rights as privileged tenants.[26] All this tended to equate the serfs with a free peasantry. Confirming the process was the intrusion of the state, especially as public justice developed at the expense of private justice, and the landholdings of serfs received recognition in the royal courts of law.[27]

What serfdom meant in the modern west was not oppressive demands, or even a lack of actual freedom, but irritating manorial regulations, usually connected with the licence fees serfs were obliged to pay their lords in order to do things that free persons did without charge. Since they often became fixed by custom, these fees tended to be objectionable because of their incidence rather than weight.[28] Such payments fell due when a serf wished to marry outside the manor, or when he wished to live elsewhere. His moveable property, moreover, was liable to a death duty; and, under the system of *mainmorte*, the lord could annex the lands and goods of serfs who happened to die without resident heirs. Serfdom in the west, moreover – the result of its genesis, and also the policies of emancipation applied in the high and late middle ages – was normally the condition of a fraction of society. Adalbéron, bishop of Laon in the eleventh century, had divided society into warriors, clerics and 'servi' (serfs), as did Beaumanoir who, two centuries later, sweepingly termed the commonalty 'les sers'. But this was the wishful thinking of one man who was a great lord and another who was a government agent.[29] The lower orders in the countryside remained a complexity of the free, the semi-free and the servile: a complexity continually increased by policies of individual manumission and partial enfranchisement. Such a state of affairs imposed its own problems upon those regarded as serfs. It was a source of social humiliation as well as of vulnerability, inciting lords to solve their financial difficulties by picking upon peasants who, by virtue of their servitude, were less protected than the free. The situation was somewhat different in the modern east where serfdom became the condition of most peasants, and therefore neither a mark of social debasement within the peasant community nor a means by which individual families could be singled out by the landlord for exploitation.

The Polish Commonwealth

Serfdom in modern Poland was authorized by a series of governmental orders: the statute of 1496 denying peasants the right to transfer from one lord to another; the edict of 1518 excusing royal courts of justice from hearing appeals against manorial jurisdiction; and the statutes of 1520–1 establishing one day per week as the minimum labour service that each full serf holding owed its lord.[30] In this manner, a system of personal subjection, already informally established, became ensconced in the law. Comprehended within it was not simply the tenantry, but every person born on the manor, unless, that is, they were of noble status or belonged to communities recognized in the law as townships rather than villages. For this reason, serfs could be labourers and artisans as well as peasants. Since they were subjected to personal rather than tenurial servitude, their lords could sell them apart from the estate.[31]

The legalization of serfdom in Poland derived from the elective nature of the monarchy; the ability of the noble order to make its wishes law; and a structural conflict within the nobility between the lesser nobles and the greater territorial magnates. Because the crown passed by election rather than inheritance – a consequence of the extinction of the Piast dynasty in 1370 – monarchs were left beholden to the nobility who, as the principal electors, could extract privileges in the run-up to an election. For almost 200 years (from 1386 to 1572), the crown remained in the hands of the Jagiellon dynasty, but only by virtue of the privileges it was prepared to grant the nobility.[32] Prominent among these privileges was a system of representation, vested in a national parliament (the Sejm) and local parliaments (*sejmiki*). Between 1454 and 1492, this parliamentary system acquired virtual control over the making of government policy and legislation, a control the nobility was able to exercise by monopolizing its membership.[33] This did not mean, however, that the Polish parliament spoke with one voice or acted in one interest.

In law the Polish nobility was egalitarian, that is, its legal privileges were equally the possession of every noble. Nonetheless, it was stratified by estate size. Moreover, it was seriously riven by a conflict of interest: between, on the one hand, the great territorial magnates, and, on the other, the nobles with small estates or no land at all. Furthermore, since, in the Sejm, the magnates were, in practice, represented by an upper chamber (the senate) and the lesser nobles by a lower chamber (the *izba*), its legislation resulted not simply from the wishes of a politically dominant nobility, but from a power struggle between two noble parties.[34]

The authority exercised by parliament obliged the crown to respect the wishes of the membership. Monarchs naturally inclined to ally with the magnates, who could be won over by grants of crown lands and the great offices of state. However, in the late fifteenth and early sixteenth centuries, this policy alienated the lesser nobility. The crown was therefore left with two alternatives: either to marginalize the lesser nobility politically, or to appease it by concession. Marginalization failed: in 1501 an attempt was made to restrict legislation to the crown and senate; but this had to be retracted four years later with the statute *Nihil Novi*. Awarding the *izba* the right of consent to all new laws, this statute laid down the principle that 'without our will and the will of our deputies, nothing new can be imposed upon us'.[35] In fact, at this time, making concessions to the lesser nobility became a vital ingredient in the political process, because of the ambitious wars that the Jagiellons were waging against Teutonic knights, Turks and Russians, and because of the parliamentary consent needed to finance the effort. Normally, in the European monarchies of the old regime, the fiscal exemption enjoyed by the nobility rendered them acquiescent in granting further taxes. Exceptionally, the Polish nobility was liable to direct taxation (at least until 1629). Therefore, to secure its consent, concessions had to be made.[36]

One of these concessions – the denial of the peasant's right of departure – laid the foundation of serfdom. This regulation was a partial response to the lesser nobility's complaint against the magnates. In the late fifteenth century, the difficulties lords had in finding tenants derived not, in the western manner, from the Black Death, but from the inclination of peasants, and sometimes peasant communities, to migrate. Generally, a very high land : labour ratio made migration irresistible and common practice. But migration was also blamed on the magnates, and the way they lured tenants from the estates of lesser nobles to their own. The 1496 prohibition of peasant migration was, then, an anti-magnate measure, rather like the ban the Sejm placed in 1504–5 on multiple office-holding and the alienation of crown lands. Essentially, they were the work of the lesser nobility acting in alliance with the crown.[37] The same was true of the regulation placed on labour services.[38] Having to compete openly with the magnates for tenants or labour, the lesser nobles stood no chance. It was therefore in their interest to create nationally applicable regulations that bound tenants and labourers to the estate with the obligation to supply weekly labour services.

The ban on migration imposed by the Piotrków Statute of 1496 was not totally unprecedented. The last of the Piasts, Casimir the Great, had legally restricted the peasant's right to leave at will in 1348. This had featured in a set of regulations which, otherwise, had safeguarded peasants' rights. Further legislation had followed, notably the Warecke Statute of 1424 and the Nieszawa Statute of 1454. They conferred upon the lords greater powers to punish runaways.[39] Yet the Piotrków Statute of 1496 was undoubtedly different in kind, since the Casimir legislation of 1348 had admitted a right of departure for those who could legally prove that they had fully acquitted their obligations to landlord or employer.[40] The 1496 statute made no such admission, confining the right of departure to one person per village per annum. To qualify for the right, this person had to be a young man leaving, with the lord's consent, for a special educational or training purpose.[41]

The problem the 1496 statute sought to solve was the frequent migration of peasants to new lands. In the thirteenth and fourteenth centuries, this process had recruited fresh blood from the west. The impact of the Black Death on western Germany, however, severely curtailed the inflow of settlers to Poland. Then, in the fifteenth century a haemorrhage to the eastern lands beyond the Vistula occurred, as peasants left the kingdom of Poland to settle on the magnate estates of Lithuania and the Ukraine. This continued throughout the early modern period in spite of the 1496 statute.[42] A consequence of the medieval migration from the west was the prevalence in Poland of beneficial tenancies, the result of a process of colonization which, in applying German law, awarded settlers rights of self-government, access to public courts and limited rents and services, all specifically defined by charter. Such terms had been concocted to attract and retain tenants: some, in newly established villages in accordance with the legislation of Casimir the Great; others, in existing villages to which lords had sold the German law freedoms, either to make money or to persuade peasants to stay. As a result, the traditionally harsh terms of tenancy found in medieval Poland and Lithuania, which derived from the conquest of heathens and their enslavement, were subsumed under an agrarian system that counter-balanced the powers of lords with well-established and legally authorized peasant rights.[43]

Medieval Poland was not directly affected, in any serious way, by the bubonic plague. For this reason, its economic development in the late middle ages differed from that of the west. Rather than a period of reces-sion and severe depopulation, the fourteenth and fifteenth centuries in Poland were a time of economic expansion and population growth: one that continued throughout the sixteenth, and into the seventeenth, century.[44] Polish lords were therefore driven to pursue different policies of estate management from those of nobles in the west, even more so because their estates were encumbered with beneficial tenures, and because serfdom hardly figured, as yet, in the Polish countryside. In the west the economic prosperity and demographic growth of the twelfth and thirteenth centuries had caused lords – seeking to maintain living standards threatened by infla-tion – to sell either manumissions from serfdom or immunities from servile exactions. They had also withdrawn from demesne farming, or had taken to cultivating their demesnes with wage labour.[45] In the fourteenth and fif-teenth centuries Polish lords did the very opposite when faced with a similar economic situation. For them, nothing was to be gained from relieving the peasantry, since, as a result of earlier concessions, all they could offer was to convert tenancy to freehold. What lords principally wanted was to benefit from the state of agricultural prosperity. This depended upon having produce to sell. Produce could be obtained either by annexing the peasants' surplus through rents in kind, or by enlisting the peasants' labour through services and hire. No matter which course they adopted, lords needed to increase their control of the tenantry. As for deciding which course to follow, an irresistible and decisive factor was the buoyant market for grain. This had been initially created by the demand from native towns. It was then pro-moted through trade with the west. Brokered by the Dutch, the grain trade to western Europe flowed along the Vistula via Danzig into the Baltic, a trade route opened up by the Jagiellons' defeat of the Teutonic state in 1466.[46] In response to the market for grain, demesne cultivation, and, along with it, demesne expansion, provided the ideal answer: it allowed nobles to incorporate vacant tenancies into the demesne, thereby reducing the tax burden on individual estates (which applied only to the tenures, not to the demesne), while realizing an easy profit from demesne cultivation. Moreover, the use of labour services came to be seen as the ideal means of working the demesne.[47] Whereas serfdom, then, had been originally imposed to retain a tenantry by preventing departure, the form it came to assume, and the conditions it created, were determined by the commercialization of the nobility: the result of their willingness to accept farming for the market as an honourable activity. This they were prepared to do in order to benefit, rather than suffer, from the long prosperity that late medieval and early modern Poland enjoyed.

Under traditional Polish law, a system of labour obligation had required tenants to provide lords with services 'whenever ordered'.[48] But settlement under German law, and also the limited needs of warrior nobles for labour, had led to annual boons rather than week-work. This changed in response to the nobility's engagement in commercial farming. By the mid-sixteenth century the weekly service exacted was well above the minimal once a week laid down in 1520, with two or three days regularly required.[49] As a result, the serfdom newly established in modern Poland became distinctly more onerous than that which had survived in the modern west.

Yet it would be entirely misleading to explain the nature of serfdom in early modern Poland in terms of a crushing defeat for the peasantry. The servile system that actually developed was, in some respects, a response to peasant needs. Just as at one level it reflected the calculations of lords and the concessions they could extract from the crown, at another it reflected the calculations of peasant communities and the concessions they could lever from lords. Although far from popular, serfdom was acceptable to its victims because of what it had to offer. Protected not in the law but, nonetheless, by a respect for custom, the tenurial rights of the peasantry survived. In spite of serfdom, peasants retained hereditary possession of their farms, along with commoning rights to the waste for grazing their livestock and collecting firewood, bracken, nuts, berries and mushrooms. And to enjoy these rights of possession and common, serfs had little rent to pay.[50] True, the law placed no restrictions upon demesne expansion or upon labour services; and it is a fact that, in the first century or so of serfdom, demesnes grew considerably, while labour services became the major obligation of the tenantry. But neither development worked totally against the peasant interest. Demesne expansion involved incorporating into the demesne the lands assigned under German law to the *sołtys* (hereditary village headmen), or adding to it freshly cultivated waste or tenures taken from the peasantry.[51] Until the late seventeenth century, the *sołtys* lands and waste were more important than tenures in enlarging the demesne. Safeguarding the tenures against demesne incorporation was the lord's dependence upon them for providing labour services with animals, either for ploughing or freightage. Such services were best provided by serfs holding full tenures (one full holding equalled 37.6 acres). To avoid having to hire labour and keep ploughs and carts, along with the oxen and horses for drawing them, the preservation of the tenures was of key importance. Consequently, even by 1700 the average proportion of demesne to the rest of the estate was only 25 per cent.[52]

In addition, the serfs had to be reasonably well off in order to perform properly the services required of them. Although enserfment allowed lords greater opportunities to exploit the peasantry than when they were free, to ensure some efficiency it had to be shown respect. Its cooperation was essential to a well-run estate. This could be preserved partly by showing reverence for custom, and partly by bringing about change through consultation and negotiation, rather than by unilateral decision and brute force. The most radical change in estate management experienced in early modern Poland came with the introduction of weekly labour services. Although established by legislative means, this change was brought about, and then extended to several days a week, by a trading-off process in which lords persuaded their serfs to comply by allowing them in return hereditary tenancy and the right to pay no more than a nominal rent.[53]

Helping serfs to defend their rights was the survival of a system of village government first established under German law. It consisted of a village parliament (*gromada*), attended by heads of households, and a governing council (*urząd*) whose members were either elected or nominated by the *gromada*. The imposition of serfdom allowed lords to intrude upon this enclave, especially as they came to purchase the office of *sołtys* and convert it into a seigneurial appointment. Lords could also control the *urząd* through bribing its members with good land and service exemptions. Yet this did not turn the system of village government into a seigneurial cipher. The *urząd* retained the power to negotiate in the village interest with lords over proposed changes in the management of the estate.[54]

Serfdom in Poland, then, was not utterly despotic, even though serfs received next to no cognizance in the law. Furthermore, serfs had at their disposal the means to resist changes that only favoured the lord. The lord's dependence upon demesne farming with labour services enabled serfs to make a powerful point by pilfering his produce and by performing badly the work he required them to do. Moreover, the shortage of labour in Poland, along with the availability of virgin soil in Lithuania and the Ukraine, incited serfs to take flight. In the early eighteenth century, a time of devastating wars, the non-cooperation practised by serfs caused a temporary disruption of the manorial regime.[55] Especially prone to departure were the landless serfs, who were a vital ingredient in the system both for filling vacant tenures and for providing cheap waged labour. In the latter capacity they were useful not only to lords but also to the landed serfs, enabling them, by hiring their labour, to cope with the double task of serving the lord and farming their own land.[56] The importance of serf labour, and the capacity of serfs to withdraw it, placed brakes upon the lengths lords could actually go to assert their serf-ownership. So did the memory of physical resistance. The instances of serf revolt were infrequent but, as they vented their fury upon lords rather than government officials, serf owners found them especially memorable. Helping to terminate serfdom in Austrian Poland was the Galician Jacquerie of 1846, an uprising not without precedent. It reflected the Human Rebellion of 1768 which broke out in the Ukraine and affected Lithuania and Silesia. Earlier there had been revolts in the east Carpathians in 1497, around Olszanica near Cracow in 1581, and others associated with the Cossack Chmielnicki Uprising of 1648.[57]

The serf–lord relationship was also determined in practice by certain external factors, notably the level of population and how it related to the labour demands of the demesne. Thus, the continued growth of the population in the sixteenth century did not alleviate serfdom simply because, under the influence of the Baltic grain trade, it was accompanied by an extension of direct demesne farming. However, Polish serfdom only became very oppressive in the late seventeenth century with the decline of the trade.[58] This was due to the depopulation caused by Swedish and Russian armies ravaging the Polish countryside in the Northern Wars of the 1650s and of 1700–21.[59] In this dramatically altered economic situation, serfdom became increasingly harsh as lords, especially the impoverished lesser nobility, desperately sought to continue farming the demesne in spite of having a much reduced work-force. As a result, the week-work required of each full holding more than doubled. In the early eighteenth century it could amount to six or seven days a week.[60] The home demand for grain to make alcoholic drinks persuaded lords to persist with demesne farming.[61] Furthermore, the tenures left vacant by the contracting population could be incorporated in the demesne. The recovery of the population in the late eighteenth and early nineteenth centuries – promoted in Poland as elsewhere by the potato – had yet another effect. By this time the resistance to excessive labour services had made its mark, persuading lords to depend instead upon hired labour, now rendered cheap by its profusion. So they disposed of troublesome and inefficient labour services by commuting them to rents in money or kind.[62]

Polish serfdom was distinguished by its freedom from public interference. This freedom was first established in the late fourteenth and fifteenth centuries when lords, operating in a piecemeal manner, removed the villages upon their estates from the public jurisdiction of the *starosta* courts, thus denying them a privilege founded on German law. It was completed in 1518 when the crown ceased to receive appeals from serfs.[63]

The way serfdom was legally defined, then, not only placed restrictions upon serfs but also left their enforcement to the lord. All this changed between 1772 and 1795 when the territories of the Polish Commonwealth – traditionally an aristocratic republic with a king – were distributed to the three adjacent absolute monarchies, Prussia, Russia and Austria. Having to operate within a very different political framework, the nature and condition of Polish serfdom inevitably changed. So far, the Polish serfs had been oppressed by their lords but not by the state. Compensating for their subjection to the nobility was the crown's failure to construct an expensive state machine. Moreover, the nobility's interest in curtailing royal taxation and the smallness of the royal standing army had minimized the fiscal and military demands made of serfs by the government. All this changed with the Partition. In Russian Poland, the serfs now suffered from a double burden, since the lords' powers were left intact while the Russian government proceeded to demand of them conscripts for the royal army and taxes for its maintenance. In Prussian and Austrian Poland, the fiscal and military demands the absolutist state made of the serfs were also heavy, yet alleviated by the system of peasant protection that the two governments had already established. This placed legal restrictions on the labour services lords could exact and upon the jurisdiction exercised in their own private courts.[64]

It would be wrong, however, to think that the regional variations evident in the nature of Polish serfdom simply came with the Partition. The political evolution of the Commonwealth – in which independent states were incorporated either by dynastic conjunction (as with Lithuania), or conquest (as with Royal Prussia) or fealty (as with Mazovia, Kurland, Livonia, Ducal Prussia and Moldavia) – had tended to confer the Polish serf system upon these territories, the native landlords appreciating the gains to be made and readily accepting the new regime. In this respect, the spectacular expansion of the Commonwealth in the late fifteenth and sixteenth centuries caused the spread of a system of serfdom in which bondage was recognized in the blood and applicable to most of the rural population; in which the government of the serfs was alienated to their lords; and in which the serfs' assigned task was principally to provide labour services for the commercial operation of demesne land. Nonetheless, economic factors ensured that, in practice, serfdom came in a variety of forms. Thus, although the oppressiveness of Polish serfdom stemmed largely from the unpaid week-work that demesne cultivation required, in parts of the Commonwealth weekly labour services did not exist. This was because the regional economy was either insufficiently commercialized or too highly commercialized. In the Carpathians or in the woodlands of Belorussia – regions where the market economy was slow to penetrate – the obligations of the serfs were restricted to rents in cash or kind. At the other extreme were parts of Royal Prussia where, in a straightforward capitalist manner, commercial farming was worked with hired labour and serfdom never became important as a means of exploiting the tenantry or of deploying its labour.[65]

The laws defining Polish serfdom, and the fact that the bulk of the population lived in villages rather than towns, meant that society was predominantly servile. For instance, in the provinces annexed by Russia in the Partition, serfs formed 72 per cent of the total male population and 83–85 per cent of the peasant population.[66] There is no reason to think the rest of the Commonwealth was all that different, apart from Royal Prussia. However, it does not follow that the labouring classes were simply serf. A distinctive feature of Polish society was the intrinsic populousness of its nobility. By 1700 it comprised 10 per cent of the whole population. No other nobility, but for that of Castile, could equal it, and normally nobles amounted to little more than 2 per cent. The very populousness of the Polish nobility meant that nobles in large numbers worked peasant holdings and even greater numbers found work as domestic servants, labourers, tradesmen and innkeepers. Noble status presumed personal freedom. This meant that the social density of serfdom was diluted by the presence of workers who were indisputably free because they were indisputably noble. Landless nobles, it is true, gravitated to the towns or inhabited the great houses, urban and rural, of other nobles; but many nobles subsisted in the countryside as peasants, on tenanted or freehold land. Thus, in sixteenth-century Mazovia, one half of its smallholdings were worked by nobles. This applied to three-quarters in Podlasie and to one-fifth of the smallholdings in Great and Little Poland. In certain parts of the Commonwealth, there were villages whose residents were wholly of noble status and therefore entirely free: ninety villages of this type were found in sixteenth-century Little Poland and as many as 1,600 in sixteenth-century Mazovia.[67]

Other peasants were free because they happened to live in towns and therefore enjoyed the rights of burghers.[68] Other legally free peasants inhabited privileged tenements, defined as such because they had once been in the possession of *sołtys*, or had been chosen to provide infantrymen for the royal service, or, in the manner of the Ollender villages of Poznan in Great Poland, belonged to communities that had been originally granted free status in order to attract settlers to them.[69]

Finally, there were semi-free peasants who lacked personal freedom in the law but possessed protection against the full weight of serfdom.[70] Some held 'bought-out' tenements, upon which money had been spent to purchase greater security of tenure. Others, like the Bojars of sixteenth-century Lithuania, were excused demesne labour services. There were also the settlers drawn to Podolia and the Ukraine who, in the traditional manner, had been granted freedom from rents and services to persuade them to come, although under Polish law they remained technically unfree.[71] This latter condition applied to a whole host of migrants lured from one estate to another, or from one region to another. Upon arrival no questions were asked. Eventually, as the problem of finding sufficient tenants disappeared, their servitude was recalled and reinstated. Finally, there existed, throughout the period of modern serfdom, large numbers of itinerant labourers who arrived for a season and then moved on, never staying long enough to become enserfed by any presumption of the law.[72]

Thanks to the Partition, serfdom endured much longer in some territories than in others. Following the Austria–Bohemian example, it was first abolished in 1794 by Kościuszko's revolutionary proclamation. Although this was undone by the Prussian occupation, further steps were taken in 1807 and 1811, when serfdom was ended by Napoleonic decree in the Duchy of

Warsaw and, then, by Hohenzollern decree in Prussian Poland. However, serfdom lasted until 1848 in Austrian Poland, and until 1861 in Russian Poland.[73]

At the end, Polish serfdom was very different from what it had been in the sixteenth and seventeenth centuries. By now the underpopulation that had brought it into being had gone. In fact, a population explosion was under way, leading to a subdivision of farms and the spawning of a large landless element in the countryside. Although the nobility continued to farm, they changed their methods under the influence of the profusion of cheap labour and in response to the growing inability of serfs with diminished farms to provide labour services with animals. They therefore preferred to employ waged workers, and to commute serf obligations from services to rents. In this way, serfdom lost its economic importance. It also lost its social purpose. Serfdom had originally developed in order to stem migrations encouraged by a competition between landlords for tenants as well as by the lure of an unsettled frontier. But the countryside was now relatively overrun with people, many of them obliged to sell their labour because they were either completely landless or lacked sufficient land to practise subsistence farming. And the traditional exodus to the east was no longer in operation.[74] The problem serfdom was meant to solve, then, had disappeared. In addition, the opportunities lords had gained from serfdom were now curtailed, not only by the entrenchment of custom but also by the imposition of state regulations. Nonetheless, deeply embedded in society, serfdom outlived its loss of function until revolutionary events forced the old order's hand. Predictably, the abolition of serfdom provoked another great migration, this time an unobjectionable one: not to the east but westwards to Germany and America.

The Habsburg Monarchy

Under Habsburg rule serfdom came in a variety of forms: personal in Hungary and Galicia; tenurial in the Austrian Territories and the lands of the Bohemian crown (Bohemia, Moravia and Silesia). In parts, it was relatively mild (most of Austria; much of Silesia); elsewhere it was relatively harsh (notably Bohemia, Moravia, parts of Hungary and Galicia). Adding to the complexity, the oppressiveness of serfdom altered a great deal over the course of time. In both Hungary and Bohemia, for example, seigneurial demands became much more exacting in the seventeenth century, a response to depopulation and the spread of direct demesne farming with serf labour.

Yet marked similarities also existed within the Monarchy, in the way serfdom developed and in the basic characteristics it assumed. Throughout the Monarchy, modern serfdom was established at roughly the same time – between 1480 and 1550 – but, in contrast to the Baltic littoral, not because of an export trade with western Europe. Furthermore, in Hungary and

Bohemia – both of them elective crowns, with noble-controlled diets exercising extensive legislative powers – serfdom was sanctioned, in the Polish manner, by the noble order through parliamentary statute; whereas in the hereditary Austrian Territories it was authorized by royal decree. Throughout the Habsburg lands, serfdom constituted a system of subjection to private lordship, so much so that the serfs' relationship with the government was indirect and depended upon the intermediation of their lords. The same subjection denied the serfs certain rights: notably to migrate from the lord's estates without his consent; to marry without the lord's permission; and to seek a new trade or training without his licence. Promoting serfdom throughout the Monarchy was the outbreak of several peasant wars, since they united nobles and government in the belief that a serf regime should be either instituted (as in Hungary after the Dózsa Uprising of 1514, and in the Austrian Territories after their involvement in the German Peasants' War of 1525), or applied with greater rigour (as in Bohemia after the uprising of 1680).

The military concerns of the Habsburgs were a vital factor in the development of serfdom, especially their long war with the Ottoman Empire. The need to provision large armies over long periods to withstand the Turk – who in 1526 took possession of part of Hungary and, on several occasions for the next one and three-quarter centuries threatened to take Vienna itself – promoted *Gutsherrschaft* (that is, direct demesne farming with serf labour), while the revenues required to pay for these military operations led to *Pfandherrschaft*. The latter was a system for raising revenue through the mortgaging of the royal estates, the collateral value of which was increased when their tenantry was enserfed.[75] In addition, serfdom allowed the Habsburgs to maintain rapport with the nobilities of two parts of the Monarchy that had a vital role to play in the Turkish wars – that is, Bohemia whose prosperity provided crucial supplies, and what was left of Hungary, which stood at the military front – and thus to exercise better control over these realms.

Only in the eighteenth century did the Habsburgs come to regard serfdom as a serious political hindrance. By now the Turkish menace had gone, and the lost parts of Hungary had been reclaimed. The new threat was the Prussian Monarchy which, in the mid-eighteenth century, seized Silesia and invaded Bohemia repeatedly. While approving of serfdom, the Habsburgs had felt, since the sixteenth century, that it was very much in their fiscal interest to ensure that the lords did not over-exploit the peasantry. Now, in the mid-eighteenth century, spurred on by a combination of military defeat, peasant revolt and the belief that a more prosperous peasantry would provide greater tax revenues and finer soldiers, the Habsburgs imposed regulations on lordly conduct and awarded serfs a means of legal action against their lords for breaking them.

This programme of agrarian reform gave serfs considerable rights in the law. But, even before it, they were not totally in the lords' power. Customary rights had partially made up for what the law had denied. Typically, these rights granted serfs hereditary tenures, fixed rents, commoning on the waste, and participation in some form of village government.

As in Poland, what serfs essentially wanted was to maintain themselves as a peasantry. First and foremost, this meant having sufficient land to cultivate. Throughout the Monarchy the system of serfdom presumed the existence of a peasantry that provided rent and unpaid labour. It also presumed the existence of a manorial system that divided the cultivated land between the dominical and the rustical, the former (i.e. the demesne) for the lord's own use, the latter (i.e. the tenures) for the use of the serfs. Although the uncultivated land was technically within the demesne, it was shared by both for grazing livestock and collecting the products of nature. In practice, then, serfdom had much to offer the peasantry in helping to preserve its way of life. A notable feature of the Monarchy was the considerable amount of land reserved for peasant cultivation. Individual families with full holdings held 30 acres or more: an advantage eventually whittled away (from the late eighteenth century) not by seigneurial exploitation but by remorseless population growth.

Nonetheless, serfdom clearly had much more to offer landlords than peasants. A free peasantry within the manorial system tended to acquire – through fixed rents, limited dues and restricted labour services – a fence of protection around its surplus which, although no safeguard against the fiscal demands of the state, was highly effective in holding off the lord. Faced by inflation or a loss of tenants and needing to sustain the value of their land-edness, the lords of free tenants were limited to leasing out the demesne, or farming with hired labour. The success of these strategies depended upon rapid population growth either to create demesne tenants prepared to pay high rents or labourers prepared to work the demesne for low wages. In other words, a contraction in the rural population tended to set the lords a major problem, unless the demesne could be leased out in large units to a few capitalist farmers.[76] In contrast, serfdom permitted a much greater flexibility in the management of estates, allowing inflationary pressures to be met by raising proceeds from the peasant tenures. This was possible because of the range of dues and fees that lords could exact from serfs to compensate for the fixed nature of the rent. In addition, lords could benefit from the price rise by working the demesne directly with compulsory serf labour, or by marketing the rents and dues serfs were obliged to pay in kind. Moreover, in periods of depopulation, serf owners were well placed to increase dues, fees and services in order to make up for the fall in the number of tenants. As for vacant tenures, they could be conveniently added to the demesne and directly farmed. In all the Habsburg lands, lords were faced with a serious handicap inherited from the high middle ages – that of a peasantry in possession of substantial tenant rights. In the severe depopulations of the late middle ages, the result of plague and war, and again in the seventeenth century, the result of the Thirty Years War and the continuing conflict with the Turk, the imposition and exploitation of serfdom was a constructive response to this problem. In addition, serfdom and the rights of rulership it conferred upon them enabled nobles to retain an aristocratic persona in an age of royal absolutism.

Finally, a distinctive feature of serfdom in the Habsburg Monarchy was the limited demands made of it by the government. In contrast to the Hohenzollerns and the Romanovs, the Habsburgs were slow in imposing regular direct taxation and conscription: the former not until 1749, the latter not until the 1770s (and later still in Hungary). Since not long afterwards serfdom was abolished, its subjection to heavy exploitation by the government lasted for a relatively brief period.[77]

Bohemia

In the kingdom of Bohemia a system of serfdom was created by one act of parliament in 1487 and confirmed by another in 1500.[78] This legislation did not introduce serfdom to the country, for much earlier, as in the medieval west, a form of personal serfdom had developed as a result of granting smallholdings to slaves.[79] What the two statutes established was a new system of serfdom, one in which peasants were bound to the lord not as persons but as tenants. Its enactment represented the earliest instance of tenurial serfdom in eastern Europe. Similar systems followed in Silesia, Moravia, Brandenburg and the Austrian Territories.[80] Essentially, tenurial serfdom applied to a much smaller proportion of the rural community than the personal serfdom that was adopted along the Baltic coast and in Poland, Hungary and Russia, since, under tenurial serfdom, the landless were free. This included the sons of serfs who failed to inherit the tenancy, as well as the daughters of serfs who failed to marry tenants. Its introduction undoubtedly marked a profound change, partly because the personal serfdom derived from slavery had never applied to more than a small segment of society, and, by this time, had largely faded away; and partly because by 1400, and thanks to extensive settlement under German law, the Bohemian peasantry had gained considerable rights of tenancy and village autonomy.[81] In other words, the act of 1487 enabled landlords to regain control of their estates.[82]

Compelling lords to take action was a great depopulation in the fourteenth and fifteenth centuries, caused by the Black Death and then the Hussite Wars.[83] As a result of it, a traditionally high land–labour ratio was made even higher. Unable to counter falling revenues by demanding more of the surviving tenants (since it might drive them to migrate to other estates), lords proceeded to deny all tenants the legal right to leave as the prelude to imposing upon them larger exactions. What enabled them to proceed in this way was the elective nature of the monarchy, a consequence of the extinction of the Premyslides dynasty in 1307, and the accession of a series of foreign monarchs, each of them obliged to grant privileges to the Bohemian nobility in order to gain election to the throne. Especially beneficial to the noble interest were the concessions granted by John of

Luxemburg in 1310, which conferred upon the Bohemian diet a law-making capacity.[84] This the nobles could control by virtue of the fact that, by the late fifteenth century, the diet comprised two chambers for the nobility and one for the towns, with a system of voting by chamber which awarded the noble order a natural majority.[85]

Serfdom in Bohemia was established before Habsburg rule. It happened during the reign of Ladislaus Jagiellon, son of the Polish monarch, Casimir IV. Both the Bohemian and Hungarian nobilities selected him to be their king, simply because he was a suitable nullity: Král Dobře ('King O.K.') as the Bohemian nobles cynically called him; or, as the Hungarian nobles put it, 'a king we can lead by the hair'.[86] In 1526 the Habsburgs secured their election to the crown; yet not until a century later were they able to establish possession by hereditary right, and this was only achieved after crushing a rebellion of the Bohemian nobility. The decree of 1627 that confirmed their hereditary right deprived the diet of the legislative powers granted in 1310.[87] Nonetheless, although Bohemia was subjected to royal absolutism, with new laws made solely by royal ordinance, the system of serfdom underwent a process of consolidation and intensification that reflected the Habsburg dependence upon the nobility as its main instrument of government.[88]

Following the battle of White Mountain in 1620, the Habsburgs remodelled not only the Bohemian constitution but also the Bohemian nobility. In the 1620s, following a large-scale emigration of Protestant nobles, half the manors of Bohemia were confiscated and redistributed. This set in motion a massive reduction of the *Ritterschaft* whose numbers fell from 1,128 families in 1620 to 228 families by 1650. The confiscated estates were given to nobles of non-Bohemian extraction. As a result, the Bohemian nobility became, mostly, a group of magnates, each of them titled, with huge estates, Habsburg court connections and a tendency to live away from their estates, in Prague or Vienna.[89] Having, for at least another century, no alternative means of government to that of aristocracy, however, the Habsburgs had to retain the support of this nobility by catering to its needs. For this reason, serfdom was preserved. The Renewed Land Ordinance of 1627 – the foundation of royal absolutism in Bohemia – confirmed the system of serfdom previously authorized by parliamentary statute. Further decrees regulated it, often following the suppression of a peasant rebellion, such as the regulatory patents of 1680, 1717 and 1775.[90] Moving the government to act was not a liberal antipathy to serfdom or nobility but its own fiscal and military dependence upon the peasantry. The nobility's exploitation of the serf system, it felt, was eroding its own resources and weakening its international position, especially in relation to Prussia. Another government concern was the political instability caused by peasant insurrections and the evident way they were incited by the nobility's abuse of its seigneurial rights.[91]

The government itself was partly responsible for the nobility's exploitation of the serfs. In 1627 it had exempted demesne land from the land tax, a concession made to the nobility. This had encouraged nobles to add rustical land to the demesne, since by doing so they freed it of tax, as well as of the rights associated with the tenures. In this way, they were able to charge higher rents.[92] The effect was to increase the burden of tax falling upon the surviving tenures. To counteract this, the government in 1717 insisted that the land transferred from tenure to demesne should remain taxable and then, in the mid-eighteenth century, it reimposed the land tax on demesnes.[93] Mainly at fault, however, for making serfdom oppressive in the seventeenth and eighteenth centuries was the way the Bohemian nobility resorted to farming the demesne instead of leasing it out.

The Bohemian nobility had a long involvement with commercial activity, but it largely concerned pisciculture, brewing and the timber trade, none of which placed a heavy demand on labour.[94] Furthermore, the revenue derived from these activities allowed lords to tolerate low rents, dues and fees from the tenantry. In these circumstances, serfdom tended to be lenient, almost benign. What is more, thanks to the population growth of the sixteenth century, tenures were easy to fill; and so departure licences were readily given, and the law banning migration went largely unenforced.[95]

The nobility's direct involvement in agriculture brought about a decisive change in the lord–serf relationship. This was largely a consequence of the Thirty Years War (1618–1648), which reduced the Bohemian population by over 40 per cent. With an excess of vacant tenures and because hired labour was scarce and costly, estate managers resorted to exploiting serfdom.[96] They did so by enforcing the 1487 statute against migration, by insisting upon the lord's monopolies and his licensing rights, and by demanding week-work.[97] The latter followed the decision to imitate the Brandenburg and Polish nobles by cultivating grain on their demesnes. As a result, the peasantry were required to provide regular labour services, which in 1680 were legally fixed at a maximum of three days a week with animals, and twice that amount for service by hand.[98] Given the tenurial nature of Bohemian serfdom, the labour services were originally exacted of the tenures. However, in the seventeenth century, and in a manner that suggested personal serfdom, regular labour service was extended to the children of tenants, even though they were free. Besides the regular services, there were irregular ones which remained unfixed until 1775.[99]

By 1700 an oppressive form of serfdom operated in Bohemia, whereas in 1600 it had been, by any standard, light. What brought about the change was the fact that, in exchange for the imposition of week-work, no relief was offered in the form of reduced rents and dues, as, for example, had happened in Poland and Brandenburg. In Bohemia the one burden was simply added to the other. Moreover, both were intensified in the late seventeenth century to counteract the effects of the great depopulation caused by the Thirty Years War.

The imposition of weekly services was accompanied by the expansion of the demesne. This, however, resulted not so much from the eviction of peasants as from the absorption into the demesne of vacant tenures and freshly cultivated land taken from the waste. Nonetheless, as the expanded demesne was subjected to direct cultivation, labour services were much increased. Furthermore, additional problems arose as the population recovered. Following its cataclysmic fall in the early seventeenth century, the population underwent a spectacular recovery. Having declined from *c.*1,700,000 in 1600 to 950,000 in 1650, it had risen to 2,400,000 by 1776.[100] With no contraction of demesne to create new tenures, this population explosion had two effects. First, it produced, by the closing years of the eighteenth century, a plenitude of free labour. Since serfs had reacted against the weight of labour services not only by revolt but also by performing them in a dilatory manner, now, in a world of cheap labour, lords chose to hire it instead, and to commute the labour services to rent.[101] Second, the peasant ambitions of the landless could be realized, and profit made from them, by renting out parts of the demesne on short-term, rack-rented leases.[102] Serfdom was seriously undermined, then, as lords adopted more advantageous methods of estate management. Coincidentally, the state intruded into the lord–serf relationship. This process culminated in the termination of serfdom in 1781, the result of a compact the nobility reached with the crown that relieved them of redundant rights while allowing them to retain an alleviated manorial system.[103]

In spite of the great demesne expansion of the seventeenth century – the result of resorting to direct cultivation in order to solve the depopulation problem – the overall proportion of dominical land in late eighteenth-century Bohemia amounted to only 16 per cent: in other words, most cultivated land remained rustical, that is, for the use of the peasantry under the protective terms of manorial custom, and therefore guaranteed low rents, hereditary tenancy and rights of common.[104] The peasantry had undoubtedly suffered from enserfment, but, in spite of it, they remained a rural elite, their social position buttressed in the late eighteenth century by the emergence of a large rural proletariat, amounting to over 40 per cent of the population.[105] In contrast to the serfs, these landless labourers were free and relatively impoverished. They found waged employment working for both lords and serfs.

The lives of the Bohemian serfs were affected not only by the development of direct demesne farming but also by the gradual intrusion of the state, the result of the government's attempt to protect its own stake in serfdom. By 1627 the imposition of serfdom had caused a marked withdrawal of the state from the countryside as manorial inhabitants became, in law, the immediate subjects of their lord.[106] This withdrawal, however, only represented the establishment of a system of indirect rule, for the government continued making demands of the peasantry, both to man and pay for its armies. By the late eighteenth century, Bohemia was of crucial importance to the Habsburgs as both a source of wealth – Bohemia yielded 40 per cent of the *Kontribution*, the main direct tax – and a strategic defence zone, given that the prime enemy was now Prussia rather than the Turk.[107] For the Habsburg government it was vital to maintain the Bohemian peasantry in a reasonable state of prosperity so that they could fulfil their fiscal and military obligations to the state, and not indulge in rebellion.[108]

There emerged, then, in the course of time a government programme of peasant protection. It began in response to peasant revolts protesting against enlarged labour services. A series of patents (1680, 1717, 1738, 1775) restricted the regular services to three days a week and to ten hours a day.[109] The programme of protection continued following the defeat of the Habsburgs in a series of wars – the War of the Austrian Succession, the Seven Years War and the War of the Bavarian Succession – all of which featured an enemy invasion of Bohemia. It was promoted by the great Bohemian famine of 1770 and 1771, as well as by the huge Bohemian peasant revolt of 1775.[110] The programme dealt not only with labour services but also with dues and judicial rights. For example, most of the seigneurial monopolies were abolished in 1738.[111] This meant that peasants no longer had to pay the lord fees for milling corn, or for baking bread, or for the sale of salt. At the same time, the lords' profitable monopoly on the manufacture and sale of beer was preserved: not surprisingly as one-third of their demesne income (which accounted for 69 per cent of their total land revenues) derived from it.[112]

The imposition of serfdom had, in effect, denied peasants access to public justice, leaving them unable to take legal action against lords for abusing their manorial authority. Appeals to the king from serf communities were effectively closed off in 1558 when the Bohemian diet enacted the punishment of peasants who did so falsely (i.e. unsuccessfully).[113] Then the reforms of the 1620s rendered peasant appeals beyond the manorial court a virtual impossibility.[114] However, long before the end of serfdom, the legal personality of the peasant was fully restored, beginning in 1717 when appeals against lords were allowed, if first addressed to the offending party. Following a bureaucratic reform of local administration between 1748 and 1751, serf appeals against lords gained a greater chance of receiving an impartial hearing. Moreover, after 1756 a reorganization of the judicial system established a tribunal to which serfs could address their complaints.[115] Administrative reforms, and the agrarian reforms they enabled the government to apply, thus altered the terms under which serfs lived and worked. However, this was a latter-day development. The earlier political reforms – notably the establishment of a hereditary, absolutist monarchy – had confirmed what an unchecked nobility had first legalized, and had then tolerated the intensification of serfdom that had resulted from the development of direct demesne farming. Furthermore, peasant protection came at a price. Moving the government to act was the belief that an effective state was founded upon the revenues and military resources furnished by the peasantry. Countering the relief the reforms offered from seigneurial exaction was an additional weight of demand from the state. In this respect, the Bohemian peasantry, like that of Brandenburg-Prussia, found itself having to bear on its back not simply the noble and clerical orders but also the bureaucratic and military apparatus of the absolutist state.

Hungary

The Hungarian nobles opted for a Polish rather than a Bohemian type of serfdom. Enserfment therefore applied to every resident of each estate, landless and landed alike, apart from those (such as nobles or clerics or members of privileged communities) whom the law exempted from servitude. As in Poland and Bohemia, a residual serfdom had survived in Hungary from the distant past, the result of acts of conquest leading to acts of enslavement, but the system prevailing after 1500 was legislated into existence by a noble-dominated parliament which, in the Polish and Bohemian manner, was empowered to exercise a special hold over the government because of the elective nature of the crown.[116]

Serfdom was enacted in 1514, a reprisal for a huge peasant revolt against landlord oppression. As the statute explained:

> And that they [the peasantry] may see for themselves what a terrible crime it is to rise against their masters, every succeeding age shall know that henceforth, with the exception of the loyal free boroughs and those peasants who maintained their loyalty, they shall lose their privilege of emigrating at will as a punishment for their treachery, and shall be subject to their respective proprietors as serfs pure and simple for all time.[117]

Verböczi contextualized this act in his 1517 codification of Hungarian law:

> The peasants [formerly] possessed the privilege, after they had paid the legal land rents and their debts, freely to move from their residences to anywhere else at their pleasure. However, they forfeited and lost their right forever during the last summer [1514] by their Kurucz conspiracy and rebellion against the whole of the nobility under the leadership of that most wicked bandit Szekely Gyorgy [i.e. George Dózsa]; [and] from now on are perpetual serfs totally subjected to their lords.[118]

Besides banning peasant migration, the act of 1514 imposed a labour service of at least one day a week. Nonetheless, the imposition of serfdom in Hungary was complicated by a further act of 1547 which restored to the rural population its traditional freedom of movement on the grounds that 'nothing has been so damaging to the once prosperous kingdom as the oppression of agricultural labour'.[119] Notwithstanding this liberation, a year later a weekly labour service of at least two days was enacted. Finally in 1608, in response to extensive depopulation caused by the Fifteen Years

War (1592–1606) against the Ottoman Turk, and following a successful noble uprising against the Habsburg government, the ban on migration was re-enacted and retained until 1791.[120]

Hungarian serfdom was shaped by the Turkish wars. Following the disastrous defeat at Mohács in 1526, one-third of Hungary was transferred to the Ottoman Empire, while the remainder was divided between the Habsburgs as monarchs of Hungary and the independent rulers of Transylvania. For almost 200 years, Hungary was a war zone on the frontier of Christendom, its resources and mentality concentrated on withstanding Muslim aggression and reclaiming lost territory, as well as on warring against the princes of Transylvania. To feed the armies and fortresses that kept the Turk at bay, the Hungarian nobility resorted to demesne farming with serf labour, as well as to extracting produce from their tenants through rents and dues in kind.[121] To man the military, heavy demands had to be made of the peasant male population. With the eviction of the Turk from Hungary and the resumption of Transylvania in 1699, a decisive turning-point was reached in Habsburg–Ottoman relations. In the Sixteen Years War to defeat the Turks, and the Eight Years War against dissident nobles that followed in 1703, half a million Hungarian lives were lost in plague or battle casualties.[122] But this simply marked the finale to a long process of depopulation that had been sustained throughout the sixteenth and seventeenth centuries by war. In the late fifteenth century, the population of Hungary had amounted to 5 million; by 1711 it stood at 2.5 million. Thereafter, it made a spectacular recovery. Aided by a massive migration of Romanians, Germans, Ruthenians and Slovaks, principally to the liberated Great Hungarian Plain, the population of Hungary by 1788 had grown to 8.5 million.[123] This demographic development undoubtedly affected the history of serfdom. The long depopulation led to its intensification as labour services rose to four days a week or more – that is, twice the minimum laid down in 1548 – and as dues and fees were increased, in number and amount, to fund private armies and fortresses.[124] In contrast, the ending of the war, coupled with the need to settle the Great Plain, improved the condition of serfs as landlords competed with each other to attract or retain tenants, and did so by offering more favourable terms.[125]

What the intensification of serfdom had failed to do was to destroy the traditional manor, with its complexity of interlocking rights and its fundamental separation of dominical and rustical land. In contrast to parts of the Baltic littoral – for example, Mecklenburg, Kurland or Livonia – where the demesne expanded to absorb virtually the whole of each estate, in Hungary, by the late eighteenth century, it amounted overall to only 27 per cent. As much as 58 per cent consisted of hereditary tenure (i.e. *sessio*, *telek*), with the remaining 19 per cent comprised of common land, to which serfs had rights of access.[126] For serfs wishing to become or remain tenants with hereditary land rights, then, the opportunities remained considerable. This only changed in the late eighteenth century as demographic growth created an excessive rural population, which could no longer be tapped off by migration, and which, given the deeply embedded agrarian nature of society, could not be sustained by industrialization or sufficiently relieved by urbanization. Adding to the problem were the huge demesnes established on the Great Hungarian Plain, following its reclamation from the Turk, which left little land for peasant tenures.[127] As well as being directly cultivated, these demesnes were rented to peasants as short-term, rack-rented leaseholds, and therefore without the customary tenurial rights. It happened so extensively that, by the 1830s, one quarter of demesne land was rented out in this manner.[128] Settling serfs on the demesne did not liberate them since serfdom was personal, not tenurial; nor did liberation result from falling into landlessness. The outcome was a serf society which predominantly consisted of demesne tenants: 51.9 per cent in 1787, against 34.1 per cent holding tenures, with 14 per cent landless servants and labourers.[129] Under pressure of population growth, and because of the demesne leaseholders' tenurial insecurity, the landless element was bound to grow. By the mid-nineteenth century, for every 100 families with land there were 147 landless families, whereas in 1767 there had been only 46.[130] In other words, serf society rapidly switched from being peasant in character to one consisting of cottagers dependent upon rural crafts or waged labour. In the sixteenth and seventeenth centuries the depopulation caused by the Turkish wars had helped to maintain the serf community as a peasantry with hereditary rights to considerable property. It had subjected serfs to an increased seigneurial control that had erased the freedoms of the late middle ages, but had not created a general state of rural destitution. In contrast, in the early nineteenth century, population growth subjected serf society to raised rents, reduced wages and a general immiseration.

The Turkish wars affected the serf interest in two other respects. Hungarian society in the early modern period became the embodiment of intransigence: the national capacity to withstand the Turk stood alongside the capacity of the noble order to resist the crown, and of peasant communities to resist the lords. Whereas noble resistance served to restrain the demands the government made of serfs, peasant resistance helped to limit the exploitation of serfs by the nobility.

Having acquired the kingdoms of Bohemia and Hungary in the early sixteenth century, the Habsburgs subjected them to a very different treatment. Bohemia was converted from an elective to a hereditary monarchy in 1547, Hungary not until 1723.[131] Bohemia was subjected to absolutist rule, but Hungary retained its constitutional polity. Whereas the Bohemian parliament lost its legislative authority, and its local assemblies ceded control of local government to centrally appointed bureaucrats, in Hungary legislation remained with the national diet, while local government continued to be run by the county assemblies, thanks to the officials they were authorized to elect. The membership of the county assemblies was exclusively noble; that of the national diet, predominantly noble. As a result, in Hungary the serf owners not only made the law but also enforced it.

This difference of treatment was undoubtedly due to the wars against the Turk, coupled with the existence of an independent and anti-Habsburg Transylvania with which the Hungarian nobles could ally. The wars obliged the Habsburg government to treat the Hungarian nobles with especial care. True, its commitment to defeating the Turk awarded it a special credit in Hungary, but this credit was conditional on showing respect for the ancient Magyar freedoms. Hungary managed to preserve its traditional polity, thanks to the noble order's ability to resist effectively whenever the Habsburgs sought to increase their control of the country.[132] Essentially, this ability was due to the enduring power and importance of the lesser nobles. In an attempt to win over the nobility, the Habsburgs had created a Hungarian peerage in the sixteenth century, awarding it in 1608 a special chamber in the national diet. As long as the war against the Turkish occupation lasted, the peers retained influence over the lesser nobility, because of their role as leaders of the reconquest. But the termination of the war in 1718 brought it to an end. As the peers gravitated to Vienna, the lesser nobility dug in to preserve their liberties against the very real prospect of Habsburg absolutism.[133] Consequently, there was little change in the basic political system, even though hereditary rule was ceded to the Habsburgs in reward for their part in repulsing the Turk. The pattern that was established in the seventeenth century – of an attempted extension of Habsburg power, followed by a noble revolt leading to a royal compromise (as in 1606 and 1681) – continued in the eighteenth century with the Treaty of Szatmar of 1711, and then with the Concord of 1790. In the latter, Leopold II admitted that 'Hungary . . . is independent and should be governed and administered according to her own laws and customs and not as other provinces', thus undoing the recent attempt, instigated by Maria Theresa and applied by Joseph II, to make it uniform with Bohemia.[134]

As a result of this noble resistance, the rule of the serfs was placed almost completely in the hands of their owners. In the late middle ages a system of village government had existed centred upon the village judge, the *biró*. With the imposition of serfdom, the village lost its former autonomy, as the *biró* became the nominee and agent of the lord, and the manor court now acted as the seat of jurisdiction for the inhabitants of the estate.[135] Complementing this process was the legislation of 1608, which not only reasserted the ban on peasant migration but also placed the regulation of all serf–lord matters in the hands of the manorial court, subject solely to oversight by the exclusively noble county assemblies.[136] Serfs lost all means of legal action against their lords since, in the various courts of appeal, they were disqualified from suing their lords, or of acting as witnesses against them.[137] In this manner, the Habsburg government delegated the protection of serfs completely to their owners. Only when the Turkish wars were over did it seek to aid the serf but, given the entrenched position of the nobility in local government and the Habsburg failure to crush its opposition decisively in the Bohemian manner, the attempt was largely ineffectual.[138]

Seigneurial exploitation was limited not so much by interference from the crown as by the resistance of the serfs. Their effectiveness owed something to the low density of the population, and the consequent need of lords to proceed leniently and respectfully of custom; otherwise they might incite their serfs to take flight. Partly, however, it was due to the recurrence of large-scale peasant rebellions, notably in the eighteenth century (for example, in 1735, 1755, 1763–4, 1784 and 1790). They took the form of violent revolts directed at the persons and property of the noble order.[139] Promoting them was the existence of military districts whose *raison d'être* was to defend the frontier of Latin Christendom against Tartar and Turk, and which were inhabited by free peasant warriors – the Transylvanian Szeklers, the Jazyg-Cumans and Hajdús.[140] The equivalent of Cossacks, these warrior communities were capable of turning upon the Habsburg government, as well as against the Muslim, especially when their liberties were under threat: notably in the eighteenth century when, no longer needed as frontier troops, they came to be regarded as a source of revenue rather than of manpower. Just as the agrarian history of early modern Russia was punctuated by peasant wars incited, organized and directed by frontier warriors, of was that of Hungary. In both countries, these rebellions were always defeated. Moreover, in Hungary's case, one of the uprisings, that of 1514, led to the original imposition of serfdom. Yet, in the long run, they helped to protect the serf interest, mainly through reminding lords of what might happen if they rejected the custom of the manor.

Because of the agrarian nature of Hungarian society, its inconsiderable urban element, and the personal nature of Hungarian serfdom, serfs formed a high proportion of the population. In 1720 they comprised between 63 and 76 per cent of taxpayers; in the late eighteenth century, 70 per cent of the peasantry.[141] This was undoubtedly a serf society, rather than a society with serfs. But diluting the prevalence of serfdom was the presence of peasants and labourers who were free. Some were inhabitants of the thirty-nine royal free cities. Yet these cities comprised no more than 5 per cent of the total population in 1720, falling to 4 per cent in 1787.[142] Others were nobles obliged by poverty to follow commoner occupations. Like Poland, Hungary possessed a populous nobility, the result of the generous ennobling policies used by the crown and magnates to reward military service: in the thirteenth and fourteenth centuries against the Tartars following their invasion of 1241, and in the sixteenth and seventeenth centuries against the Turkish occupation. The Hungarian nobility amounted in 1787 to 4.8 per cent of the population, with much greater concentrations in certain counties such as Maramaros (16.6 per cent) or Borsod (15.2 per cent); and in certain villages all the resident families were noble. The census of 1720 revealed the existence of 1,228 noble villages. In them nobles worked without shame as peasants, craftsmen and traders. The nobility's very density ensured that many nobles had to work in ignoble occupations. In fact, by the mid-eighteenth century they comprised over half the noble membership. Peasant nobles were categorized as *armalis* or *curialis*: both worked a peasant tenure, the former as tenants, the latter as owners. All were safeguarded against enserfment by virtue of their noble status. Adding to their numbers in the eighteenth century was the use landlords made of ennoblement to attract fugitive serfs. Lured onto an estate by the freedom that ennoblement offered, they became attached to it, paradoxically, by an act of emancipation, and the protection that noble status guaranteed against seigneurial exploitation.[143]

Another limit on serfdom were the free communities established to guard the frontier: the Szeklers and Jazyg-Cumans founded in the middle ages to fight the Tartar, and also the Serbian, Grenzer and Hajdú communities founded in the early modern period to combat the Turk.[144] Although reduced in numbers during the eighteenth century, as some were ennobled and others enserfed, they constituted 13.5 per cent of the total population in 1780.[145]

Combating the weight of serfdom were the rights that serfs managed to retain. These related to security of tenure; fixed obligations set out in *urbaria*; access to the uncultivated parts of the manor; participation in the running of the manorial regime; and the right to occupy a fixed proportion of the manor outside the demesne. The serf's security of tenure was neatly defined in Verböczi's codification: 'Beyond fees and rewards for his work, the peasant has no right whatsoever to his lord's land, except the right of inheritance; full ownership of the land belongs exclusively to the land-lord.'[146] This basically implied that, although legal ownership of the whole estate lay with the lord, possession of the tenures lay with the serfs. As a result, the lord had no right of eviction unless the serf failed to fulfil his tenurial obligations. Otherwise, the serf was entitled not only to hold his farm for life but also to transmit it to his children. One consequence of this right was the lack of an entry fine, the seigneurial device used to convert a tenancy at will into an inheritable tenure. Hereditary rights also applied to goods and chattels. As a result, serfs were not required to pay a heriot.[147] In addition, the lord had no right to take away from the serf community the cultivated land originally assigned to its use and lying outside the demesne.[148] One way of removing the serfs' hereditary rights was to incorporate their holdings into the demesne. This the law forbade. Lords, however, were entitled to lease out their demesnes. They did so when tenants could be found and when the commercial openings for direct farming were limited. Demesne leasing created serf tenants without security of tenure. The practice was promoted by rapid population growth, the absence of which, until the late eighteenth century, meant that serfs, in the early modern period, mainly belonged to families holding land by hereditary right.

A second important right enjoyed by serfs was to have their obligations to the lord specified in written regulations (i.e. *urbaria*).[149] Originally, these obligations were defined in contracts produced by individual manors.

However, in the early modern period they also came to be defined by parliamentary acts and royal decrees, notably the acts of 1514, 1548 and 1608,
and the decree of 1767. The annual rent was fixed at 1 florin per annum in
1514 and confirmed at this amount in 1767; as was an annual smoke fee, a
private hearth tax due from every household on the estate.[150] In addition,
an annual due of one-ninth of the harvest and of newborn calves (*nona*,
kilenced) had to be paid. Originally introduced in 1351, it was confirmed
in 1514 and 1767.[151] Also associated with serfdom were annual gifts to the
lord; and gifts for special occasions such as the lord's ransom, marriage
or first mass. The annual gifts were made obligatory in 1514, the special
gifts in 1548. The laws introducing these gifts defined them: for example,
each tenure owed one chicken per month and two geese per year in 1514,
altered in 1767 to an annual payment of two hens, two capons, eggs and
butter.[152] Unfixed for much of the history of serfdom were the labour
services, essentially because the regulations of 1514 and 1548 only laid
down a minimal requirement. All this, however, changed in 1767 when the
minimum was made the maximum. As a result, the labour service for each
holding was limited to one day a week with animals, and two days a week
by hand.[153]

A further important serf right granted access to the common land. This
ancient right certainly underwent restriction under serfdom, especially
when hunting and fowling (in 1514) and fishing (in 1729) were turned into
seigneurial monopolies. To safeguard themselves against the charge of
poaching, serfs now had to pay a licence fee.[154] Likewise, pannage – the right
to feed pigs on the woodland – was also subjected to a payment, along with
the right to collect fruit and nuts.[155] Other commoning rights, moreover,
were made conditional upon service. Access to the lord's forests to collect
fuel and timber was granted, in return for supplying the manor house with
wood; as was access to marshland to cut reeds, in return for supplying a
portion to the lord.[156] The serf's one free right was access to the manorial
pastures for grazing his cattle.[157] His rights of common, then, were hedged
in by seigneurial monopolies, probably to a greater extent than in most
modern serf societies, but not to the point of complete denial. As a result,
the serfs had at their disposal not only their own land but also the waste,
which, on average by the late eighteenth century, amounted to one-fifth of
the manor.[158]

Although serfdom limited the peasants' control of their own community,
it did not deny them a say in how it was run. The lord imposed himself
through the village headman (*bíró*), who formerly had been simply chosen
by the villagers and now, under serfdom, became a nominee of the lord.
However, the villagers were not completely excluded since they were
allowed to elect him from the shortlist nominated by the lord. True, they
could not dismiss him – that was the lord's prerogative – but, as his term
of office only lasted for one year, this did not matter. Moreover, upon
appointment, he had to swear before the villagers to carry out his office
properly, which meant showing respect for the rights and obligations of the

village. Furthermore, in running the village he had to act in cooperation with the jurors and the village notary, all of whom were chosen by the villagers.[159] Entrenched within the serf regime then – at the village if not at the county or national level – was a system of representation and official answerability, which enabled serfs to defend and preserve the customs that safeguarded their interest.

Characteristic of the manorial system in Hungary was the extensive range of exactions that lords were entitled to make. Besides the dues in kind, besides the licence fees charged for access to the waste and permission to marry, to change a trade, to commute labour services and to leave the estate, lords enjoyed a series of profitable monopolies: the usual milling and distilling rights; rights of pre-emption that enabled them to purchase goods from their tenants at low prices; and rights of sole sale within the manor, which allowed them to charge what they liked for meat and, at certain periods of the year, for wine as well.[160]

The immunity nobles enjoyed from customs dues – first granted in 1543 and made all-inclusive in 1574 – encouraged them to engage in the cattle trade to Austria and Bohemia, in the wine trade to Poland and Silesia and, eventually, in the corn trade throughout the Habsburg Monarchy.[161] But this entrepreneurial activity did not necessarily involve them in direct farming, since the goods they traded were frequently extracted from the peasantry by means of dues in kind and pre-emption rights.[162] In other words, the commercial activities of the Hungarian nobility were not heavily reliant – in the Bohemian and Polish manner – upon extending the demesne at the expense of the tenures, or upon increasing labour services for its cultivation. Hungarian lords undoubtedly became engaged in demesne farming, in response to the Turkish wars, and to feed the troops and garrisons involved in them. Once they were over, they supplied produce to Austria, and then responded to demands created by the Napoleonic Wars. In parts, directly farmed demesnes could exceed 40 per cent of the estate, especially on the reclaimed Great Hungarian Plain, Croatia and Transylvania.[163] But extensive pastoral farming on the demesne, coupled with the ability of lords to tap peasant production through seigneurial dues, kept labour services relatively low.[164] Carrying services were important for taking produce to market, as was castle maintenance in the sixteenth and seventeenth centuries; yet neither sufficiently counteracted the low demand for field work to make services heavy.[165] Serfs were protected from gross exploitation, then, by the following: the limited extent of demesne farming; the profits nobles made from trading; the way dues were fixed by custom or law; the hereditary rights appertaining to serf tenures; and the serfs' ability to purchase freedoms through the payment of a licence fee. This was even the case when depopulation obliged lords to increase their demands of the survivors in order to maintain the value of their land revenues.

The condition of the Hungarian serfs was also relieved by the nobility's resistance to royal absolutism. Rather like the Polish serfs before the

Partition, the Hungarian serfs remained lightly taxed. From 1724, their liability to direct government taxation increased, but, for this purpose, their wealth was under-assessed. A standing army was introduced in 1715 and serfs, along with the free cities, had to provide it with food and lodging; but the serfs were not made liable to conscription until 1785–6, and, even then, call-up was repeatedly postponed by noble opposition.[166]

The days of serfdom were numbered when the Habsburg Monarchy, as part of a programme of modernization, became committed to agrarian reform. In Hungary, however, it encountered fierce resistance in the diet from the nobility, and when it sought to proceed by decree, it met with effective non-cooperation. Since the government could only make its mark by reaching a compromise with the noble interest, serfdom gained a much longer lease of life in Hungary than in Bohemia and Austria.

Two decrees were issued which were of great moment for the Hungarian serfs. The first was the Urbarial Patent of 1767; the second, the *Leibeigenschaftspatent* of 1785.[167] The former standardized throughout the kingdom the exactions lords were entitled to make. It also sought to place greater restrictions on the seigneurial interest, partly through defining services in terms of maxima rather than minima, and partly by banning certain exactions, notably irregular gifts.[168] Yet, since the Urbarial Patent had not been authorized by the diet and was therefore unacceptable to the county administration, its enforcement proved impossible. In an attempt to assert itself, the Habsburg government refused to summon the Hungarian diet between 1765 and 1790; in 1785, it even dissolved the county assemblies:[169] but all in vain. In 1785–6 Joseph II sought to replace the old county system with a centrally controlled bureaucratic apparatus resting upon ten new districts administered by commissars. This, however, only resulted in political disjunction.[170] The same problems affected the *Leibeigenschaftspatent* of 1785, which abolished serfdom by granting a right of free migration.

Upon Joseph's death in 1790, his successor, Leopold II, sought to re-establish a workable relationship with Hungary, in the well-tried manner, by respecting the traditional polity – that is, a legislative diet and a county administration, both answerable to the county assemblies – and by requiring parliamentary consent for the two agrarian patents. The Urbarial Patent was accepted; allowing, at long last, an agrarian reform initiated by the government to stand some chance of implementation.[171] The *Leibeigenschaftspatent*, however, was neither accepted nor rejected, thanks to a compromise that allowed serfs to migrate, but only if the lord and the acting head of the county administration (the *alispán*) deemed it unharmful to the seigneurial economy and the county tax returns. In other words, a legal right to migrate was re-established, but only with the consent of seigneur and local government. Without this consent, the migrant was liable to punishment as a runaway.[172] Bearing this in mind, along with the survival of the labour services and patrimonial jurisdiction, a system of serfdom appeared to endure into the nineteenth century. Confirming its existence was yet another compromise, as the Habsburg government in 1798, and again in 1821, removed itself from the relationship between lord and serf, allowing issues between them to be determined not by government order but by what was agreeable to the two interests.[173]

Upheld in this manner, a sort of serfdom lasted until 1853, although it was subjected to further restriction of the lord's powers. Rather than being imposed by the government, these restrictions were granted by a liberal nobility (notably in 1836). Now able to farm its demesnes with waged labour, it no longer had need of serf labour services. Moreover, it had to establish a better relationship with the peasantry in order to strengthen its hand in the nationalist struggle against Habsburg rule. The same nobles in the revolution of 1848 even abolished serfdom – along with the rest of the seigneurial system – but the suppression of this revolution allowed a further stay of sentence. Serfdom, in fact, was finally terminated five years later by an act of royal absolutism, committed to enlist peasant support for the Habsburg cause.[174]

The Russian Empire

The imposition of serfdom in Russia typically involved a prohibition on departure. This ban was permanently applied in 1649 to all non-noble and non-clerical residents of privately owned land. Before that, it had been imposed since 1580 on an occasional annual basis, and since 1603 on a recurring annual basis.[175] The problem addressed was the usual one of depopulation, caused by disease, war and the flight of peasants to newly settled lands.[176] Compounding the problem was a traditionally under-populated society, the result of a very high ratio of land to people. Driven by the need to escape the high taxation of Ivan the Terrible in the late sixteenth century, and then lured south to new lands – which, in the early seventeenth century, the construction of the Belgorod Defence Line had secured from Tartar and nomad attack – the peasantry of Muscovy proceeded to liberate itself, settling on the black soil south of Moscow in the late seventeenth and early eighteenth centuries, then in Left Bank Ukraine and beyond (Little Russia and New Russia) in the late eighteenth century, and, finally, in North Caucasus and the trans-Volga region in the early nineteenth century.[177]

Serfdom proved quite incapable of stemming this migratory flow. Rather than abandoning serfdom as a failure, however, the government simply extended it to the new territories once they were settled and subjected to lordship. In this way, serfdom became a basic instrument of imperial rule. In some of the newly annexed regions, however, it already existed: for example, the territories taken from Poland in the late seventeenth and late eighteenth centuries (Belorussia, Right Bank Ukraine, Kurland, Lithuania) and the Baltic provinces of Estonia and Livonia, formerly in the possession of the Teutonic Order and acquired by the tsar from Sweden after the

Northern War of 1700–21. In these regions serfdom was preserved as a means of maintaining the native nobilities' allegiance to the tsar.

All the serf regimes located within the Russian Empire were systems of personal serfdom.[178] Like Hungarian and Polish serfs, Russian serfs and their offspring were owned by the lord, irrespective of whether or not they held land of him. Essentially they were bound in the blood. The personal nature of serfdom was established by the code of 1649. It was demonstrated in the legislation of 1701 and 1773 which permitted the sale and mortgaging of serfs, a practice that remained legal until 1843.[179] Recognition by serfs of their personal bondage was vividly illustrated in 1819 when the liberal noble I. D. Yakushkin proposed to turn his serfs into free tenants, each of them renting from him the land they then worked, and was met with the objection 'we are yours, but the land is ours': in other words, they had no right to be free because they were Yakushkin's personal property, while he had no proprietary rights to the land that they had traditionally cultivated for their own use.[180] They were hereditary chattels, then; but did this render them slave-like?

In early modern Russia hereditary slaves existed, both for domestic work and demesne labour, the result of capture in war, purchase or self-donation. In addition, there were non-hereditary slaves, the result of debt bondage and a criminal code that allowed the death sentence to be commuted to slavery for life. During the sixteenth and seventeenth centuries, slaves amounted to 7–8 per cent of the population in the Russian heartland, providing something like 10 per cent of its agricultural labour. Some of them underwent a process of enserfment in the fifteenth and sixteenth centuries, through being granted smallholdings.[181] What distinguished slavery from serfdom was the slave's immunity to government taxation. This distinction, however, was removed in 1680 when slaves with their own households were taxed as if they were serfs. Moreover, in 1719 all male slaves, like all male serfs, were subjected to the poll tax.[182] As a result, they became formally merged into one serf order, although with certain retained differences. On the one hand were the field serfs; on the other the so-called household serfs (*dvorovye liudi*) who worked as skilled craftsmen, unskilled labourers or servants. Whereas the field serfs subsisted on the land that they farmed in their own right, the landless household serfs were sustained on rations dispensed by the lord. These comprised a monthly grain allowance and monetary payment to buy other foods, plus a sheepskin coat every three years.[183] Field serfs were clearly far removed from slaves, but household serfs and slaves strongly resembled each other. Of the two, the household serfs were in a small minority, comprising 7 per cent of the serf population. Their numbers were sustained, however, by an extensive practice, started in the late seventeenth century, of buying and selling serfs apart from the land. Landless serfs were also produced by a practice, begun in the mid-eighteenth century, of employing serfs in the metallurgical industries of the Urals, where they worked for wages and a grain ration as factory hands or miners.[184] Eroding the numbers of household serfs was their greater proclivity to flight. This was because they had no landed commitment to keep them attached to any one particular lord.

In the typical manner, most Russian serfs were distinguished from slaves in being peasants.[185] Slaves in the modern period may have had strong peasant ambitions but, before emancipation, they failed to form peasant societies, and rarely achieved, in the peasant manner, the autonomy of self-subsistence. Where slaves comprised a substantial part of society they were inevitably non-peasant; only when they were in a small minority was it possible for them to subscribe to the peasant ideal. In contrast, most Russian serfs could take the peasant way of life for granted. It was part of their very nature, a view accepted by lord and tsar alike. They were distinguished from slaves, moreover, by their hereditary rights to the land. Although not warranted by law, their claim 'the land is ours' was a customary fact, so much so that, throughout the history of Russian serfdom, a great deal of the cultivated land on private estates was set aside for the exclusive use of the serf community. All this makes it quite inappropriate to regard the Russian serf as a sort of slave, or to regard Russian serfdom as comparable in nature with American slavery.[186]

The Russian serfs were distinctly different from the other unfree peasantries of eastern and central Europe. This was largely for three reasons. Until the late eighteenth century, Russian serfdom was predominantly a source of income rather than labour, the result of the late development of commercial demesne farming. To describe it as essentially 'a system of labour' is therefore misleading.[187] Then, in the late eighteenth and early nineteenth centuries, a division emerged between the Russian heartland, where serfs remained a source of income from rent, and the central and southern steppes, where the development of commercial farming caused serfs to be regarded as a source of labour. In spite of the massive growth of demesne farming in the late eighteenth and early nineteenth centuries, by 1850 those owing labour rather than rent comprised only 55 per cent of the serf population.[188]

Russian serfdom was also distinguished by the prevalence of communally held land and the attendant practice of repartition. Rather than being in the ownership of individual families, the land resided with the village, and was subjected to reallocation in accordance with family needs.[189] This allowed younger sons to become landholders. It also meant an absence of the transfer charges that normally fell due when a son succeeded his father to a holding, or when holdings were conveyed from one family to another. The obligations that Russian serfs owed the lord were relatively simple: usually, either rent or labour service; occasionally, a combination of the two.

A further distinctive feature of Russian serfdom lay in the relatively low proportion of serfs to the population as a whole. Systems of personal serfdom might be expected to include a much larger share of the population than systems of tenurial serfdom, simply because serf status was transmitted to all the offspring, not just the eldest son. This was certainly the case in Poland, the Baltic provinces and Hungary, where the proportion stood at well over 70 per cent; but not in Russia, where the proportion was more akin to the tenurial serf regimes of Brandenburg or Austria-Bohemia, whose serfs comprised less than 50 per cent of the population. This had nothing to do with the size of Russia's urban population: at 3 per cent in 1724, it had risen only to 4.4 per cent in 1812 and to 7.8 per cent in 1851. Russian society, in fact, was just as agrarian as that of Hungary or Poland.[190] Nor did it have anything to do with capitalist farming or industrial capitalism, since in Russia both operated through serf labour. Nor did it stem from the existence of free military communities, for they existed in all three countries. What rendered Russia different was its high proportion of state/crown (appanage) peasants: that is, peasants not subjected to private landlordship but answerable to the tsar or his family for rent and jurisdiction as well as for taxes and military service.

Between 1678 and 1857 the proportion of serfs in the Russian peasantry fell from 60 to 40 per cent. In the same period, the state peasantry rose from 12 to 50 per cent,[191] an increase for which Catherine the Great's seizure of ecclesiastical property in 1763 was responsible. The residents of church land comprised 18 per cent of the peasantry. Instead of giving them away, she converted them into state peasants.[192] The proportion of state peasants was also enlarged by military service. This happened not only in the seventeenth century, as serfs fled to the southern frontier and became free military servitors, but also in the eighteenth and nineteenth centuries: for, following the establishment of a large standing army manned by conscripts, serfs, along with their wives and children, were granted freedom in reward for serving in it.[193]

The existence of state peasants affected Russian serfdom not only because it reduced the proportion of serfs in rural society but also because it provided serfs with an emancipatory ideal. Presented with the two alternatives to serfdom – a state peasantry and the Cossacks – it was not difficult for serf communities to appreciate the advantages of freedom over servitude.[194]

Serfdom was not simply imposed upon the Russian peasantry in the early seventeenth century and thereafter left to waste away. For much of the late seventeenth and early eighteenth centuries, the proportion of serfs to the total population was on the increase, partly because the law was changed to convert free persons – orphans, foundlings, bastards, even servants – into serfs; and partly because the government was inclined to use state and crown lands as a form of patronage for favourites and officials, a practice of reward which converted their inhabitants into serfs. As a result, the serfs increased from 60 per cent of the peasantry in 1678 to 70 per cent in 1719–21. Then, in the late eighteenth century, the proportion contracted sharply, comprising 54 per cent in 1795–6. The earlier growth was the work of the government, especially that of Peter the Great.[195]

These figures, however, relate only to the Russian core. In the Russian Empire as a whole, the proportion of serfs continued to increase during the late eighteenth century as the government, by means of decrees enserfing the residents of private estates, extended serfdom to the Ukraine in 1784, and to the territories between it and the Black Sea (New Russia) and the Caucasus in 1796.[196] Furthermore, Russia's acquisition, in the eighteenth century, of the Baltic Provinces and the eastern parts of the Polish Commonwealth added societies in which, by the 1790s, serfs comprised at least 85 per cent of the peasantry.[197] Within the Russian Empire, then, serfdom remained a living, expanding organism into the nineteenth century, although, within Russia itself, it was contracting fast at least a century before the final abolition.[198]

How did the condition of the Russian serf compare with that of other serfs? Russian serfs had few rights in the law.[199] And these the government found it virtually impossible to enforce, simply because mediatized between the serfs and the state were their owners, the nobility, through whom the government was obliged to operate. Unable to call upon impartial royal officials to protect them, the serfs therefore had to resort to their own devices, the most potent of which was non-cooperation.

Most Russian serfs lived on large estates with absentee owners.[200] Subjected to the management of a bailiff, who lacked the resources to enforce his total domination, each serf community was, in practice, left to look after itself. Just as the state operated through an alliance with the serf owners, the serf owners operated through an alliance with the village elders.[201] Non-cooperation, either by nobles or serfs, could easily be crushed by government troops; but this was necessarily an emergency measure, to be employed only in the extreme situation of rebellion. Non-cooperation, however, could be exercised by serfs in a variety of subtle and effective ways that failed to justify military action: for example, by malperformance of labour services, the theft of grain and timber, the non-payment of rent, and flight.[202] To safeguard against this non-violent type of resistance, lords and their managers were obliged to follow a policy of respecting custom and village autonomy. Changes that infringed custom – such as a rise in rent, or the cultivation of a new crop, or an increase in labour services, or a conversion of rent to labour services, or a conversion of rent from money to kind – were best achieved by negotiation and concession. If discipline had to be applied, it was best administered, other than for crimes, by the serf community itself through the institution of the commune, an assembly of household heads from whom the village officials were appointed by election.[203] A system of despotism existed, then, tempered, if not undone, by delegation. Just as the government operated through the lord's private authority, the lord operated through the authority of the commune. Within this scheme of things, the lord informed the village of the services and payments required of it, but allowed the commune to allocate these requirements within the serf community. The performance of labour services, the allocation of rent, the amount of government tax families had to pay, the selection of conscripts for the tsar's army were all decided from within.[204] Underlining the need for cooperation beween lord and serf was the memory of peasant rebellion. The outcome was the preservation of certain rights and liberties which rendered serf status, for those subjected to it, a social impediment rather than a source of economic exploitation. The lord's respect for serf rights, however, did not necessarily make the system of serfdom function efficiently: labour services were performed without dedication; a great deal of flogging was necessary to keep serfs up to the mark; and rents often fell into arrears, with lords and their agents unable to do much about it when the whole community refused to pay.[205]

Following the permanent ban on migration in 1649, serfdom was intensified by further legislation, thanks to a succession of government decrees. Some denied rights to serfs, for example, to make legally recognized transactions, as in 1731 and 1761; or to bring legal actions against their lords, as in 1649 and 1767. Others extended seigneurial authority over the sale and punishment of serfs, for example, the dispatch of disobedient serfs to Siberia in 1760.[206] But there is no reason to believe that this process worsened the serf's lot. Likewise, there is no reason to believe that it was alleviated by the rights the government eventually conferred upon serfs: for example, in allowing them to make formal complaints against their lords (1796), in forbidding excessive labour services (1797, 1832, 1853), in limiting the punishment lords could administer (1845, 1857), in defining serf obligations (1845–8), in restricting serf sales (1721, 1771, 1833, 1841) and in ordering lords to leave serfs with enough land for peasant farming (1827).[207]

Of greater import were the massive changes affecting the Russian economy in the late eighteenth century, especially with the development of noble farming (direct demesne cultivation) on the southern steppes, and the establishment of large industrial complexes in the Urals. Manned by serf labour, both developments worked against the interest of millions of serfs; but with what effect?

Noble farming caused demesnes to expand and rent payments to convert to labour services. As a result, in parts of the black soil region the ratio of demesne to peasant land decreased from 1:5 in 1780 to 1:1 in 1850.[208] Attendant population growth, coupled with repartitional systems which allocated land according to the number of *tiagla* (man and wife plough teams), kept labour services within reasonable bounds, but also created a need in peasant communities for additional land. As this was something demesne expansion tended to deny, individual holdings had to contract. Furthermore, even when demesne expansion occurred simply at the expense of the waste, as it often did, it still harmed the serf community in reducing the extent of forest and pasture to which its commoning rights applied.[209] Nonetheless, while noble farming was clearly not in the serf's interest, it is far from certain that it resulted in hardship. Moreover, a noble farming system allowed serfs greater chances of reprisal, through foot-dragging and the pilfering of demesne produce, and therefore greater leverage in calling the lord to order.[210] And rarely did it threaten to depeasantize the serfs. Normally, they remained with sufficient land – 22 acres, 32 acres are the figures given, and in addition access to meadows and forests – to continue as self-subsistent farmers.[211]

At the close, in 1861, serfs were associated not only with agriculture but also with industry. In many instances the association was mixed, notably in the heartland north of Moscow where serfs remained as peasant farmers, while also engaging in the cottage industries of weaving and nail-making, and working for wages in the textile and metal trades. Industrial employment, in this respect, was a source of peasant maintenance, even of wealth and prosperity.[212] But, from the early eighteenth century, serfs became involved in the huge metallurgical enterprises of the Urals. Some were local peasants whose service obligations involved them in providing unpaid auxiliary work. Many, however, were a proletariat working for wages in the factories and mines.[213] Shifted from a peasant world, they became tied to an industrial one. In peasant eyes, the move must have seemed a demotion. But did it cause hardship? The condition of industrial serfs related to the prosperity of the firm for which they worked. If the firm fell on hard times, they suffered through being tied to the business – much more so than free workers who could look elsewhere for work. However, if the firm prospered, the serfs did reasonably well. Wages, true, were probably three or four times less than those paid to free workers, but the rewards serfs received consisted of a range of other benefits. These included a specific allotment of rye flour, free housing, free fuel and timber, a free garden plot, free pasturing, free health care, exemption from taxation and military service (for which the firm had to pay), even old age and disability pensions. Judged by eyewitness accounts and government reports, their standard of living was high, at least in the early nineteenth century, with good housing, ample food and sufficient free benefits to compensate for the low wage.[214]

In fact, the hardships suffered by Russian serfs had little to do with their unfree status. More to blame were the periodic famines – for example in 1821–2, 1833–4, 1848–9 – which affected the peasantry generally.[215] Arguably, serfs were better protected against famine than the rest of the peasantry, because of the obligations their lords were under to provide them with relief. However, this depended upon whether the lords had sufficient resources of spare grain.[216] Furthermore, famine relief was beneficial in the short term but not in the long term, because of the population growth it failed to check. Yet, throughout the history of Russian serfdom, land hunger was not a serious problem: even in the period 1750–1860, when the population of Russia increased fourfold and, coincidentally in the black soil region, the extension of noble farming restricted the amount of land available for peasant cultivation.[217] Nonetheless, the substantial acreage retained by average holdings and, thanks to the repartitional system, the practice of reallocating land in accordance with family need, meant that the self-subsistent peasant way of life did not come under threat before emancipation (1861). The families of serfs who fell into poverty did so largely because of personal failings such as drunkenness, or because of bad fortune such as the death of a horse or having no children of working age.[218] Other serf families achieved considerable wealth, usually because of their off-farm activities as traders, carriers and craftsmen.[219] Serfs generally in this period retained, in the traditional manner, a standard of living that failed to impair their fertility or reduce their life expectancy.

Russian serfdom only proved oppressive because it became subjected to a double demand, from the government and the seigneur, with neither party prepared to offer compensation for what the other exacted. In contrast, for the state peasants, the quitrent charged took into account the weight of taxation. On the other hand, seigneurial demands upon serfs were not necessarily heavy. Because of repartition, serfs lacked the opportunity, present in central Europe, of employing on low wages the landless to carry out the demesne services, but this did not render their services unbearable. In fact, the growing numbers available to provide labour services made them lighter. As for the rent that serfs paid as an alternative to service, this often became fixed by custom and, if commuted to money, was gradually devalued by inflation. Generally speaking, the plight of the serf was worse than that of the state peasant, although this had nothing to do with being tied to the estate since, following the establishment of the poll tax in the 1720s, state peasants had also been denied a right of departure.[220]

The burden of seigneurial exaction and unfreedom that serfs actually suffered rested upon a number of considerations. Lords reliant upon labour services had to impose greater control than those reliant upon rent, simply to get the work done. Serfs on rent were given considerable freedom to leave the estate in search of paid work, and to do whatever they wished, so long as their dues and taxes were paid. Nonetheless, what was demanded of serfs in labour service required the consent of the commune; otherwise, a train of resistance would start up which could be highly inconvenient for the lord. Undoubtedly, lords sought to increase their demands in the early nineteenth century as opportunities beckoned and inflation pressed. The result was a high level of serf disobedience amounting to revolt.[221] But it does not follow that the serfs who attacked their lords and their property were heavily oppressed. While serious grievances and good grounds for action existed, the ensuing conflict was arguably more of a constitutional than a bread-and-butter issue, caused not by destitution but by the lord's attempt to breach custom, or to introduce changes without first securing his serfs' consent. In response, serfs could insist upon having their obligations fixed, preferably by law; or, more radically, they might hope to be released from seigneurial control and become state peasants.[222]

Rumours of emancipation circulated in Russia as early as 1761, at the accession of Peter III. They resurfaced thereafter on the accession of each new tsar.[223] Yet Russian serfdom was almost the last of the serf regimes to be abolished, surviving in spite of the examples set by the Hohenzollern and Habsburg governments, the latter in 1781, the former in 1807. Long before 1861, however, the Russian government had approved emancipations within the empire, both in its Baltic provinces and in some of its Polish territories. In the Baltic provinces, it eventually complied with an initiative taken by the native nobilities of Kurland, Livonia and Estonia and sanctioned in their noble-dominated diets between 1805 and 1817. Moving these nobilities to act was what had happened further west during the revolutionary years, as well as a fear of peasant revolution. A policy of rewarding serfs with legally recognized hereditary holdings gave way to one of rewarding them with emancipation but without landholding rights.[224] Moreover, when Napoleon's creation, the Duchy of Warsaw, was placed under the rule of the tsar in 1815, the Napoleonic decrees of 1807 – which had freed the serfs while enabling the lords to own the land – were preserved since they accorded with what the nobles wanted.[225] When deliberating on Russian serfdom in the mid-nineteenth century, then, the Russian government was not without direct experience of emancipation. Furthermore, in the opening decade of the nineteenth century, it had turned sharply against serfdom, first, by refraining to impose it upon newly acquired territories, notably Finland and Bessarabia; second, by ending the practice of enserfing state or crown peasants by giving them away to subjects; third, by authorizing nobles to liberate their serfs if they so wished. The first two measures prevented the further extension of serfdom, but the last had little effect. Of the 10 million or so serfs, only 150,000 were freed in this manner, largely because the nobles were obliged to grant the serfs they liberated sufficient land to continue as peasant farmers.[226]

Essentially the abolition of Russian serfdom, as with its original establishment, was a government initiative, carried out to serve the interests of the state and implemented by royal decree. Moved by the memory of the great peasant wars of the seventeenth and eighteenth centuries, and the revelation of peasant power associated with the French Revolution, the government took more seriously than it needed the rural disturbances of the early nineteenth century. These happened with greater frequency than the great Russian peasant rebellions of the past, although not on the same individual scale. In abolishing serfdom, the government was also moved to thoughts of reform by a deep concern for its international standing, following its defeat in the Crimean War.[227] Elsewhere in eastern Europe, the abolition of serfdom was rendered acceptable to the nobility by the government's willingness to continue the seigneurial system, for it enabled them to preserve the lordship central to their social code and their traditional *raison d'être*. A vestige of this procedure was used in Russia where, according to the terms of the 1861 emancipation, peasants were allowed to redeem themselves from the seigneurial system only with the lord's consent – that is, until 1881, when redemption became compulsory for all serfs.[228] Attractive to the Russian nobles was a settlement that awarded them a considerable amount of land, as well as compensation for the property that now entered the legal ownership of the former serf communities.[229] All this took time as the government agonized over what to do. It accepted from the 1840s that 'serfdom . . . is an evil' and that 'the present state of affairs cannot go on for ever', but, frightened of undoing society and unleashing mob rule, it sought 'a gradual transition to a new state of affairs' that was impossible to realize.[230] As a result, it found itself a dinosaur among the great powers. Suddenly, in 1861, it decided to remove part of the old regime so as to save the remainder: serfdom was abolished in order to preserve a peasant society, a noble order and an absolute monarchy.

10
Islamic Slavery

Africa and Asia

In the early modern period, a prolonged war between the Austrian Habsburgs and the Ottoman Turks pitted against each other two systems of servitude, the one based on serfdom, the other on slavery. For the Habsburgs, serfdom furnished taxes and troops; for the Ottomans, slavery provided military leadership and crack professional troops. The dependence of both upon servitude underlined its historical importance, since the epic struggle between the two powers held the fate of Latin Christendom in the balance for much of the early modern period. Having taken Constantinople in 1453, the Ottoman Turks in the next 100 years completely annexed the Balkans, took possession of one-third of Hungary, and even threatened Vienna itself. Led by slaves and stiffened by highly trained slave soldiers, their armies proved almost invincible. Modern slavery, then, had the capacity to generate not only enormous wealth, through the plantation systems of the New World, but also enormous power, through the military slave regime of the Ottoman Empire.

The Ottoman slave system was not unique but typified the servitude found in the Islamic world. In certain basic respects, Islamic slavery had much in common with the Christian slavery of the New World. In both cases, most slaves were in private ownership, engaged as domestic servants, artisans, porters and farmhands.[1] From a legal point of view, they had no identity other than as the property of their master. True, the law recognized them as persons, but it defined them as disposable goods.[2] Slave status was regarded as degrading, no matter what benefits it conferred.[3] Usually, the slaves were outsiders, uprooted from other societies. To maintain sufficient numbers, a slave trade and a continual process of enslavement were necessary. Like Christians, Muslims opposed the enslavement of co-religionists but did not allow the enslaved to liberate themselves automatically by conversion.[4] Finally, even though they possessed few legal rights, slaves under both systems were permitted to enjoy rights and liberties by customary usage, largely to encourage efficient and compliant work.

But these similarities form only part of the picture, for Islamic slavery differed from New World slavery in several essential respects. Although commonly found in the Americas, plantation slavery was largely absent from the Islamic world. The slave plantations – found, for example, growing cotton in nineteenth-century upper Egypt, sorghum in the middle Niger valley, and cloves on the African east coast, in and around Zanzibar – were exceptional and mostly latter-day developments.[5] Agricultural slavery in the Islamic world normally took the form of serfdom, with slaves granted small farms in return for labour services or sharecropped rent. The extensiveness of free peasant farming, however, meant that this occurred less frequently than in eastern Europe. Islamic slavery tended to be an urban rather than a rural phenomenon, with slaves benefiting from the opportunities towndwellers had to make money as petty traders, porters and craftsmen.[6]

Slaves were found as soldiers in the New World, notably in the American War of Independence, in the British Caribbean during the Napoleonic Wars, and in the American Civil War.[7] But there was no equivalent of Islamic military slavery, a system in which slaves were carefully trained to serve as a ruling elite. Whereas the upper classes of the New World were exclusively composed of freemen, Islamic slaves were found at both ends of the social spectrum. At the top were the military slaves who, as the arm of the ruler, enjoyed considerable power and wealth; at the bottom were the worker slaves owned by subjects and, for the most part, poor and powerless. Also absent in the New World, but prevalent throughout the world of Islam, was the slave harem. Islamic slave elites comprised not only officials and soldiers charged with running and defending the state, but also slaves required to service the master's sexual needs. Some were wives; others concubines. Both were protected by slave eunuchs. All inhabited the harem and were well placed to exercise influence over the master and to enjoy, thanks to his wealth, a leisured and luxuriant existence.[8]

The regular demand for concubines and domestic servants meant that the slave trade to the Islamic world was somewhat different from that to the Americas. In the latter, there was little demand for women, and young male adults predominated, whereas, in the former, young females had the priority. This difference was reflected in the price, which was higher for females in the Islamic world and higher for males in the New World.[9] In addition, the military slave institution placed priority on importing children to be trained as officials, soldiers and servants, whereas plantation slavery in the Americas called for adults capable of working long hours in the field.

Race provided a further difference between the two slave systems. Whites served as bondsmen in the New World but were servants not slaves. Apart from a few Indians, slavery was reserved for blacks. In contrast, the Islamic world enslaved both whites and blacks, the former normally serving as elite slaves in the ruler's service and harem, the blacks employed as household servants and labourers. Race, then, helped to determine the two extremes of the Islamic slave spectrum, but not to distinguish the free from the unfree.

In both worlds, slavery suffered a high wastage rate; but whereas in the New World this was due to high death-rates and low birth-rates, in the Islamic world manumission was the more important reducing agent.[10] The members of Islamic slave elites stood a good chance of emancipation, either for themselves in reward for service or for their children through being Muslim-born.[11] In this respect, Islamic slavery was far more assimilative than American slavery, with the enslaved, especially whites, regularly undergoing conversion to the culture and religion of their Muslim masters and then becoming, via manumission, free subjects. Promoting the assimilative process were, apart from the marital relations established with slave women, the pressures traditionally brought upon the slaves to convert to Islam, coupled with their willingness to comply.[12] In the New World the readiness of masters to admit slaves to their own religion was a late development; and the slaves themselves were none too keen to embrace Christianity. However, much depends on the region studied. Notably in Spanish America, where attitudes to slavery had been influenced by Islamic Moorish practices, and where the plantation system was less dominant, manumission was easier to achieve than in the British Caribbean or upon the North American mainland. Nonetheless, differences between New World and Islamic slavery remain, since manumission in Spanish America was never as great as in the Islamic world, while Islamic slavery remained vitally different from US slavery because it remained heavily dependent upon the external slave trade: so much so that, from the late nineteenth century, it suffered badly as diplomatic, moral and military measures taken by the West successfully curtailed the flow; whereas in the USA the capacity of slavery to achieve natural growth left it unaffected when the imports from Africa stopped in 1808.[13]

Two further differences between Islamic and American slavery need to be noted. Islamic slaves tended to be less harshly treated than New World slaves. It was commented upon by European travellers in the nineteenth century. Thus John Lewis Burkhardt wrote of Egypt and Arabia: 'Slavery had little dreadful in it but the name', and Gustav Nachtigal, who lived for five years in the Islamic Sudan and, at one point in his travels, was almost enslaved himself, reported: 'Everywhere Islam brings with it a mild administration of the institution of slavery.'[14] This may have had something to do with Islamic law and its injunction that masters treat converted slaves as 'God's people like unto you'.[15] It certainly had something to do with the absence of a slave-operated sugar industry. The tendency of Islamic slaves to be more frequently engaged in service than in production also helped to alleviate their condition.[16]

The other notable difference between Islamic and New World slavery lies in the former's longevity. An unbroken practice reached from the early days of the Caliphate to the twentieth century. Sustaining this tradition was the sanction of the Koran, the absence of a native abolitionist movement, and, until the late nineteenth century, a continual supply of fresh slaves from the adjacent, well-populated Pagan or infidel regions, notably Africa and the southern steppes of Russia, which could be ethically plundered on the pretext of waging a jihad against non-believers, and whose peoples could be justifiably enslaved as a means of saving their souls.[17]

Military slavery

From the ninth to the nineteenth centuries, Islamic regimes often possessed an elite of military slaves whose function extended from protecting the ruler to running the state.[18] Entry to it was by enslavement, careful selection and military training.[19] When these elites operated in their prime, the native-born were excluded from them. This applied both to the off-spring of the slave elite, as well as to all free subjects. As a result, its membership exclusively comprised men born in a foreign land and into a faith other than the religion of Islam.[20] Often they were recruited as children, on account of the importance attached to a rigorous and lengthy training. Preferably white, over the centuries they were drawn from Turkish, Slav, Greek, Armenian, Georgian and Circassian backgrounds.[21] Mostly belonging to rulers, they were public rather than private slaves.[22] Nonetheless, military slaves could also be privately owned, especially by subjects under obligation to provide the ruler with the military service of a number of troops, as, for example, in Mughal India or in the nineteenth-century Sudanese kingdom of Bornu.[23]

The more prominent modern examples of military slavery include the Delhi sultanate which ended in 1555, giving way to the Mughal Empire which, by the late seventeenth century, ruled virtually the whole of India and then fell apart in the early eighteenth century. Dominating the Middle East were the Ottoman and Safavid empires, the former spreading over northern Africa, the Balkans, Anatolia, Armenia and Arabia in the fifteenth and sixteenth centuries and surviving until the First World War; the latter ruling Persia between 1501 and 1732. Both possessed a slave institution that served a civil, as well as a military, purpose, the Safavid system developing in imitation of the Ottoman one.[24] Dominating North Africa were the Islamic states of Morocco and Egypt. Egypt with its Syrian empire fell to the Ottoman Turk in 1517, but preserved its military slave system under Ottoman rule until the early nineteenth century. Dominating central Africa – especially the savannahs of the Sudan – were the Islamic states of Songhai, the Fulani emirates of the Sokoto Empire, Dar Fur, Sinnar, Bornu, Bagirmi and Wadai. All possessed a military slave system of some sort, as did, possibly in imitation, some of the Pagan warrior kingdoms.[25] Fortunes waxed and waned among these Islamic regimes, but the prevalent polity, until the European scramble for Africa in the 1880s and 1890s, centred upon military slavery. The number and size of these Islamic regimes in Africa and Asia, coupled with their proclivity to use slave soldiers, meant that military slavery was not some peculiar, topsy-turvy, local practice but a major aspect of modern servitude.[26]

Once established as an Islamic institution – first in North Africa, then in Moorish Spain and under the Caliphate – military slavery continued to be employed because it was appreciated as a traditional device sanctioned by long and familiar usage. But it could also serve a very useful political purpose, providing an instrument of military power – for both achieving foreign conquests and preventing dynastic overthrow – that was much more effective than either the tribal levies of Africa and Asia or the feudal armies of Europe. What is more, as professional troops, military slaves were far superior to mercenaries; and as a method of imperial rule they were without equal. When functioning properly, military slavery supplied rulers with an unrivalled means of subduing their own subjects and defeating foreign powers.[27] Rarely, however, was the military slave institution sufficient in itself to man the ruler's armies, or to staff his government. Native interests usually remained an integral part of the polity. Rather than a complete system of rule, military slavery offered a means of assertion within a broader regime that allowed some political or military role for indigenous elites. Alternatively, it provided a system of overrule which, in practice, allowed local communities to govern themselves.[28]

To offer some examples: the Safavids took control of Persia at the start of the sixteenth century, thanks to its invasion by a confederation of Turkmen tribes, the Qizilbash. By the end of the century the Safavid shahs had established a system of government that was equipped with a regular army of slave soldiers. Financially and administratively, the system was based upon the crown lands, which were administered by slaves from the royal household. This military slave institution served two purposes: it provided a means of effectively combating the aggression of Ottoman Turks with a device very similar to the one they employed; and a means of reducing the shah's dependence upon the Qizilbash. Yet its introduction did not transform the polity, since the Qizilbash cavalry remained an important element in the army, and, outside the crown lands, the Turkmen tribal chiefs remained a vital part of local government. Likewise, the Persian interest continued to monopolize the positions of the pen and therefore provided the officials that ran the Muslim institution and the chancellery.[29]

At the other extreme was an Islamic system of government that had no more than an indirect reliance on military slaves. This came about when free subjects were allowed to fulfil their military service to the ruler by placing at his disposal their own slave troops. In contrast to the Delhi sultanate which it replaced, the Mughal Empire was ruled through an order of free *mansahdars*, some of whom were hereditary nobles, although many were outsiders appointed by the emperor. In return for military service they were awarded *jagirs*, or the right to take for their own use taxes from a given area.

With this revenue they could employ mercenaries. Frequently, however, they chose to maintain military slaves instead.[30]

In between the Safavid and Mughal extremes were the military slave systems employed, between the sixteenth and nineteenth centuries, in the savannah sultanates of central Africa. Each of these sultanates was a predatory state that thrived on the slaves taken in war from neighbouring kingdoms or rounded up in slave hunts carried out in the Pagan regions to the south. Slaves were a source of wealth and power: of wealth, because of their value in the trans-Saharan trade; of power, because rulers could use them to override the native interest, by providing a fund of external talent to compensate for the principle of birthright and the limitations it placed upon their choice of officers and officials. But in no instance did the ruler's reliance on military slaves render the native polity redundant, or reduce his subjects to the role of mere taxpayers. Thus the Funj dynasty ruled the upper Nile kingdom of Sinnar with the aid of slave officials, slave military commanders and slave troops, but the traveller James Bruce was quite wrong to assert that in the 1770s 'slavery in Sinnar is the only true nobility'. Below the hereditary sultan were the hereditary lesser princes, each with his own province divided into hereditary lordships. The regime of each prince mirrored that of the sultan, centring upon an earth castle which housed not only his family but also his slave troops and slave officials. In addition, there was a hereditary nobility of mounted and chain-mailed warriors. Furthermore, the armies of the sultan comprised both slave and free troops, consisting of a regular slave bodyguard; the units of cavalry provided by the princes (composed of slave and free warriors); and the free fighting men provided by subject nomadic tribes.[31]

Each of the savannah kingdoms comprised a complexity of communities, often with their own tribal affiliation and local autonomy. Political devices were therefore required to link them with the sultan. The employment of slave forces and officials, acting in the name of the sultan, was one of them. In the highly sophisticated manner of Ottoman Turkey and Safavid Persia, slave boys in the Keira kingdom of Dar Fur were trained in a school (*som*) situated in the sultan's household (*fashir*). In the course of time they became leading court officials and military commanders. But attending the same school, and receiving the same education, were free pages drawn from various native tribes who, having been trained in loyalty and reverence to the sultan, were sent home to become tribal rulers. The Dar Fur sultan's court, moreover, was attended by title-holders, some of whom were free while others were slaves. The former had become a hereditary group, maintained not by salaries but on revenues exacted from the estates they held of the sultan. In addition, the sultans of Dar Fur intruded upon the localities through intendants commissioned to visit a region as the sultan's representative. As Nachtigal reported: 'any official, whether slave or free, could be appointed to this office'. As in Sinnar, the Dar Fur kingdom was divided into provinces which could be ruled by slaves or hereditary title-holders. At the district level in Dar Fur, administration lay in the hands of the *shartay* who held his office by hereditary right and ruled through the medium of free village chiefs. The system of government, then, was a mixture of offices, some appointed and others held by right of birth. The appointees were usually slaves. It was similar with the military. Preserving this mixed slave–free system was the hereditary title-holders' ability to resist the sultan whenever he tried to shift the balance of power in his favour by increasing his reliance on slaves.[32] A salutary lesson lay in the fate of Sultan Abu'l-Qasim who, in the late eighteenth century, sought to rely completely on slave troops, slave courtiers and slave governors, but was stopped in his tracks and deposed.[33] The Bornu kingdom was very similar, at least in the nineteenth century following the Al-Kanemi dynasty's usurpation of the throne. It possessed an aristocratic element in the *kogonas*, who were courtiers with local affiliations resting on the fiefs they held of the sultan. A non-slave source of military power lay with the warriors on horseback (*furmas*) and the warriors on foot (*waladi*), who were retained by the *kogonas*. Although dependent upon the *kogonas*, however, the sultan was not without his own means of action, which lay in his household slaves, his slave generals and a standing army of slaves. In turn, the *kogonas* also operated through slave officials and slave troops, as did even the village chiefs.[34] In each of these examples, however, the military slave was no substitute for the free servitor. Instead, he served as an additional device, designed to provide the sultan with a means of independent action, and also to reduce the chances of his dynastic overthrow by allowing him access to the service of outsiders.

The drawbacks of military slavery were considerable. To work well, it required frequent and fresh recruitment. This usually entailed a policy of conquest to allow an injection of new blood from prisoners of war (through enslavement) or conquered territories (through slave tribute). Countering the reverence to the ruler that the training of slaves instilled was the *esprit de corps* imparted by their military service. Military slaves tended to acquire a corporate loyalty which the ruler had to respect; for, if he did not, he could face a mutiny that he would be powerless to quell, other than by apology and concession. Rather than serving the ruler as a source of strength, the military slaves could easily cause his overthrow, or, at least, take charge of government policy.[35]

A second major drawback of the military slave institution lay in the difficulty of maintaining it in pristine condition: that is, manned by slaves trained from childhood to serve the ruler alone. Priority had to be placed on recruiting children from beyond the bounds of Islam and on ensuring that the children of military slaves were kept out: otherwise it would become corrupted by native interests. At times this was achievable but, understandably, not for long. As a result, institutions of military slavery were prone to degeneration. However, when operating in their prime, they could become a magnificent instrument of power, as the Ottoman state revealed in the late medieval and early modern period.

The Ottoman system

Nowhere else in the Islamic world was there a military slave institution as sophisticated in its organization, as comprehensive in its purpose, as effective in its impact. After originating, in the typical manner – as a bodyguard, which was eventually expanded to form a regular, professional army – Ottoman military slavery underwent two vital, interrelated changes in the late fifteenth century.[36] Having taken Constantinople in 1453, and turned it into Istanbul – the capital of his empire – Sultan Mohammed II established there the Palace School for training his slaves. At the same time, he began to appoint slaves to leading offices in central and provincial government.[37] Significantly, the office next to the sultanate, the grand viziership, was transferred from free, Turkish-born hands to those of a slave. This was no temporary measure: slaves continued to hold the office for the next three centuries.[38] Moreover, by the early sixteenth century, the leading officers of the empire – the *sancak beyis*, the *beylerbeyis*, the viziers central and provincial, the commanders of the regular army – were nearly all slaves meticulously groomed for office in the Palace School.[39]

Recruitment to the Palace School was principally through the white boy levy (*devshirme*). This the Ottoman government exacted from the Christian regions of its empire, which were largely situated in the Balkans. Taken to Istanbul, the enslaved boys were converted to the Muslim religion, circumcised and tested for aptitude. They were then segregated into one contingent earmarked for a palace training and another destined to serve as ordinary troops in the regular infantry (the janissaries). The second contingent was placed with Turkish farmers in Anatolia, working for them as labourers and learning from them the Turkish language and Turkish customs. After seven years these slaves were recalled to the capital.[40] Designated novices, they had to spend another seven years in manual work, in and around the palace, before finally becoming enrolled as janissaries, whereupon they were garrisoned in the major cities of the empire. As the special instrument of the sultan, they were directly answerable to him and beyond the control of the provincial administration.[41]

The janissary contingent took nine-tenths of each tribute. Until qualified, they were treated very much like the slaves of the New World, with the important difference that the unskilled manual labour required of them was not on plantations. As for the other tenth, their education and career prospects were totally different. After spending up to eight years in preparatory schools, those falling below the mark – that is, the majority – were assigned to the regular household cavalry (the spahis of the Porte); the remaining handful entered the inner service of the sultan's palace to receive a four-year training in one of its vocational colleges, under the supervision of the White Eunuchs. Those deemed to fail at college were also dispatched to the household cavalry, but were rewarded with generous salaries and the prospect of promotion to important regimental commands. The successful graduands were kept on in the palace. All were destined for high office, some in the inner service, which placed them close to the sultan and at the centre of palace politics, the rest in the outer service, which opened up careers as provincial governors and high-ranking officers in the regular army.[42]

In this manner the sultan's slaves came to control not only palace affairs and the regular army, but also central and provincial government. As provincial governors (i.e. *beylerbeyis* and *sancak beyis*), they took command of the irregular provincial cavalry, which was provided by the timariots, that is, native-born Muslims who were allowed assignments of tax (*tīmārs*) in return for providing mounted service when required.[43] Slaves were able to infiltrate this force as the sultan's slaves were allowed to acquire *tīmārs*, and also because each timariot was expected to serve with an average of four additional horsemen, who could be his own slaves; but Muslim-born freemen also continued to serve in the provincial cavalry, sometimes electing non-slave *alay beyis*, whose function was to muster the cavalry and command it under the slave *sancak beyis*.[44]

In fact, the military slave institution, even in its prime, applied to only certain parts of the governmental system. Free of the slave presence – apart from its oversight by the grand vizier acting in the name of the sultan – was the system of jurisdiction for the Muslim-born. Just as the palace produced the office-holding slaves, the Ulemā (i.e. Muslim Institution) produced not only the priests but also the judicial officers – the jurists (*muftīs*) and judges (*kādīs*) – whom it educated in the same systematic way that the Palace School trained its slave officers and officials.[45] Whereas the palace recruited its members from abroad through the slave tribute, the Ulemā recruited its members at home through family patronage.[46] Two other important parts of the administration – the treasury with its *defterdārs* and the chancellery with its *nishāngîs* – were recruited from both the Ulemā and the palace. In this respect, slaves were found as officials not only in the domain of 'the men of the sword' but also in that of 'the men of the pen'.[47]

The distinctiveness of the Ottoman system of government caused sixteenth-century Europeans to compare it with their own aristocratic polities. Machiavelli in *The Prince* contrasted the government of France, which he characterized as ruled by a prince through his barons, with that of the Ottoman Turks, which he presented as ruled by a prince through his slaves. Ogier Ghiselin de Busbecq, the imperial ambassador to Istanbul in the time of Suleiman the Magnificent, made the same distinction in his *Turkish Letters*, stating that the essential means of government in Europe was the nobility, whereas the Ottoman sultan had his slaves.[48] These comparisons, however, are highly misleading, especially because they imply that the military slave institution allowed the Ottoman government to sever all relationship between state and society. Essentially, the socio-political system of the Ottomans rested upon a legal separation of two social groups, the rulers (*askarī*) and ruled (*ré'āyā*), which resembled the distinction that the European notion of the society of orders made between nobility and commonalty.[49] In both cases tax exemption was the reward offered to the ruling group in return for the official and military duties it was required to perform. The *askarī*, however, formed a much more complicated group than the European nobility. Within it was (as with the nobility) a hereditary element, composed of the timariots and their families, who remained *askarī* unless formally redefined as *ré'āyā*. The same was true of the families of officials associated with the Ulemā. But also within the *askarī* was a sizeable 'new blood' group recruited from the military slave institution.[50] This meant two things: a high injection of newcomers, recruited through the tribute system from the Balkans and southern Russia; and also the existence of slaves in considerable numbers, who, far from being outside recognized society, were an important part of its upper stratum. Furthermore, the military slavery of the Ottomans was essentially an imperial device, enabling the regime to function with an overall efficiency. Locally, regionally, there existed systems of self-government which the military slave institution did not disturb. In Anatolia rule was by village council for the settled communities and by tribal institutions for the nomads. At the regional level and state level, tribal chiefs or landed aristocrats ruled, in both cases by hereditary right, the former, for example, in Armenia, Kurdistan and Albania; the latter in Transylvania, Hungary, Montenegro, Wallachia and Moldavia.[51]

Two developments inexorably undermined the Ottoman military slave institution: one was the way the Turkish-born managed to penetrate its ranks; the other was the way the military slaves could abandon their loyalty to the sultan. By the end of the sixteenth century, large parts of the regular army, the janissaries and spahis of the Porte, had ceased to consist of troops enlisted and trained as slaves and were mainly composed of free Muslims. Some were the sons of military slaves, freed by virtue of having been born into the Muslim religion. This stemmed from the permission Selim I (1512–20) granted the janissaries to marry, followed by the permission Selim II (1566–74) granted them to enrol their sons in the corps.[52] Other free recruits were drawn from the native population, who were allowed to enter the janissaries in large numbers in the 1580s and 1590s.[53] Then, in the early seventeenth century, Murad IV (1623–40) suspended the tribute from the Balkans, previously a major source of slave recruitment to the regular army.[54] Furthermore, the provincial cavalry faded away in the early seventeenth century, the result of inflation devaluing the fixed incomes of the timariots, so that they could no longer afford to serve, and of the government's policy of reclaiming *tīmārs* in order to use them, through tax farming, as a source of revenue rather than service. As the regular army expanded in compensation, the inadequate supply of fresh slaves obliged the sultan to look to his subjects.[55] The original basis of the military slave institution therefore ceased to be authentically slave, and the garrisons of janissaries came to be manned by the local population.[56]

With the slave tribute from the Balkans terminated, the Palace School had to look elsewhere for its intake; but, some time before that, and at least from the closing years of Suleiman the Magnificent (1520–66), the sons of slaves and of free subjects were being admitted.[57] They presented themselves as the sultan's slaves, but this was no more than a conceit of the court, to which they happily subscribed because of the rewards it proffered. The practice of pretending to be the sultan's slave had a very long history. Its existence in 1480 was revealed by a stilted exchange between the duke of Savoy and an Ottoman official. Asked by the duke: 'What is your status? Are you a *kul* [a slave, or servant] of the sultan?' the official responded: 'I am.' But when asked: 'What is your descent?', he replied: 'I am Turkish-born.' Baffled, the duke rightly pointed out: 'One who is Turkish-born cannot be the sultan's *kul*.' In response, the official replied: 'Your excellency is right. But I am the son of a *kul*: I eat the sultan's bread, and so I count as his *kul*.'[58] In the late sixteenth and early seventeenth centuries, this form of slave pretence came to be frequently practised. It clearly had a profound effect upon the household cavalry, which was traditionally recruited from the Palace School.[59] But what effect did it have on the holders of the highest offices? In the course of the eighteenth century the grand viziership reverted to Turkish-born hands; but in the early nineteenth century, as European visitors observed, slaves still predominated in high office. Adolphus Slade reported in the 1830s that four out of five of the sultan's ministers were genuine slaves, and, in his opinion, so were many of the provincial governors.[60]

As Slade also revealed, all the slaves in these high positions had been originally purchased. Since large numbers of slaves were not needed to maintain this aspect of the military slave institution, it had managed to outlive the ending of the Balkans boy levy. Nonetheless, in the previous decade the three remaining props of elite slavery had been kicked away: in 1826 the sultan abolished the janissaries, closed the Palace School as a training college for government service, and ended the royal slave household.[61] Over the centuries the political control that the sultan's slaves were able to exert had resided in the influence exercised by them, not only as members of the regular army and as top officials but also as close contacts of the sultan – who himself was normally the son and husband of a slave. Central to this association had been the harem, with its slave wives, concubines and eunuchs, which Suleiman had admitted to the palace in the sixteenth century. Now, in 1826, this association was severed.[62] A final blow to elite slavery came in the reforms of 1838–9, when the sultan relinquished his right to own the persons and property of his officers and officials, and thus disposed of a final relic of the military slave system.[63]

Military slaves were notoriously difficult to handle. Given an expansive policy of conquest and the opportunities to loot and pillage, all went reasonably well; but left idle and inadequately rewarded, they could turn upon the master like an unfed beast. Slaves had even been known to overthrow reigning dynasties and seize the throne for themselves, as in the thirteenth-century sultanates of Egypt and Delhi.[64] This was not the fate of the Ottoman sultans. Yet several were overthrown, notably Bayezid II in 1512 and Osman II in 1622. Others were brought to the throne by slave support, in dynastic struggles caused by a succession that was not automatically determined by the rule of primogeniture, and by an abundance of heirs spawned by the practice of polygamy. Unless pre-empted by the discreet use of the silken bowstring, contenders used slaves to wage a war of succession upon each sultan's death.[65]

Even conquering sultans could be successfully opposed by their military slaves. This happened to Selim I, whose Persian campaign the janissaries terminated by refusing to go any further after the victory of Caldiran in 1514. The same thing happened to Suleiman the Magnificent, who had to raise the siege of Vienna in 1529 when the janissaries demanded to go home.[66] Essentially, the service of the military slaves had to be bought with generous salaries and large accession payments. But even this proved insufficient in the late sixteenth and early seventeenth centuries as debasements of the coinage devalued their pay, leaving them continually dissatisfied, untrustworthy, troublesome, and inclined to favour the present sultan's overthrow in order to bring forward the next accession payment.[67] The sultan's attempted solution to the problem was to convert the janissaries into a free native army, by stopping the major source of slave recruitment, the tribute levy from the Balkans, and by admitting to the corps the free sons of slaves as well as large numbers of Turks. This solution was ineffectual, since the janissaries continued to upturn their kettles in demonstrable complaint until finally disbanded in 1826.[68] But its effect upon the nature of the Ottoman state was profound. By transforming the regular army from a body of slaves into one of freemen, the government's dependence upon slavery was considerably reduced.

Needless to say, Ottoman slavery did not consist simply of the military slave institution. Besides the public slaves, who served the sultan and his leading officials in carrying out the military and civil tasks of government, there existed a much greater number of private slaves, who worked as domestic servants and labourers. Moreover, at times, a substantial number of the sultan's slaves – usually those taken in war – were placed on crown lands to work in agriculture as sharecropping serfs. However, they tended to undergo rapid assimilation into the free peasantry by adopting the Muslim faith, marrying free persons, and acquiring inheritable plots of land.[69] Private slaves were also engaged in agriculture, but much depended upon whether peasant farmers could afford to buy them. This, in turn, depended upon the supply. Moreover, in sixteenth-century Anatolia, the need to purchase private slaves was ruled out by the agricultural use to which the sultan's janissaries were put before they were committed to military service. However, this labour supply disappeared in the seventeenth century as the janissaries ceased to be recruited by enslavement.[70] Private slaves also worked as urban artisans, notably in the manufacture of luxury goods; as did enrolled janissaries when held in reserve.[71] Yet the former tended to work on manumission contracts, purchasing their freedom by producing a given quantity of goods; and the latter was ruled out by the expansion of the janissary corps in the sixteenth century, which left no scope for a slave reserve.[72] Private slaves were mostly engaged in domestic service.[73] Whereas state service placed a priority on young white boys, domestic service created a high demand for young black girls.[74]

In the normal Islamic manner, private and public slavery was a transient state, thanks to the frequency with which manumission was granted – partly to earn virtue, partly because of the willingness of the manumitted to remain attached to the master's service – and the freedom conferred upon slaves born into the faith.[75] The high incidence of deslavement rendered the slave trade vital for the continuation of slavery in the Ottoman Empire.[76] In this respect, the curtailment of this trade decided the fate of Ottoman slavery. Within the empire, no abolitionist movement developed, and when it collapsed during the First World War, slavery still remained a legitimate activity, although no longer extensively practised.[77]

The Turks had drawn fresh slaves from three main sources. At first, they were recruited as prisoners of war, whose execution was stayed in return for enslavement and conversion to the Muslim faith.[78] The foreign aggression of the Ottoman Turks ensured that capture in war was a major supplier of slaves, not only in the fifteenth and sixteenth centuries, when they were scoring spectacular victories over Christians and Shiite Muslims, but also in the seventeenth and eighteenth centuries: for example, 80,000 were taken in the Vienna campaign of 1683 and another 50,000 in 1788 following the Austrian defeat at Klausenberg.[79]

Capture in war remained a means of recruiting slaves until the 1830s. By this date another vital source of recruitment was about to end. From the fifteenth century, the Ottomans had demanded a tribute in slaves from parts of their empire and from client states. Slaves had been exacted, then, not only from the Balkans but also from the Crimea, the Caucasus and Tunisia. Although the Balkans levy was ended in the early seventeenth century, the other tributes continued to be exacted until the late eighteenth century. Then, Russia's annexation of the Crimea and Georgia left Tunisia as the only remaining source, which was finally closed, under Western diplomatic pressure, in 1842.[80]

By the late nineteenth century, private purchase had become the only means of acquiring fresh slaves.[81] For centuries, the slave market had been an important provider, an essential counter to individual enfranchisement. For much of the nineteenth century, it supplied new slaves at an average rate of 10,000 a year.[82] However, from the mid-nineteenth century the purchase of slaves became increasingly difficult, the result of restrictions the Ottoman government was obliged to place on the trade in response to the pressures the British and French managed to impose because it needed to maintain them as allies.[83] Consequently, the slave market in Istanbul was closed in 1846; the slave trade into the Ottoman Empire from the Persian Gulf was outlawed in 1847; the importation of black slaves was banned in

1857; and that of white slaves in 1908.[84] As a result of increasing the price of slaves, the prohibitions placed upon the slave trade confined their acquisition to a contracting segment of society. Because of the high wastage rate caused by frequent manumission and virtually nil reproductiveness, these prohibitions seriously undermined the practice of slavery in the empire, even in the absence of a native moral objection.[85]

Part III

Emancipation and After

11

Abolition in Europe and the Americas

The rejection of serfdom and slavery compared

A major event in the history of modern servitude was the coincidental termination of New World slavery and European serfdom. Although both remained in their prime and virtually unchallenged in 1765, a hundred years later they were in terminal decline and had been, for the most part, obliterated. As acceptable systems of labour, they were both undermined by the Enlightenment which, notwithstanding strains of elitist conservatism, ambivalent rationalism and ironic ambiguity, created a new code of values which proposed that, rather than being concordant with civilized behaviour – as the examples of ancient Greece and Rome would suggest – servitude was barbaric. In contrast, free societies were presented as, *ipso facto*, polished and refined. Also associated with the Enlightenment was a radically revised attitude towards capitalism. This was propounded by the French physiocrats Turgot, Boncerf and Quesnay; the Scottish political economists Hutcheson and Smith; and the central European cameralists von Justi and von Sonnenfels. By appreciating capitalism as a source of public and private wealth, happiness and efficiency, they challenged the traditional view, held by noble and peasant alike, that it was the derogatory work of unscrupulous merchants and moneylenders bent on exploiting the rest of society. Revisable rents and waged labour now came to be seen as respectable and rational, while the fixed rents, hereditary tenures, compulsory labour and lordly rule of the manorial system were dismissed as lacking in political, social and economic utility. Promoting these Enlightenment ideas was the prosperity of the regions that had already put them into practice: notably, parts of Britain, northern France, the Low Countries and the New England colonies of North America.[1] The same ideas were propagated by the American and French revolutions. By repudiating differential privileges in the law

– the linchpin of the society of orders – and 'despotism', they also added to the general condemnation of servitude a heightened appreciation of juridical equality and political liberty.

These new attitudes, however, were not in themselves sufficient to bring New World slavery and European serfdom to an end. Enlightened masters and lords proceeded to free their subjects as a result of the books they read, but the overall effect was minimal; in fact, it was little different from the limited ability of Christianity in the modern period to persuade the owners of serfs and slaves that manumission should be granted because it was the way to piety and salvation. The individual initiatives of owners left the system intact. In this respect, the modern emancipations differed radically from those of the middle ages. Then, first slavery and eventually serfdom had faded away, the result of landowners choosing to adopt new policies of estate management. Slavery in the New World and serfdom in modern eastern Europe, in sharp contrast, were ended by a series of acts of state that simply made them illegal. Compulsion of this sort was necessary because, well into the nineteenth century, both remained extremely useful as a source of wealth and social control, and therefore, from the point of view of master and lord, worthy of preservation, no matter how morally dubious.

Serfdom and slavery were undermined in the late eighteenth and early nineteenth centuries not only by a change in attitude to labour but also by a change in the labour situation. The rise of modern slavery and serfdom had stemmed from a scarcity of free labour. For this reason, commercial farming became closely associated with systems of forced labour, in both eastern Europe and the Americas. By the mid-nineteenth century, however, the labour situation had undergone a fundamental change as population growth in Europe and Asia, policies of emancipation, and the migration of free labour had created in these servile economies the prospect of a sufficiency of waged labour. Commercial operators therefore were strongly placed to question their dependence upon systems of forced labour which for a variety of reasons – moral disapproval, cost, inefficiency, problems of control – had become increasingly unsatisfactory.

Violence played a vital part in the termination of European serfdom and New World slavery. In both cases, the opposition of the servile was insistent and effective. It took the form of armed rebellion as well as the more subtle, erosive protests of flight and poor work. Thus, the serf revolts of 1775 in Bohemia, and of 1846 in Galicia, were major factors in ending serfdom in the Habsburg Monarchy, just as the many revolts that occurred in the Russian countryside during the early nineteenth century led to the Emancipation of 1861. Likewise, slave revolts in the Caribbean, notably in Haiti and Jamaica, were directly linked with emancipation in the French and British colonial empires. The non-cooperation of the servile also played a crucial part in the process of abolition: for example, during the American Civil War when slaves undermined the war effort in the South by refusing to work or by fleeing to Union lines, and when, in the 1870s and 1880s, the slaves of Cuba and Brazil fled from the plantations.[2] Moreover, contributing to the termination of serfdom, in both the medieval and modern periods, had been the dilatory manner in which serfs fulfilled their labour obligations to the lord.

The key device for ending both European serfdom and New World slavery was a people in arms bent on an anti-aristocratic mission. Decisively, the revolutionary armies of France imposed their own country's rejection of serfdom upon the rest of Europe: directly through conquest and annexation, as in western Germany and the Low Countries; indirectly, over the next half century, through inspiring agrarian reform – much of it the work of counter-revolution – in the territories of the Hohenzollerns, Romanovs and Habsburgs. With equal decisiveness, the armies of the Union in the 1860s imposed slave emancipation upon the US South. Yet the actual achievement of emancipation was often the by-product of a larger conflict, which, manipulatively, used the prospect of freedom to secure some political advantage: whether it be French revolutionaries in 1789, making a bid for peasant support; or the English aristocracy, seeking to retain its control over the political system by offering some concession to popular pressure; or the North, seeking to crush the South in the American Civil War; or colonies, engaged in wars to secure their national independence, as in North America in the late eighteenth century, or in nineteenth-century Spanish America.

Yet, given the differences that existed between the character of New World slavery and that of European serfdom, the termination of the two could not be completely alike. New World slavery was undermined by the measures taken to stop the transatlantic slave trade. Reducing the supply of new slaves from Africa made slave labour more expensive by raising its replacement cost. In the USA, the prohibition of the external slave trade in 1808 was countered by a vigorous internal trade between the old slave areas of tobacco and rice and the new cotton belt; and in Brazil, the shifting of slaves from the sugar region in the north-east to the coffee region in the south-east served the same purpose, after the slave trade with Africa was finally stopped in 1850. However, in the Caribbean and Spanish America, the low reproductivity of the existing slave population, now compounded by the problem of replacement, caused a serious contraction in the slave work-force.

Although European serfdom and New World slavery were similarly affected by an increasing supply of free labour, the demographic reasons for their termination were quite different. A trade in serfs had never figured importantly in upholding serfdom. Replacement was adequately provided, in the course of time, by serf reproductivity. In fact, from the late eighteenth century, serf populations became more than capable of sustaining themselves. A spectacular natural increase in the rural population occurred which, in conjunction with other factors such as serf resistance, questioned the economic usefulness of serfdom by spawning a mass of cheap waged labour and would-be tenants. It suddenly appeared in the lord's interest either to work his estate as a fully-fledged capitalist farm – that is, with waged rather than compulsory labour – or to turn himself into a rentier capitalist by converting the servile tenures – with their protective fixed rents and rights of inheritance – into short-term rack-rented leaseholds, in order to benefit from the competition for tenancies that the enlargement of the rural population had created. With ex-serfs prepared to continue doing the work they had performed as serfs, emancipation in Europe was less fraught with difficulty than in the Americas. There, not only ex-slaves were averse to working on plantations: so were whites, and for the same reason – its association with slavery.

Furthermore, the social pressures for terminating European serfdom and New World slavery were quite different. The enlistment of popular support was important in ending both, but it came from different sources and had different causes. The anti-slavery movement was backed by the urban population. Moved by the conviction that slavery was evil, it impressed itself by petition and demonstration, calling for an end initially to the slave trade and then, with that achieved, to slavery itself. Much of the impetus came from religious groups, notably Quakers, Methodists, Baptists, Presbyterians and Evangelical Anglicans. Serfs, in contrast, had mostly to trust to themselves. Serfdom in the West was opposed by the Protestant belief that serfdom was against God's law, since Christ had purchased the freedom of all with his sacrifice: a point made in article three of the Memmingen petition produced by the German Peasants' War of 1525, and in article 16 of the petition produced by Ket's Rebellion of 1549. Moreover, certain Russian sects opposed enserfment, such as the Old Believers, the Dukhobortsy and the Molokane.[3] But no equivalent religious crusade developed to demand an end to serfdom. Urban groups were mostly indifferent, except in the circumstances of revolution when they backed agrarian reform as a means of enlisting peasant support. In the eastern borderlands, Cossacks during the seventeenth and eighteenth centuries had behaved similarly when struggling to defend their liberties against governmental encroachment.

Again, because of the differing natures of European serfdom and New World slavery, the attitude and actions of the government had a different role to play in bringing them to an end. With serfs owing obligations to the state, governments had a strong motive for limiting what the lords could exact of them. A conflict of interest was perceived between rents and taxes on the one hand, and labour services and military service on the other. The government's willingness to intervene stemmed from the extent to which the apparatus and policies of the state had to rely upon the taxes, manpower and loyalty of the peasantry. By the late eighteenth century, this reliance was considerable as, subjected to the development of professional bureaucracies and standing armies and the growing cost of war, the machinery of state became much more expensive to maintain. In response, governments, moved principally by political considerations, proceeded to abolish serfdom. With slavery it was a somewhat different matter, simply because slaves were not subjects of the state and therefore, apart from owing obedience, they were without political obligation. For this reason, the drive towards slave emancipation was imposed not by government upon society but rather by society upon government. With serf emancipation, it was the other way round.

Finally, serf emancipation did not adversely affect the profitability of farming; whereas slave emancipation frequently transformed a period of agricultural prosperity into one of economic decline. Furthermore, serf emancipation often led to proletarianization as the landlords engrossed peasant farms in order to extend the area that they directly cultivated, in effect, turning their estates into plantations operated for a purely commercial purpose with labour that was hired. In contrast, slave emancipation often worked against the plantation and led to its partial replacement by peasant or small-scale commercial farming. Unwilling to work as labourers on the former plantations, ex-slaves frequently opted to farm smallholdings, into which estates that could no longer be operated in the old plantation manner came to be divided: as in Haiti, Jamaica, Trinidad, the Windwards, Guadeloupe, the US South, Cuba and Brazil.

Neither slaves nor serfs appeared to derive much material benefit from emancipation. For ex-serfs, rapid population growth caused subdivision of holdings, increased rent on leased land and reduced agricultural wages, thus removing the gains imparted by the conversion of tenancy to freehold. For ex-slaves, the problem lay in having to survive in societies beset by white racism.[4]

The emancipation of the European serfs

Jerome Blum in a justly famous study, *The End of the Old Order in Rural Europe*, proposed a thesis of serf emancipation that provocatively played down the usually recognized factors – the impact of the French Revolution, peasant revolt, population growth and bourgeois capitalism – elevating instead the ability of absolute monarchs to overrule the nobility.[5]

No one could doubt the importance of royal absolutism in disposing of serfdom, especially in the light of the Habsburg edict of 1781 that abolished serfdom in Austria and Bohemia; the Hohenzollern edict of 1807 that abolished serfdom in the Prussian monarchy; the Romanov edict of 1861 that abolished serfdom in the Russian Empire. Yet the vital questions of 'how?' and 'why?' summon up a host of other agents, notably those diminished by Blum: revolution, peasant revolt, population growth, and the willingness of nobles to concede the end of serfdom because it served their interest. Furthermore, it could not be said that absolute monarchs willingly embraced emancipation. Rather, it was forced upon them by shattering defeat in war. Significant in the process of emancipation were Prussia's defeat of Austria in the Seven Years War, Prussia's defeat by France at Jena in 1806, and Russia's defeat by France, Britain and Turkey in the Crimean War of 1854–6. In each case a terrible blow to the monarch's honour and pride, coupled with a realistic appreciation of the peasantry as the bedrock of the state, led, in accordance with Enlightened thinking, to a royal attempt to ameliorate the condition of the rural population, on the understanding that, once free from serfdom and therefore less vulnerable to seigneurial exploitation, peasants would become more prosperous and therefore better providers of taxes and troops.

The process of emancipation began in 1771 in Savoy. By the outbreak of the French Revolution in 1789, serfdom had been banned in Austria-Bohemia (1781), Baden (1783) and Denmark (1788).[6] In each case, absolute monarchy took rights away from the nobility, but did not seriously damage the noble interest. Royal absolutism from the start was based on an alliance between crown and nobility, and emancipation did not mark its severance. In return for ceding their right to own serfs, the nobles retained a great deal, especially the privileges of their order and, if they were landlords, manorial rights. The old regime's preference for nobility remained, allowing them to fill the offices of state and to continue exercising control over local government through rights of lordship. Nobles, moreover, had several good reasons for accepting emancipation. Originally, serfdom had addressed the problem of underpopulation and its exacerbation by peasant flight. Its basic aim was to preserve a sufficiently populated estate. Later, its purpose was to provide labour for demesne farming, in the relative absence of labour for hire. By the end of the eighteenth century, these preconditions had faded away. With more would-be tenants than tenures, and with a landless labour force now available, serfdom ceased to have much point. Furthermore, serfdom had obvious drawbacks from the lord's point of view, in sanctioning hereditary tenures and fixed dues, and in providing labour services that were often poorly performed. One solution for the lords was to give up demesne farming; another was to pursue it more vigorously with waged workers, and to extend the demesne at the expense of the tenures, which now became unnecessary as a source of labour. Left to themselves, nobles were slow to act in emancipating their peasants; but, pressed by the crown, they had no good reason to resist.[7]

A major step in the abolition of serfdom was undoubtedly the French Revolution, for the example of agrarian reform that it set was not only effective in France but also enormously influential in the rest of Europe.[8] Central to the French Revolution was a programme of agrarian reform which was authorized by the National Assembly on 4 August 1789. Inspired by physiocratic ideas and Voltaire's personal campaign against *mainmorte*, it was implemented in response to the widespread peasant revolts of the previous spring. Its purpose was to convert a militant peasantry to the revolutionary cause. Besides the abolition of serfdom, which by this time affected little more than the eastern border provinces of France, the August legislation proposed to demolish the manorial system by terminating seigneurial rights of jurisdiction and by allowing the *censitaires* (copy-holders) to convert themselves into freeholders. Conversion involved the payment of redemption to the former lords. However, this was found objectionable by the peasantry, who refused to pay and continued to rebel: so much so that in 1793, in a further bid to retain peasant support, redemption was abolished. These reforms did not benefit the whole peasantry, for those who leased demesne remained unprotected tenants; yet they represented a new type of agrarian settlement that had enormous appeal to peasants, free and serf. For the latter, the prospect of receiving not only free status but also freehold land was a great improvement on the emancipations that had preceded the French Revolution, which had left peasant land under manorial lordship.[9]

There is no reason to believe that such radical reform was, in the first instance, a simple response to peasant demands. The revolts from which the reforms first sprang – the disturbances of early 1789 – had objected to aspects of the manorial system but had not demanded its complete abolition, largely because peasant communities had much to gain from its continuation, notably in the form of hereditary tenures, fixed rents and rights of common. However, offered freeholds in place of *censives*, they had no reason to object. Educated by the legislation of 4 August to accept the demolition of the manorial system, a central pillar of the old regime, the peasantry quickly adapted their aims to ensure that, by opposing redemption, it would cost them nothing.

In this manner, a policy of agrarian reform was created which must have appealed strongly to the peasantry, if not to the lords. It was carried beyond the French borders as the French revolutionary armies conquered and occupied. By 1815 not only the serf remnants of western Europe but also the predominantly serf societies of certain parts of Poland had been liberated with land, the result of the French occupation of the Low Countries and the Rhenish states, followed by Napoleon's establishment of the Kingdom of Westphalia and the Duchy of Warsaw.[10] The impact of the French agrarian programme reached even further as the surviving *anciens régimes* were driven to apply agrarian reforms in the cause of self-preservation. Defeated by the French in 1806, the Hohenzollerns in the following year abolished serfdom; threatened by Napoleon, the Romanovs sanctioned serf emancipation in Estonia, after its nobility had proposed it as a means of pacifying peasant revolt, and later extended the same terms to the other Baltic provinces.[11]

Following Napoleon's fall, agrarian reforms were undone as the *ancien régime* re-established itself; but the process of reaction was far from complete. Influencing the attitude of governments to serfdom in the early nineteenth century were two basic policies of agrarian reform: one simultaneously gave serfs freehold land and free status; the other – first applied in Austria-Bohemia prior to the French Revolution, and then in Prussia and the Baltic provinces – relieved serfs of their subject status but did not, coincidentally, improve their security of tenure. In Prussia, as in Austria-Bohemia, the freed peasants were left with their manorial holdings; in the Baltic provinces, the freed peasants were redefined as leaseholders, irrespective of whether or not they occupied demesne land, but remained under manorial lordship. The retention of the manorial system, then, provided another reason for the nobility to accept the abolition of serfdom.[12]

The process of serf emancipation was taken a stage further by another bout of revolution. The coincidence of peasant militancy and political revolution in 1848 helped to dismantle the manorial system completely. In the circumstances, revolutionary and conservative governments were constrained to act alike. Consequently, counter-revolution could not recover what revolution had jettisoned. To appeal to the peasantry, the manorial system had to be destroyed but some equivalent of their manorial rights had to be preserved.[13] Thus, in the Habsburg and Hohenzollern lands, peasants, who had been emancipated many years before, received in 1848 freehold rights to their farms, in return for making redemption payments to their former lords. Exceptionally in Hungary, Habsburg attempts at emancipation in the late eighteenth century had failed in the face of noble opposition. In 1848, however, the Hungarian nobles needed to enlist peasant support in their nationalist resistance to Habsburg rule. To create a consensus with the peasantry, they therefore conceded emancipation along with the conferment of freehold rights. The termination of the Hungarian Revolution by Habsburg force did not undo these agrarian reforms but led to their confirmation, as the Habsburg government applied the same policy in order to persuade the peasantry to accept its rule.[14]

By the mid-1850s, serfdom still survived in Europe – to the extent of over 10 million serfs – but it was largely confined to Russia (including Lithuania) and Romania. In both cases the revolutionary era had left its mark; and the basic question now was not how best to retain serfdom but how best to dispose of it. In Russia, the evident disadvantages of serfdom – in a European world that had rejected it – became utterly clear as peasants repeatedly rebelled and as Russia was soundly defeated in the Crimean War. In the light of what had already happened, the options open to the Russian government were limited. To please the nobles, it would have been best to emancipate the serfs without land rights, but the government was fully aware that this policy had already been applied with disastrous consequences in the Baltic provinces; and, moved by the memory of the great peasant wars of the seventeenth and eighteenth centuries, it could not afford to risk provoking further rural unrest.[15] And so, when military defeat appeared to justify reform, it proceeded, in the French revolutionary manner, to abolish serfdom and manorialism at the same time, offering, however, in compensation to the nobility, either the right to retain the latter if they so wished, or, if they chose to give it up, to receive a redemption payment, plus a generous allocation of forest and waste. The emancipation of 1861, moreover, occurred at a time of rapid population growth which guaranteed for the nobles the opportunity to pay low wages and charge high rents.

European serfdom was terminated by Romania's Rural Law of 14 August 1864. Besides being the last country in Europe to get rid of serfdom, Romania had been the first to ban personal bondage (*Leibeigenschaft*): in

1746 for Wallachia and in 1749 for Moldavia. The aim had been to attract home the peasants who had fled from the war of 1736–9 between Russia, Austria and Turkey, which was mostly fought on Wallachian soil. Serfdom remained, however, in tenurial form, with peasants tied to the estate. This was first authorized by the binding settlement of 1595, yet another response to peasant flight.[16]

Since the 1830s, Wallachia and Moldavia had been under a Russian protectorate; but this ended in 1856, a consequence of Russia's defeat in the Crimean War. The Romanian serfs had engaged in the revolutions of 1848, but no agrarian reforms had resulted since Russian and Turkish troops had marched into the country and restored order. Thereafter agrarian reform was barred by the Romanian nobles who put up a successful resistance, both in 1858, when international pressure placed it within a programme of modernization designed to establish a strong independent buffer state between Russia and Turkey, and in 1862, when the noble-dominated national assembly of the new state of Romania rejected the government's plans to relieve the peasants' lot. Responsible for terminating the Romanian serf regime was the recently elected prince, Alexander John Cuza. He was hardly an enlightened despot but rather a radical lesser noble who, having studied in Paris and participated in the Moldavian Revolution of 1848, was heir to the French revolutionary tradition on agrarian reform. Following the example of Louis Napoleon, he proceeded by *coup d'état* in March 1864, when he dismissed the resistant Romanian national assembly. He then secured, through a plebiscite, the authority to act by decree, which he used – in the manner originally created by the French revolutionaries of the 1790s, and recently applied in Russia – to grant the Romanian peasantry not only free status but also freehold rights to the lands they farmed. This reform passed into law following the establishment of a new national assembly that was less dominated by the noble interest.[17]

Responsible, then, for ending serfdom in Europe were three elements of the old order, each acting to defend its self-interest in the unsettling circumstances of revolution and a rapid population growth that was yet to be alleviated by urbanization, industrialization or emigration to America. The moving ideology stemmed from the Enlightenment, transmuted by the French Revolution.[18] First, the crown took action often with policies formulated by ministers who were landless nobles. Before the French Revolution, it did so in order to acquire a larger share of the peasantry's surplus through reducing the proportion the nobility exacted as serf owners. It also felt that the state would become less vulnerable internationally if it rested upon a prosperous peasantry and was not disrupted by peasant rebellion. The answer seemed to lie in the abolition of serfdom. After the French Revolution, monarchs took action to save themselves from an alliance between peasants and revolutionaries, as well as to modernize the old regime. Second, serfdom came under attack from peasants made militant by land hunger, landlord oppression, and rumours of emancipation elsewhere or in prospect. Peasant revolt had already proved effective in disposing of serfdom before the French Revolution, thanks to the way the Habsburgs had responded to it in Bohemia and Austria. It became even more potent in the situation of revolution when measures to redress agrarian discontent were seen as a vital means of enlisting popular support. In addition, emancipation could be promoted by serf owners, usually members of the noble order, who, as leaders of nationalist struggles – for example, in Poland against the consequences of Partition, in Hungary against Habsburg rule – could propose it to secure peasant backing for their cause or, as in the Baltic provinces, to improve the management of their estates. Elsewhere, they were won over by generous emancipation settlements, which allowed them to retain their manorial rights in spite of the termination of serfdom; or granted them considerable rewards, in the form of redemption payments from the liberated peasants; or awarded them the right to clear the freed peasants off the land. Generally, they were won over by the realization that their farming enterprises could be more efficiently worked with hired labour and that, as landlords, they stood to benefit from substituting free leasehold for servile tenures. Arguably, although suggested by the Enlightenment and triggered by revolution, serfdom was abolished because the old order no longer had any real need of it.[19] As Jerome Blum suggested, of little import in the process of abolition was the impact of a capitalist bourgeoisie. Industrial or agricultural revolutions had little effect, largely because, in the servile lands, industrialization had yet to take place, while commercial farming had been established centuries before in connection with serfdom. As for the bourgeois revolutionaries who questioned the manorial system, they tended to be professional men advocating agrarian reform for political rather than economic reasons.[20]

The termination of New World slavery

New World slavery was another victim of revolution. Yet it demonstrated a remarkable capacity to survive in the face of moral outrage and attempts at abolition. This was not only because of its economic usefulness, but also because whites found it difficult to accept that blacks were, intrinsically, no different from themselves. In addition, an abiding respect for the rights of property played its part. Sustaining American slavery in the early nineteenth century was the strong demand for sugar and cotton, a consequence of urbanization and industrialization in the north-eastern states of the USA and north-western Europe. To meet this demand, the slave trade continued, transporting over 3 million slaves from Africa. Another 1,300,000 slaves figured in the internal slave trades of the USA and Brazil. In the early nineteenth century, the slave plantation remained a vigorous and profitable business, not only in the Deep South but also in Cuba, Puerto Rico and Brazil. Slave numbers in the Americas increased from 3 to 6 million between 1800 and 1860. The amount of land worked as slave plantations likewise doubled, thanks to expansion in the USA, Cuba and Brazil.[21]

Slavery was also sustained by the belated development of an anti-slave movement, coupled with the moderation of its initial demands for reform. Before the mid-eighteenth century the protests made by whites against enslavement were few and far between, but then, from the mid-eighteenth century, slavery came to be criticized by the Scottish political economists (notably George Wallace, Francis Hutcheson, Adam Smith and John Millar), somewhat ambivalently by Montesquieu, and more directly by the French physiocrats. In his *Spirit of Laws* (1748), Montesquieu had declared slavery to be intrinsically bad. This was because it awarded neither slaves nor masters cause to treat each other in a civilized manner – the slaves lacking 'a motive of virtue', the masters lacking any restraint upon their cruelty. He also condemned slavery as unnatural on the grounds that 'all men are born equal', arguing that it was therefore alien to all political systems, except for a despotism that ruled the free as if they were slaves. But then, instead of advocating the termination of slavery, he seemed to suggest that, in certain circumstances, it might be justified. Focusing upon black slavery in the Americas, he even offered reasons for its maintenance. Finally, he proposed no other remedy than careful regulation.[22]

Pursuing the utility argument, the Scottish political economists and the French physiocrats proceeded to show that, compared with free labour, slave labour was not particularly advantageous. Waged workers, they argued, were more productive than slaves and, because of high mortality and naturally poor work, slave labour was not cheap but dear. All of them presented slavery as a primitive mode of production, something associated with barbarism rather than civilization. Added to the objection based on economic efficiency, then, was one of style.[23] Yet these arguments failed to make slave owners alter their ways. After all, the latter knew that, contrary to these academic reservations, slavery in the Americas formed an integral part of a highly profitable system of agriculture. Their faith in slave labour was confirmed by the disastrous effects of emancipation upon the economies of St Domingue (Haiti) in the 1790s and of the British West Indies in the 1830s. They were also aware of the terrible plight of free factory workers in the US North and in Britain. In comparison with them, slaves appeared to be well off.[24] And did not the example of ancient Greece and Rome demonstrate how slavery and civilization could walk hand in hand?

In the late eighteenth century, there also emerged a Christian objection to slavery. This started with the Quaker claim that *all* men were equal before God. By the late 1780s, it was also voiced by Methodists, Presbyterians, Evangelical Anglicans and Unitarians. The religious objection presented slavery as utterly wicked, a terrible taint on the individuals who practised it and the nations that tolerated its existence.[25] The key work was John Wesley's *Thoughts on Slavery* (1774), the effectiveness of which derived partly from personal experience (for Wesley had spent time in Georgia and, by revealing that whites were just as capable as blacks of working in the tropical heat, he could cast serious doubt upon one main justification for slavery), and partly from the breadth of his attack.[26] Slavery was presented as totally unchristian since Christians should surely do unto *all* others as they would be done by; but it was also condemned on secular grounds. The tract approved of Blackstone's opinion that the classical justifications for enslavement – that is, captivity in war, sale and birth – were 'built upon false foundations'. It concluded that no form of slavery was 'consistent with any degree of natural justice'.[27] It also related slavery to the English libertarian tradition by proclaiming: 'liberty is the right of every human creature . . . Give liberty to whom liberty is due: that is, to every child of man, to every partaker of human nature.'[28] It condemned the conduct of both slave-traders and planters as brutish.[29] In contrast with the objections of the Enlightenment, Wesley's were unequivocal. Moreover, he simply but cleverly showed that Christianity had gone back on itself: having heroically liberated Europe from the slavery imparted by Greeks, Romans and the German tribes, it had now despicably imposed it upon the Americas.[30] The only remedy, he proposed, was to abandon slavery in the New World; otherwise, at the Day of Judgement, 'the great God [will] deal with you as you have dealt with [the slaves], and require all their blood at your hands'.[31]

The breadth and directness of Wesley's attack on slavery allowed it to influence the attitude of Enlightened thought. This was evident in its impact upon another highly influential criticism, a brief essay entitled 'African slavery in America' that appeared in 1775, published in the *Pennsylvania Journal* by someone who signed himself 'Justice and Humanity'. The essay was clearly beholden to Wesley, using his phrase 'man-stealers' to condemn slavery as theft. It also employed Wesley's arguments for showing that slavery was alien to Christianity. The author was Thomas Paine, who at the time was busy implanting the English libertarian tradition in the North American colonies in the attempt to persuade them to break free of the English crown. In the same essay, he addressed Americans with the pertinent question: since they were seeking to avoid enslavement, how could they justify imposing it upon others?[32] The outcome of the essay was the establishment of the first anti-slavery society in the world, formed in Philadelphia on 14 April 1775. The essay's effectiveness did not stop there, for the first emancipation ever enacted, in Pennsylvania five years later, contained a preamble based upon it.[33]

Stirred by these intellectual and moral objections, a popular anti-slavery movement had developed by the late 1780s, in Britain and North America. It became especially strong in Britain where, in 1791–2, 400,000 adults – one out of every eleven – signed petitions calling for Parliament to abolish the slave trade. In 1814, one out of every eight adults, 750,000 signatories, petitioned the government to secure an international agreement to end the slave trade at the Congress of Vienna; while, in 1832–3, Parliament received petitions signed by 1.5 million adults – one out of every seven – to end slavery altogether.[34] Anti-slavery, not surprisingly, had a more chequered and less effective career in the USA. In the South, where the slave planta-tion was clearly a source of great wealth, closing down the external slave trade posed no problem, given the capacity of the slave population to more than reproduce itself; but to end slavery itself was regarded as inconceivable: a view fully justified, it was felt, by the economic decline the Caribbean emancipations of the 1790s and the 1830s had precipitated. In the North a combination of Enlightenment thinking and religious evangelism generated anti-slavery sentiment, just as it had done in England. But the anti-slavery movement in the USA encountered major stumbling-blocks – notably its total incapacity to move the South, and the tendency in the North to give priority to issues of self-interest.[35]

The reform proposed by most of these movements did not, to begin with, demand immediate abolition. The initial mode of attack was obliquely to call for the ending of the slave trade and better treatment of slaves. The former, it was felt, would lead to the latter. If emancipation was considered at all, it was to be gradual: to be granted to the children of slaves upon attaining a certain age, rather than to be immediately extended to all slaves. Against the complete removal of slavery was the feeling, shared by reformers and planters, that slaves were not ready for liberation. Regarded as subhuman because of their blackness, it was felt that, at least for the time being, they were best left in bondage. Also held against them was their propertylessness. To give them the social right of freedom was thought, at least in Britain, to be as dire and dangerous as granting political rights to the unpropertied white masses – the swinish multitude. Also barring the way to abolition was the slave's legal definition as a piece of property. Compulsory emancipation would therefore affront property rights: something immoral and totally unjust. The offence to property could be avoided, but only by a system of owner consent and compensation, a slow and expensive process. Since slaves in general, unlike serfs, could not be expected to find a financial means of redemption, the money would have to come from taxation, another serious snag. This problem was eventually solved by obliging slaves to redeem themselves through labour. Thus, although freed in 1880, Cuban slaves had to indemnify their masters by serving them for another six years. The Cuban *patronato* had its equivalent in the British 'apprenticeship' system which, in 1834, had likewise imposed upon the freed a further six-year service to their former masters.

As with the termination of serfdom, so with the end of slavery, political revolution played a vital part. Establishing the idea that slavery should be removed completely was first the American Revolution and its impact upon the northern and central states of the Union. Taking the message of the new constitution to heart, and able to dispense with slavery because their citizens found it of limited economic value, all these states formulated policies for ending slavery between 1780 and 1804; as did the new states of Latin America when they rejected Spanish rule in the nineteenth century.[36] Yet this was very much an American affair. Apart from Spain, it had little effect upon the European slave-owning powers. In persuading them to ban slavery, the conjunction of two other revolutions – the French and the Haitian – was of outstanding importance.

The Caribbean Republic of Haiti was established in 1804. Previously it had been the slave colony of St Domingue, a French possession attached to the slave colony of Santo Domingo, a Spanish possession. In 1789 St Domingue was the largest and most productive colony in the Caribbean, inhabited by 500,000 slaves, 30,000 whites and 28,000 free coloured. The French Revolution itself did not produce an immediate demand for the abolition of slavery, just as it did not produce an immediate demand for the abolition of serfdom either. These demands were imposed upon it, the one by the popular pressure of peasant revolts at home, the other by slave revolt on St Domingue. The latter revolt flourished in the circumstances of conflict between the National Assembly in Paris and the royalist planters of St Domingue, as well as between the planters and the free coloured on the island who, moved by the French Revolution, were demanding the same civil rights as the white settlers. The slave revolt was clearly moved by the French Revolution, and this was evident in its slogan: 'Listen to the voice of liberty which speaks in the hearts of all.' It involved thousands of slaves who besieged the colonial assembly in Le Cap and raided the plantations, where they slaughtered the white planters and their overseers. In June 1793, following attempts by the English and Spanish to annex St Domingue, and acting in the belief that the security of the colony lay with the slaves – since they had already proved their military effectiveness – the French revolutionary commissioners in St Domingue offered arms and liberty to the rebel bands, and a month later decreed the liberation of all slaves within the colony. The decree had the desired effect in retaining the colony under French rule. In April 1794 the leader of the blacks, Toussaint L'Ouverture, who, having been previously manumitted, was a slave owner himself, as well as a monarchist, became a republican upon learning that, on 4 February, the French Convention had decreed the abolition of slavery throughout the French colonies. The outcome was a sustained war in the Caribbean, the French revolutionary government allied with the former slaves, while the British expeditionary forces supported the planters. Militarily, the French strategy proved correct. By early 1798, the English military position had collapsed. But then, with their control of St Domingue and the other French colonies assured, the French sought to restore slavery in 1802. This precipitated a black revolt against colonial rule, with the rebel armies of St Domingue tearing the white band from the tricolour and fighting under a red and blue standard, the initials R.F. (i.e. République Française) replaced by the motto 'Liberty and Death'. Having cleared the British troops off the island in 1798, the black army now, in the course of 1803–4, removed the French.[37] In January 1804 the independent Republic of Haiti was established which restored the emancipation first achieved a decade earlier and retracted in 1802. This abolition represented the first to occur in a society where slavery remained central to the economy. It liberated 80 per cent of the slaves living in the French Caribbean.[38]

In Haiti, then, emancipation resulted from the overthrow by a radical black revolution of a conservatizing white revolution. Elsewhere in the

French Caribbean, slavery was restored and persisted until the French revolution of 1848 when – out of the blue, but presumably in recollection of the undone emancipation of 1793, and undoubtedly in response to slave disorders aroused by rumours of imminent emancipation – another emancipation decree was issued with immediate effect in Martinique, Guadeloupe and French Guiana. By July 1849 abolition had been formalized in the French Caribbean, the former slave owners receiving a generous compensation of half the value of each slave. The emancipation in Haiti, and the violent manner in which it was achieved, had reverberated throughout the Caribbean, making it clear to planters what resistant slaves could achieve, and revealing to slaves that complete emancipation was a distinct possibility. Fears and expectations were thus placed on a more credible plane. Of similar effect in the Caribbean was the French revolution of 1848. As rumours of actual and impending emancipation incited slave revolts in the Dutch Virgin Islands and the Danish island of Ste Croix – revolts that the planters were unable to quell – slavery was abolished in the bid to restore order, leaving slavery in the Caribbean confined to the Spanish colonies of Cuba and Puerto Rico.[39]

The abolition of Caribbean slavery was furthered by the parliamentary act of 1833 outlawing slavery in all British colonies. In Britain, anti-slavery movements were, by this time, fifty years old. Mostly, they had emphasized the need for reform rather than outright emancipation. The advocated policy of stopping the supply of fresh slaves from Africa had been highly successful: producing the statute of 1807, which forbade the importation of African slaves to the British colonies, and the joint decision reached at the Congress of Vienna (1815) to condemn the Atlantic slave trade. At this time, however, and in reaction to the emancipation policy followed by revolutionary France, the liberation of slaves – rather like republicanism, democracy and atheism – was seen as a highly dangerous concept; and, like the extension of the franchise, it could only be granted when seen as necessary to preserve the aristocracy's control of the political system. The point was made by the leading British anti-slaver William Wilberforce who, bearing in mind the savagery associated with slave revolts, considered the blacks not yet 'fit . . . to bear emancipation': a response he made when gradual emancipation was proposed during the parliamentary passage of the Slave Trade Bill in 1807. Along with many others, Wilberforce thought that the termination of the trade would solve the problem of slavery, by obliging the owners to take better care of their slaves. In the meantime, he felt that, in preparation for their eventual liberation – he had hopes that they would be 'gradually transmitted into a free peasantry' – slaves should have the chance to civilize themselves by converting to Christianity, while planters needed to be reminded of their Christian duty.[40]

Nonetheless, the transatlantic slave trade continued to flourish in the early nineteenth century, allowing the French to restock their Caribbean colonies and enabling Cuba and Brazil to extend their slave plantations. This failure to stem the trade not only kept the anti-slave movement very much alive but also drove it to pursue other policies. Thus in 1823, Wilberforce, Lord Brougham and other veteran opponents of the slave trade established the catchily named Society for Mitigating and Gradually Abolishing the State of Slavery throughout the British Dominions. Its emphasis was upon persuading slave owners to manumit worthy slaves, to reduce working hours, especially on Sundays, to limit corporal punishment, to permit a free-womb policy, and to increase slave rights. Yet no sooner was this ameliorative policy formulated than it was dramatically confronted with the shocking demand for immediate emancipation. This was made in the pamphlet 'Immediate not Gradual Abolition'. Composed by Elizabeth Heyricke, it was supported by a number of women's groups, who were partly reacting against Wilberforce's disapproval of female involvement in the anti-slavery movement.[41] By 1830, the Society for Mitigation had been replaced by the Anti-Slavery Society, which was dedicated to the cause of immediate freedom for all slaves and which, in the early 1830s, commanded many more followers than the related movement for extending the parliamentary franchise.[42] Sustaining the 'emancipation now' movement was not simply moral outrage against an aristocracy of planters but also the practical consideration that, if slaves became wage-earners, the Caribbean colonies might provide a better market for British manufactures.

Emancipation in the British colonies followed the 1832 Reform Act, which made Parliament more susceptible to public pressure; but it was achieved thanks to the huge concessions granted to the planters: a compensation payment of £20 million, plus the requirement that slaves should remain attached to their former master and work a ten-hour day unpaid for another six years.[43]

Yet it would be misleading to explain the emancipation settlement simply in terms of peaceful pressures, negotiated terms and parliamentary deliberation. Slave revolts played a vital part, notably in 1823 on the plantations east of the Demarera River in British Guiana, and, most important of all, at Christmas 1831 in western Jamaica – a huge uprising involving 20,000 slaves led by the Baptist lay preacher, Sam Sharpe.[44] Intensifying the rage of the slaves was the belief that the planters were increasing their labour services, in compensation for the decline in the slave population the stoppage of the transatlantic slave trade had caused. In this respect, the abolition of the slave trade appeared to be having just the opposite effect to that predicted by Wilberforce. What moved the Jamaican slaves to take direct action – the Demarera slaves had been similarly affected – was the rumour that in London measures of slave amelioration had been passed which the planters were ignoring. The impact of this revolt was so great that, upon hearing of it, the British government decided to free the slaves, even though, in April 1831, it had declared that it 'would have nothing to do with immediate emancipation'.[45]

Although the slave-trade abolitionists appeared somewhat misguided in believing that their policy would radically improve the lot of the slaves, those who thought it would undermine slavery, through making slave regimes more difficult to run, were close to the mark. The undermining process took time, but in Cuba (with the external trade ended in 1867 and slavery abolished in 1880), Brazil (with the external trade effectively ended in 1851 and slavery abolished in 1888), and the British West Indies (with the trade ended in 1807 and slavery abolished in 1834), stopping the transatlantic slave trade undoubtedly prepared for the ending of slavery. This was due to the labour problems the planters faced as high mortality, low fertility and manumission seriously reduced the slave population.[46] Yet exceptions existed. In Barbados, the slave population actually increased between 1808 and the 1830s, from 75,000 to 85,000; and, in all likelihood, Jamaica would have achieved a similar growth if slavery had not been outlawed when it was.[47] In this respect, the Emancipation Act of 1833 came just in the nick of time, terminating a system that would have become sustainable once the slave population had acquired the ability to reproduce itself. This is exactly what happened in the US slave states, where the ending of the transatlantic slave trade in 1808 was followed by a four-fold increase in the slave population. Moreover, since in the US South no prohibition was placed on the internal slave trade, the termination of the external slave trade had next to no effect in preparing the way for emancipation.

But while slavery continued to flourish in the southern states, various immediate and gradualist policies of emancipation limited its scope elsewhere in the Union. Following the American Revolution of the 1770s and the 1780s, and acting in accordance with its precepts of equality and liberty for 'all men', slavery was outlawed in Vermont and Massachusetts, as well as excluded from the North-West Territories. It was also phased out in Rhode Island, Connecticut, Pennsylvania, New York and New Jersey, by means of laws that declared children born of slave mothers to be free, while requiring them to serve their mother's master until the age of twenty-eight.[48] From the government's point of view, the advantage of a gradualist system of emancipation was that it avoided the need to offer slave owners financial compensation for loss of property. From the slave owners' point of view, it conveniently allowed them to retain the labour of those freed by birth until they were in their late twenties. The free-womb policy was not confined to the USA. It was widely applied in Latin America where, during the anti-colonial revolutions of the early nineteenth century, the republicans used various measures of emancipation to persuade the slaves to serve in their armies. It was eventually adopted in Cuba, Puerto Rico (both in 1870) and Brazil (1871).[49] Where it notably failed to take root was in the US South.

Contradictory policies of emancipation and tolerance created within the United States two very different, even alien, societies.[50] Binding them together until the 1840s was the economic importance of the slave South, and also the fact that both societies were mainly rural and agricultural. But then the economic bond was severed as a rapidly industrialized and urbanized north-east established a special complementary relationship with the agricultural Midwest.[51] Holding North and South together had also been the political dominance the South had held in the Union through its ability to control the majority of seats in Congress, and regularly to fill the presidency with one of its own.[52] But this suddenly lapsed in 1860 when the Republican party was able to take charge with electoral support confined to the North.[53] Not even religion preserved a bond between North and South since, specifically on the issue of slave abolition, the Methodists, Baptists and Presbyterians – all the evangelical fruit of the Second Great Awakening – had divided on a regional basis, the northern division objecting to slavery, the southern division approving its preservation.[54]

Since it was no longer dependent on it, why should the North have objected when the South sought to secede in 1861? The issue of slave emancipation was not the cause, since, in the first instance, the federal government was prepared to concede the continuation of slavery if the South rejoined the Union.[55] To the fore, however, was an animus against southern society which was seen as 'old order': aristocratic, unprogressive, violent, economically stagnant, corrupt, idle, licentious – in fact, 'one great Sodom'.[56] As the South held out, principally in fear that the North would seek to reform it, the North became resolved upon its reincorporation for that very purpose. During the course of the consequent war, slave emancipation emerged as a card well worth playing, especially in view of slave discontent and desertion in the South, and the need to remotivate the northern troops. Emancipation, then, became a political device for winning the war, its use encouraged partly by the centrality of slavery to southern culture, but also by the evident way slave resistance was sapping the strength of the South. Emancipation also became worth supporting because it provided a platform that the various interests in the Republican coalition could share with some commitment. Although absent at the start, slave emancipation had emerged, by early 1863, as a leading aim of the war.[57] As for the final abolition of North American slavery in 1865, and the form it assumed, this was simply due to the North's conquest of the slave South and its willingness, from the vantage of victory, to impose an emancipation settlement which concessively preserved the great estate and white supremacy, replacing slavery with segregation, but granted no compensation whatsoever to the former masters, either in labour obligations from the freed or in redemption money from the state.

The victory of the North over the South released from slavery 4 million human beings, but over 2 million slaves still remained in the Americas: at least 300,000 in Cuba and 1,700,000 in Brazil. In Cuba the abolition of slavery was achieved, in the typical American manner, as the by-product of an anti-colonial war. Moreover, in that it resulted from a military struggle between the planters of the west and the non-plantation society of the east, it bore some resemblance to what had happened in the American Civil War.[58]

Central to the process of abolition in Cuba was the Ten Years War (1868–78). During it, the two sides – the Spanish government and the eastern rebels – made competitive concessions to the enslaved in order to strengthen their own position on the island. Thus, by mid-1870, the Spanish government had passed the Moret Law which authorized a free-womb policy and liberated all slaves at the age of sixty. So as not to alienate the planters, the law allowed them to retain their other slaves, as well as the unpaid labour of newborn slave children until their eighteenth birthday. The essential purpose of the law was to persuade both slaves and the free coloured not to become anti-colonial rebels.[59] Its specific aim was to counter the rebel reforms, which, in December 1868, had promised the slaves abolition once the revolution had succeeded, and then, in February 1869, had decreed immediate liberation with some redemption payment to the masters. By July, this had been altered to immediate liberation conditional upon the ex-slaves remaining tied for a time to a master. Such reforms and revisions were clearly designed to appeal to various interests: not just those of the slaves and free blacks but also those of the slave owners, even the US government. Faced by the Moret Law of July 1870, the rebels were driven a step further. The following December they granted immediate, complete and unconditional freedom.[60] In the early 1870s, compelled by a vigorous abolitionist movement in Spain, the Spanish government proceeded to stamp out slavery in Puerto Rico in 1873, which raised hopes and fears in Cuba. But before the latter could follow suit, the military *coup* in Spain of 1874 suspended the Spanish *cortes* and banned further public meetings of the Spanish Abolitionist Society, a ban that lasted until 1879.[61]

In undermining Cuban slavery, the Moret Law was undoubtedly important, especially in conjunction with the effective stoppage the Spanish government placed upon the external slave trade in 1867. Between 1840 and 1866, 246,800 slaves were imported into Cuba, mostly from Africa, causing a 13.8 per cent increase in the island's slave population between 1846 and 1861, and helping to maintain the island's slave system in a flourishing state. With the external trade stopped, the slave population began to contract, largely because of the high rate of manumission, at a time when Cuba's sugar industry was still expanding. This created the imminent prospect of a severe labour problem – if, that is, the plantations continued to rely upon slave labour.[62] The contraction was quickened by the Moret Law, so much so that the slave population fell by a dramatic 46 per cent between 1862 and 1877: from over 300,000 to under 200,000. True, an internal trade maintained a means of replenishing the sugar plantations, but, with slaves increasingly expensive to buy, thanks to the Moret Law and the ending of the external slave trade, it came at a price.[63] Other sources of labour undoubtedly existed. The white population was growing rapidly in the late nineteenth century – by 73.4 per cent between 1846 and 1861, and by a further 22 per cent between 1862 and 1877 – as was the population of free coloureds, with an increase of 48 per cent between 1846 and 1861.[64] But neither offered much scope for plantation field work while it continued to be associated with slave labour. Coming to the planters' rescue, it seemed, was servile Chinese labour. By 1861, 34,000 Chinese worked as indentured labourers on Cuban plantations, and between 1847 and 1874, 125,000 had been imported on eight-year contracts. But then, reacting to reports of maltreatment, the Chinese government prohibited this trade, leaving a major problem still to be solved.[65]

The anti-colonial revolution failed, for the rebels were obliged to sign the Pact of Zanjon in 1878 and to accept that Cuba would remain within the Spanish Empire. This submission annulled the rebels' anti-slavery legislation. Nonetheless, the abrupt reinstatement of bondage was too much for the slaves to accept, even more so as the terms of the pact freed those slaves who had served as soldiers on both sides, to the number of 16,000. By desertion, strikes and cane-burning – to the cry 'No freedom, no cane' – slaves in 1878–9 mounted a further wave of resistance to the planter regime.[66] In reaction, and fearing a resurgence of anti-colonialism, the Spanish government acted promptly. It abolished slavery in January 1880 but, to appease the planters, it required the freed, as a means of redeeming themselves through labour, to serve their former masters for a further eight years, thus allowing a respite for solving the labour problem that now hung over Cuba's plantation economy.[67]

In Brazil, the cause of slave abolition lacked the chance to promote itself through the medium of an anti-colonial revolution. Independence from Portugal had been simply and uniquely achieved in the 1820s by a *coup d'état* in which a member of the Portuguese royal family assumed the title of emperor of Brazil and, acting upon that authority, took possession of the country as an independent state. Consequently, an anti-slave movement was a very late development: hardly existent, in fact, before the 1860s, and of little effect before the 1880s. Not until 1880 was the Brazilian Anti-Slavery Society founded.[68]

Proposals for the reform of the slave system initially came from outside or from above. The reforms initiated outside the country were delayed in effect, largely because of the lack of internal commitment. Thus, the British persuaded the Brazilian government to prohibit its external slave trade in 1830, but this trade brazenly continued, and was only terminated in 1850 when a British naval squadron obliged the Brazilian government to enforce the law of 1830 and stamp out the profitable contraband in African slaves.[69] The reforms from above largely followed the example set by other countries. Moved by emancipation in the USA, Emperor Pedro II in the 1860s backed the idea of reforming the Brazilian slave system. However, he had to tread carefully so as not to provoke a Republican backlash from the Brazilian planters.[70] Following the Spanish example set in Cuba and Puerto Rico, the Brazilian government proposed a free-womb policy that became the Rio Branco Law of 1871. This gave masters the choice of receiving compensation either in state bonds or in the right to use the unpaid labour of the freed slave children until their twenty-first birthday.[71]

Like Cuba, Brazil had been heavily dependent on the African slave trade. With the trade stopped, the slave population contracted fast. Having peaked at 2.5 million in 1850, it fell to 1,715,000 in 1864, 1,500,000 in 1872, 1,241,000 in 1884 and 723,400 in 1887.[72] The effect of this contraction was mixed, however, because of the survival of an internal, interprovincial slave trade which allowed the more prosperous plantations, especially those in the south-central coffee-growing regions of São Paulo and Rio de Janeiro, to replenish their slave populations.[73] Nonetheless, unlike Cuban slavery – which had to be legally abolished before it was effectively terminated – Brazilian slavery faded away; so much so that the Abolition Act of 1888 simply recognized a *fait accompli*.[74] Instrumental in this evaporating process was, first, a powerful abolitionist movement which operated piecemeal in the localities, rather than by seeking to control politicians and influence government policy. This was a consequence of the political system, which was confined in 1884 to an electorate of 140,000 in a total population of 12,000,000. Whereas the population generally was indifferent to, or against, slavery, the political nation had a vested interest in its preservation.[75] As a result, the abolitionists had no choice but to focus upon reforming local-ities. Their approach was to secure the emancipation of all resident slaves within a given area, such as a street, a township, a district or a province. This was accomplished by persuading masters to manumit their slaves, something they were prepared to do to avoid social censure. Making it easier for masters to free their slaves was the fact that the latter's market value had fallen sharply, the result of the abolitionists' success in dissuading Brazilians from seeking to acquire them. But also important in eliminating slavery was the willingness of slaves in large numbers to flee the plantations. Encouraging them to commit this illicit act was the establishment of free zones, where they could take refuge, as well as the aid secretly offered by abolitionists.

The abolitionist movement recruited from the entire range of society. Most supporters were undoubtedly driven to act by their own perception of the horrors of slavery, but they were also moved by a sense of national shame, and the concomitant belief that, for its salvation, Brazil had to be rescued from the clutches of a self-serving aristocracy. Bearing in mind Brazil's international isolation as a slave regime in the 1880s, the abolition-ists' intent was to redeem and modernize the country, initially by liberating it from slavery.[76]

The earliest successes of the movement were, not surprisingly, secured in provinces where slavery was of limited importance, notably in the far northerly province of Ceara which, between 1882 and 1884, was established as a *terra da luz*: free of slavery and a refuge for slaves fleeing from the old sugar provinces of Bahía, Pernambuco, Paraíba and Rio Grande do Norte. All this resulted from the arrival in the province of an abolitionist leader, José do Patrocinio, the descendant of a slave, along with his strategy of liberating specific areas, and the popular enthusiasm his approach and presence inspired.[77] Other provinces followed suit in 1884: Amazonas in the north-west, and Rio Grande do Sul in the far south. Amazonas had few slaves, and, what is more, they were mostly disposable since they tended to work in domestic service rather than production; but Rio Grande do Sul had 60,000 slaves, mostly employed in the beef industry. Caught up in the emancipatory fervour of the 1880s that originated in Ceara, two-thirds of its slaves were manumitted in August and September 1884.[78]

Yet the abolitionist cause was only won on a national scale thanks to the conversion of the rich, coffee-growing province of São Paulo. This happened in the period 1885–7. It again followed the procedure of establishing internal free zones, notably at Santos in 1886, and by encouraging slaves to leave the plantations and take refuge in them. By 1887, whole slave communities were on the move, either transferring to plantations that accepted them as free wage-earners or migrating to free zones. What is more, the army was now refusing to hunt down runaways. The danger of losing their labour force obliged the planters to propose abolition themselves, under terms that might allow them to retain it. To begin with, they freed the slaves on their own estates, placing them instead on labour contracts. But this did not stem the exodus. Eventually, planters cooperated to propose policies of abolition to the government.[79] The volte-face of the São Paulo planters caused the planters of other provinces, who likewise remained heavily dependent upon slave labour – in Bahía, Pernambuco, Minas Gerais and Rio de Janeiro – to follow their example.[80]

Making it relatively easy for planters to adapt to abolition at this late stage was the coincidental arrival of free labour from Italy – 32,000 in 1887, 90,000 in 1888. In addition, there was the massive untapped resource of free labour native to Brazil. The free population of Brazil had risen from 1,888,000 in 1817 to 8,530,000 in 1864. Much of it was impoverished but capable of surviving on the fruits of the forest, or by servicing the large townships. It had therefore remained independent of the plantations, which had traditionally preferred slaves to paying out wages. With slavery phased out by slave flight, and planters now driven to employ waged labour, the existence of this traditional resource, coupled with the arrival of Italians in large numbers, allowed the planters a practical means of breaking free of slave labour.[81] As a result, the planters made little objection to the Abolition Act of May 1888, even though it offered them no compensation whatsoever. In this latter respect, abolition followed the respectful but rigorous US pattern.[82]

Following the abolition of serfdom in Europe, peasants remained exploited by high rents and workers remained exploited by low wages, but this no longer had anything to do with legal status. All were equally free. In contrast, the termination of slavery generated servitude in other forms. Slave emancipation led to a slump in plantation production, the result of the failure to secure sufficient waged labour to maintain plantations running at their former cost efficiency. This stemmed from the antipathy of ex-slaves to work on plantations – the understandable result of bitter memories – the unwillingness of planters to pay reasonable wages, and the ability of former slaves to find an alternative livelihood, often as smallholders, artisans, traders and fishermen. To save the plantation economy, several devices were created, the effect of which was to replace slave labour with other forms of servile labour. Thus, to make ex-slaves work on the plantations, the law obliged them to continue in the employment of their former masters. Moreover, to ensure that wages were kept low, systems of indentured labour and debt bondage were widely used for importing foreign workers, mostly from Asia, whose labour was owned by those who bought it. All this meant that the abolition of slavery gave servitude a further lease of life, one that extended into the twentieth century. Furthermore, the abolition of serfdom released European societies from servitude only for a time. It returned with a vengeance in the form of the concentration camp.

12

The Survival of Servitude

Instead of slavery

Slavery in the Western world did not come to an end because it ceased to be economically viable. In the years leading up to abolition, the slave-operated plantation flourished as never before. The profitability of sugar, cotton, coffee and cocoa all justified its continuation, even its expansion.[1]

If slave labour were done away with, what would replace it? In the era of abolition an overpopulated Europe – with 145 million in 1750, reaching 265 million by 1850, and 440 million by 1900 – was shedding its surplus, much of it passing freely to the Americas or the overseas colonies, as shipping charges were reduced, as voyages became, thanks to the introduction of the steamship, shorter and less arduous, and as overseas governments, in search of white settlers, were prepared to provide Europeans with assisted passage. Yet European emigrants tended to go to temperate zones, whereas the plantations were mostly situated in the tropics. The exception was Brazil. There the province of São Paulo, a region of coffee plantations, attracted 800,000 Europeans, mostly Italians, between the late 1880s and 1907.[2]

Parts of Asia, notably China (with a population of 300 million in 1779, reaching 430 million by 1850) and India (with a population of 185 million in 1800, and of 285 million in 1900), also acquired surplus populations. Driven to emigrate in search of work, they were less averse than Europeans to tropical conditions. The problem, however, was to get Asian workers to plantations thousands of miles from home, for poverty mostly prevented them from funding their own passage; and, in their case, governments were unwilling to foot the bill, partly for racist reasons, partly in the belief that, as the major beneficiaries, the planters should make some contribution.[3] As for the planters, they were accustomed to paying a work-force with rations, not wages, and to controlling it through rights of chattel ownership. Conversion to a system in which the work-force owned, and disposed of, its own labour presented the planters, inevitably, with a major challenge, especially as slave labour had proved so profitable and convenient, whereas free labour threatened them with wage bills of crippling proportions. Once deprived of slavery, planters not surprisingly resorted to other systems of servitude.

Slave labour, in the first instance, was frequently replaced by an apprenticeship arrangement. This was sanctioned by the laws abolishing slavery, but limited to a non-renewable period. In addition, planters resorted to indentured service, a device previously used to increase the white population of the Americas and now employed to supply plantations in the Caribbean, the Indian Ocean and the Pacific with Asian and Melanesian labour. Debt bondage was a further device for persuading workers to travel great distances in order to work on plantations or down mines. Finally, convicts were also used as a slave substitute, although on a relatively small scale. None of these devices amounted to plantation slavery. All tended to be short-term. Moreover, indentured service and debt bondage, which accounted for the majority of workers involved, were systems of consent and of waged labour. Nonetheless, bound to their employers and prevented from competing in a free market, these servile workers were far removed from the labour ideal that the devotees of capitalism advocated.

The apprenticeship of ex-slaves began with the introduction of free-womb laws that liberated the children of slaves while requiring them to serve their mother's master, as if they were still slaves, for a specified time. The first of these laws was enacted in Pennsylvania in 1780. It rigorously required slave children to remain bonded until the age of twenty-eight. Other laws allowed liberation at the age of twenty-one. The final examples, enacted for Cuba and Brazil in 1870–1, permitted freedom to commence at the age of eighteen.[4] By this time, apprenticeship had also become a standard part of the procedure for the complete termination of slavery, the precedent set by the British statute of 1833, which required all ex-slaves in the British colonies to serve their former masters for another six years (twelve years were proposed in the original bill), with the obligation to provide forty hours' unpaid labour each week. This procedure was followed, for example, by the Portuguese in Angola in 1858 with a twenty-year apprenticeship, by the Dutch in 1863 with a ten-year apprenticeship, and by the Spanish (in 1873 for Puerto Rico and in 1880 for Cuba), with an eight-year apprenticeship. But apprenticeship was not common to all abolitions.[5] The French failed to make use of it. Further notable exceptions were the USA and Brazil, in the former, because abolition was enforced by military defeat, in the latter, because, by the time it happened (in 1888), other precedents – especially emancipation in the United States – had made their mark. What is more, in Brazil alternative sources of free labour were now available, and planters had come to realize, in the light of massive slave desertions, that, since slavery no longer served to bind labour effectively to their estates, apprenticeship would stand even less chance of doing so.[6]

Apprenticeship had a two-fold purpose: partly to oblige the ex-slave to compensate the former master for a capital asset lost through emancipation; partly to preserve for the planters a supply of labour. In effect, when used to close down a slave system rather than to liberate slave offspring, it caused nothing but trouble. The legacy of plantation slavery was the bitter antipathy ex-slaves felt for their former work, even when it was paid. True freedom for them meant not simply the end of slavery but also escape from the plantation labour regime. When the latter was forestalled by the terms of abolition, it raised the charge that what the law had granted practice had denied. This evident act of hypocrisy revived the wrath of abolitionists, as well as driving ex-slaves to even greater acts of non-cooperation than had been committed under slavery. The British apprenticeship system was a failure and had to be withdrawn after four years.[7]

Various means were used to make the ex-slaves work the plantations, such as the confinement of housing to plantation land; vagrancy laws; debt bondage; taxation to flush them out of subsistence farming into earning wages; even morcellizing the plantation land so that it could be worked through a system of commercial tenant farming dependent on family labour. These devices sometimes achieved their purpose.[8] But if former slaves had the opportunity to escape the plantation – by working their own subsistence plots, artisan work or petty trading – they took it, placing those who were prepared to do plantation work in a stronger position, because of their scarcity value, to command high wages.[9] It therefore became clear to the planters that it was best to sever their dependency upon the ex-slaves by seeking an alternative source of labour. This they found in indentured service and debt bondage.

In the period 1834–1922, at least 2.5 million workers migrated under terms of indentured service, binding themselves to employers usually on five-year contracts, with wages and maintenance agreed, but with no say over the work to be done and no right to leave their employer until the contract ran out.[10] The work was unskilled hard labour, chiefly on sugar plantations (in Mauritius, Réunion, Jamaica, Trinidad, British and Dutch Guiana, Natal, Fiji, Hawaii, Queensland, Cuba, and the French Caribbean), but also in mining (the guano quarries of Peru, the gold mines of the Transvaal and French Guiana, the gold, nickel and phosphate mines of Australia) and on railway construction (in East Africa, Panama and Peru).[11]

The British Empire had a major role to play in the development of this labour system, as supplier, employer and regulator. Much the largest contingent of indentured servants was provided by the British Raj. It authorized the export of about 1,400,000 Indians between the late 1830s and 1916 when, finally admitting that indentured service represented the continuation of slavery in another guise, it banned this form of emigration.[12] The British also had a leading role in furnishing the second largest emigration of indentured servants: the 400,000 Chinese exported between 1843 and 1910; for it followed the Opium Wars of 1839–41 and 1856–60, through which the British opened up China to the world, and was initially promoted by the British shipping firms, Tait and Company and Syme, Muir and Company.[13] The British were also involved in providing Africans and Pacific islanders for plantation work: the former between 1834 and 1870, when Africans rescued from the slave trade were sent to the Caribbean under indenture; the latter, from the 1860s, when Melanesians, largely drawn from the Solomon Islands and New Hebrides, were sent to work the new sugar plantations of Fiji, Queensland, Samoa and Tahiti.[14]

Most Indian indentured labour went to plantations in the British colonies: notably Mauritius (455,000), British Guiana (239,000), Natal (153,000), Trinidad (150,000) and Fiji (61,000). Some went to the French colonies (75,000 to Réunion and 79,000 to Martinique and Guadeloupe); but this trade was stopped in the mid-1880s by the government of India, in response to reports of worker maltreatment.[15] Presumably because the Raj had proved so fruitful, the British colonies made little use of Chinese indentured labour, whose major beneficiaries were Cuba (138,000, mostly between 1850 and 1880) and Peru (117,400, between the 1840s and 1870s), that is, until the first decade of the twentieth century when, between 1904 and 1907, 70,000 Chinese were briefly employed in the British Transvaal.[16] After the British, the chief users of indentured labour were the French, employing in their Caribbean and Mescarene colonies 70,000 Africans between 1850 and 1900, and 154,000 Indians between the 1840s and 1880s. As *engagés à temps*, they also employed 140,000 Chinese in France towards the end of the First World War.[17] After Peru and Spanish Cuba came the Portuguese. Following the abolition of slavery in 1858, the Portuguese shipped 80–100,000 indentured Africans from Angola to the offshore cocoa plantations of São Tomé and Principe.[18] The Dutch employed 53,800 indentured servants in Dutch Guiana, with 35,500 Indians imported between the 1870s and 1916, plus 19,300 shipped from their colony of Java, mostly between the 1890s and 1920; while Germany employed an unknown amount of indentured labour in New Guinea at the close of the century.[19]

Notably uninvolved in the indentured labour trade was the USA, which, in 1867, shortly after abolishing slavery, banned indentured service and other forms of 'voluntary servitude' from all its territories.[20] And notably insignificant in the indentured labour trade were white workers, although 56,000 (mostly Portuguese, with some French and Germans) were exported under these terms: 41,000 to the British Caribbean between the 1830s and 1850s, and 13,400 to Hawaii, mostly in the 1880s.[21]

Generally, the employment of indentured labour, in this second phase, began in the 1830s and 1840s, peaked in the 1860s (419,000), continued to provide substantial recruits (over 200,000 per decade) between the 1870s and 1910, tailed off in the next decade (71,000), and virtually disappeared thereafter. The largest contingent (752,000) went to the Caribbean; with 564,000 going to the Mescarenes (Mauritius and Réunion); 255,000 to southern Africa; 118,000 to Peru; and 115,000 to Hawaii.[22] The Caribbean, the Mescarenes and Peru received most of their indentured labour before 1870; with Queensland, Fiji, Natal, the Transvaal, Uganda and Hawaii receiving most of theirs between 1870 and 1910.

The extensive employment of indentured labour resulted from the abolition of plantation slavery. It either followed the abolition of the slave trade, as in Cuba and Peru, where it was initially used to compensate for the contracting slave population, or resulted from the abolition of slavery itself – as in the British, French, Dutch and Portuguese plantation colonies.[23] Promoting its use was a huge expansion of the sugar cane industry in the Caribbean, the Indian Ocean and the Pacific, as well as enduring methods of plantation organization.[24] For much of the nineteenth century, the abiding ideal remained the Caribbean model of the large, autonomously processed, directly operated plantation. This applied not only in the ex-slave sugar colonies but also in the new sugar regions that had never known plantation slavery: Hawaii, Fiji, Natal and Queensland.[25] In the absence of slavery, the work-force had to be paid. In addition, substantial numbers of unskilled labourers were required, capable of continuous work and reliable attendance, something the resident labour tended to lack. The problem was not insufficient population – as it had been with the original establishment of serfdom, plantation slavery and the first phase of indentured service – but unwillingness to comply with the planters' labour demands.[26] It was difficult to persuade former slaves to continue with plantation work; it was far from easy to persuade native peoples radically to adapt their way of life and work full-time for wages. Much depended upon the availability of land for peasant cultivation. On the small, intensely cultivated island of Barbados, for example, where plantations had absorbed most of the farm land, the ex-slave population, with no alternative means of survival, had to plod on as plantation workers. But elsewhere in the Caribbean, the plantation system stood alongside a complexity of smallholdings. In this situation, plantation labour had to be imported.[27] Likewise, in the new, post-slavery sugar regions – where the natives preferred to follow their own traditional means of subsistence, whether it be peasant or hunter-gatherer, and showed contempt for the wage-slavery of plantation work – indentured labour filled the breach.[28] The presence of indentured servants helped to keep wages low; and the bondage to which their contracts subjected them awarded the planters considerable control, especially as these contracts were enforced by harsh penal laws.[29] Nonetheless, problems remained, the chief of which was the shortness of the contract, coupled with the normal right of indentured servants to be repatriated free of charge upon its expiration. The length of a typical indenture was five years. In the British colonies an extra five years was at first required before repatriation could be claimed. However, this was ended in 1862. The degree of actual repatriation was low in the sugar colonies: it averaged 27 per cent for the Caribbean islands, Guiana and Hawaii, and 31 per cent for Mauritius and Natal.[30] But this resulted from the concessions the planters were obliged to make – in the form of higher wages, cash bonuses or grants of land – either to persuade the indentured to renew the contract, or to stay on as free labourers. However, thanks to a low rate of reproductivity among the immigrants which, in the former slave manner, was due to an excess of men over women, as well as to the antipathies dividing the ex-slaves of African extraction from the Asian newcomers, and also to the high wastage rate caused by desertion and the high mortality that came of shifting from one epidemiological zone to another, the only practical solution was to import more of the same.[31]

Indentured service resulted from a plantation demand for cheap, reliable labour. The reason for its origin, then, was the same as that of New World slavery. The trade in servants, moreover, resembled the slave trade. It transported people across enormous distances to alien worlds where they were sold on disembarkation, and mostly set to work in the fields under a closely supervised and demanding regime, enforced by fierce legal penalties for desertion and insubordination. But there the similarity ends. The African slave trade was an act of compulsory recruitment. Men and women did not subject themselves to enslavement in order to secure a free trip to the Americas. In contrast, the Asian servant trade was mostly an act of voluntary enlistment, its terms and conditions carefully regulated at least by the British. Unlike slavery, indentured service was temporary.[32] Responsible for its recruitment was not simply the planter's demand for labour but also the labourer's search for work. Underpinning it were the excessive populations of China, India, Japan and Java, the primitive nature of their home economies, and the existence of advanced economies that required the unskilled labour Asia possessed in profusion and could not employ. On the other hand, this was not the case with Africa or the Pacific islands, where the pull factor was stronger than the push. Workers had to be lured away from comfortable homes, sometimes by force. Nonetheless, false promises and the pressure of colonial taxes, which obliged them to earn wages, normally did the trick.[33]

The use of indentured labour in the nineteenth century spread the Asian population throughout the plantation world: so much so that by the 1920s, 43 per cent of the population of Hawaii was Japanese; 40 per cent of the population of Fiji was Indian, as was 71 per cent of the population of Mauritius, and 33 per cent and 42 per cent respectively of the populations of Trinidad and British Guiana. Since these labourers rarely exercised their right to return home, their importation also increased the permanent population in these colonies, and established in them a profound ethnic discord.[34] Furthermore, its importance in boosting sugar production during a long trend of falling sugar prices – in British Guiana, Trinidad, Mauritius, Natal, Hawaii, Cuba, Peru, Queensland and Fiji – cannot be doubted. Within the sugar cane industry, the overall productivity of indentured labour remained below that of slavery. But, between 1870 and 1880, the proportion of the world's sugar cane it produced increased from 23 per cent to 29 per cent. In doing so, it partially compensated for a decline in slave production from 52 per cent to 37 per cent, helping to ensure that, even in the early 1880s, at least 66 per cent of the world's sugar cane remained the product of bonded labour.[35] The usefulness of indentured service – for securing the necessary labour to man plantations and carry out deeply unpleasant tasks such as mining and railway construction – was clearly evident throughout the late nineteenth century. Why then should it fall into disuse?

Besides being useful to planters and mine owners, indentured service was of considerable benefit to the labourers themselves. It offered free passage to the plantations, enabling otherwise unaffordable, long-distance voyages to be made, and usually a free return. Conditions of work were often bad, especially in the early days when what was expected of indentured labourers was measured against what was previously demanded of slaves; and, in punishment for failing to complete assigned tasks, wages were docked, whippings were administered and indentures extended. In addition, conditions deteriorated during periodic slumps in the sugar industry, notably in the 1840s and during the 1880s and 1890s, when wage rates were again reduced.[36] Yet the material rewards were much greater than those on offer at home. If the work on the plantations had been unbearable, the indentured would have seized the opportunity to return home once their contract had ended, but, in the overseas regions, many more stayed on than returned, and re-indenture frequently occurred. Furthermore, news of adverse conditions would have deterred others from coming. Throughout the late nineteenth century and into the early twentieth century indentured service provided an opportunity for the ambitious and dynamic poor to better themselves.[37] Spurred on by inexorable population growth, there was no shortage of takers. In other words, indentured service did not fade away because workers turned against it. It did so because the governments of the supplying societies banned its export, and because the governments of the receiving societies banned its import. Whereas nationalism contributed to the former, racism was responsible for the latter.[38]

From the 1830s to the early 1860s, there was little opposition to the export of indentured labour, even though it was frequently viewed as a variant of slavery, and atrocious conditions and extreme maltreatment came to be associated with it. Accusations of shanghaiing were made, as were reports of poor accommodation, long hours of work, reduced or delayed wages, along with whippings and imprisonment for labour offences.[39] But then, in response to these reports, the British in the early 1870s established commissions of inquiry and enacted protective regulations to restrain the planters, even creating a colonial inspectorate to see to the welfare of the indentured. Furthermore, accounts of the evils of the trade led to several suspensions: in 1862 when the import of Chinese contract labour to the USA was forbidden; in 1868, when the Japanese government suspended exports of indentured labour to Hawaii; in 1874, when the imperial government of China, subject to pressure from the British, banned all exports of Chinese indentured labour; in the mid-1880s, when shipments from British India to the French colonies were stopped, a suspension extended to the German colonies in 1911, and to the rest of the world in 1916.[40] Some of these suspensions were eventually repealed, notably by the Chinese in 1893 and by the Japanese in 1885.[41] Nonetheless, for several decades their effect was to curtail the trade at a time when the demand for indentured labour remained strong. Moreover, the British restrictions remained permanently in force, confining and eventually cutting off the largest supply of indentured labour in the world.

In 1910 the Sanderson Committee reported on Indian indentured labour. Its brief was to test the charge that it was a new form of slavery, an accusation brought by Gandhi and other Indian nationalists, who had been antagonized by the treatment of indentured Indians in Natal and the Transvaal. After due deliberation, the committee declared indentured labour to be free not slave. Because the conditions of the workers 'leave little to be desired' by way of improvement, it provocatively recommended continuation. This sparked off more nationalist protest, under the pressure of which the government, concessively, maintained the ban on exporting Indian indentured labour to the French colonies when it came up for review in 1911, and extended the prohibition to the German colonies in Africa. Further protest led to a volte-face in imperial policy. This was signalled in 1915 when Lord Hardinge, viceroy of India, condemned indentured service as 'a system of forced labour . . . differing but little from a form of slavery'.[42] This admission left the British, by virtue of their heroic struggle against the slave trade, with no choice but to ban future exports of indentured labour from India: an act that reduced from a flood to a trickle the flow of contract labour to the plantations of the world.

By this time, the plantation colonies had reconsidered the wisdom of employing indentured labour. Their concern had stemmed from the inclination of workers who had migrated under indenture not to return home when the term expired. Originally this was welcomed as a solution to the labour problem. Eventually, however, it was deplored, notably in colonies of extensive European settlement, where whites placed a fear of being racially subsumed before their concern for cheap labour. This white reaction first declared itself in the USA with its anti-peonage law of 1867, which applied to both indentured labour and debt bondage, and with its exclusion laws of the 1880s, which banned the further immigration of Chinese workers. The same laws were applied to Hawaii when the USA annexed it in 1900.[43] A similar response was made during the 1890s in British Natal where, to reduce the proportion of Asians in the native population, Indians were discouraged from permanent settlement by a fiscal policy that imposed a special

tax on free Indian residents, followed by a ban on further imports of indentured labour.[44] Queensland applied a ban on all new indentures in 1901. This
not only prevented fresh imports but also put a stop to the practice of re-
indenture. The aim was to stem the influx of Pacific islanders. This policy
of exclusion was completed in 1906–7 when a programme of repatriation
dispatched the islanders home as their indentures expired.[45] A similar repatriation policy was applied in Kenya to get rid of the Indian labour admitted by indenture between 1896 and 1902 to build the Uganda railway.[46]
Moved by the racist concerns of the white settlers, and its own reputation
as an opponent of the slave trade, the British government terminated indentured service in the Transvaal in 1906. Then, in 1916, it complemented the
recent ban upon exporting indentured servants from India by refusing
Chinese contract labourers employment on British territory – at the time,
a quarter of the world.[47]

The indentured labour of the late nineteenth century was mainly
connected with the sugar industry. Helping to phase it out was the reorganization of this industry from the 1880s, a response to the slump in world
sugar prices. In place of the large, discrete plantation with its own processing machinery and an army of waged field hands, there developed
a centralized processing system that serviced a multitude of small, sugar-
producing farms. A report of 1900 on the sugar industry in Mauritius –
previously a heavy user of indentured labour – described what had recently
happened: 'The parcelling out of so many estates lately has furnished
old immigrants with the opportunity of becoming small landed proprietors.' Such reorganization had the double virtue of fulfilling the landed
ambitions of the work-force and of massively reducing the number of waged
labourers needed. It was adopted in most other sugar colonies: for
example, in Cuba, British Guiana, Trinidad and Fiji. In colonies of white
settlement, the small farms created by morcellization fell to white farmers:
as in Queensland and Natal.[48] In this way, the sugar industry liberated
itself from bonded labour, allowing imperial and colonial governments,
under pressure from humanitarian and racist sentiments, the opportunity to abolish indentured service without causing too much economic
harm.

Nonetheless, the majority of migrants from India and China in the late
nineteenth century were not indentured. In fact, at least two-thirds of
Indian emigrants and four-fifths of Chinese emigrants travelled abroad by
other means.[49] But this was not because they could pay their own passage
and therefore were able to work abroad as free men. Many had to become
debt bondsmen. In India the *kangani* and *maistry* systems allowed labourers to pay for their passage to foreign plantations retrospectively, out of
the wages received for working on them. Until they had done so, they
were bound to work at someone else's command. In China the credit-ticket
system created a similar arrangement. The person or company who paid
for the worker's passage abroad had control over his labour until the debt
was acquitted.[50] Like indentured service, and in contrast to slavery, this

type of debt bondage, when not subjected to abuse, was short-term, waged and voluntary. It differed from indentured labour, however, in being unsupervised by official authority and in lacking legal warranty. It was much more of an informal, private and even secret arrangement: in the case of Indian labour, between a broker who recruited it and then hired it out to planters; in the case of Chinese labour, between the person who, having bought it from a broker, had full use of it until the purchase price had been recovered from the wages earned. Neither employer nor worker could call upon the law to enforce their respective rights. The condition of work therefore depended upon the benevolence of the owner and the opportunities for workers to desert. As with indentured service and slavery, debt bondage involved the employer in making an advance payment. To recoup this payment, he not only needed to retain the labour he had bought but he also had to ensure that the work was efficiently done. This could easily lead to severe punishment when labour was withdrawn through absenteeism or foot-dragging or insubordination; but it could also lead to paternalism. Needless to say, its very nature, which prevented the bonded from being officially distinguished from the free, renders impossible the task of defining statistically the extent to which it was ever employed, or how it really operated.

For migrant labour, debt bondage in China had a somewhat different purpose from that of India. In India debt bondage complemented indentured service. Whereas indentured service was chiefly employed to reach distant plantations in the Caribbean, the Pacific and the Indian Ocean, mainly to grow sugar, debt bondage was used to convey workers to plantations much closer to home – notably Ceylon, Burma and Malaya – and principally to cultivate tea, rice and rubber. In contrast to indentured servants, Indian debt bondsmen migrated for a much shorter period of time and, except for those who went to Ceylon, they tended to return home.[51] With the Chinese, however, debt bondage was used to convey workers on massive, overseas journeys, notably to California, Australia and Hawaii. In this respect, it served the same purpose as indentured service, and had similar consequences. When used to pay for a journey that removed labourers thousands of miles from home, with the term of service necessarily extended over several years, debt bondage ensured that they did not return.[52]

The essential privacy of debt bondage allowed it to flourish in spite of being banned by law. Thus, the US Anti-peonage Act of 1867 had no effect upon the inflow of Chinese who went to California under debt bondage to work as miners and on railway construction. Likewise, the outlawing of debt bondage by written contract in India in 1860, and in Malaya in 1883 – both the result of British imperial policy – was ineffectual in curtailing the use of debt bondage to fund short-term labour migrations to Southeast Asia.[53] As well as resulting from the abolition of slavery, debt bondage was promoted by government attempts to end the trade in indentured labour. This was much more susceptible to effective prohibition because it rested upon

legal evidence. Thus, the flow of debt bondsmen to California followed the
US ban on indentured immigration in 1862. It was only stopped by the
Exclusion Laws of 1882 and 1884, which denied further entry to all Chinese
workers, free and unfree.[54] The American experience of receiving debt
bondsmen instead of indentured servants was replicated elsewhere. The
restrictions placed on the export of Chinese indentured labour in the early
1870s caused large numbers of workers to leave the country by credit-ticket.
The same thing happened to Japanese labour whenever steps were taken to
ban its export under indenture. Where indentured migrant labour was outlawed, debt bondage became the principal means by which the Asian poor
found work in foreign parts: that is, until Asian families abroad were able to
fund the outward passage of relatives left in the home country. Until the
latter happened, the only limitation effectively placed on the use of debt
bondage to fund labour migrations was fierce immigration legislation
which, in the manner of the US Exclusion Laws, banned entry on grounds
of race.[55]

Besides allowing planters or miners to compensate for the inadequacies of native labour by importing foreign workers, debt bondage also
served to recruit and control native labour. Although illicit after 1867, it was
found on US plantations, a device to affix the labour of ex-slaves. It was
notably practised in late nineteenth-century Spanish America. From the
employers' point of view, the problem lay with the lands and natural
resources communally owned by the Amerindian villages which deterred
their inhabitants from seeking work elsewhere. Over the centuries a number
of devices came into use to extract and deploy this labour: notably, enslavement; grants of Indian communities to individual settlers (*encomiendas*);
tribute systems – for example, the *mita* in Peru, the *repartimiento* in Mexico,
the *mandemiento* in Guatemala – which required Indian communities to
furnish labour not only for public works but also for private estates and
mines; assigned Indian convict labour; and service tenure, which enabled
Indians to receive estate land in return for providing labour services.
However, disapproval by the Spanish government soon phased out Indian
enslavement, while both *encomiendas* and labour tribute faded away in the
sixteenth and seventeenth centuries, the result of the great depopulation
and government restriction.[56] Following restrictions upon the import of
foreign labour in the nineteenth century – first by the termination of the
transatlantic slave trade and then by constraints placed upon the trade in
indentured labour from Asia – it became a matter of top priority to enlist
native Indian labour, which now existed in profusion. But how was it to be
made available?

One solution was to persuade Indians to leave their communities and
settle permanently on estate land.[57] When Indian villages had a surplus
population and suffered land hunger, this was easier to achieve than otherwise; but even then there could be problems in recruiting and retaining
labour, especially if other employment opportunities existed, such as
in mining or seasonal plantation work, or if (as, for example, in early

nineteenth-century Mexico) there was a strong demand for tenants, a consequence of a downturn in the profitability of commercial farming which caused landowners to rent out their estates rather than cultivate them directly.[58] When the landowners' demand for tenants exceeded supply, debt bondage became a device for binding them to the estate. It took the form of debt enserfment.[59] Thus, Indians were lured onto the estate by the offer of land, then placed in debt through a policy of generous credit, and in this manner affixed until the debt had been cleared. This device had been used under Spanish colonial rule and was widely employed in the nineteenth century. Phasing it out were two distinctive developments of the period 1870–1940: rapid population growth and a change in estate management, as landowners chose to farm directly a much larger share of their land. In this situation, Indian demand for tenancies came to exceed the supply. Since tenants could now be easily replaced, landowners no longer needed to bind them to the estate.[60]

Debt bondage came to the landowner's aid in a second sense, for it was also used to recruit temporary labour, through a system of debt peonage.[61] Agents of the landowners would visit the Indian villages and offer wages in advance. Having taken the *moneda sonante* (jingling coin), the Indians placed themselves under an obligation of work for a given period. As to whether the Indians had to be forced to enter such arrangements, this depended upon the nature of the work. Following the disappearance of slavery, and as restraints came to be placed on the importation of Chinese contract workers, debt peonage became a major means of securing labour, as it was used to bring Indians down from the sierras for seasonal work on the sugar plantations of coastal Peru or the cotton plantations of Laguna in Mexico.[62] Viewed as a labour migration, it was not too different from that of free waged labour. Little enticement was required because the rewards were obvious and the enterprise was beneficient not only to the planters but also to the Indian communities whose basic resources it enlarged. However, drawing Indian labour into the guano mining of the Peruvian coast or the mahogany timbering of Tabasco and Chiapas was a different matter, in view of the unpleasantness of the work, its non-seasonal nature, and the Indian reluctance to take it on. Here, the debt peonage used to recruit labour degenerated into a system of enforcement, with Indians tricked against their wills into long-term bondage through being duped into debt.[63]

Debt peonage became of great value in the late nineteenth century as, under the impact of the world economy – to which Mexico, especially, was exposed by railroad construction, the steamship and the government policies of Porfiro Diaz (1876–1911) – capitalist agriculture entered an advanced stage, but did so before undergoing real proletarianization. While labour remained in the peasant mode and directed by peasant aspirations, debt peonage for a time played a vital economic role as a recruiter of labour. Eventually reducing its importance was the tendency of plantations to annex the independent resources of the Indian villages: commoning rights, water rights and community land. This happened, moreover, when a rapidly growing Indian population needed more land to maintain its traditional way of life. Deprived of self-subsistence by these two pressures, Indians in large numbers were obliged to seek plantation work. In other words, they no longer needed to be enticed or attached. As the plantation took over the countryside, debt bondage in its two basic forms, debt peonage and debt enserfment, became redundant; for what was left was an Indian society increasingly obliged to abandon its peasant ideals – hence the peasant proverb 'Poor Mexico! So far from God and so near the United States' – and work as a proletariat. In this respect, the establishment of a fully-fledged capitalist society in Spanish America made debt bondage unnecessary.[64] When it came to be generally outlawed, the consequence of the Mexican Revolution (1910–20) and the impact of *Zapatista* peasant movements upon its course, debt peonage was rapidly falling into disuse.[65]

All these servile devices represented a demand for labour that arose from the abolition of slavery, the extension of large-scale commercial farming or mining operations, and the unwillingness of resident populations to respond to the work opportunities that these developments created. Moreover, all were key devices in the network of economic imperialism spun by British and American capitalism. But coming in the wake of slave emancipation, all were rendered dubious through being branded as forms of slavery, so much so that governments, moved by humanitarian pressures and a sense of reputation, were driven to opposed them in law. Eventually, international bodies also proceeded against them: notably the League of Nations Convention of 1926, which condemned not only slavery but also 'slave-like labour practices'; the Convention of the International Labour Conference of 1939, which sought to impose an upper limit on labour contracts; and the First Asian Relations Conference of 1947, which called for the abolition of bonded service. But their mutual benefit to capital and labour made abolition a difficult and prolonged task, especially as debt bondage was extremely hard to identify.[66] Effective abolition only became possible either under the impact of large-scale capitalist production, when a combination of mechanization and free waged labour proved sufficient, or if plantations morcellized into tenant farms operated through family labour. Paradoxically, the bonded labour systems which replaced plantation slavery were finally phased out, on the one hand by proletarianization, the result of the creation of a free labour market, and on the other by a bastard form of peasantization, in which family farms emerged seeking self-subsistence through the cultivation of a cash crop.

The colonial accommodation

For much of the nineteenth century the trade in Africans – the essential prop of slavery in the Americas and the Muslim world – remained a highly productive one, transporting 3,300,000 across the Atlantic, 1,250,000 across the Sahara, almost half a million across the Red Sea, and yet another half million across the Indian Ocean.[67] Supplying this trade with fresh slaves were the warrior states of the African savannah, as they plucked Pagans from the forests to the south and plundered each other for human chattels. Nonetheless, in the course of the century certain critical impediments were placed upon the trade, the effect of which cast serious doubts on the future of slavery.

The first impediment came with the sustained onslaught, naval and diplomatic, that the British waged against the trade by sea. By the 1850s the transatlantic trade had been virtually brought to a halt. Of the Africans transported to the Americas during the course of the nineteenth century, only 5 per cent went after 1850; and next to none after 1866 when the trade to Cuba ceased. Furthermore, from the mid-nineteenth century, the British also proceeded successfully against the trades – via the Mediterranean, the Red Sea and the Persian Gulf – that had traditionally furnished the Ottoman Empire with black slaves. To secure their support against Russia, the Ottoman government was obliged to comply with French and British demands for limiting the slave trade. No longer capable of recruiting slaves by tribute or war, Ottoman slavery slid into terminal decline.[68]

A second impediment came with the founding of British and French colonies in Africa. In the 1880s and 1890s the two powers became entrenched there not simply as traders, missionaries and owners of coastal stations but as rulers of two massive territorial empires. This allowed them to oppose the slave trade at its source, as well as to interrupt it as it passed along the overland routes to the Mediterrean, the Red Sea and the Indian Ocean.

A third impediment came with the collapse of the Ottoman Empire. By 1921, its possessions in north Africa had fallen to the French or the British; its possessions in the Middle East had become mandates under British and French control.[69] In this manner, a region highly sympathetic to slavery, because it was seen as an integral part of Islam, underwent direct or indirect interference by two European powers which regarded slavery as a horrendous crime against humanity. The outcome, however, was not the complete obliteration of slavery but its adaptation and survival.

Following its abolition in the Western world, slavery continued to flourish elsewhere, especially in Africa. Under the stimulus of the export trade in slaves and commodities, and because of the usefulness of slaves as a source of wealth, status and power, slavery in late nineteenth-century Africa was no fringe phenomenon but something central to many societies, Islamic and Pagan. Slaves typically formed majorities in the plantation regions and substantial minorities elsewhere.[70] Yet by 1930 African slavery was very different in character from what it had been in 1880. Four types of slavery had disappeared: plantation slavery, military slavery, sacrificial slavery and slavery as currency.

Plantation slavery had recently developed in parts of western and eastern Africa, largely in response to the European demand for cloves, cotton and palm oil. As in the slave plantations of the Americas, it depended very much on access to fresh supplies of slaves. For this reason, it had benefited from the ending of the transatlantic slave trade, which left a surplus of slaves for African use. However, plantation slavery was then badly damaged by the British and French missionary and colonial presence, which not only curtailed the internal slave trade but also incited slaves to flee the plantations.[71]

Slave soldiers had for centuries featured in the warrior societies of northern and central Africa. Both Pagan and Islamic warrior states had thrived on the wealth made from slave-trading. They had also depended upon slaves as soldiers and officials. Although very much alive in 1880, this world was virtually dead forty years on.[72] Essentially, it had flourished on the slave trade and the freedom to wage war and indulge in plunder. With the slave trade severely limited, and some order imposed by colonial rule, the warrior state lost its *modus vivendi*. Military slaves transferred to the service of the colonial state. As colonial policemen and soldiers, they helped to quell the disorder previously generated by them as warriors in the service of princes, chiefs and Muslim religious leaders.[73]

Sacrificial slavery was also phased out. Central to traditional African slave practices was the belief that benefits could be gained by putting slaves to death. In this way deceased rulers could be attended in the afterlife; gods could be propitiated or persuaded to dispense favours; messages could be received from, and sent to, the gods; warriors could be fortified before battle on human flesh, and pacts between different states could be sealed with blood. Long before its disappearance, slave sacrifice in Africa had been restricted by the spread of Islam which, like Christianity, strongly disapproved of the practice.[74] Then, in the course of the nineteenth century, Christian missionaries exposed it to the world as an evil canker suppurating at the heart of darkness. Finally, it was prohibited as the Pagan societies that practised it were subjected to Christian colonial rule. And the closing down of the slave trade removed the surplus of slaves upon which it had thrived.

Following the effective abolition of the slave trade, the practice of using slaves as a currency substitute ceased: cowrie shells, thanks to devaluation, had become extremely difficult and costly to convey; slaves, in contrast, carried themselves and, in doing so, could also carry other goods. In traditional Africa, slaves had been categorized as household slaves and commodity slaves, the former normally kept for service, the latter used as a means of commercial transaction.[75] Commodity slavery came to be ruled out partly by the spread of European currencies but also by a drying up of the supply of new slaves, coupled with the penalties imposed by colonial powers on slave sales.

Nonetheless, slavery and related forms of bonded labour remained entrenched in African societies well into the twentieth century. This was especially true of reproductive slavery and voluntary bondage. The former consisted of slaves attached to private households as domestics or settled on the land like serfs. Both types of slave had rights to families and reproduced the next generation of slaves.[76] The only means of quickly terminating this 'benign' form of slavery lay with the slaves themselves and their willingness to take flight. Alongside slavery, African servitude, especially in non-Islamic parts, had traditionally featured a system of pawnship which allowed debts to be acquitted through a temporary submission to bondage.[77] Pawnship could degenerate into slavery, thanks to chronic indebtedness and its re-interpretation by Muslim and Christian slave-traders. However, it differed from slavery in certain important essentials, and therefore had a much better chance of survival. In the first place, pawnship rested upon agreement; in the second, the relationship between master and pawn was between members of the same community, whereas the relationship between master and slave was with an alien, or the offspring of an alien. Unlike slavery, pawnship had never depended upon a trade in labour. Essentially, it was a local arrangement for allowing the poor to raise credit through the security of a labour service. In the absence of charity, welfare or waged employment, it usefully served a social need. For all these reasons, pawnship endured, even though condemned by international commissions as a variant of slavery.

Debt bondage sometimes replaced slavery when the latter was outlawed. This was the case in India following the Anti-Slavery Act of 1843. In 1841 Sir Bartle Frere reckoned that, in the whole of India, there existed something like 16 million slaves – twice the number to be found in the Americas and rivalled only by Africa.[78] Some were in domestic service; others in agriculture. The former had been concentrated in the great cities and attached as workers and attendants to royal, noble, professional and mer-cantile households. This type of slave had been traditionally imported, notably from Africa and Southeast Asia; but many were native-born, recruited from self-sale and child-sale: in other words, the acts of despera-tion committed by the poor to survive periods of terrible famine. Besides sanctioning these practices, Hindu law allowed enslavement for certain crimes such as incest, adultery, abortion and rebellion. In the case of murder and tax default, enslavement could also apply to the criminal's family.[79] Indigenous slavery of this sort was affected by caste only in the sense that brahmins were exempt from enslavement and untouchables were barred from domestic service.[80] Untouchables, however, were the major source of recruitment for field or agrestic slavery. They comprised the bulk of the slave population found in the countryside. In the absence of plantations, these slaves were predominantly serfs, bound to their owner's land and obliged to provide him with unpaid labour services for ever more. As with the rest of the slave system, this stemmed from Hindu law, particularly the ruling that certain low-caste social groups could not own land. Access to it was gained through enslavement. Whereas domestic slavery had been dependent on the slave market, agrestic slavery was, in the serf manner, self-perpetuating, the children of slaves eventually replacing their parents in bondage.[81]

In the African manner, however, servitude in India had traditionally included debt bondage, the result of pawning labour to acquit a debt. In India, debt bondage had frequently rested upon a written contract; and the term of servitude was usually finite. In this respect, it differed from slavery.[82] However, it resembled slavery quite closely in that it was hereditary and therefore not simply by consent. This was because the contract applied to the debt bondsman's family. If he were unable to acquit the debt – through death, illness or old age – the obligation fell upon his wife and children. Until the debt was cleared, then, the whole family remained in the creditor's control.[83]

Bonded labour thrived in colonial India. For it to do so, only minor shifts and adjustments were required. Thus, with slavery abolished in 1843, ex-slaves were transformed into debt bondsmen. Domestics were now seen as indebted to their masters and therefore obliged to serve them. Agricultural workers were now seen as bound to the land by the debt they had incurred from their master's generosity in allowing them to work it.[84] A further shift resulted from the Indian Penal Code of 1860 which not only made keeping slaves a criminal offence but even placed a ban on debt-bonded labour. The latter legitimized itself, however, simply by dispensing with written contracts.[85] In addition to tolerating debt bondage, the British introduced indentured service. Authorized in 1837, it became an imperial device not only to convey Indian workers abroad but also to attach them to the tea plantations of Assam. To make the indentures fully binding in India, the Workman's Breach of Contract Act was passed in 1859, rendering any violation of contract by the indentured labourer a punishable offence. This system of bonded labour remained in legitimate use until 1915.[86]

Because of the usefulness of debt bondage in maintaining servitude in a legally amenable guise – thus allowing tradition to be preserved and the caste system of Vedic law respected – and in offering the poor special provision for raising credit, it managed not only to outlive British rule in India but also to survive the attempts made at abolition in the late twentieth century. Although declared illegal in the whole of India in 1976, in 1981 it remained the fate of 2,617,000 Indians, most of them untouchables. Bearing in mind that debt bondage applied to the bondsman's immediate family, the total figure for those affected, directly or indirectly, probably amounted to something like 10 million persons.[87]

Elsewhere in the Far East, slavery had been especially concentrated in Southeast Asia where, in the Indian and African manner, it existed alongside debt bondage. Slaves could be recruited indigenously as punishment for crime, or through entering an inescapable state of indebtedness, or through self-sale. But usually they were acquired by capture, the result of civilized, settled urban regions raiding the primitive hunter-gatherer or swidden-cultivating societies of the forests and uplands. Alternatively, they were bought from abroad. As for debt bondage, traditionally, this had been a purely indigenous institution. It had accounted for the majority in servitude. In the late nineteenth century it was also used as a means of importing Indians to labour temporarily on the plantations of Burma and Malaya. Furthermore, indigenous debt bondage became even more prominent in the late nineteenth and early twentieth centuries as colonial governments – the British in Burma and Malaya, the Dutch in Indonesia, the French in Vietnam – swept slavery under the carpet by allowing its redefinition as debt bondage. Moreover, independent regions such as Thailand, in the bid to stave off colonial take-over, sought to present a modern image to the outside world by declaring slavery illegal while continuing to sanction debt bondage. The bondage that survived usefully allowed the poor to extend their credit and cope with debt. It also served the needs of employers in a society that continued to regard waged labour as demeaning.[88]

The colonial approach to the termination of servitude was an ambivalent one. Of the powers that acquired territory in the partition of Africa, the Portuguese, the Belgians, the Germans and the Italians appeared not much interested in ending slavery. However, all were ready to stop the export of Africans from their own colonies as a means of conserving a basic labour resource, and therefore opposed the slave trade.[89] Moreover, while the British and the French appeared much more dedicated to the abolition of slavery, both could find reasons for permitting its survival. Considerations of power and wealth demoted the moral mission to second place. Yet certain colonial policies – applied by both the committed and the less committed – undermined the slave system and prepared for its demise: notably attempts to stop the slave trade; the construction of railways and roads, which reduced the need for slave porterage; the imposition and maintenance of order, especially through the curtailment of the raiding activities of warrior bands, which had previously sustained slavery by supplying it with fresh blood; the increase in the use of European currencies, which made slaves less useful as money-substitutes; the promotion of waged employment – in connection with building roads and railways, commercial farming and the colonial service – thus providing ex-slaves with a means of survival if they left their masters; and the issue of anti-slavery declarations which persuaded slaves to flee from their masters and seek the sanctity of the flag or the mission. For all these reasons, the decay of slavery in the late nineteenth and early twentieth centuries was undoubtedly a consequence of colonial rule and its effectiveness, on the one hand because it directly challenged societies that retained a firm belief in slavery with the abolitionist beliefs of western Europe and, on the other, because it promoted economic systems predicated on a free labour market. Slave regimes that remained free of colonial rule, as in Ethiopia, managed to preserve themselves much more successfully than those that became subjected to it.[90]

However, between the establishment of colonial rule in Africa and the elimination of bonded labour there was a considerable time lag. This can be explained partly in terms of the ingrained nature of bondage, partly in terms of the ineffectiveness of colonial rule, and partly in terms of the willingness of colonial authorities to tolerate what they had been taught to abhor. The successes colonial rule had scored in curbing the slave trade encouraged a toleration of slavery. Without the further recruitment of slaves, colonial administrations felt that the more obnoxious forms of slavery – those, for example, connected with plantations and sacrifice – would gradually fade way, leaving an acceptable and harmless residue. It was also felt that slavery could be best eradicated by developing the economy and through a process of social evolution, rather than by a sudden act of political enforcement.[91] To impose abolition, it was feared, would not only cause disorder and weaken colonial control but also harm the colonial economy which, in its present state, depended upon forced labour. As colonial officials became more educated in native ways, they grew to accept that slavery was not wholly bad and that bonded labour could even be justified.[92]

From 1848 the law of France explicitly condemned slavery in its colonies. This rested on the principle that French citizenship and slavery were completely incompatible and the willingness to make it applicable to all 'the colonies and possessions of the Republic'.[93] Nonetheless, the responsibilities accompanying the acquisition of a huge territorial empire in West Africa led the French to reinterpret the law: rather than being accepted as French citizens, colonial inhabitants came to be seen as subjects, and therefore unaffected by the anti-slave legislation of 1848.[94] By the late 1890s French colonial officials and experts were convinced of the need to preserve slavery for the time being. In 1895 the governor of Senegal, Colonel Trentinian, had warned against an enforced abolition: 'The issue of slavery requires infinite tact and prudence, if one does not wish to turn the land topsy-turvy and result in its complete economic ruin.' This was echoed by William Ponty, the governor of Haut Sénégal and Moyen Niger, in 1901. He was prepared to concede that, given French beliefs and principles, 'we cannot recognize the condition in which people are called captives, slaves or non-free', but felt the need to stress, in the cause of practicality: 'Above all, we must not forget that to act *ex abrupto* would suddenly provoke large political disorder.' Contrary to public opinion in France, which felt strongly that the legislation of 1848 had to be applied, the colonial administration believed that slavery was necessary for the good of the empire.[95]

For roughly the same reasons, the British followed the same policy. British colonies were rendered free of slavery by the act of 1833. However, the African territories acquired in the late nineteenth century were often defined as protectorates and therefore removed from its scope.[96] As the British became overlords of enormous territories, they adopted a tolerant attitude to the existence of slavery, which became even more permissive as time went by. This was very much to do with the scramble for Africa, and followed upon the sudden acquisition of huge territories which its colonial administration was incapable of effectively ruling. To consolidate control, it was vitally necessary to establish firm alliances with native elites.[97] By this time, missionaries were following a similar strategy, placing priority on the conversion of the socially and politically prominent and therefore inclined to go slow on abolition. As the Reverend Duff MacDonald of the Church of Scotland Mission in central Africa put it in 1880: 'I saw that our reception of runaway slaves had alienated many excellent men who might have been our best friends and who were better able to rule slaves than we.'[98]

The British toleration of slavery was neatly illustrated by the gradualist policies adopted towards the Gold Coast Protectorate, Sierra Leone, Zanzibar, British East Africa and Anglo-Egyptian Sudan. In the Gold Coast Protectorate an anti-slavery ordinance was issued in 1874.[99] Rather than abolish slavery outright, it implemented a free-womb policy. In addition, it outlawed further enslavement and denied claims to slave-ownership cognizance in the courts. In 1890, the same year that it was made a protectorate, a similar policy was applied in Zanzibar, with provision for liberation at birth and a ban on slave sales, and with an additional clause allowing slaves to purchase manumission at a reasonable price. But, faced with objection from the slave owners, the British backed off. Arthur Hardinge issued a solemn warning that the economy would collapse if emancipation was not applied gradually. A massive public protest in Britain followed against this attempt to harbour slavery under the British flag. Needing to steer a course between the Scylla of the Zanzibar slave owners and the Charybdis of the British abolitionists, a policy was formulated in 1897 that permitted slaves the right to apply for manumission, accepting that, if they did so, the former master was to be compensated while, if they did not, the master would retain possession as before but without a legal means of enforcing his ownership. A similar policy was applied in British East Africa.[100] With the foundation of the Sierra Leone Protectorate in 1896 the anti-slave ordinances issued were even more permissive.[101] Slavery was officially recognized. All that was done was to ban the sale of slaves and to offer slaves some legal protection against maltreatment. The occupation of the upper Nile in 1896 allowed the British the chance to get to grips with the slave systems of the savannahs. From 1900 war was waged against the Sokoto caliphate which fell in 1903. Yet no attempt was made to abolish slavery completely. Such a policy was dismissed by Lugard as 'administrative folly'. The slavery practised was appreciated as an integral part of Islam and therefore worthy of respect. And so instead a slow, undermining policy was applied that rested upon banning slave sales and granting freedom to the newborn.[102]

Not until 1928 was slavery abolished in Sierra Leone. And with what effect? If the colonial powers could evade the anti-slavery laws enacted at home, so could colonial subjects. As the Vei chief put it: 'No, we don't have slaves now; we have cousins.'[103] Slave trading was relatively easy to root out; but slave practices were not. A great deal of African slavery was self-reproductive and therefore could easily outlive the termination of the trade. Furthermore, much of it was relatively inoffensive, the result of slaves employed as domestic servants, or as agricultural workers resembling serfs rather than plantation field hands. If the bonded were prepared to stay with their masters, little could be done to free them. As a result, the laws of abolition which were eventually enacted tended to have little immediate effect. The capacity of slave systems to survive their abolition was vividly illustrated in the Cox Report on Sierra Leone for 1956. Of the thousands liberated in 1928, it stated that 'many returned to the houses and farms of their former proprietors there to give free [i.e. unpaid] labour from time to time in return for the use of the lands they occupy and the shelter they receive'.[104] In White Nile Province in southern Sudan, 13,000 domestic servants were offered freedom certificates in 1929 but only 3,000 took them up. In Zanzibar ten years after the 'abolition' decreed in 1897, only 17,000 slaves had applied for emancipation while 140,000 remained in slavery.[105] This state of affairs colonial governments readily accepted as they backed away from an apparently impossible, and perhaps pointless, task.

Nonetheless, the colonial presence of the French and the British did precipitate the flight of slaves. Their intrusion, both as rulers and Christian missionaries, profoundly affected the institution of slavery in Africa not only by limiting the slave trade but also by inspiring slaves to leave their masters in large numbers.[106] The mass flight of slaves became a source of discontent among indigenous elites. It was also seen as a cause of economic disruption. Colonial authorities therefore did their best to stem the exodus with vagrancy laws and a policy of returning captured slaves to their owners.[107] But tougher action to contain the runaways was ruled out by the need of both the French and British to keep their abolitionist reputations untarnished, and by the pressure upon government of public opinion at home. They also had to consider the gains to be made from employing runaways. Their colonial administrations had a pressing need for indigenous labour and service, something the self-liberated slave population could easily supply. The laying of an infrastructure of roads, railways and bridges became very much dependent upon the labour of former slaves; as was the development of colonial police forces and frontier guards. Work on construction projects provided fleeing slaves with a means of survival and helped to turn them into a labour force accustomed to working for wages.[108] By entering the colonial military service, they continued in the tradition of the slave-recruited warrior bands of the past, with the difference that, by doing so, they were securing automatic freedom; and, rather than upholding the slave system by providing it with fresh slaves, they were now dedicated to opposing the interest of slave master and slave-trader – to a greater extent than the colonial authorities were.[109] Slavery, then, was allowed to continue in

Africa by a process of consent. This was permitted at one extreme by colonial rule and, at the other, by the slaves themselves. However, the intrusion of the British and French as colonial powers, and its effect both in curtailing the slave trade and in undermining reproductive slavery by encouraging slaves to flee, meant that, rather than continuing to flourish, slavery was destined to linger on in a vestigial and evanescent state. In contrast, debt bondage continued to fulfil its traditional role in providing relief for the poor, as well as in drawing and attaching labour to plantations and mines.

The outcome of the scramble for Africa was not only a carving up of the continent into colonies opposed to slave-trading, but also the establishment of international agreements critical of slavery. The original purpose of these agreements was to apply moral gloss to a process of imperial expansion clearly bent on wealth and power. Thus, an international conference in 1890 produced the Brussels Act which secured agreement for banning the slave trade in Africa. The act was rescinded in 1919 when the Allied Powers committed themselves to the abolition of slavery 'in all its forms'. This led on to the Geneva Slave Convention of 1926, the work of the League of Nations, which obtained the ratification of forty-one states for the complete abolition not only of slavery but of all forms of slave-like forced labour. The latter agreement was confirmed by the Forced Labour Convention of 1931. The 1926 Slave Convention was later revised with a Supplementary Convention on the Abolition of Slavery, the Slave Trade and Institutions and Practices Similar to Slavery. Agreement was reached in 1956 – the work of the United Nations. Arising from the 1926 and 1956 conventions, and the committees of experts on slavery established first in 1932 and again in 1949, was a wealth of evidence, collected and publicized, as to which states had abolished slavery and which had not. The outcome was to create an internationally accepted moral code that condemned slavery as either evil or a mark of backwardness.[110] The effect was not only to encourage colonial powers to issue acts of abolition as a sign of enlightenment, but also to persuade independent slave-holding states to do likewise in a bid to obtain credibility as 'modern societies'. Prominent among the latter were the Arab states of the Middle East. For, by the 1930s, Arabia was the one remaining area where slavery could be said to thrive. The Muslim religion inspired no popular movement for the abolition of either slave-trading or slavery itself. Yet, inspired by the international agreement reached at Geneva in the 1920s, the Muslim World Conference held at Mecca in 1926 committed itself to the condemnation of slavery. Inspired by the Geneva agreement of 1956, another Muslim World Conference, held at Mogadishu in 1964, explicitly resolved: 'Islam condemns enslavement of men by men.'[111] Subjected to these pressures, Saudi Arabia, the largest user of slaves in the Middle East, shifted its ground. In 1970 it declared slavery illegal. The Yemen acted likewise in the same year. Slavery was not necessarily terminated in Arabia by an act of abolition, but, now outlawed, its continuation was only possible under the subterfuge of calling slaves servants or wives.[112]

In the totalitarian state

The use of forced labour in the twentieth century reached its peak in Nazi Germany and Stalinist Russia, where it served not just to assert political control but also to meet the economic needs of the state. Between the 1930s and 1950s, the labour of millions of Europeans was compulsorily requisitioned: either because they were foreigners defeated in war and conscripted to work for the victor, or because they were native Germans and Russians who had lost their freedom as a result of being declared enemies of the state. In Germany's case, most forced labourers were 'defeated foreigners', the result of its military successes in western and eastern Europe.[113] In Russia's case, most were simply citizens deemed to be 'enemies of the people' and sentenced to hard labour for having broken the law. In both cases, the forced labour used was not totally penal labour in the strictest sense of the term. Of the forced civilian workers employed by the Nazis, only a small proportion had actually fallen foul of the law. Most of them, it is true, were accommodated in fenced and guarded barracks with tight regulations and barbed-wire perimeters, but they were not legally defined as convicts, and their barracks, although far from pleasant, were not concentration camps. They were even paid wages. Originally these wages were pitched well below the rate for Germans, but to stop firms from preferring to employ foreigners to Germans, in 1940 the rate of pay for the two was made uniform, with the foreigners now disadvantaged through having imposed upon their wages an additional 15 per cent 'social compensation' tax. Nonetheless, the conscripted foreigners were not free workers, having been recruited under compulsion, given non-negotiable wages, denied the chance to change jobs, and allowed no choice as to the work. In Russia, among the forced labourers were the exiles placed in labour settlements. They were not seen as serving a prison sentence, but were often held behind barbed wire, and had to provide labour for the state. Both groups, moreover, were vulnerable to being siphoned off, through conviction for petty work offences, to prison work camps. As for the labour provided by convicted prisoners, it was performed under conditions that were much worse than those normally associated with prison. Typically housed in concentration camps, the workers were at the absolute mercy of the camp officials and guards, whose treatment of them was, in practice, completely unfettered by law.[114]

At the end of the Second World War, the two powers between them employed about 10 million forced labourers: over 2 million by Soviet Russia and about 7.7 million by Nazi Germany. Of this number, over 2 million were in concentration camps. Moreover, over 5 million were Russians, with 2.8

million of them worked by the Nazis as prisoners of war and conscripted labourers.[115]

In the Third Reich and Soviet Russia, thousands of camps sprang up to accommodate this work-force, and both regimes became heavily dependent upon its labour: in Nazi Germany, principally because of the extent of the war effort, coupled with the government's inability to turn the female population into an industrial substitute for the menfolk as they were called up to fight; in Soviet Russia, not only because of the war effort but also because, before and after the Second World War, it lacked a work-force capable of meeting – simply as a proletariat – the demands of an industrialization programme that, it felt, was urgently needed to defend itself against the capitalist world.

The system of forced labour used by Nazi Germany derived from two precedents. The first came from the First World War, during which the Germans employed the labour of 2,500,000 prisoners of war.[116] In addition, civilians were compulsorily recruited at that time, originally by preventing Poles resident in Germany when war broke out from returning home; and then by obliging people in the eastern occupied territories to provide involuntary work for the Kaiserreich.[117] Finally, in late 1916 and early 1917, 60,000 Belgians were deported to Germany. Much of this forced labour came to be housed in curfewed and barbed-wire camps. If they were Poles, they had to wear badges. Shirking was punished with imprisonment and reduced rations.[118] In other words, the forced labour plans of the Nazis were first tested in the First World War. Resulting from the massive call-up of 3 million Germans in 1914, their purpose was to make up for the consequent shortage of manpower in agriculture and industry. Largely, they failed. The prisoners of war managed to achieve a very low rate of productivity. They also required a great deal of guarding: in the occupied eastern territories, the conscripted labour was especially prone to abscond. What is more, the transportation of Belgian workers to Germany encountered international objection; and the unwilling conscripts effectively made their point with a very poor work rate.[119]

Created as a device of war, these work camps ended with the peace. A second precedent was set with the establishment of concentration camps in 1933, a reprisal against political dissidents following the burning down of the Reichstag.[120] During the course of the Second World War, they acquired two basic functions: extermination and labour exploitation. By the start of the war, this system – a conjunction of death and work camps – was established in embryo.[121] It simply required revival and further development. By 1941 it had become a central pillar of the Nazi state and an essential part of its racist policies and the war economy.[122]

The Nazi regime was driven by the need to upturn the liberal values created in the eighteenth century and applied thereafter. For this reason, it easily warmed to the concept of forced labour, taking note of what could be done by observing the racial servitude employed, during the previous century, in the Americas and the British Empire. It gave some consideration to the idea of resting the Third Reich upon a system of enslavement. Early in the 1930s, Hitler had remarked to Rauschning: 'Human culture cannot be developed any further without creating a certain modern form of bondage – or, if you like, of slavery.'[123] Over the years this idea surfaced on several occasions, usually in connection with the distinction the Nazis made between people of German stock and the racially alien, and the belief that, if necessary, the latter should be made to serve the former. Thus, a long-term plan for incorporating Poland into the post-war Reich – entitled the Peacetime Programme of the SS Reichsführer – was produced by Hans Kammler in December 1941. It proposed the creation of 12,000 camps to accommodate for German usage 4 million Slavs. In 1942 Kammler's plans were incorporated in a post-war construction programme for eastern Europe that entailed 14.6 million forced workers. Albert Speer interpreted the plan to imply that, when the war was won, a huge system of slavery would be established; and that the Third Reich would become, permanently, a 'slave state' under the rule of the SS.[124]

The Nazis' appreciation of slavery was assumed at the Nuremberg Trials. The International Military Tribunal described as a 'programme of slave labour' the forced foreign labour that the Nazis had organized and assigned to leading German companies such as Flick, IG-Farben and Krupp.[125] But were the forced labour schemes of the Nazis part of a plan to establish a permanent slave institution? Were they even an exercise in temporary slavery? Or, as in the First World War, were they simply a practical response to the labour problem created by a massive military mobilization, their use determined not by any far-reaching plan but by factors and events that steered the Nazis in that direction through a process whereby other solutions came to be eliminated?

The use to which forced labour was put during the Second World War complied with a principle Hitler propounded in his final war plans of May 1939: 'The population of non-German territories does not perform military service and is available for labour.'[126] In 1941, nearly 3 million foreigners were employed as forced labourers. This had risen to well over 7 million by 1944.[127] The defeat of Poland and France and the early victories over the Soviet Union contributed to the massive deployment of foreigners. Spectacular victories against all three placed enormous numbers of war prisoners in German hands.[128] However, the Nazis' labour policy was largely shaped by their failure to defeat Russia in late 1941, and the great amount of German manpower which was thereafter engaged in that lost cause. Also highly influential in the policy's formulation were several constraints and missed opportunities that sprang from ideological beliefs, vindictiveness and incompetence. One major constraint was the Nazi party's unwillingness to employ German female labour. In 1939 Germany possessed 3.5 million unemployed women, only half a million less than the 4 million Germans who had been called up to fight by May 1940.[129] Yet, as the Nazi, Eduard Willeke, sincerely and typically believed, to 'deploy more women' would endanger 'the folk-biological strength of the German people'.[130] The issue of female employment was pressed by Speer in 1942, as the labour problem became acute; but to employ German women in industry was seen as removing them from their natural habitat of children, kitchen and church; and with so many foreigners of alien race about, and the vital need to prevent miscegenation, keeping women at home became even more important. A minor concession was eventually made in the spring of 1943, when Hitler permitted the recruitment of 800,000 German women for industrial employment, but only on condition that they worked part time.[131]

The second major constraint shaping the Nazis' labour programme was their unwillingness to use Jewish labour. Having decided that Jews were harmful to the German nation, the Nazis interned them as aliens. The work to which they were deliberately put was not seen as economically useful but a retributive and humiliating preparation for death. Exceptionally in 1944, 100,000 Hungarian Jews were employed building underground bunkers; but otherwise the Nazis stuck to a policy of extermination 'in accordance with the Führer's wishes' (Himmler).[132]

The preference for holocaust left the labour problem unsolved. Yet it was not as if the Nazis were without other means of remedy. After all, the Nazis enjoyed a bonanza of prisoners of war: 1 million from Poland in 1939, 1.2 million from the west in 1940; 3.5 million taken from Russia in the winter of 1941–2. By May 1944, as many as 5 million Russian troops were in German hands.[133] The Geneva Convention forbade their use in industries connected with the war, and at first the Nazis abided by this. Prisoners of war were mostly assigned to agriculture where they were much needed, simply because the military build-up in the late 1930s had caused a flight of labour to industry. A shortage of labour in the farming sector had existed even before the war started. However, by November 1941 the Geneva Convention had been repudiated, especially to allow German industry to make use of the Russian and French prisoners of war.[134] Yet this massive resource of manpower was squandered. Only one-third of the Polish prisoners were used as labourers. Of the prisoners of war from the west, only the French and the Walloons were kept to work in the Reich, presumably because they were racially alien. Those regarded as of German stock (from Denmark, Norway and Holland) were sent home.[135] Of the prisoners of war taken in the Russian campaign, the Nazis allowed huge numbers to die – for reasons of national animus, ethnic contempt, fear of Bolshevism, vindictiveness as the war on the eastern front turned against them, and the sheer inability to cope with such massive numbers. The slaughter caused by starvation, disease and brutality had reduced the 3.5 million captured at the start to 1,100,000 by February 1942. Of these, only 166,881 were used as labour. Of the 5 million Russians taken by May 1944, only 1,900,000 managed to survive, and only 875,000 of them were actually put to work.[136]

With these options ruled out or wasted, the Nazi government had no real choice but to recruit foreign labour. Initially, this was done on the basis of consent. Anti-communist, anti-Russian or anti-Jewish sympathies were fertile recruiters, notably in Lithuania and the Ukraine, but the contemptuous and segregated treatment the workers received in Germany discouraged this source of supply. When the volunteers failed to sign on in sufficient numbers, compulsion was substituted. By early 1943, conscription and coercion had become the principal means of extracting labour from the occupied territories in both the east and west.[137] The programme was carried out on such a great scale that, by August 1944, the labour provided by prisoners of war – which in 1941 had comprised a substantial 39 per cent of the foreign work-force in the Reich – now stood at 25 per cent: against 1.9 million prisoners of war, there were 5.7 million civilian conscripts, 4 million of whom were Slavs from Poland and Russia.[138] But were they treated as slaves?

The Nazi treatment of conscripted civilians largely sprang from the policies they first drew up for the Poles and then applied to the Russians. They were set out in the *Polenerlasse* (Polish Decrees) of March 1940 and the *Ostarbeitererlasse* (Eastern Worker Decrees) of 1942, the latter modelled on the former. The *Polenerlasse* insisted on the following: a work permit; the letter P to be prominently displayed on clothing; a curfew after dark; and segregation from the German community. Polish workers were banned from using public transport, from attending the social, cultural and religious functions of the German community, and from entering German bars and restaurants. The penalty for sexual intercourse with a German was death.[139] At this stage, there was no insistence upon placing the workers under security in closed camps. However, this was explicitly provided in the regulations decreed for eastern workers in February and August 1942, which had conscripted Russians in mind. They were to be accommodated as 'civil prisoners': that is, in fenced camps and under guard, without freedom to leave the camp except for work.[140] This proposal materialized in a massive camp-construction programme in late 1942, planned and overseen by Speer. Since the 'P' badge was now inadequate, it was replaced by 'Ost'.[141]

The Polish labour regulations of March 1940, amazingly, had been issued when recruitment for work in the Reich was still on a voluntary basis. A month later, however, conscription had been brought in. All Poles born between 1915 and 1925 were called up. Whenever the local quota was not fulfilled, exemplary reprisals were taken, by the confiscation of farm animals and other goods. Then, a new deadline was set for the missing conscripts. As peasants took refuge in the forests, the SS organized manhunts to track them down. They also conducted surprise dawn attacks on villages and towns, to catch the inhabitants before they had time to flee.[142] This procedure, of operating through age cohorts backed up by tough action to meet the quotas, set the pattern for elsewhere.

Poles were regarded as only fit for agriculture. To secure sufficient industrial workers, conscription was applied to Russia in mid-1942, and to France in February 1943.[143] This was part of a massive labour recruitment drive conducted by Fritz Sauckel acting as Plenipotentiary General for the Utilization of Labour, aided by Albert Speer, Reich Minister of Munitions. As a result, 5,400,000 foreign workers were deported to the Reich between 1942 and 1944.[144] The policy of conscription led to a great deal of brutality, not only in recruitment but also in controlling the work-force, both in the camps and on the factory floor. Some of it came from officers and police, but a great deal was applied in the workplace by German workers who took it upon themselves to beat up recalcitrant Slavs. In the Krupp steelworks at Essen, for example, plant squads were set up in July 1942. All were employees, equipped with steel helmets, white armbands and leather truncheons. Assembled by siren, they declared the superiority of the *Herrenmensch* by attacking chiefly Russian workers. Driving them to this violent aggression must have been anxieties generated by the presence of large numbers of sullen foreigners. In early 1943 – before the allied bombing raids severely reduced their numbers – the latter comprised 40 per cent of the work-force.[145]

The Nazis deployed foreign labour through three types of camp. First, there was the prisoner-of-war camp, to which captured soldiers were sent after registration and vetting in Stalags. These prison camps were situated near the place of work. The inmates were kept under the surveillance of the army. Firms applied to use this labour which was allocated to them for a sum of money. Out of this income, the prisoners received a small allowance, but no wage.[146] Second, there was the barracks camp. Here the conscripted civilians were lodged, travelling daily to nearby factories and farms. The barracks camp had become the typical abode by late 1942. Earlier, accommodation had been the responsibility of the employers, with the workers lodged in a variety of places, including private housing. Now, for the eastern workers, the great majority of conscripted civilians, the barracks took over. For the Russian workers, the camps were fenced and guarded.[147] Third, there was the punishment camp – concentration camps for the long term, labour education camps for the short term.[148] They played an essential part in controlling the conscripted foreign labour, since the penalty for disobedience was committal to one of them.

In the course of time, the concentration camps became providers of labour in their own right, with inmates taken to work outside, or put to work within. Certain concentration camps were designated industrial plants in March 1942, specifically to make armaments. Their industrial importance grew as the SS, who ran them, became deeply engaged in aircraft and rocket production from late 1943, and recruited the necessary manpower by committing to them captured runaways from the prisoner-of-war and barracks camps. In the first half of 1944, for example, 204,000 were committed.[149] The population of the industrial concentration camps grew considerably between April 1943, when it stood at 171,000, and January 1945, when it stood at 714,200.[150] The flagship of this industrial empire was Central Works, established in 1943–4. It was situated underground in the Harz Mountains and engaged in building rockets. Here, as in the other concentration camp factories, the working conditions were terrible. A death-rate of 5.7 per cent per month was recorded for Central Works in December 1943. Speer claimed that the conditions improved greatly when he intervened in 1944 and arranged for the workers to be housed above ground. But the death-rate still remained at 10 per cent per year.[151] In the concentration camps a policy of working labour to death was pursued, the work-force driven on by brutality and docked rations. Such a policy had been alien to the slave systems of the past since it wasted capital. Responsible for it was partly the urgency of the work but also the belief that replacements were easily obtainable from the large supply of embittered conscript labour already in the Reich. For the latter, transference to a concentration camp was a descent into hell. But how did the majority fare who managed to avoid that fate?

From the start, the Nazi regime could not resist the temptation to humiliate its foreign workers: for example, by making them wear badges, by placing them in camps fenced with barbed wire, by assuming them to be subhuman (i.e. the *Untermensch*). This attitude of contempt had alienated foreign volunteers, obliging the Nazis to resort to conscription. Conscription instilled in foreign workers poor motivation and a spirit of resistance. The existence of both hardened the Germans' hostile attitude towards them. At times, ham-fisted attempts were made to win over the foreign labour force. Sauckel, for example, ordered the removal of badges from April 1944 and sought to get rid of barbed-wire fencing. Incentive schemes were also established, involving payment for piece-work and more food.[152] But Sauckel's attempts at liberalization tended to be ignored; and the incentive schemes relating to food could only have effect if the work-force was inadequately fed: as the authorities were well aware, for the rewarded workers were obliged to eat their special treats, usually well-filled, doorstep sandwiches, in front of their fellow inmates. Characterizing the system were long working hours; poor food (e.g. turnip soup for breakfast, lunch and dinner); inadequate clothing (in 1943 a uniform was introduced for eastern workers made from rags or cellulose); the frequent and deliberate practice of making skilled workers carry out unsuitable tasks (e.g. electricians were made to grease coach wheels); inappropriate punishments for minor offences (such as flogging, hosing down in freezing conditions, or solitary confinement); and an absence of medical care.[153] Eastern workers were treated much worse than western workers: their food rations were less, and, while the former came to be confined in camps, the latter were sometimes accommodated in private housing.[154] Conditions deteriorated in the closing stages of the war, especially from 1943. This was partly due to the success of Sauckel's recruitment drives, which led to gross overcrowding in the barracks camps.[155] It also resulted from the disintegration of the

Nazi regime, as it was driven back by the Russians and pounded from the air by the Allies. Eventually, it became incapable of running the forced labour system it had created. A great deal of hardship occurred in the resulting chaos.

Humiliated and overworked, the forced foreign labour reacted with a great deal of resistance: not by acts of rebellion but by extensive disobedience. As a result, German industry was plagued with *Arbeitsbummelei* (go-slows, absenteeism, self-mutilation, low productivity) and *Arbeitsflucht* (absconsion). In addition, the camps acquired their own inner autonomy, based on barter, petty theft and trading in worker-made goods, as well as the forging of work and leave permits. Licensed by corruption among camp officials, it was something the authorities were powerless to stop.[156] They reacted to worker disobedience with a programme of punishment which failed to root out the problem while worsening the worker's lot. Coupled with the danger of falling into the hands of the SS through being dispatched to a concentration camp, there was the danger of being arrested by the Gestapo. From 1943 the Gestapo waged a relentless campaign against foot-dragging, arresting 260,000 foreign workers for this offence in the first five months of the year. They dispatched them to labour education camps, where conditions were similar to those of the concentration camps.[157]

Absconsion had inevitably increased as conscription was introduced. Thus, the Poles were noted fugitives from 1940. With other foreigners, it only became a problem from late 1942. By the end of 1943, 45,000 a month went missing. One major cause of flight was Allied bombing raids. Especially vulnerable were the foreign workers attached to industrial plants, notably in the Ruhr where heavy bombing began in March 1943 and continued in early 1944. The camps were close to the factories, the focus of the bombing. They lacked their own air raid shelters. Since the eastern workers were not admitted to the large public shelters, the death toll among them was enormous. Foreign workers, not surprisingly, fled to the countryside, looting houses *en route*. In doing so, they came under a massive onslaught from the police and army who set up road checks and hunted them down. Those captured – 30–40,000 were taken each month in 1944, with possibly half a million arrests made in the course of the year – fell to the Gestapo, who by late 1944 were handing them over to the SS. They were then placed in industrial concentration camps.[158]

This failed to stem the exodus as, responding to the Allied slogan 'To the Countryside', thousands of foreign workers in the autumn of 1944 took to the fields and woods, liberating themselves as the authorities lost the capacity not only to stop, but even to monitor, their flight. Nonetheless, the Gestapo continued to make arrests, so much so that by March 1945 their prisons were bursting with eastern workers. To solve this problem, it resorted to mass executions.[159]

Like the wars between the Ottoman and Habsburg empires in the sixteenth and seventeenth centuries, the military conflict between Nazi

Germany and Soviet Russia pitted against each other two systems of servitude. On both sides, the war effort relied heavily upon the forced labour of millions of men and women, whose basic role was to compensate for the labour lost to the military. However, in the Soviet Union convicts also served as troops at the front. Volunteering for war service, either to escape the work camps or hopefully to expunge their criminal record through acts of bravery on the battlefield, 1 million fought in penal battalions, which, predictably, were assigned to the most dangerous operations – such as clearing minefields or storming impregnable positions – and therefore suffered the highest casualties in the Red Army.[160] Those convicts engaged in civilian work during the war amounted to 1.9 million in 1941, falling to 1.5 million in 1945.[161] Most worked in the mines, factories, farms and fisheries directly run by the secret service (the NKVD), but a quarter of a million were allocated to concerns run by other commissariats. For this reason, in the manner of the conscripted foreigners in Germany, some Soviet convicts laboured alongside free workers. No matter where they worked, they fell under the administrative control of the Gulag (i.e. Chief Administration for Camps). Some were placed in Corrective Labour Camps, others in Corrective Labour Colonies. The former were concentration camps, meant for long-term prisoners (those sentenced to three or more years); the latter were defined as 'places of general imprisonment', and were intended for those serving less than three years. In addition, there were labour settlements for those sent into exile. These labour settlers also tended to be kept behind wire. Like the convicts, they came under the Gulag administration, with an obligation to work for the NKVD. For foreign soldiers captured in battle, there were the usual prisoner-of-war camps; for Russian soldiers who had fallen into enemy hands, there were Verification and Filtration Camps to greet them on their return to the motherland.[162]

In Soviet Russia, this system of penal labour preceded and postdated the Second World War. Before the war, it was much more highly developed than the German system. In 1938, the Soviet Union already possessed a penal labour force of 1.9 million which was heavily engaged in production under an extreme regime of long working hours and wretched living conditions.[163] This penal system was a continuation of the one used in Tsarist Russia, where, in the nineteenth century, over 1 million criminals and political dissidents had been employed to develop Siberia, some in exile, others in prison camps.[164] The Bolsheviks resorted to it as they sought to consolidate their assumption of power. Concentration camps were authorized by decree in September 1918 and April 1919. Following the civil war, sixty-five camps existed by 1922, but mostly in the vicinity of Moscow and Leningrad. In the following year they were reduced to twenty-three.[165] These camps were, essentially, for punishment, not production. However, in the late 1920s they were shifted away into the wild and became work camps for exploiting the natural resources of the far north. By 1926 a number had been established on Solovetsky Island in the region of Archangel, where the prisoners were housed in monasteries, and their labour was employed in agriculture, timbering and fishing.[166] The second major step in establishing the Gulag system was taken in the early 1930s following a proposal to the Politburo in 1929 that – in view of overcrowding in the prisons – long-term convicts should be used to develop the northern regions, principally by constructing a network of railways and roads for the extraction of timber and minerals. The outcome was the establishment of the Northern Camps of Special Designation. In 1930 several camps had been located not only in the north but also in Siberia, and in the far east of the Soviet Empire.[167] Their role was vital to the Soviet economy. It was to supply from traditionally inaccessible regions, where free labour could not be persuaded to go, the resources needed for a programme of rapid industrialization.[168]

To fulfil this difficult task, considerable manpower was required. And, as the enterprise became outstandingly profitable, with its organizers, the NKVD, making more money than any other commissariat, the urge to find enough forced labour became overpowering and unstoppable; so much so that economic needs came to determine the level of imprisonment, with prosecution quotas set which were decided simply by the camp and colony demand for workers.[169] At the disposal of the NKVD's recruitment drives were certain state regulations and policies. From 1926, there was article 58 of the Criminal Code, which gave a very broad definition to what constituted a crime against the state.[170] In 1932, a law was passed in defence of state property – largely to back up the programme of collectivization – making the theft of small amounts of goods, such as farm produce, liable to ten years' imprisonment. The enforcement of this one law alone yielded, over the next four years, a labour force of 127,000.[171] Another labour-productive law was the absenteeism and tardiness legislation introduced in 1940 to discipline the industrial work-force. Late arrival at work – twenty-one minutes or more – became a criminal offence, qualifying the offender for imprisonment in a work camp. Within the first six months of its operation, it recruited 29,000 workers.[172] But before this law was made, the NKVD had already created a huge fund of forced labour through a series of major purges, the first against the peasantry, the second against 'bourgeois specialists'.

For allegedly resisting collectivization, 5 million peasants were proceeded against between 1930 and 1933. Not all, however, were sent to prison or to work camps. Over 2 million were defined as 'special migrants' (*spetsposelentsy*). They were deported to remote areas for ever and put to work by the Gulag. The remainder served sentences, some in prison but most in Corrective Labour Camps and Colonies.[173]

The second great purge occurred in 1936–8, sweeping into the camps and colonies a large segment of the professional bourgeoisie. Convicted of acts or words against the Stalinist government, officials, officers and the intelligentsia of writers, academics and teachers were, overnight, transmuted into manual workers. In 1938, 1.9 million prisoners were placed under labour service in this manner.[174] So far, most condemned to penal labour had been Russian citizens. This changed, following the Nazi–Soviet Pact of 1939, when the Baltic states of Finland, Estonia and Latvia were added to the Soviet Union, as were eastern Poland and Bessarabia. To root out nationalist dissidents, the work camps acquired yet a further use, with 1 million men and women dispatched to them in 1939 and 1940.[175]

The Soviet work camps were ideally suited to fulfil their economic purpose, which was initially to build an infrastructure of communications in primitive, unpopulated regions, and then to extract from them ore and timber. This much was demonstrated in the late 1930s. The labour was undoubtedly cheap. For 1932–3, it was calculated that the upkeep of prisoners cost 500 roubles per annum, whereas an equivalent wage was 1,500 roubles.[176] Also, the necessary investment in capital was low. Unlike slaves, prisoners did not have to be purchased. Moreover, the supply was so plentiful that there was little need of draught animals or machinery, apart from trains to bring in fresh workers. The system also provided a work-force that could be firmly controlled and easily shifted from area to area.[177]

Within each camp, the guards were highly motivated both to prevent workers from escaping and to meet production targets, since, subjected to surveillance by the Operational Department of the NKVD, failure could mean, via criminal prosecution, condemnation to prison or work camp, usually as a guard without pay.[178] For the prisoners, there was the incentive of promotion, since prisoners, in reward for good work, could become freed employees, continuing in the camps as paid doctors, administrators, mechanics and engineers. Cases were known of ex-prisoners entering the ranks of the NKVD as guards, directors of camps and leading officials.[179] This social mobility between the servile and the custodians made the Russian system of penal servitude distinctly different from that of the Nazis, and also from New World slavery and Old World serfdom. For the prisoners, however, the main motivation to work and obey came from being kept in a state of semi-starvation. In other words, the camps were run on a deliberate food policy that, on the one hand, reduced the running costs and, on the other, promoted production. It was described by S. Swianiewicz, an ex-prison labourer: 'The general food policy in the camps is to keep the men in a state of semi-starvation, and, by holding out hopes of slightly better food, to give them an incentive for doing more work.'[180] This policy also distinguished Soviet, and likewise Nazi, prison labour from serf and slave systems, and overcame the problem identified by Adam Smith and Karl Marx of how to make an unwaged work-force efficient. Smith proposed that coercion through the whip was the only solution: a flawed one, in his opinion, since it kept slaves in order but did not encourage them to do their best.[181] Deprivation of food, however, while a more effective motivator of work than the whip, also had its drawbacks. These stemmed from another difference between slavery and Soviet penal labour. In so much as the price of the slave encouraged masters to show him or her some respect for life, this consideration was absent in the Soviet work camps, where there was no practical safeguard to prevent prisoners from being worked to death. The fact that replacements were easily obtainable – it was simply a matter of using the criminal law to raid the free population – caused the work-force to be regarded as disposable. This meant that the food rations underpinning the system of worker motivation tended to be pitched too low, since it did not matter if some died of starvation. As a result, the motivation inspired by the desire for food was countered by the physical state to which the work-force was reduced by a vicious combination of hard labour, atrocious conditions and malnutrition.[182]

Yet to explain the Soviet prisoner's incentive to work only in terms of his stomach or the prospect of promotion within the Gulag would be inadequate. In addition, the camp authorities divided the workers into 'shirkers' and 'shock troops', the latter receiving favours denied the former. Workers, moreover, were arranged in competitive teams, with remuneration dependent upon what the team produced, putting pressure upon individuals to discipline, and be disciplined by, their team-mates. The fear of punishment also spurred on the workers: not just a reduction in rations but also being placed in the *shizo*, an unheated solitary confinement cell, or pegged out for the mosquitoes to drain dry.[183] All this provided the prisoner with a strong incentive to respond positively to set tasks; but what motivated him in the long term was the hope of liberation and the ability to bring the prospect closer by securing, in reward for work or providing information against other prisoners, a shortening of the sentence. This, of course, was a feature of slave systems frequently found both in the New World and in the world of Islam, although rarely in the British Caribbean or the USA. For this reason, among many others, US slavery and USSR penal labour were worlds apart. And for the same reason, among many others, Soviet penal servitude and the slave-serf practices of Tsarist Russia were very different from each other.

The economic achievements of Soviet penal labour did not end with the pre-war industrialization programme. Nor were they limited to infrastructural development and primary production. With Russia's involvement in the Second World War, the camps became a vital source of industrial as well as agricultural labour, an inevitable consequence of the massive call-up for military service – with 7.5 million mobilized in 1941, 10.9 million in 1942 and 11.1 million in 1943 – at a time when, faced by the Nazi onslaught, the free working population was contracting fast, from 72.8 million in 1941 to 55.6 million in 1943. Prisoners were quickly turned to the manufacture of ammunition: M-50 mortars, RGD-33 grenades and shells. By early 1944, 17 per cent of ammunition produced in the Soviet Union was made by prison labour, which was also engaged in making uniforms, gas masks and field telephones. In addition, the prisoners became much more involved in agriculture. The land they worked increased from 250,000 hectares in 1941 to 441,000 hectares in 1944. They also continued with their construction work, building railways, roads, aerodromes and factories, and with mining.[184] All this was achieved at low cost, but also at an enormous price. In the heroic national struggle to withstand the Nazi invasion – between the moment when the Germans reached Moscow in September 1941 and the moment in May 1945 when the Red Army took Berlin – the Soviet convicts came low down in the order of priorities. The urgency of the work and their lack of food and adequate clothing caused high mortality. It increased on average from 3 per cent a year before the war to 25 per cent in 1942–3, with something like one-third of the penal work-force unable to work through physical frailty.[185] Nonetheless, the Gulag remained throughout a highly productive regime and a major part of the war effort.[186]

Unlike the Nazi system of forced labour, the Gulag did not end once the war was over. With Stalin still in control, it went from strength to strength in the following eight years. During the war, the prison labour force had fallen dramatically, the result of the release of convicts to fight at the front and a very high death-rate in the camps: so much so that, between 1941 and 1944, it fell by 40 per cent.[187] But, in the last year of the war, the prison population began to recover – the result of large-scale arrests made in the regions liberated from Nazi rule. Placed in the camps were collaborators and Germans, prisoners of war and civilians. The prison population increased by 25 per cent between January 1944 and January 1945, although, by the latter date, it stood at less than half its total in 1941.[188] With the end of the war, the Gulag achieved a new order of magnitude. This related both to its control over prisoners put to labour and to people exiled as labour settlers. From 1935 to 1947, the prisoners under sentence of labour remained, in any one year, between 1 and 2 million. However, between 1948 and 1953, it reached between 2 and 2.6 million. The total of 510,300 in 1934 had risen to 2.5 million on Stalin's death, boosted by the post-war action taken against suspect nationalities.[189] What is more, the proportion of prisoners sentenced to three years or more rose steeply. Although sentences of three or more years had easily exceeded those of less than three years in 1939 (79 against 21 per cent), by 1945 the former was exceeded slightly by the latter (49 against 51 per cent), reflecting the increase in the numbers of prisoners used on ordinary factory and construction sites. However, by 1953 the ratio was 70 per cent against 30 per cent, indicating not only an increase in longer sentences but also that more of the work was carried out in concentration camps.[190] In addition, the numbers placed in exile rose. As a result of the opposition to collectivization, the population of labour settlers achieved a figure of 1.3 million in 1932 and 1 million in 1936. It gradually fell away, as the exiles were called up for military service, standing at only 653,000 in December 1944. With the peace, however, the trend was reversed. By 1949, the labour settlers had reached 2.3 million, an all-time record.[191] This meant that the sum total of those subjected to forced labour in 1949 stood at 3.5

million. This exceeded the previous highest figure – that for 1939 – by over 900,000.[192]

Nor did penal servitude end with Stalin's death, although an amnesty of 1956 appeared to reduce the prison camp population by two-thirds. The camps survived until the late 1980s, if in a very undermanned state.[193] This continued reliance on forced labour in the post-war years stemmed partly from the incapacity of the Soviet state to establish a proper rapport with Russian society – the Tsarist state had suffered from the same problem – but it was also a consequence of two other factors: the fear that capitalist powers were plotting to overthrow its communist regime, and an appreciation of prison labour as an indispensable economic asset for exploiting the natural resources of outlying regions where the permafrost and the mosquito reigned supreme.

Conclusion: The Significance of Modern Servitude

Servitude is undoubtedly a terrible tale of man's inhumanity to man. Most crimes against humanity have consisted of tortures, mutilations, killings and pillage inflicted in a situation of war. Justifying, or at least excusing, these crimes was the belief that the enemy had committed, or was about to commit, similar atrocities. Yet an outstanding exception to this equation of inhumanity with war lies in the practice of servitude. True, some forms of it, notably slavery and penal servitude, had military associations: for example, the enslaved were often prisoners of war and, in the twentieth century, political prisoners, defined as internal enemies of the state, have been subjected to hard labour to sustain the war effort. The philosopher John Locke even saw slavery as akin to war because, lying outside the social contract, the relationship between slave and master likewise rested upon a suspension of normal society. But, for the most part, modern servitude had little to do with war. It was usually imposed in time of peace. New slaves were mostly bought, after being acquired by theft or plunder. Its imposition in modern times was predominantly the work of civilized societies which were under no great pressure to place men, women and children in bondage, and which often subscribed to ideologies (democratic, capitalist, communist, Christian) that strongly disapproved of the practice. As well as an inexcusable crime, then, modern servitude stands as one of the most outrageous acts of collective hypocrisy ever committed.

Yet modern servitude was not simply the mark of evil. In the development of the modern world, it had a practical function of vital importance: as a supplier of labour and a delegator of authority, the former allowing capitalist production to develop before the creation of a proletariat, the latter allowing states to undergo centralization before acquiring the bureaucratic apparatus necessary to bring it about. In key situations, then, servitude made up for the deficiencies of the capitalist economy and the modern state. What is more, it continued to do so into the twentieth century, supplying labour for unpleasant work in inhospitable regions and acting as a means of enforcing submission to totalitarian regimes.

Subjection to servitude usually implies victimization. But to regard it just in this light overlooks a vital feature: the capacity of the servile to establish protective barriers that their lords, masters and employers needed to respect. It also overlooks the variety of forms servitude could assume, as well as the variety of conditions found within each form. To use slavery as a metaphor for the whole range of servitude tempts one to ignore the gains workers could make as serfs or as indentured servants, and the advantages transported convicts could draw from a free passage to North America or Australia. It also causes one to underestimate the terrible hardships, physical and mental, suffered by the internees of twentieth-century concentration camps. Furthermore, using the image of plantation slavery to encapsulate the essence of slavery misrepresents the conditions under which many slaves actually lived.

Condemning servitude is an act of virtue but hardly a means of understanding the subject. It overlooks the fact that, prior to the late eighteenth century, the societies which permitted slavery saw nothing wrong in it. Merely by reference to religious authority, they could easily justify the practice as perfectly ethical. It also overlooks the fact that, rather than being compulsorily imposed, servitude was often voluntarily accepted, whether it was domestic slavery in Africa, serfdom in Latin America and Europe, or indentured service and debt bondage in Asia. This was because people either opted for protection rather than freedom, or agreed to trade their liberty for a free passage abroad. Furthermore, the millions of Africans transported against their wills to the Americas or the Middle East came from societies that practised slavery. Their objection was not to the principle of slavery but to being its victims rather than its beneficiaries, and, in the process, to undergoing compulsory and permanent exile in an alien world. Having suffered this awful plight, however, slaves in the Americas proceeded to shape the system in their own interest. This they successfully accomplished in spite of the legal and economic advantages that the masters enjoyed. What was consequently established in practice was far removed from the ideal expectations held by their owners. Yet it was something the latter had to tolerate in order to make the system work. In this respect, an accommodation was often reached because of what the masters had to concede; and, as a result, slaves came to accept a regime that had been initially forced upon them but which subsequently they had helped to make.

Much of the actual meaning of servitude was lost as the Western world turned against it in the late eighteenth century and, in the bid to get it abolished, erected a monumental edifice of condemnation. The problem is to view servitude independently of abolitionism: an extremely difficult task. This is because much of the surviving evidence relating to slavery, serfdom, indentured service and debt bondage was produced to make the case for emancipation.

Impeding a realistic understanding of servitude are two key concepts. Originally created by abolitionism, they were adopted by scholars for a variety of unscholarly reasons. The one equates servitude with the extremes of exploitation; the other regards it as tantamount to social death. However, servitude and exploitation were never simply related. Compared with free workers, the servile were often relatively well off; so much so that what essentially distinguished one from the other was not grinding poverty but legal restriction. Nor did their unfree status necessarily place the servile completely beyond the social pale. Serfs, after all, comprised society; enslavement was often a means of admission to an alien society; penal servitude was a state of social sleep, not of social death. Indentured servants and debt bondsmen were only temporarily out. When their bondage was up, they either returned to their native societies or entered the free society of their adopted country. As for the slaves of the New World, to what extent was their social ostracization the result of bondage? After all, in predominantly white societies it continued unabated after abolition, suggesting that it had more to do with race. The outcome was not social death but the creation of self-contained black societies: something established under slavery and preserved after emancipation. The black society, under slavery and after, was as valid a part of the whole society as that of the whites. It only differed in being disconnected from the political system. In this respect, it gave an extended lease of life to the *ancien régime* in which, typically, the political nation embraced a fragment of the population and the rest suffered political exclusion – but not social death.

There can be no doubt that servitude was a major force in shaping the modern world. This was largely because of its role in the global spread of commercial agriculture, and the part this development played in the general process of modernization. Until the nineteenth century, commercial farming largely operated through pre-capitalist modes of production. Rather than based on a free market for waged labour, it was slave- or peasant-based, the latter reliant either on serfs under obligation to farm the demesne or on free sharecroppers. The commercial agriculture dependent upon servile labour, moreover, led to the creation of several peripheries of primary production, whose function was to supply the more advanced economies with food and raw materials. Coincidentally in the early modern period, one periphery developed in eastern Europe and another in the Americas to meet the essentially urban needs of western Europe. Then in the nineteenth and twentieth centuries yet another developed in the Third World to supply commodities to the industrialized societies of North America, Europe and Japan. In the process, primitive economies were suddenly modernized as a result of becoming linked up with a world market through their capacity to produce cash crops. In each case, the transformation happened before the development of native societies capable of managing and servicing the new economic regime. Making this modernization possible was the importation of large amounts of labour. Some of this labour consisted of free settlers, who took capitalism with them; but much of it comprised bondsmen and bondswomen, most of whom passed under compulsion from pre-capitalist societies into a capitalist world. These migrations of bonded labour were connected not simply with slavery but also with the use of pre- and post-slavery forms of servitude: debt bondage, indentured service and convict labour. The whole process had its beginnings in the late fifteenth century and extended into the early twentieth century. Responsible for it was the spread of plantation farming, initially in the Americas and eventually in Asia and Africa.

The development and extension of this system of commercial agriculture was reliant upon a sufficient supply of labour. This was essentially provided by servitude. The impact of servitude, in turn, depended upon the importance acquired by the plantations of the periphery in the modern world. This rested upon their linkage with other major developments, notably urbanization and industrialization. Before the advent of industrialization, a major urban development took place in Europe as the number of large cities – that is, those with populations of over 100,000 – increased from four to seventeen. Promoting this increase was the role of towns as centres of government and commerce, but enabling it to occur were the serf granaries of central and eastern Europe and the supplies of corn they dispatched to western Europe via the Baltic. This stage of urbanization in turn promoted commercial farming in the hinterlands of the great cities, as capitalist farming with waged labour, and sharecropping with family labour, developed to feed the inhabitants. As for the relationship between servitude and industrialization, this rested upon the commercial wealth generated in the seventeenth and eighteenth centuries by the transatlantic slave trade, and the importance of certain raw materials that servile labour came to produce. The connection inevitably was made by cotton, the bulk of which was produced by slaves. In addition, servitude influenced the global development of industrialization by helping to create two worlds: the one centred upon the production of manufactured goods and financial services, the other upon the production of raw materials; the one subjected to economic overdevelopment, the other to economic underdevelopment; the one a world of wealth, the other a world of poverty. Although interrelated, the two worlds were not complementary or reciprocal since the benefits flowed only one way. Colonial rule and economic imperialism merely upheld this dichotomy. Its very creation stemmed from the slave plantation which established a society that, internally, maximized supply but minimized demand; and ensured that what it produced was principally for export.

Socially, modern servitude made its mark in five basic respects. In the first place, the concept of personal freedom as it developed in the West was undoubtedly promoted by the practice of servitude. Yet other factors must have played a part, notably the libertarian ideas the English acquired in opposition to Stuart despotism, and their transmission to North America in opposition to Hanoverian despotism: ideas that became impressed upon the world by virtue of the power these two societies acquired thanks to industrialization. In the second place, because of slavery, servitude created in the

Americas new societies that were not simply governed by class, even though wealth was monopolized by the free. Central to them was the distinction made in the law between the free and the unfree. This meant that among the free was a large element – the poor whites – whose sense of status owed nothing to their lack of wealth. The same was true of the unfree, whose lack of status had nothing basically to do with poverty. As well as providing poor whites in the New World with status, servitude also supplied the poor in the Old World with a taste for luxury, since slavery, indentured service and debt bondage were very much involved in producing non-essential goods such as sugar, tobacco, coffee, chocolate and tea. Through the democratization of luxury, servitude was involved in the early development of consumerism. In the fourth place, servitude was a major source of cultural intermixing, the result of transporting millions of people to parts of the world with which they had no cultural identity. Finally, the use of bonded workers – first slaves, then indentured servants – in conjunction with the sugar plantation, rested upon a contempt not only for labour but also for the resources of nature. Extreme monocultural production, in which profit surmounted all considerations of ecological consequence, had its beginnings in modern servitude.

Politically, the continuation of servitude into the twentieth century exposed the inadequacies of the modern state. In all its basic forms – royal absolutism, the democratic state, the colonial state, totalitarianism – it had to rely, at least for a time, upon some form of servitude, although subscribing to principles that appeared to repudiate the practice. Despite its emphasis upon direct, centralized rule through public institutions, royal absolutism in central and eastern Europe depended upon serfdom, a system of delegated, privatized authority. For the first century of its existence, the democratic United States relied upon the wealth generated by the slave South, its constitutional principles of equality and liberty rendered a nonsense in practice unless seen as predicated on race. As colonial powers in the nineteenth and twentieth centuries, the French and the British compromised their reputations as crusaders against slavery by tolerating its existence, for the sake of preserving imperial order and prosperity. Despite the fact that they were based on a philosophy designed to liberate the worker from exploitation, communist regimes felt obliged to place millions under penal servitude. And despite the fact that it was founded on a philosophy of racial purity, Nazi Germany was obliged to rely heavily upon the forced labour of imported Slavs, even though their presence on German soil posed a massive threat of miscegenation. In view of its economic, social and political impact, then, modern servitude has to be noted for its long-term importance, rather than simply deplored and dismissed as a crime.

A Bibliographical Essay

The intention here is not to cover the subject thoroughly – a virtually impossible task – but merely to identify key contributions and suggest further reading. Needless to say, this is very much an arbitrary and impressionistic exercise. In concentrating upon the basic forms of servitude, the essay fails to relate the reading to the issues of development, impact and termination; but remedy for this shortcoming lies in consulting the endnotes.

Comparative analysis of the different forms of servitude is, arguably, still in its infancy. The same could be said for the comparative study of the varieties of servility found within each form. In comparing the forms of servitude the following are especially useful: Abbot E. Smith's *Colonists in Bondage: White Servitude and Convict Labour in America, 1607–1776* (Chapel Hill, 1947); W. Kloosterboer, *Involuntary Labour since the Abolition of Slavery* (Leiden, 1960); Bruno Lasker, *Human Bondage in Southeast Asia* (Chapel Hill, 1950); Claude Meillassoux, *The Anthropology of Slavery* (London, 1991), pt 1, ch. 4 (for slavery and serfdom); Stanley Engerman, 'Slavery, serfdom and other forms of coerced labour', *Serfdom and Slavery*, ed. M. L. Bush (London, 1996), ch. 2; Peter Kolchin, *Unfree Labour: American Slavery and Russian Serfdom* (London, 1987). Fruitful in its provocativeness is Stanley Elkin's unconvincing comparison of slavery with concentration camp internment in his *Slavery: a Problem in American Institutional and Intellectual Life* (Chicago, 1959).

The outstanding work on New World slavery is Robin Blackburn's *The Overthrow of Colonial Slavery* (London, 1988), and its prelude *The Making of New World Slavery* (London, 1997), although omitted – necessarily because of the structure – is an examination of the US slave system in its prime. This can be found in Robert W. Fogel's *Without Consent or Contract* (New York, 1989) and Peter Kolchin's *American Slavery* (London, 1993). Further useful studies of North American slavery are Betty Wood, *Origins of American Slavery* (New York, 1997); Ira Berlin, *Many Thousands Gone: the First Two Centuries of Slavery in North America* (Cambridge, Mass., 1998); Philip D. Morgan, *Slave Counterpoint: Black Culture in the Eighteenth-Century Chesapeake and Lowcountry* (University of North Carolina Press, 1998); Alan Kulikoff, *Tobacco and Slaves: the Development of Southern Cultures in the Chesapeake, 1680–1800* (Chapel Hill, 1986); Joe Gray Taylor, *Negro Slavery in Louisiana* (New York, 1963); D. C. Littlefield, *Rice and Slaves* (Baton Rouge, 1981); William Dusinberre, *Them Dark Days: Slavery in the American Rice Swamps* (Oxford, 1996). Especially important is Michael Tadman's *Speculators and Slaves: Masters, Traders and Slaves in the Old South* (Wisconsin, 1989). By studying the extent of the internal slave trade, he throws new light on the nature of slave control in the USA. Helpful comparisons between North American slavery and the slavery found elsewhere in the New World are provided by Herbert S. Klein in *African Slavery in Latin America and the Caribbean* (Oxford, 1986) and *Slavery in the Americas: a Comparative Study of Virginia and Cuba* (Chicago, 1967); by Carl N. Degler's *Neither Black nor White: Slavery and Race Relations in Brazil and the United States* (New York, 1971); and by James Walvin's *Questioning Slavery* (London, 1996). For slavery in Latin America, there is Colin A. Palmer, *Slaves of the White God: Blacks in Mexico, 1570–1650* (Cambridge, Mass, 1976); F. P. Bowser, *The African Slave in Colonial Peru, 1524–1650* (Stanford, 1974); Peter Blanchard, *Slavery and Abolition in Early Republican Peru* (Delaware, 1992); George R. Andrews, *The Afro-Argentinians of Buenos Aires, 1800–1900* (Wisconsin, 1980); William F. Sharp, *Slavery in the Spanish Frontier: the Colombian Choco, 1680–1810* (Oklahoma University Press, 1976); Stuart B. Schwartz, *Sugar Plantations in the Formation of Brazilian Society: Bahia, 1550–1835* (Cambridge, 1985); R. B. Martins, *Growing in Silence: the Slave Economy of Nineteenth-Century Minas Gerais, Brazil* (Ph.D., Vanderbilt University, 1980); Mary C. Kurasch, *Slave Life in Rio de Janeiro, 1808–1850* (Princeton, 1987); Robert Conrad, *World of Sorrow* (Baton Rouge, 1986). For slavery in the Caribbean, there is Barbara Bush, *Slave Women in Caribbean Society, 1650–1838* (London, 1990); Hilary M. Beckles, *Natural Rebels: a Social History of Enslaved Black Women in Barbados* (New Brunswick, 1989); Elsa V. Goveia, *Slave Society in the British Leeward Islands at the End of the Eighteenth Century* (New Haven, 1965); Orlando Patterson, *The Sociology of Slavery: an Analysis of the Origins, Development and Structure of Negro Slave Society in Jamaica* (London, 1967); J. R. Ward, *British West Indian Slavery, 1750–1834* (Oxford, 1988); Richard S. Dunn, *Sugar and Slaves: the Rise of the Planter Class in the English West Indies* (London, 1973); Clarence J. Munford, *The Black Ordeal of Slavery and Slave Trading in the French West Indies* (New York, 1991), vols 2 and 3; F. W. Knight, *Slave Society in Cuba during the Nineteenth Century* (Madison, 1970); Rebecca J. Scott, *Slave Emancipation in Cuba* (Princeton, 1985).

For African and Asian slavery, see James L. Watson (ed.), *Asian and African Systems of Slavery* (Oxford, 1980); Martin A. Klein (ed.), *Breaking the Chains: Slavery, Bondage and Emancipation in Modern Africa and Asia* (Madison, 1993). For further reading on India, see Tanika Sarkar, 'Bondage in the colonial context', *Chains of Servitude: Bondage and Slavery in India*, ed. Utsa Patnaik and Manjari Dingwaney (London, 1985), ch. 3. For further reading on Southeast Asia, see Anthony Reid, 'Closed and open slave systems in pre-colonial Southeast Asia', *Slavery, Bondage and Dependency in Southeast Asia*, ed. Reid (St Lucia, Queensland, 1983), ch. 7. For further reading on Africa, see the brilliant account by Claude Meillassoux in his *The Anthropology of Slavery* (London, 1991); Paul E. Lovejoy, *Transformations in Slavery: a History of Slavery in Africa* (Cambridge, 1983); John Grace, *Domestic Slavery in West Africa* (New York, 1975); Allan G. B. Fisher and Humphrey J. Fisher, *Slavery and Muslim Society in Africa* (London, 1970); R. S. O'Fahey and J. L. Spaulding, *Kingdoms of the Sudan* (London, 1974); Richard L. Roberts, *Warriors, Merchants and Slaves* (Stanford, 1987).

For further studies of Islamic slavery, see Murray Gordon, *Slavery in the Arab World* (New York, 1989); Daniel Pipes, *Slave Soldiers and Islam* (New Haven, 1981); Y. Hakan Erdem, *Slavery in the Ottoman Empire and its Demise, 1800–1909* (London, 1996); Halil Inalcik, *The Ottoman Empire in the Classical Age, 1300–1600* (London, 1994); I. K. Kunt, *The Sultan's Servants: the Transformation of Ottoman Provincial Government, 1550–1650* (New York, 1983); Barnette Miller, *The Palace School of Muhammad the Conqueror* (Cambridge, Mass., 1941); N. Itzkowitz, *The Ottoman Empire and Islamic Tradition* (New York, 1972); A. H. Lybyer, *The Government of the Ottoman Empire in the Time of Suleiman the Magnificent* (Cambridge, Mass., 1913); Cornel H. Fleischer, *Bureaucrat and Intellectual in the Ottoman Empire* (Princeton, 1986).

For serfdom in modern Europe, see the outstanding, if flawed, overview by Jerome Blum, *The End of the Old Order in Rural Europe* (Princeton, 1978). A useful coverage of eastern Europe is provided in a special issue of *Slavic Review*, 34 (1975), with contributions by A. Kaminski, B. K. Kiraly, W. E. Wright and L. Makkai. Key reinterpretative work on the nature of serfdom has been done by Steven L. Hoch in his *Serfdom and Social Control in Russia* (Chicago, 1986); by W. W. Hagen in both his article 'How mighty the Junkers? Peasant rents and seigneurial profits in sixteenth-century Brandenburg', *Past and Present*, 108 (1985), and his essay 'The Junkers' faithless servants: peasant insubordination and the breakdown of serfdom in Brandenburg-Prussia, 1763–1811', *The German Peasantry*, ed. R. J. Evans and W. R. Lee (London, 1986); by Edgar Melton in his 'The decline of Prussian Gutsherrschaft and the rise of the Junker as rural patron, 1750–1806', *German History*, 12 (1994). For Polish serfdom, see J. C. Miller, *The Nobility in Polish Renaissance Society, 1548–1571* (dissertation, Indiana University, 1977); J. Lukowski, *Liberty's Folly: the Polish–Lithuanian Commonwealth in the Eighteenth Century* (London, 1991); W. Kula, *An Economic Theory of the Feudal System: towards a Model of the Polish Economy, 1500–1800* (London, 1976); W. W. Hagen, 'Subject farmers in Brandenburg-Prussia and Poland', in Bush (ed.), *Serfdom and Slavery*, ch. 15. For Hungarian serfdom, there is A. J. Janos, *The Politics of Back-wardness: Hungary 1825–1945* (Princeton, 1982); B. K. Kiraly, *Hungary in the Late Eighteenth Century* (London, 1969). For Bohemian serfdom, there is William E. Wright, *Serf, Seigneur and Sovereign* (Minneapolis, 1966); A. Klima, 'Agrarian class structure and economic development in pre-industrial Bohemia', *Past and Present*, 85 (1979). For Russian serfdom, there is, besides Hoch (see above), Edgar Melton, 'The Russian peasantries, 1450–1860', *The Peasantries of Europe*, ed. Tom Scott (London, 1998), ch. 8; Isabel de Madariaga, 'Catherine II and the serfs', *Slavonic and East European Review*, 52 (1974); David Moon, 'Reassessing Russian serfdom', *European History Quarterly*, 26 (1996).

For pre-nineteenth century indentured service, there is David W. Galenson, *White Servitude in Colonial America* (Cambridge, 1981); Sharon V. Salinger, *To Serve Well and Faithfully: Labour and Indentured Service in Pennsylvania* (Cambridge, 1987); Hilary M. Beckles, *White Servitude and Black Slavery in Barbados, 1627–1715* (Knoxville, 1989). For nineteenth- and twentieth-century indentured service, there is David Northrup's outstanding survey *Indentured Labour in the Age of Imperialism, 1834–1922* (Cambridge, 1995); Watt Stewart, *Chinese Bondage in Peru: a History of the Chinese Coolies in Peru, 1849–1874* (Durham, North Carolina, 1951); Hugh Tinker, *A New System of Slavery: the Experience of Indian Labour Overseas, 1830–1920* (London, 1974); Kay Saunders, *Workers in Bondage: the Origins and Bases of Unfree Labour in Queensland, 1824–1916* (St Lucia, Queensland, 1982); Kay Saunders (ed.), *Indentured Labour in the British Empire, 1834–1920* (London, 1984); Doug Monro, 'The Pacific Islands labour trade: approaches, methologies, debates', *Slavery and Abolition*, 14 (1993); Stanley Engerman, 'Contract labour in sugar and technology in the nineteenth century', *Journal of Economic History*, 43 (1983).

For debt bondage, there is the reinterpretative essay by Arnold J. Bauer, 'Rural workers in Spanish America: problems of peonage and oppression', *Hispanic American History Review*, 59 (1979); and another by Alan Knight, 'Debt bondage in Latin America', *Slavery and other Forms of Unfree Labour*, ed. Leonie Archer (London, 1988). There is also N. D. Kamble, *Bonded Labour in India* (New Delhi, 1981); Gyam Prakash, *Bonded Histories: Genealogies of Labour Servitude in Colonial India* (Cambridge, 1990); Bruno Lasker, *Human Bondage in Southeast Asia* (Chapel Hill, 1950), ch. 3; Toyin Falola and Paul E. Lovejoy (eds), *Pawnship in Africa: Debt Bondage in Historical Perspective* (Oxford, 1994); Gunther Barth, *Bitter Strength: a History of the Chinese in the United States, 1850–1870* (Cambridge, Mass., 1964); Patricia Cloud and David W. Galenson, 'Chinese immigration and contract labour in the late nineteenth century', *Explorations in Economic History*, 24 (1987).

For penal servitude before the twentieth century, there is A. R. Ekirch, *Bound for America: the Transportation of British Convicts to the Colonies, 1718–1775* (Oxford, 1990); J. B. Hirst, *Convict Society and its Enemies: an Early History of New South Wales* (London, 1983); Stephen Nicholas (ed.),

Convict Workers: Reinterpreting Australia's Past (Cambridge, 1988); Ian Duffield and James Bradley (eds), *Representing Convicts* (London, 1997). For convict labour in Soviet Russia, there is David J. Dalin and Boris I. Nicolaevsky, *Forced Labour in Soviet Russia* (New York, 1974 repr.); Edwin Bacon, *The Gulag at War* (London, 1994); Robert Conquest, *The Great Terror: a Reassessment* (London, 1968); Alexander Solzhenitsyn, *The Gulag Archipelago* (London, 1974). For forced labour in Nazi Germany, there is Edward L. Homze's pioneering study, *Foreign Labour in Nazi Germany* (Princeton, 1967); Ulrich Herbert, *Hitler's Foreign Workers: Enforced Foreign Labour in Germany under the Third Reich* (Cambridge, 1997); Daniel Goldhagen, *Hitler's Willing Executioners: Ordinary Germans and the Holocaust* (London, 1996); Albert Speer, *The Slave State: Heinrich Himmler's Master-Plan for SS Supremacy* (London, 1981).

Notes

Part I   The Forms of Legal Bondage

1 See Orlando Patterson, *Slavery and Social Death: a Comparative Study* (Cambridge, Mass., 1982); Robert W. Fogel and Stanley L. Engerman, *Time on the Cross: the Economics of American Negro Slavery* (New York, 1974); Eugene D. Genovese, *Roll, Jordan, Roll: the World the Slaves Made* (New York, 1974); Joseph C. Miller, *Way of Death: Merchant Capitalism and the Angolan Slave Trade, 1730–1830* (London, 1988). For an example of 'cold war' discourse, see Peter Kolchin, *Unfree Labour: American Slavery and Russian Serfdom* (London, 1987), p. 149.

2 According to Patterson, a slave by definition is 'a socially dead person'. See his *Slavery and Social Death*, p. 5.

3 Ibid., p. 331.

4 For India, see Lionel Caplan, 'Power and status in South Asian slavery', *Asian and African Systems of Slavery*, ed. James L. Watson (Oxford, 1980), pp. 181–2. For Southeast Asia, see Anthony Reid (ed.), *Slavery, Bondage and Dependency in Southeast Asia* (St. Lucia, Queensland, 1983), p. 23. For Africa, see D. C. Little-field, *Rice and Slaves* (Baton Rouge, 1981), pp. 78–9, n. 11; A. G. B. Fisher and H. J. Fisher, *Slavery and Muslim Society in Africa* (London, 1970), pp. 111–13; Claude Meillassoux, *The Anthropology of Slavery* (London, 1991), pt 1, ch. 6.

5 See Patterson, *Slavery and Social Death*, pp. 2, 4, 331.

6 See below, pp. 79–81 (Chocó), 89 (Minas Gerais).

7 For consideration that such slaves were not really slaves at all, see Ehud R. Toledano, 'Ottoman concepts of slavery in the period of reform, 1830s–1880s', *Breaking of the Chains*, ed. Martin A. Klein (Madison, 1993), pp. 39–40.

8 James L. Watson, 'Slavery as an institution, open and closed systems' in Watson (ed.), *Asian and African Systems*, ch. 1; Klein (ed.), *Breaking the Chains*, pp. 14–15.

9 See below, p. 73.

10 Patterson, *Slavery and Social Death*, pp. 43, 127.

11 Robert W. Fogel, *Without Consent or Contract* (New York, 1989), pp. 12–18.

12 See Keith Hopkins, *Conquerors and Slaves* (Cambridge, 1978), p. 99. For modern applications of the distinction, see Philip D. Morgan, 'British encounters with Africans and Africa in America, c. 1600–1780', *Strangers within the Realm*, ed.

Bernard Bailyn and Philip D. Morgan (Chapel Hill, 1991), pp. 163–4; Ira Berlin, *Many Thousands Gone* (Cambridge, Mass., 1998), pp. 8–9, 17ff, 95ff.

13 Patterson, *Slavery and Social Death*, ch. 6.

14 See Adam Smith, *An Inquiry into the Nature and Causes of the Wealth of Nations*, 6th edn (London, 1791), II, p. 88.

15 Michael Bush, 'Serfdom in medieval and modern Europe: a comparison', *Serfdom and Slavery: Studies in Legal Bondage*, ed. M. L. Bush (London, 1996), pp. 215–16.

16 For genuine serfs in Latin America, see Andrew Pearse, *The Latin American Peasant* (London, 1975), pp. 32–4. For 'serfs' bound by debt bondage in Latin America, see ibid., pp. 30–1 and below, n. 61.

17 M. L. Bush, 'Tenant right and the peasantries of Europe under the old regime', *Social Orders and Social Classes in Europe since 1500: Studies in Social Stratification*, ed. M. L. Bush (London, 1992), pp. 137–8; Bush, 'Serfdom', pp. 206–7.

18 Ibid., pp. 215–16; Michael Bush, *Noble Privilege* (Manchester, 1983), pp. 165–9.

19 Bush, 'Serfdom', pp. 200–6.

20 Ibid., p. 214.

21 Ibid., p. 207.

22 Bush, 'Tenant right', p. 148.

23 E.g. the study by Steven Hoch, *Serfdom and Social Control in Russia: Petrovskoe, a Village in Tambov* (London, 1986).

24 Bush, 'Serfdom', p. 209.

25 See below, pp. 135, 140–1.

26 See below, pp. 181–4.

27 Bush, 'Serfdom', pp. 213–14, 217; Bush, *Noble Privilege*, pp. 147–8.

28 Jerome Blum, *The End of the Old Order in Rural Europe* (Princeton, 1978), p. 96.

29 See below, pp. 123–5.

30 Bush, 'Tenant right', p. 144. For leasing, also see Immanuel Wallerstein, *The Modern World-System* (New York, 1974), ch. 2.

31 Bush, 'Serfdom', p. 215.

32 Bush, 'Tenant right', p. 142; William W. Hagen, 'Subject farmers in Brandenburg-Prussia and Poland' in Bush (ed.), *Serfdom and Slavery*, pp. 304–5, 308; Stephen L. Hoch, 'The serf economy and the social order in Russia' in Bush (ed.), *Serfdom and Slavery*, pp. 316–17.

33 See Blum, *End of the Old Order*, pp. 65–70.

34 For an exploration of the differences between serfdom and slavery, see Kolchin, *Unfree Labour*, pp. 151–2. He nonetheless agrees with Jerome Blum's assertion that 'the Russian serf was scarcely distinguishable from a chattel slave', adding that Russian serfdom 'was a form of slavery', but with certain significant differences. For the view that Russian serfs were very different from slaves, see Hoch, *Serfdom and Social Control*, passim.

35 For first phase, see below, ch. 7. For second phase, see below, ch. 12.

36 For 'first phase' figure, see David W. Galenson, *White Servitude in Colonial America* (Cambridge, 1981), p. 17. Following Smith, he claims that 300,000–400,000 migrants went as indentured servants. Smith, however, included convicts in his figures (see Abbot E. Smith, *Colonists in Bondage* (Chapel Hill, 1947), p. 316) and presumably migrants who went as bonded servants according to the custom of the country (i.e. not with a specific indenture). This would suggest – if Smith is right in saying that one half to two-thirds of all white settlers went originally as bondspersons – that the actual number of indentured servants should be nearer 300,000 than 400,000. For 'second phase' figures, see David Northrup, *Indentured Labour in the Age of Imperialism, 1834–1922* (Cambridge, 1995), table A1, which provides recruitment regions and destination of recruits. That there were a few white indentured servants in the second phase, see ibid. Northrup's grand total is an underestimation: see below, ch. 12, n. 10.

37 Hugh Tinker, *A New System of Slavery: the Export of Indian Labour Overseas, 1830–1920* (London, 1974), pp. 217–19.

38 For statement, see F. W. Knight, *Slave Society in Cuba during the Nineteenth Century* (Madison, 1970), p. 116. For first term, see the title of Tinker's book (above, n. 37); for second term, see Ravindra K. Jain, *Indian Communities Abroad* (New Delhi, 1993), p. 7. For an examination of the similarity between seventeenth-century indentured service and slavery, see Hilary M. Beckles, *White Servitude and Black Slavery in Barbados, 1627–1715* (Knoxville, 1989), ch. 3.

39 See Sharon V. Salinger, *'To Serve Well and Faithfully':Labour and Indentured Servants* (Cambridge, 1987), p. 73. For a similar ratio in seventeenth-century Barbados, see Beckles, *White Servitude and Black Slavery*, p. 117.

40 See Galenson, *White Servitude*, p. 6.

41 See ibid., pp. 6–8; Beckles, *White Servitude and Black Slavery*, pp. 71–3.

42 See below, ch. 5.

43 See Smith, *Colonists in Bondage*, pp. 20–2.

44 For Peru, see Watt Stewart, *Chinese Bondage in Peru: a History of the Chinese Coolies in Peru, 1849–1874* (Durham, North Carolina, 1951), pp. 42–4. For Cuba, see Knight, *Slave Society in Cuba*, p. 116; Rebecca J. Scott, *Slave Emancipation in Cuba: the Transition to Free Labour, 1860–1899* (Princeton, 1985), pp. 29–35.

45 See below, ch. 6.

46 For resistance, see Northrup, *Indentured Labour*, pp. 118–19, 127.

47 Tinker, *New System of Slavery*, ch. 7.

48 Northrup, *Indentured Labour*, pp. 143–4, 146–7.

49 For returns, see Tinker, *New System of Slavery*, p. 232. For peasantization, see Northrup, *Indentured Labour*, p. 151; Tinker, *New System of Slavery*, pp. 234–5.

50 But see reservations, above, n. 36.

51 See Stanley Engerman, 'Contract labour in sugar and technology in the nineteenth century', *Journal of Economic History*, 43 (1983), pp. 652–3; Northrup, *Indentured Labour*, pp. 29–40.

52 Northrup, *Indentured Labour*, pp. 117–19.

53 Tinker, *New System of Slavery*, pp. 34, 234–5.

54 Northrup, *Indentured Labour*, pp. 64–7.

55 Alternative terms to debt bondage are 'pawnship', as used in relation to traditional African societies, and 'debt peonage', as used in relation to Spanish America.

56 Bruno Lasker, *Human Bondage in Southeast Asia* (Chapel Hill, 1950), pp. 137, 146.

57 For Africa, see Klein (ed.), *Breaking the Chains*, p. 5; Toyin Falola and Paul E. Lovejoy (eds), *Pawnship in Africa: Debt Bondage in Historical Perspective* (Oxford, 1994), ch. 1. For China, see Watson (ed.), *Asian and African Systems*, p. 13. For India, see Caplan, 'Power and status', pp. 172–82; D. Kumar, 'Colonialism, bondage and caste in British India' in Klein (ed.), *Breaking the Chains*, p. 122. For Philippines, see Lasker, *Human Bondage*, pp. 131, 135. For Cambodia, see ibid., p. 155. For Thailand, see Andrew Turton, 'Thai institutions of slavery' in Watson (ed.), *Asian and African Systems*, pp. 263–5.

58 Lasker, *Human Bondage*, pp. 154–5, 159.

59 See William Glade, *The Latin American Economy* (New York, 1969), p. 125; Lasker, *Human Bondage*, p. 131; Sarma Marla, *Bonded Labour in India* (New Delhi, 1981), p. 7.

60 Tinker, *New System of Slavery*, pp. 179–80; Northrup, *Indentured Labour*, pp. 11–12.

61 See W. Kloosterboer, *Involuntary Labour since the Abolition of Slavery* (Leiden, 1960), pp. 98ff. For attachment to haciendas, see Glade, *Latin American Economy*, pp. 125–6; Alan Knight, 'Debt bondage in Latin America', *Slavery and Other Forms of Unfree Labour*, ed. Leonie Archer (London, 1988), pp. 108–9. For attach-

ment to plantation work, see Glade, *Latin American Economy*, p. 240; Knight, 'Debt bondage', pp. 106–7. For serving as slave-substitutes, see below, pp. 215–17.

62 Northrup, *Indentured Labour*, p. 11; P. C. Campbell, *Chinese Coolie Emigration to Countries within the British Empire* (London, 1923), p. xvii.

63 For all three systems, see Northrup, *Indentured Labour*, pp. 11–12. For *kangani*, see Ravindra K. Jain, 'South Indian Labour in Malaya, 1840–1920', *Indentured Labour in the British Empire, 1834–1920*, ed. Kay Saunders (London, 1984), p. 171; Tinker, *New System of Slavery*, p. 179. For *maistry*, see Lasker, *Human Bondage*, p. 147. For credit-ticket, see Campbell, *Chinese Coolie Emigration*, p. 147.

64 Arnold J. Bauer, 'Rural workers in Spanish America: problems of peonage and oppression', *Hispanic American Historical Review*, 59 (1979), pp. 37–8.

65 Patricia Cloud and David W. Galenson, 'Chinese immigration and contract labour in the late nineteenth century', *Explorations in Economic History*, 24 (1987), pp. 24–9, 39–40; Gunther Barth, *Bitter Strength: a History of the Chinese in the United States, 1850–1870* (Cambridge, Mass., 1964), chs 3–5.

66 For Java, see Lasker, *Human Bondage*, p. 127. For Latin America, see Knight, 'Debt bondage', p. 111.

67 For the first formulation, see Knight, 'Debt bondage', p. 102. For the second, see Bauer, 'Rural workers', p. 36.

68 See Knight, 'Debt bondage', p. 107.

69 For commutation of slavery, see Lasker, *Human Bondage*, p. 154. For creditor adoption, see ibid., p. 150; Falola and Lovejoy (eds), *Pawnship in Africa*, pp. 7–8, 11.

70 Lasker, *Human Bondage*, p. 154–5.

71 Tinker, *New System of Slavery*, p. 179.

72 See Knight, 'Debt bondage', pp. 111–14; Kloosterboer, *Involuntary Labour*, pp. 97–104.

73 Cloud and Galenson, 'Chinese immigration', pp. 24, 39–40; Northrup, *Indentured Labour*, p. 74.

74 Lasker, *Human Bondage*, pp. 122, 147, 159–60; Kloosterboer, *Involuntary Labour*, p. 104.

75 See Edward L. Homze, *Foreign Labour in Nazi Germany* (Princeton, 1967), pp. 47–8, 237.

76 A. R. Ekirch, *Bound for America: the Transportation of British Convicts to the Colonies, 1718–1775* (Oxford, 1990), chs 3, 4. For terms of service, see ibid., pp. 124–5, 155.

77 P. J. Byrne, *Criminal Law and Colonial Subjects* (Cambridge, 1993), pp. 20–1; J. B. Hirst, *Convict Society and its Enemies: an Early History of New South Wales* (London, 1983), pp. 128–33; A. G. L. Shaw, *Convicts and the Colonies: a Study of Penal Transportation from Great Britain and Ireland to Australia and Other Parts of the British Empire* (London, 1966), pp. 92–4; Hamish Maxwell-Stewart, 'Convict workers, "penal labour" and Sarah Island: life at Macquarie Harbour, 1822–1834', *Representing Convicts*, ed. Ian Duffield and James Bradley (London, 1997), p. 146.

78 For a consideration of convict assignment as a slave system, see Hirst, *Convict Society*, p. 31; Shaw, *Convicts and the Colonies*, p. 270.

79 Edwin Bacon, *The Gulag at War* (London, 1994), p. 148; Albert Speer, *The Slave State: Henrich Himmler's Master-Plan* (London, 1981), p. 212.

80 Bacon, *Gulag at War*, pp. 66, 69; Daniel Goldhagen, *Hitler's Willing Executioners: Ordinary Germans and the Holocaust* (London, 1996), pp. 174–5; David J. Dalin and Boris I. Nicolaevsky, *Forced Labour in Soviet Russia*, repr. (New York, 1974), pp. 100–3.

81 Hirst, *Convict Society*, ch. 2; Shaw, *Convicts and the Colonies*, p. 229.

82 For America, see Ekirch, *Bound for America*, p. 150. For Australia, see Shaw, *Convicts and the Colonies*, pp. 72–3, 203, 215.

83 Joy Damousi, 'Headshaving and convict women in the female factories, 1820s–1840s' in Duffield and Bradley (eds), *Representing Convicts*, ch. 11.
84 Hirst, *Convict Society*, p. 58; Byrne, *Criminal Law*, p. 21.
85 For punishment, see Shaw, *Convicts and the Colonies*, p. 228. For flogging, see ibid, p. 202; Hirst, *Convict Society*, pp. 108–9. For legal personality, see Hirst, *Convict Society*, pp. 81–2.
86 For France and Spain, see Stephen Nicholas (ed.), *Convict Workers: Reinterpreting Australia's Past* (Cambridge, 1988), pp. 34–5. For Russia, see ibid., pp. 36–7.
87 Patterson, *Slavery and Social Death*, p. 5.
88 Ekirch, *Bound for America*, pp. 52–3; Duffield and Bradley (eds), *Representing Convicts*, pp. 9–10.
89 Shaw, *Convicts in the Colonies*, pp. 153, 170–2, 178, 183.
90 Bacon, *Gulag at War*, p. 51; Albert Speer, *Inside the Third Reich: Memoirs* (London, 1970), p. 343; Speer, *Slave State*, p. 49. For the Nazi labour policies towards the Jews, see Goldhagen, *Hitler's Willing Executioners*, pp. 290–2.
91 Gitta Sereny, *Albert Speer: His Battle with the Truth* (London, 1995), p. 332.
92 Ulrich Herbert, *Hitler's Foreign Workers: Enforced Foreign Labour in Germany under the Third Reich* (Cambridge, 1997; 1st edn 1985), p. 1; Speer, *Slave State*, p. 47; Bacon, *Gulag at War*, pp. 37, 126 and table 2:1 (p. 24).
93 For figures, see Nicholas (ed.), *Convict Workers*, pp. 29–30. The French transported *c*.36,000 to French Guiana and New Caledonia. For North America, see Smith, *Colonists in Bondage*, pp. 95–6; Ekirch, *Bound for America*, p. 166.
94 For America, see Ekirch, *Bound for America*, p. 166. For Australia, see Nicholas (ed.), *Convict Workers*, table 4.3 (p. 53).
95 Smith, *Colonists in Bondage*, chs 8, 9; Shaw, *Convicts in the Colonies*, pp. 152–3, 183.
96 Smith, *Colonists in Bondage*, p. 92.
97 Byrne, *Criminal Law*, p. 51ff.
98 Robert Conquest, *The Great Terror: a Reassessment* (London, 1968), ch. 11; Bacon, *Gulag at War*, p. 72.
99 Bacon, *Gulag at War*, pp. 134–5.
100 Herbert, *Hitler's Foreign Workers*, p. 239; Speer, *The Slave State*, pp. 16–17, 34, 205–12; Speer, *Inside the Third Reich*, p. 370.
101 Shaw, *Convicts in the Colonies*, pp. 231–2.
102 Dalin and Nicolaevsky, *Forced Labour*, ch. 5.
103 Ekirch, *Bound for America*, p. 194 and ch. 7; Hirst, *Convict Society*, ch. 2.
104 Shaw, *Convicts and the Colonies*, p. 221.
105 Ekirch, *Bound for America*, pp. 122–4.
106 For Russia, see Bacon, *Gulag at War*, pp. 134, 143; Dalin and Nicolaevsky, *Forced Labour*, pp. 105–6. For Germany, see Speer, *The Slave State*, pp. 36, 212.
107 Shaw, *Convicts and the Colonies*, p. 51.
108 Ekirch, *Bound for America*, p. 152.
109 Ibid., pp. 59–68.
110 See Goldhagen, *Hitler's Willing Executioners*, pp. 174–5; Conquest, *The Great Terror*, ch. 11.

Part II Emergence and Development

Chapter 7 White Servitude in the Americas

1 Abbot E. Smith, *Colonists in Bondage: White Servitude and Convict Labour in America, 1607–1776* (Chapel Hill, 1947); Richard B. Morris, *Government and Labour in Early America* (New York, 1946); David W. Galenson, *White Servitude in*

Colonial America (Cambridge, 1981); Sharon V. Salinger, *'To Serve Well and Faithfully': Labour and Indentured Servants in Pennsylvania* (Cambridge, 1987); Hilary M. Beckles, *White Servitude and Black Slavery in Barbados, 1627–1715* (Knoxville, 1989); A. R. Ekirch, *Bound for America: the Transportation of British Convicts to the Colonies, 1718–1775* (Oxford, 1990).

2 Herbert S. Klein, *African Slavery in Latin America and the Caribbean* (Oxford, 1986), p. 49; Robin Blackburn, *The Making of New World Slavery* (London, 1997), pp. 281–3.

3 Smith, *Colonists in Bondage*, pp. 236, 296–7; Beckles, *White Servitude and Black Slavery*, p. 39; Galenson, *White Servitude*, p. 17.

4 Smith, *Colonists in Bondage*, p. 4.

5 Galenson, *White Servitude*, pp. 13, 97–8; Morris, *Government and Labour*, pp. 390–2; Salinger, *Labour and Indentured Servants*, pp. 10–11; Smith, *Colonists in Bondage*, pp. 18–22, 227–9, 231, 244; E. I. McCormac, *White Servitude in Maryland* (Baltimore, 1904), pp. 37–8.

6 For spiriting, see Morris, *Government and Labour*, pp. 337–45; Salinger, *Labour and Indentured Servants*, pp. 9–10; Beckles, *White Servitude and Black Slavery*, pp. 50–2. For transported convicts, see Ekirch, *Bound for America*, passim; Beckles, *White Servitude and Black Slavery*, pp. 52–8.

7 Morris, *Government and Labour*, pp. 345–9, 354–61.

8 Beckles, *White Servitude and Black Slavery*, pp. 5–6; Salinger, *Labour and Indentured Servants*, table 3.2 (p. 80); Galenson, *White Servitude*, pp. 102–3.

9 D. W. Galenson, 'The rise and fall of indentured servitude in the Americas', *Journal of Economic History*, 44 (1984), p. 3; Smith, *Colonists in Bondage*, p. 16; Galenson, *White Servitude*, p. 4.

10 Galenson, *White Servitude*, app. B; Salinger, *Labour and Indentured Servants*, p. 9.

11 Smith, *Colonists in Bondage*, pp. 20–2, 224, 240–1.

12 Galenson, *White Servitude*, pp. 86, 126, 139, 156.

13 Galenson, *White Servitude*, pp. 85–6. And see his table 8.7 (p. 125). These percentages, however, do not relate to total arrivals but only to the smallish sample taken by Galenson. See his app. A.

14 Ibid., compare tables 8.2 (p. 120) and 8.7 (p. 125).

15 Ibid., pp. 117, 126–8, 139; Beckles, *White Servitude and Black Slavery*, pp. 125–30.

16 Galenson, *White Servitude*, p. 137; Richard S. Dunn, *Sugar and Slaves: the Rise of the Planter Class in the English West Indies* (London, 1973), pp. 49–69; Smith, *Colonists in Bondage*, p. 293; Beckles, *White Servitude and Black Slavery*, pp. 123–5, 135–9.

17 Smith, *Colonists in Bondage*, pp. 27, 35, 39; Galenson, *White Servitude*, pp. 151–2; Salinger, *Labour and Indentured Servants*, p. 2. For relative prices of servants and slaves, see Salinger, *Labour and Indentured Servants*, p. 73.

18 Galenson, 'Rise and fall of indentured servitude', pp. 6–9; Galenson, *White Servitude*, pp. 98–9, 143–5; Salinger, *Labour and Indentured Servants*, p. 10; Smith, *Colonists in Bondage*, p. 236.

19 Smith, *Colonists in Bondage*, pp. 264–6; Galenson, *White Servitude*, pp. 7–8; Beckles, *White Servitude and Black Slavery*, p. 84.

20 Salinger, *Labour and Indentured Servants*, p. 6. For conversion of slaves into indentured servants, see ibid., pp. 3–4, 147.

21 Morris, *Government and Labour*, pp. 500–1.

22 Salinger, *Labour and Indentured Servants*, pp. 9–10.

23 Dunn, *Sugar and Slaves*, pp. 239–40.

24 Smith, *Colonists in Bondage*, pp. 233–6, 278–9; McCormac, *White Servitude in Maryland*, p. 30.

25 Salinger, *Labour and Indentured Servants*, p. 6.

26 Dunn, *Sugar and Slaves*, pp. 239–40.

27 Galenson, *White Servitude*, pp. 3, 171; Smith, *Colonists in Bondage*, p. 234–5; Morris, *Government and Labour*, pp. 500–2.

28 Salinger, *Labour and Indentured Servants*, p. 73; Smith, *Colonists in Bondage*, pp. 233–4; Morris, *Government and Labour*, p. 412. For treatment of runaways, see Morris, *Government and Labour*, pp. 435–59; Smith, *Colonists in Bondage*, pp. 264–6; Galenson, *White Servitude*, pp. 8, 100, 171.

29 Smith, *Colonists in Bondage*, pp. 257–9; Galenson, *White Servitude*, pp. 117, 126–8, 159, 163, table 6.6; Salinger, *Labour and Indentured Servants*, pp. 143–5; Beckles, *White Servitude and Black Slavery*, ch. 5.

30 Smith, *Colonists in Bondage*, pp. 238–41; Salinger, *Labour and Indentured Servants*, pp. 35–6. For headright, see Morris, *Labour and Government*, pp. 397–8; Blackburn, *Making of New World Slavery*, pp. 227–8; E. S. Morgan 'Headrights and head counts', *Virginia Magazine*, 80 (1972), pp. 361–71.

31 Smith, *Colonists in Bondage*, pp. 238–41, 299; Beckles, *White Servitude and Black Slavery*, ch. 6. For the Virginian quote, see Morgan, 'Headrights and head counts', pp. 370–1.

32 Galenson, *White Servitude*, p. 179; Morris, *Government and Labour*, p. 322; Salinger, *Labour and Indentured Servants*, pp. 15, 137–8.

33 Salinger, *Labour and Indentured Servants*, pp. 145, 152; McCormac, *White Servitude in Maryland*, pp. 109–10; Morris, *Government and Labour*, p. 322; Galenson, *White Servitude*, pp. 179–80; David Eltis, 'Free and coerced transatlantic migration: some comparisons', *American Historical Review*, 88 (1983), pp. 255, 258, 272.

34 Smith, *Colonists in Bondage*, p. 27; Salinger, *Labour and Indentured Servants*, p. 73.

35 Galenson, *White Servitude*, pp. 82, 95, 117.

36 Mildred Campbell, 'English emigration on the eve of the American Revolution', *American Historical Review*, 61 (1955), pp. 4–5.

37 Smith, *Colonists in Bondage*, pp. 3, 20; Salinger, *Labour and Indentured Servants*, pp. 3, 118.

38 Smith, *Colonists in Bondage*, pp. 48, 50–1; Salinger, *Labour and Indentured Servants*, pp. 54–6.

39 Smith, *Colonists in Bondage*, pp. 92–3; Morris, *Government and Labour*, p. 324. For the 1662 Act, see 13/14 Charles II, c. 12 (23).

40 Smith, *Colonists in Bondage*, pp. 92–103 and chs. 8–9. Smith's figures need to be revised in the light of the 4,000 convicts known to have been transported to Barbados. See Beckles, *White Servitude and Black Slavery*, p. 58.

41 Ekirch, *Bound for America*, pp. 134–40; Smith, *Colonists in Bondage*, p. 104.

42 Ekirch, *Bound for America*, pp. 23–7, 113–14; Smith, *Colonists in Bondage*, pp. 100–4, 117–19; Salinger, *Labour and Indentured Servants*, pp. 77–8.

43 Smith, *Colonists in Bondage*, pp. 110–13; Ekirch, *Bound for America*, pp. 17–18, 22, 118, 120.

44 Smith, *Colonists in Bondage*, pp. 131–2; Ekirch, *Bound for America*, p. 118.

45 Ekirch, *Bound for America*, pp. 150, 154. For the colonial convicts, see Morris, *Government and Labour*, pp. 345–8, 354–61.

46 Smith, *Colonists in Bondage*, p. 131; Ekirch, *Bound for America*, pp. 54, 155.

47 Ekirch, *Bound for America*, pp. 122–4, 141–2.

48 Ibid., pp. 150, 194–5, 206, 208.

49 Ibid., pp. 146, 152.

50 Morris, *Government and Labour*, p. 349.

Chapter 8   New World Slavery

1 Orlando Patterson, *Slavery and Social Death* (Cambridge, Mass., 1982), pp. 84, 106–7, 191; Robert H. Ruby and John A. Brown, *Indian Slavery in the Pacific Northwest* (Washington, 1993), ch. 1.

2 D. Eltis, 'Free and coerced transatlantic migration', *American Historical Review*, 88 (1983), p. 258.
3 Herbert S. Klein, *African Slavery in Latin America and the Caribbean* (Oxford, 1986), p. 60.
4 Ibid., p. 62.
5 Peter Kolchin, *American Slavery* (London, 1993), pp. 24–5. For cotton exports, see William B. Dana, *Cotton from Seed to Loom* (New York, 1878), pp. 29, 35.
6 Kolchin, *American Slavery*, p. 22; Robert W. Fogel, *Without Consent or Contract* (London, 1989), p. 18. For further consideration of numbers leaving Africa for the Americas and their destinations, see David Eltis and David Richardson, 'The "numbers game" and routes to slavery', *Routes to Slavery*, ed. Eltis and Richardson (London, 1997), pp. 1–2, 6. Differences between calculations appear to be largely created by the length of the period taken into account and how the death toll during the passage is estimated.
7 Paul E. Lovejoy, *Transformations in Slavery: a History of Slavery in Africa* (Cambridge, 1983), p. 19.
8 Kolchin, *American Slavery*, pp. 96–8. Also see below, pp. 107–8.
9 For Peru, see below, n. 34 (Blanchard). For Brazil, see Robert Conrad, *World of Sorrow* (Baton Rouge, 1986), pp. 172–5.
10 Kolchin, *American Slavery*, p. 93.
11 Eltis, 'Free and coerced transatlantic migration', p. 255.
12 Colin A. Palmer, *Slaves of the White God: Blacks in Mexico, 1570–1650* (Cambridge, Mass., 1976), pp. 2–3; F. P. Bowser, *The African Slave in Colonial Peru, 1524–1650* (Stanford, 1974), pp. 76–8.
13 For Mexico, see Palmer, *Slaves of the White God*, p. 40; Klein, *African Slavery*, p. 36. For Peru, see Bowser, *African Slave in Peru*, pp. 338, 341.
14 For Brazil, see below, p. 82.
15 Palmer, *Slaves of the White God*, pp. 43, 60–73; Bowser, *African Slave in Peru*, pp. 100, 125–6; Klein, *African Slavery*, pp. 34–6; George R. Andrews, *The Afro-Argentines of Buenos Aires, 1800–1900* (Wisconsin, 1980), p. 32.
16 Bowser, *African Slave in Peru*, ch. 6.
17 Palmer, *Slaves of the White God*, pp. 44–5; Bowser, *African Slave in Peru*, p. 125.
18 Bowser, *African Slave in Peru*, pp. 125, 138–9.
19 Palmer, *Slaves of the White God*, p. 40; Bowser, *African Slave in Peru*, p. 75.
20 Bowser, *African Slave in Peru*, pp. 88–9; Andrews, *Afro-Argentines*, p. 38.
21 Palmer, *Slaves of the White God*, pp. 65–6; Bowser, *African Slave in Peru*, p. 19.
22 *The Cambridge World History of Human Diseases*, ed. Kenneth F. Kiple (Cambridge, 1993), p. 40.
23 For the banning of Indian slavery, see Palmer, *Slaves of the White God*, p. 62; Bowser, *African Slave in Peru*, p. 12.
24 Palmer, *Slaves of the White God*, pp. 65–7.
25 Bowser, *African Slave in Peru*, pp. 90, 119–20.
26 Ibid., pp. 14, 19.
27 Ibid., p. 20.
28 Ibid., p. 90.
29 Klein, *African Slavery*, pp. 34–5.
30 For 1570, see Palmer, *Slaves of the White God*, table 13 (p. 76). For 1597, see ibid., table 14 (p. 80).
31 Klein, *African Slavery*, pp. 34–6; Palmer, *Slaves of the White God*, pp. 73, 82–3.
32 Klein, *African Slavery*, p. 36; Palmer, *Slaves of the White God*, pp. 187–8; Robin Blackburn, *The Making of New World Slavery* (London, 1997), p. 499.
33 Klein, *African Slavery*, p. 36; Peter Blanchard, *Slavery and Abolition in Early Republican Peru* (Delaware, 1992), p. 14.
34 Blackburn, *Making of New World Slavery*, p. 499; Blanchard, *Slavery and Abolition*, pp. 1, 3–4.

35 See below, p. 87.
36 Palmer, *Slaves of the White God*, pp. 86–7; Bowser, *African Slave in Peru*, pp. 222–3, 254.
37 Bowser, *African Slave in Peru*, p. 233; Palmer, *Slaves of the White God*, pp. 53, 56.
38 Bowser, *African Slave in Peru*, pp. 259, 261, 263–5.
39 Palmer, *Slaves of the White God*, p. 86.
40 Ibid., pp. 56–7; Bowser, *African Slave in Peru*, pp. 235, 255.
41 Palmer, *Slaves of the White God*, pp. 53–4; Bowser, *African Slave in Peru*, pp. 243, 256.
42 Palmer, *Slaves of the White God*, p. 44; Bowser, *African Slave in Peru*, p. 328.
43 Klein, *African Slavery*, pp. 34–5.
44 Bowser, *African Slave in Peru*, pp. 88–9.
45 Ibid., p. 88.
46 Blackburn, *Making of New World Slavery*, p. 497.
47 William F. Sharp, *Slavery on the Spanish Frontier: the Colombian Chocó, 1680–1810* (Oklahoma University Press, 1976), pp. 20, 22.
48 Ibid., pp. 134–5, 143–4.
49 E.g. for Lima, see Bowser, *African Slave in Peru*, p. 103; and for Buenos Aires, see Andrews, *Afro-Argentines*, pp. 34–5.
50 Palmer, *Slaves of the White God*, ch. 6.
51 Ibid., p. 146.
52 Ibid., ch. 7; Bowser, *African Slave in Peru*, pp. 274, 278–81.
53 Palmer, *Slaves of the White God*, p. 178; Bowser, *African Slave in Peru*, p. 301.
54 Bowser, *African Slave in Peru*, pp. 282–3, 286, 298.
55 For *coartación*, see Sharp, *Slavery on the Spanish Frontier*, pp. 143–4 and below, pp. 101–2.
56 Palmer, *Slaves of the White God*, pp. 47–8.
57 Blackburn, *Making of New World Slavery*, pp. 143, 168, 230–1.
58 Palmer, *Slaves of the White God*, p. 3; Klein, *African Slavery*, p. 37.
59 Palmer, *Slaves of the White God*, pp. 187–8; Klein, *African Slavery*, pp. 36–7.
60 Bowser, *African Slave in Peru*, p. 75; Blanchard, *Slavery and Abolition*, pp. 1, 14.
61 Bowser, *African Slave in Peru*, p. 124.
62 Blackburn, *Making of New World Slavery*, pp. 498–9.
63 Conrad, *World of Sorrow*, p. 1.
64 Blackburn, *Making of New World Slavery*, pp. 174, 485.
65 Klein, *African Slavery*, p. 37.
66 Stuart B. Schwartz, *Sugar Plantations in the Formation of Brazilian Society: Bahia, 1550–1835* (Cambridge, 1985), pp. 16, 19.
67 Blackburn, *Making of New World Slavery*, pp. 172, 485.
68 R. B. Martins, *Growing in Silence: the Slave Economy of Nineteenth-Century Minas Gerais, Brazil* (Ph.D., Vanderbilt University 1980), pp. 23–9.
69 Ibid., pp. 97–8.
70 Schwartz, *Sugar Plantations*, pp. 29–30, 32, 35.
71 Ibid., p. 33.
72 Ibid., p. 43.
73 Ibid., pp. 33, 37.
74 Ibid., pp. 53, 70–1.
75 Ibid., pp. 43–5.
76 Ibid., pp. 39–43.
77 Klein, *African Slavery*, p. 23; Martins, *Growing in Silence*, p. 10.
78 Conrad, *World of Sorrow*, pp. 172–3; Martins, *Growing in Silence*, pp. 179–81.
79 Schwartz, *Sugar Plantations*, p. 6.
80 Blackburn, *Making of New World Slavery*, pp. 174–7.
81 Schwartz, *Sugar Plantations*, pp. 65–6.
82 Blackburn, *Making of New World Slavery*, p. 384.

83 Conrad, *World of Sorrow*, pp. 25, 34, 28–9, 31, 34.
84 Martins, *Growing in Silence*, p. 176.
85 Conrad, *World of Sorrow*, p. 22.
86 Robert Conrad, *The Destruction of Brazilian Slavery, 1850–1888* (Berkeley, 1972), p. xiii; Conrad, *World of Sorrow*, p. 22.
87 Conrad, *World of Sorrow*, pp. 9–10.
88 For sexual imbalance, see Schwartz, *Sugar Plantations*, p. 350. For high mortality, see ibid., ch. 13; Mary C. Karasch, *Slave Life in Rio de Janeiro, 1808–1850* (Princeton, 1987), ch. 4, pp. 126ff, ch. 6.
89 Schwartz, *Sugar Plantations*, p. 369.
90 Ibid., pp. 157–8, 331–2; Blackburn, *Making of New World Slavery*, p. 492; Carl N. Degler, *Neither Black nor White: Slavery and Race Relations in Brazil and the United States* (New York, 1971), pp. 44, 71, 75–7.
91 Schwartz, *Sugar Plantations*, p. 350; Conrad, *World of Sorrow*, p. 14; Degler, *Neither Black nor White*, pp. 51–60, 92.
92 Schwartz, *Sugar Plantations*, p. 462; Conrad, *Destruction of Brazilian Slavery*, p. xiii. For roles of freed men, see Degler, *Neither Black nor White*, p. 84.
93 Schwartz, *Sugar Plantations*, chs 9, 10.
94 Ibid., pp. 450, 461.
95 Ibid., p. 305.
96 Ibid., p. 302.
97 Ibid., p. 453.
98 Ibid., p. 390.
99 Martins, *Growing in Silence*, p. 169; Blackburn, *Making of New World Slavery*, pp. 485–9.
100 Martins, *Growing in Silence*, table 35 (p. 170).
101 Ibid., pp. 91, 148.
102 Ibid., pp. 248–9.
103 Ibid., pp. 286, 291, 302.
104 Ibid., pp. 315–16.
105 Ibid., pp. 248–53.
106 Ibid., table 72 (p. 322).
107 For cotton factories, see ibid., pp. 292–4. For ironworks, see ibid., p. 312.
108 Ibid., table 17 (p. 96); ibid., pp. 314–16.
109 Ibid., p. 314.
110 For Rio, see Karasch, *Slave Life*, table 3.6 (p. 66). For Salvador, see Schwartz, *Sugar Plantations*, p. 87.
111 Karasch, *Slave Life*, p. xxii; Blackburn, *Making of New World Slavery*, p. 206.
112 Schwartz, *Sugar Plantations*, pp. 456–7; Conrad, *Destruction of Brazilian Slavery*, pp. 11–15; Blackburn, *Making of New World Slavery*, p. 493.
113 Schwartz, *Sugar Plantations*, p. 412; Karasch, *Slave Life*, pp. 116–17; Degler, *Neither Black nor White*, pp. 26–37.
114 Conrad, *World of Sorrow*, pp. 20–1; Karasch, *Slave Life*, pp. 311–15; Degler, *Neither Black nor White*, p. 51.
115 Schwartz, *Sugar Plantations*, pp. 158–9. A case for the benign nature of Brazilian slavery was vividly made by Gilberto Freyre in his classic *The Masters and the Slaves: a Study in the Development of Brazilian Civilization* (New York, 1946), but it was dubiously made to rest on the benevolent paternalism of the masters and the physical intimacy that existed between the master's family and the slaves. Arguably he attached too much emphasis to the domestic slavery in the Big House, and not enough to field slavery on the plantation.
116 Ibid., p. 342; Karasch, *Slave Life*, ch. 8, pp. 261–3.
117 Schwartz, *Sugar Plantations*, p. 390.
118 Ibid., pp. 137, 157; Blackburn, *Making of New World Slavery*, p. 340.
119 Schwartz, *Sugar Plantations*, p. 157; Karasch, *Slave Life*, p. 89.

120 Karasch, *Slave Life*, pp. 89–90.
121 Ibid., pp. 206–7.
122 Schwartz, *Sugar Plantations*, p. 154; Martins, *Growing in Silence*, p. 118.
123 Schwartz, *Sugar Plantations*, p. 158; Karasch, *Slave Life*, pp. 210–11.
124 Blackburn, *Making of New World Slavery*, p. 206; Karasch, *Slave Life*, pp. 189, 199–200.
125 Schwartz, *Sugar Plantations*, pp. 331–2; Degler, *Neither Black nor White*, pp. 40–4.
126 Degler, *Neither Black nor White*, p. 83.
127 For amelioration, see J. R. Ward, *British West Indian Slavery, 1750–1834* (Oxford, 1988), pp. 194–207.
128 Richard Sheridan, *The Development of the Plantations to 1750* (Jamaica, 1970), p. 33; Ward, *British West Indian Slavery*, p. 8, Klein, *African Slavery*, pp. 45–9; Hilary M. Beckles, *A History of Barbados* (Cambridge, 1990), p. 20.
129 Ward, *British West Indian Slavery*, pp. 9–11.
130 See Elsa V. Goveia, *Slave Society in the British Leeward Islands at the End of the Eighteenth Century* (New Haven, 1965), pp. 103–5; Richard S. Dunn, *Sugar and Slaves: the Rise of the Planter Class in the English West Indies* (London, 1973), p. 131.
131 Blackburn, *Making of New World Slavery*, p. 294; Dunn, *Sugar and Slaves*, p. 237.
132 Goveia, *Slave Society*, pp. 106–10; Orlando Patterson, *The Sociology of Slavery: an Analysis of the Origins, Development and Structure of Negro Slave Society in Jamaica* (London, 1967), p. 36.
133 Ward, *British West Indian Slavery*, pp. 23–4, 105; Goveia, *Slave Society*, p. 234; Hilary M. Beckles, *Natural Rebels: a Social History of Enslaved Black Women in Barbados* (New Brunswick, 1989), pp. 35, 45–7.
134 For Jamaica, see Patterson, *Jamaica*, pp. 266ff. For St Domingue, see David Geggus, *Slavery, War and Revolution* (Oxford, 1982), p. 27. For Cuba, see Franklin W. Knight, *Slave Society in Cuba during the Nineteenth Century* (Madison, 1970), p. 80; Herbert S. Klein, *Slavery in the Americas: a Comparative Study of Virginia and Cuba* (Chicago, 1967), p. 72.
135 Blackburn, *Making of New World Slavery*, pp. 416–19; Beckles, *Barbados*, pp. 59–61; James Walvin, *Questioning Slavery* (London, 1996), ch. 8.
136 Blackburn, *Making of New World Slavery*, pp. 411–12.
137 Patterson, *Jamaica*, pp. 216–20, 224–6; Goveia, *Slave Society*, pp. 226–7; Barbara Bush, *Slave Women in Caribbean Society, 1650–1838* (London, 1990), pp. 46–50; Beckles, *Natural Rebels*, p. 81.
138 Ward, *British West Indian Slavery*, pp. 111–16.
139 Ibid., pp. 223–4.
140 Patterson, *Jamaica*, pp. 77–9, 84; Bush, *Slave Women*, p. 29; Ward, *British West Indian Slavery*, p. 167.
141 Ward, *British West Indian Slavery*, p. 38.
142 Ibid., pp. 85, 91.
143 Knight, *Slave Society in Cuba*, pp. 25–6; Rebecca J. Scott, *Slave Emancipation in Cuba* (Princeton, 1985), tables 1 and 3.
144 For the Caribbean, see Blackburn, *Making of New World Slavery*, p. 332. For Brazil, see above, p. 82. For North American colonies, with 4 per cent of the population enslaved in 1650 and 22 per cent in 1770, see Fogel, *Without Consent*, p. 30.
145 Kolchin, *American Slavery*, app. table 3.
146 For Leewards, see Goveia, *Slave Society*, p. 203. For Jamaica, see Blackburn, *Making of New World Slavery*, pp. 403–4. For Cuba, see Knight, *Slave Society in Cuba*, pp. 22, 180–1; Scott, *Slave Emancipation in Cuba*, pp. 6–7 (table 1).
147 Blackburn, *Making of New World Slavery*, p. 229; Klein, *African Slavery*, p. 131; Walvin, *Questioning Slavery*, p. 2.
148 See above, p. 58.

149 Ward, *British West Indian Slavery*, pp. 9–11; Patterson, *Jamaica*, pp. 23–4; Goveia, *Slave Society*, pp. 82–3, 104–5, 147; Beckles, *Natural Rebels*, pp. 29, 37; David W. Galenson, *White Servitude in Colonial America* (Cambridge, 1981), pp. 132–3.

150 Beckles, *Barbados*, p. 23.

151 See above, pp. 80–1, 85, 95.

152 For proportion of free blacks in Caribbean, see Goveia, *Slave Society*, p. 203; Blackburn, *Making of New World Slavery*, table X.3 (p. 405). For US free blacks, see Kolchin, *American Slavery*, app. table 2. For French and Spanish Caribbean, see below, p. 100.

153 Blackburn, *Making of New World Slavery*, p. 260; Patterson, *Jamaica*, pp. 66–9.

154 See above, p. 86.

155 Ward, *British West Indian Slavery*, p. 23; Beckles, *Barbados*, pp. 47–8, 35; Goveia, *Slave Society*, p. 234.

156 Dunn, *Sugar and Slaves*, p. 229. Also see Eltis and Richardson, 'The numbers game', p. 6.

157 Ward, *British West Indian Slavery*, pp. 121–2.

158 Kolchin, *American Slavery*, p. 93.

159 See above, pp. 77, 80–1.

160 Patterson, *Jamaica*, pp. 98–107; Ward, *British West Indian Slavery*, pp. 179–80; Blackburn, *Making of New World Slavery*, pp. 423–6; Geggus, *Slavery, War and Revolution*, p. 24.

161 Ward, *British West Indian Slavery*, pp. 121–2, 141, 148–55; Beckles, *Barbados*, pp. 75–7; Goveia, *Slave Society*, pp. 124–5.

162 Ward, *British West Indian Slavery*, pp. 179–80.

163 For proportions of Africans, see ibid., pp. 210–11; Beckles, *Natural Rebels*, p. 21. For infusion of African culture, see Goveia, *Slave Society*, pp. 240–2.

164 See Goveia, *Slave Society*, pp. 52–3; Patterson, *Jamaica*, pp. 70, 93.

165 Bush, *Slave Women*, pp. 27–8; Blackburn, *Making of New World Slavery*, p. 290; Knight, *Slave Society in Cuba*, p. 123.

166 For enforcement difficulties, see Geggus, *Slavery, War and Revolution*, p. 24; Knight, *Slave Society in Cuba*, pp. 106–7.

167 Bush, *Slave Women*, p. 29; Patterson, *Jamaica*, p. 77; Blackburn, *Making of New World Slavery*, pp. 346–7.

168 Klein, *African Slavery*, p. 56; Geggus, *Slavery, War and Revolution*, p. 19; Blackburn, *Making of New World Slavery*, p. 439; Knight, *Slave Society in Cuba*, p. 86; Scott, *Slave Emancipation in Cuba*, table 1 (p. 7).

169 For small planters, see Ward, *British West Indian Slavery*, pp. 210–11; Sheridan, *Development of Plantations*, pp. 36, 48; Blackburn, *Making of New World Slavery*, p. 439; Knight, *Slave Society in Cuba*, p. 86; Scott, *Slave Emancipation in Cuba*, p. 8. For mulattos and manumission, see Geggus, *Slavery, War and Revolution*, pp. 19–20.

170 For French colonies, see Sheridan, *Development of Plantations*, pp. 35–8, 48. For Cuba, see Knight, *Slave Society in Cuba*, pp. 63–7; Scott, *Slave Emancipation in Cuba*, p. 11.

171 See Ward, *British West Indian Slavery*, pp. 210–11; Knight, *Slave Society in Cuba*, p. 134. A transfer to large plantations occurred in Cuba after 1838, following the construction of a railway system, as the island converted to a cash crop economy based on sugar (ibid., p. 39). Until then, coffee growing had upheld the small, slave-operated plantation (ibid., pp. 65–6).

172 For public works on St Domingue, see Sheridan, *Development of Plantations*, pp. 51–2. For public works in Cuba, see Knight, *Slave Society in Cuba*, pp. 31–3, 38–9.

173 Knight, *Slave Society in Cuba*, pp. 4–6, 86, 132; Scott, *Slave Emancipation in Cuba*, table 1 (p. 7).

174 Knight, *Slave Society in Cuba*, pp. 86, 130–2; Klein, *Virginia and Cuba*, pt V, ch. 9. For some reservations about the liberating effects of *coartación*, see Scott, *Slave Emancipation in Cuba*, pp. 13–14.
175 Ward, *British West Indian Slavery*, p. 7, n. 18.
176 For limited cultivation of food, see Goveia, *Slave Society*, p. 148; Beckles, *Natural Rebels*, p. 48. For population density, see Beckles, *Natural Rebels*, p. 41.
177 Hilary M. Beckles, *White Servitude and Black Slavery in Barbados, 1627–1715* (Knoxville, 1989), table C1 (p. 173); Goveia, *Slave Society*, p. 203; Sheridan, *Development of Plantations*, p. 28; Patterson, *Jamaica*, p. 93.
178 Beckles, *Barbados*, pp. 21, 33, 51–2, 56; Blackburn, *Making of New World Slavery*, p. 344.
179 Beckles, *Barbados*, pp. 35–40, 55–6, 59–61.
180 Ibid., pp. 56, 59.
181 Patterson, *Jamaica*, pp. 266ff.
182 See above, pp. 99–100.
183 Beckles, *Barbados*, p. 34; Patterson, *Jamaica*, p. 84.
184 Beckles, *Barbados*, p. 60; Patterson, *Jamaica*, pp. 224–6.
185 Beckles, *Barbados*, p. 34.
186 Patterson, *Jamaica*, p. 80.
187 Ibid., pp. 77–8, 84.
188 Beckles, *Barbados*, pp. 57–8; Blackburn, *Making of New World Slavery*, pp. 416–19; Bush, *Slave Women*, pp. 151–60; Patterson, *Jamaica*, chs 7, 8.
189 For external pressures on planters, see Ward, *British West Indian Slavery*, p. 208. For effect of amelioration on slaves, see ibid., pp. 194, 198, 207.
190 Fogel, *Without Consent*, p. 29; Kolchin, *American Slavery*, app. table 3.
191 See Joe Gray Taylor, *Negro Slavery in Louisiana* (New York, 1963), pp. 68–9.
192 For tobacco, see Philip D. Morgan, *Slave Counterpoint* (University of North Carolina, 1998), p. 7; Alan Kulikoff, *Tobacco and Slaves* (Chapel Hill, 1986), pp. 37–8; Ira Berlin, *Many Thousands Gone* (Cambridge, Mass., 1998), ch. 5. For rice, see Peter H. Wood, *Black Majority* (New York, 1974), p. 36; D. C. Littlefield, *Rice and Slaves* (Baton Rouge, 1981), passim; Betty Wood, *The Origins of American Slavery* (New York, 1997), pp. 64–5; Berlin, *Many Thousands Gone*, ch. 6. For cotton, see Kolchin, *American Slavery*, pp. 95–6; Taylor, *Negro Slavery*, p. ix.
193 Herbert G. Gutman, *The Black Family in Slavery and Freedom, 1750–1925* (New York, 1976), p. 328; Eugene Genovese, *Roll, Jordan, Roll* (New York, 1974), p. 5.
194 Kulikoff, *Tobacco and Slaves*, p. 71; Blackburn, *Making of New World Slavery*, p. 461.
195 Kolchin, *American Slavery*, p. 23.
196 Littlefield, *Rice and Slaves*, p. 67.
197 Blackburn, *Making of New World Slavery*, pp. 470–1.
198 Kulikoff, *Tobacco and Slaves*, pp. 392–3; Peter Kolchin, *Unfree Labour* (Cambridge, Mass., 1987), pp. 135–7. For Caribbean, see above, p. 92.
199 Kulikoff, *Tobacco and Slaves*, p. 71; Morgan, *Slave Counterpoint*, pp. 81–95; ibid., table 21 (p. 92).
200 Kolchin, *American Slavery*, p. 37; Morgan, *Slave Counterpoint*, table 10 (p. 61).
201 The story is told in Michael Tadman's *Speculators and Slaves* (Wisconsin, 1989).
202 See Genovese, *Roll, Jordan*, p. 9; Kulikoff, *Tobacco and Slaves*, p. 359; Morgan, *Slave Counterpoint*, pp. 512–15, 521.
203 Kolchin, *American Slavery*, pp. 156–60; Genovese, *Roll, Jordan*, pp. 589–94; Walvin, *Questioning Slavery*, pp. 122–3.
204 Kolchin, *American Slavery*, pp. 151–6; Kulikoff, *Tobacco and Slaves*, p. 381; Genovese, *Roll, Jordan*, p. 48. For the Indian factor, see Morgan, *Slave Counterpoint*, pp. 477–85.

205 Kolchin, *American Slavery*, pp. 96–7. The original exporting states were Delaware, Virginia and Maryland. By the 1820s they had been joined by the Carolinas and Kentucky; and by the 1850s by Tennessee, plus parts of Missouri, Georgia and Alabama. From the 1820s the main importing states were Alabama, Mississippi, Louisiana, Texas, Arkansas and Florida. See Tadman, *Speculators and Slaves*, pp. 6–7.

206 Tadman, *Speculators and Slaves*, p. 31.

207 Ibid., pp. 112, 147, 153.

208 Ibid., p. 112.

209 Ibid., p. 113.

210 Kulikoff, *Tobacco and Slaves*, pp. 430–2.

211 Kolchin, *American Slavery*, pp. 78–9.

212 Tadman, *Speculators and Slaves*, p. 113.

213 Kulikoff, *Tobbaco and Slaves*, p. 292; Genovese, *Roll, Jordan*, pp. 535–40; Ira Berlin and Philip D. Morgan (eds), *The Slave Economy* (London, 1991), p. 6. For horses, see Philip D. Morgan 'Work and culture', *William and Mary Quarterly*, 3rd ser., 39 (1982), pp. 588–90. Exceptions to very limited free time were found in South Carolina and Louisiana, in the former thanks to the task system which could leave the afternoons free, and in the latter thanks to having Saturdays as well as Sundays off. See Morgan, *Slave Counterpoint*, pp. 186–7 and Taylor, *Negro Slavery*, pp. 15–16.

214 Berlin and Morgan (eds), *The Slave Economy*, p. 12; Genovese, *Roll, Jordan*, pp. 535–7. For trading by slaves, see Morgan, *Slave Counterpoint*, pp. 251–2, 371–2; Taylor, *Negro Slavery*, pp. 84–5; Kulikoff, *Tobacco and Slaves*, pp. 339–40. For slaves selling to masters, see Morgan, *Slave Counterpoint*, pp. 359–64.

215 Genovese, *Roll, Jordan*, pp. 313–14.

216 For plantation size, see Kolchin, *American Slavery*, app. tables 4 and 5; Morgan, *Slave Counterpoint*, tables 1 and 2 (pp. 40–1); Genovese, *Roll, Jordan*, pp. 7–8. For master residence, see Genovese, *Roll, Jordan*, pp. 11–12. Exceptionally large plantations with absentee masters that resembled the Caribbean form were to be found in lowcountry South Carolina, Alabama and the Mississippi valley. See Genovese, *Roll, Jordan*, p. 31. For the unusual cultural autonomy of the slaves in lowcountry South Carolina, see Morgan, *Slave Counterpoint*, p. 23, table 1 (p. 40). The theme runs through the book.

217 Edmund S. Morgan, *American Slavery, American Freedom* (New York, 1973), p. 329; Klein, *Virginia and Cuba*, p. 50.

218 Genovese, *Roll, Jordan*, pp. 184–93, 232–3, 235.

219 For the African connection, see ibid., pp. 197–201, 210–11.

220 Ibid., pp. 163, 207, 213, 245–6, 252.

221 For own congregations, see ibid., pp. 236–7. For own preachers, see ibid., pp. 255–79. For own funeral service, see ibid., pp. 197–9; Morgan, *Slave Counterpoint*, pp. 640–4. For own church service, see Genovese, *Roll, Jordan*, pp. 232–55.

222 Genovese, *Roll, Jordan*, pp. 189, 236–7. Also see Kolchin, *Unfree Labour*, pp. 220ff.

223 Gutman, *The Black Family*, pp. 270, 274–6; Morgan, *Slave Counterpoint*, pp. 104–8.

224 For slave marriage, see Gutman, *Black Family*, chs 1–4, 7.

225 For partners living on different estates, see below, n. 233. Hiring out affected 5–10 per cent of slaves at any one time in mid-nineteenth century. See Genovese, *Roll, Jordan*, pp. 390–2. Also see Morgan, *Slave Counterpoint*, pp. 515–16.

226 See below, ns. 227, 231.

227 For privacy of quarters, see Kolchin, *American Slavery*, pp. 149–50; Morgan, *Slave Counterpoint*, pp. 113, 120–4. For masks, see Bertram Wyatt-Brown, 'The mask of obedience: male slave psychology in the Old South', *American Historical Review*, 93 (1988), pp. 1228–1252. For surnames, see Morgan, *Slave Counterpoint*, pp. 556–7; Gutman, *Black Family*, ch. 6. Also see Genovese, *Roll, Jordan*, p. 93.

228 Genovese, *Roll, Jordan*, pp. 539–40, 567, 573; Taylor, *Negro Slavery in Louisiana*, pp. 127–8; Morgan, *Slave Counterpoint*, p. 185.

229 For non-cooperation, see Kolchin, *American Slavery*, pp. 157–9; Genovese, *Roll, Jordan*, pp. 620–1, 648–56. For formal complaints by slaves, see Morgan, *Slave Counterpoint*, pp. 192, 327–9, 332. For the 'negotiated' relationship, see Berlin, *Many Thousands Gone*, pp. 2–3.

230 Genovese, *Roll, Jordan*, p. 567.

231 For customs of inheritance, see Morgan, 'Work and culture', *William and Mary Quarterly*, 3rd ser., 39 (1982), pp. 592–3; Genovese, *Roll, Jordan*, pp. 537–8.

232 Genovese, *Roll, Jordan*, pp. 486–7; Taylor, *Negro Slavery*, pp. 108, 126; Morgan, *Slave Counterpoint*, pp. 138–9.

233 For visiting, see Kulikoff, *Tobacco and Slaves*, p. 11; Morgan, *Slave Counterpoint*, pp. 524–30, 508–9.

234 For task work, see Kolchin, *American Slavery*, pp. 31–2; Morgan 'Work and culture', p. 564. For gang work, see Kulikoff, *Tobacco and Slaves*, pp. 381–410. For establishing customary limits on work, see Morgan, *Slave Counterpoint*, p. 192. For self-hire, see Taylor, *Negro Slavery*, pp. 15–16; Genovese, *Roll, Jordan*, pp. 313–14; Kulikoff, *Tobacco and Slaves*, pp. 396–8, 414, 416; Morgan, *Slave Counterpoint*, pp. 351–2.

235 E.g. Taylor, *Negro Slavery*, pp. 128–31. Also see Walvin, *Questioning Slavery*, pp. 142–3.

236 Littlefield, *Rice and Slaves*, p. 2, n. 3.

237 E.g. Klein, *Virginia and Cuba*, pp. 50, 55–6.

238 Morgan, *Slave Counterpoint*, pp. 257–300. Also see ibid., chs 6 and 7.

239 Genovese, *Roll, Jordan*, pp. 430–1.

240 For Louisiana free blacks, see Kolchin, *American Slavery*, app. table 2. For restrictions placed on manumission once Louisiana passed to the USA, see Taylor, *Negro Slavery*, ch. 7.

241 Morgan, *American Slavery, American Freedom*, p. 337.

242 Klein, *Virginia and Cuba*, pp. 183, 187; Kulikoff, *Tobacco and Slaves*, p. 432.

243 Kolchin, *American Slavery*, app. table 2.

244 Blackburn, *Making of New World Slavery*, pp. 482–3.

245 Kulikoff, *Tobacco and Slaves*, pp. 418–19, 432.

246 Genovese, *Roll, Jordan*, p. 408.

247 Kolchin, *American Slavery*, app. table 2.

248 Ibid.

249 Ibid. Upper South comprises Delaware, Dist. of Columbia, Maryland, Virginia, North Carolina, Kentucky, Missouri, Tennessee. Deep South comprises South Carolina, Georgia, Florida, Arkansas, Alabama, Louisiana, Mississippi, Texas.

250 Berlin, *Many Thousands Gone*, table 1 (pp. 370–1).

251 Kolchin, *American Slavery*, app. table 1.

252 For 1770, see ibid. For 1860, see ibid., table 3. For mid-eighteenth-century northern colonies, see Berlin, *Many Thousands Gone*, table 1 (p. 370).

253 Blackburn, *Making of New World Slavery*, pp. 476–7. For a substantial picture of northern slavery, see Berlin, *Many Thousands Gone*, chs 2, 7, 9.

254 Kolchin, *American Slavery*, pp. 26–7, 30; Blackburn, *Making of New World Slavery*, pp. 239, 476–7; Betty Wood, *Origins*, ch. 5; Philip D. Morgan, 'British encounters with Africans and African-Americans, c. 1600–1780', *Strangers within the Realm*, ed. Bernard Bailyn and Philip D. Morgan (Chapel Hill, 1991), p. 167.

255 Walvin, *Questioning Slavery*, p. 123. For eighteenth-century percentages in all states, see Berlin, *Many Thousands Gone*, table 1 (pp. 370–1).

256 For Virginia, see Kulikoff, *Tobacco and Slaves*, p. 340. For lowcountry, see Morgan, *Slave Counterpoint*, p. 95. For states of South Carolina and Mississippi in 1860, see Kolchin, *American Slavery*, app. table 3 and p. 73.

257 Kolchin, *American Slavery*, app. tables 1 and 3.
258 See above, p. 86.
259 See above, pp. 84–5, 90.

Chapter 9   European Serfdom

1 For similarities and differences, see Michael Bush, 'Serfdom in medieval and modern Europe: a comparison', *Serfdom and Slavery*, ed. M. L. Bush (Harlow, 1996), ch. 11.
2 Ibid., pp. 200–6. Also see above, ch. 3.
3 M. L. Bush, *Noble Privilege* (Manchester, 1983), pp. 147–8, 165, 168–9; Bush, 'Serfdom', pp. 219–20.
4 For the east, see Isabel de Madariaga, 'Catherine II and the serfs: a reconsideration of some problems', *Slavonic and East European Review*, 52 (1974), pp. 32, 36–7; Jerome Blum, *The End of the Old Order in Rural Europe* (Princeton, 1978), pp. 30–3. For the west, see P. L. Fossier, *Peasant Life in the Medieval West* (Oxford, 1988), p. 157.
5 Bush, 'Serfdom', pp. 203–6.
6 See Bush, *Noble Privilege*, p. 165; below, pp. 128, 139–40, 149, 153.
7 See M. L. Bush, 'Tenant right and the peasantries of Europe under the old regime', *Social Orders and Social Classes in Europe since 1500*, ed. M. L. Bush (Harlow, 1992), ch. 8. A vigorous and bitter debate on this subject of differential development has opposed the factor of depopulation against that of class struggle, with both sides, nonetheless, claiming in defence of their position to accept a multicausal explanation that regards demography, social structure and political position as all playing an interactive part. See *The Brenner Debate*, ed. T. H. Aston and C. H. E. Philpin (Cambridge, 1985) and Robert Brenner's 'The rises and declines of serfdom in medieval and early modern Europe' in Bush (ed.), *Serfdom and Slavery*, ch. 13. However, even when all these factors are included in the equation they fail to account for the difference of direction in which eastern and western Europe developed with regards to serfdom. In explaining why the one should adopt serfdom and the other reject it, previous historical experience has to be taken into account, plus the fact that serfdom when introduced in the east offered advantages to the peasant as well as to the lord. In addition, the western resort to leasehold conferred upon lords a more advantageous device than the gains they would have made from attempting to revive serfdom.
8 Blum, *End of the Old Order*, p. 96; Hartmut Harnisch, 'Peasants and markets', in *The German Peasantry*, ed. R. J. Evans and W. R. Lee (London, 1986), p. 46.
9 Bush, *Noble Privilege*, pp. 158–60.
10 Ibid., p. 165.
11 Blum, *End of the Old Order*, chs 10, 11.
12 Bush, 'Serfdom', p. 205.
13 Ibid., p. 201. For slaves enserfed to stop flight, see Pierre Bonnassie, *From Slavery to Feudalism in South-West Europe* (Cambridge, 1991), pp. 47–8.
14 Bush, 'Serfdom', p. 201.
15 Ibid., pp. 219–20, and fn. 66.
16 Werner Rosener, *Peasants in the Middle Ages* (Oxford, 1985), p. 268; David W. Sabean, *Power in the Blood* (Cambridge, 1984), pp. 4–5; Blum, *End of the Old Order*, p. 37. For general process of enserfment in the late medieval West, see H. Wunder, 'Serfdom in later medieval and early modern Germany', *Social Relations and Ideas*, ed. T. H. Aston et al. (Cambridge, 1983), pp. 251–2, 257–8; Peter Blickle, *The Revolution of 1525* (Baltimore, 1981), pp. 29–35; Thomas Robisheau, *Rural Society and the Search for Order in Early Modern Germany* (Cambridge, 1989), p. 35.

17 Bush, 'Serfdom', pp. 204, 219; Georges Duby, *Rural Economy and Country Life in the Medieval West* (London, 1968), p. 250; W. C. Jordan, *From Servitude to Freedom* (Philadelphia, 1986), p. 98.
18 Jordan, *From Servitude*, pp. 28–9.
19 Theodore Evergates, *Feudal Society in the Bailliage of Troyes* (Baltimore, 1979), pp. 28–9, 144.
20 Marc Bloch, *French Rural History* (London, 1966), pp. 111–12; Bush, 'Serfdom', p. 218; Richard N. Britnell, *The Commercialisation of English Society 1000–1500* (Manchester, 1996), ch. 9.
21 Rosener, *Peasants*, p. 218; Bush, 'Tenant right', pp. 143–4.
22 P. Freedman, *The Origins of Penal Servitude in Medieval Catalonia* (Cambridge, 1991), ch. 7.
23 Blum, *End of the Old Order*, pp. 217–18, 228; T. C. W. Blanning, *Reformation and Revolution in Mainz, 1743–1803* (Cambridge, 1974), p. 89; David W. Sabean, *Property, Production and Family in Neckerhausen* (Cambridge, 1990), p. 47.
24 For general overview, see Blum, *End of the Old Order*, p. 35. In Dutch Republic: I. J. Brugmans, 'La Fin de la féodalité aux Pays-Bas', *L'Abolition de la féodalité dans le monde occidental* (Paris, 1971), I, pp. 222–3. In France: Bloch, *French Rural History*, p. 111. In Germany: Wunder, 'Serfdom in late medieval and early modern Germany', pp. 254–61; G. Benecke, *Society and Politics in Germany, 1500–1750* (London, 1974), pp. 76–81, 177–8; Blanning, *Reformation and Revolution*, pp. 88–9; Tom Scott, *Freiburg and the Breisgau* (Oxford, 1986), p. 79; Robisheau, *Rural Society and the Search*, p. 35; Sabean, *Property, Production and Family*, p. 47; Gregory W. Pedlow, *The Survival of the Hessian Nobility, 1770–1870* (Princeton, 1988), p. 118.
25 Bush, 'Tenant right', pp. 144–5; Sabean, *Power*, pp. 4–5.
26 For impact of proto-industrialization, see Rudolf Vierhaus, *Germany in the Age of Absolutism* (Cambridge, 1988), pp. 48–50.
27 For the intrusion of the state, see Thomas Robisheau, 'The peasantries of Western Germany, 1300–1750', *The Peasantries of Europe*, ed. Tom Scott (Harlow, 1998), pp. 133–7.
28 Bush, *Noble Privilege*, p. 152; Blum, *End of the Old Order*, pp. 36–7.
29 Bush, 'Serfdom', pp. 221–2.
30 J. Lukowski, *Liberty's Folly: the Polish-Lithuanian Commonwealth in the Eighteenth Century* (London, 1991), p. 38; J. C. Miller, *The Nobility in Polish Renaissance Society, 1548–1571* (dissertation, Indiana University, 1977), pp. 206, 210; William W. Hagen, 'Village Life in East-Elbian Germany and Poland, 1400–1800' in Scott (ed.), *The Peasantries of Europe*, p. 158 (n. 14). In 1562–3 the minimum labour service was raised by statute to at least two days a week. See Miller, *Nobility in Polish Renaissance Society*, pp. 233–4. But this reverted to one day a week ten years later. See J. Topolski, 'Sixteenth-century Poland and the turning point in European economic development', *A Republic of Nobles*, ed. J. K. Fedorowicz (Cambridge, 1982), p. 76.
31 Bush 'Serfdom', p. 205; Hagen, 'Village life', p. 158. For sales, see Miller, *Nobility in Polish Renaissance Society*, p. 246.
32 Bush, *Noble Privilege*, pp. 11–12.
33 Ibid., pp. 103–7.
34 Michael Bush, *Rich Noble, Poor Noble* (Manchester, 1988), pp. 44–5.
35 Ibid., p. 45.
36 Bush, *Noble Privilege*, p. 29.
37 Miller, *Nobility in Polish Renaissance Society*, pp. 210–12.
38 Ibid., p. 210.
39 Ibid., p. 209; A. Kaminski, 'Neo-serfdom in Poland and Lithuania', *Slavic Review*, 34 (1975), p. 267.
40 Miller, *Nobility in Polish Renaissance Society*, p. 171.

41 Ibid., p. 210; Fedorowicz (ed.), *Republic of Nobles*, p. 71; Norman Davies, *God's Playground: a History of Poland* (Oxford, 1981), I, p. 281.

42 Miller, *Nobility in Polish Renaissance Society*, pp. 171–2; Hagen, 'Village life', pp. 156, 172.

43 For beneficial tenures, see Miller, *Nobility in Polish Renaissance Society*, pp. 170–1. For slavery, see R. A. French, 'The three-field system of sixteenth-century Lithuania', *Agricultural History Review*, 18 (1970), p. 111; G. V. Vernadsky, *Russia at the Dawn of the Modern Age* (New Haven, 1959), IV, p. 201.

44 Miller, *Nobility in Polish Renaissance Society*, pp. 170, 174; Hagen, 'Village life', 156, 160, 163–4.

45 See above, pp. 123–4.

46 For connection beween Polish serfdom and the Baltic grain trade to western Europe, see M. Malowist, 'The economic and social development of the Baltic countries from the fifteenth to the seventeenth century', *Economic History Review*, 2nd ser., 12 (1959), pp. 183–6; Hagen, 'Village life', p. 164. For stressing the importance of internal demand, as opposed to foreign trade, in the generation of serfdom, see Miller, *Nobility in Polish Renaissance Society*, pp. 173, 210–12; Topolski, 'Sixteenth-century Poland', p. 82; Robert I. Frost, 'The nobility of Poland-Lithuania, 1569–1795', *The European Nobilities in the Seventeenth and Eighteenth Centuries*, ed. H. M. Scott (London, 1995), II, p. 200.

47 For the fiscal advantage, see Miller, *Nobility in Polish Renaissance Society*, pp. 295–6.

48 Ibid., p. 218.

49 Hagen, 'Village life', p. 170; Miller, *Nobility in Polish Renaissance Society*, 223–4; Topolski, 'Sixteenth-century Poland', p. 76. For the range of service required, see Lukowski, *Liberty's Folly*, p. 41. For a long-term overview, see Davies, *God's Playground*, I, p. 284.

50 For tenant rights, see S. Kieniewicz, *The Emancipation of the Polish Peasantry* (Chicago, 1969), p. 15; Kaminski, 'Neo-serfdom in Poland', p. 267; W. I. Thomas and F. Znanieki, *The Polish Peasant in Europe and America*, 2nd edn (New York, 1958), I, pp. 158–9. For commoning rights, see ibid., p. 187. For rents, see Hagen, 'Village life', pp. 170, 178; Kaminski, 'Neo-serfdom in Poland', p. 267.

51 Fedorowicz (ed.), *Republic of Nobles*, p. 71; Topolski, 'Sixteenth-century Poland', p. 76; Kaminski, 'Neo-serfdom in Poland', p. 258.

52 Lukowski, *Liberty's Folly*, p. 38.

53 Kaminski, 'Neo-serfdom in Poland', p. 267. For a broader view of the relationship, see W. Kula, *An Economic Theory of the Feudal System: Towards a Model of the Polish Economy, 1500–1800* (London, 1976), pp. 64–5. For the replacement of rents by labour services, see Hagen, 'Village life', p. 178.

54 Lukowski, *Liberty's Folly*, p. 56; Miller, *Nobility in Polish Renaissance Society*, p. 194.

55 Kaminski, 'Neo-serfdom in Poland', p. 262; Lukowski, *Liberty's Folly*, pp. 58–60. For the temporary breakdown of the manorial regime, see Hagen, 'Village life', p. 172.

56 Hagen, 'Village life', p. 158.

57 See Miller, *Nobility in Polish Renaissance Society*, pp. 208, 211; Lukowski, *Liberty's Folly*, pp. 58–60; R. I. Frost, *After the Deluge: Poland-Lithuania and the Second Northern War, 1655–1660* (Cambridge, 1993), pp. 7–8; Kieniewicz, *Emancipation*, p. 19 and ch. 9.

58 Sheldon J. Watts, *A Social History of Western Europe, 1450–1720* (London, 1984), p. 137; Topolski, 'Sixteenth-century Poland', pp. 83–4; Davies, *God's Playground*, I, pp. 287–91.

59 Hagen, 'Village life', pp. 171–2, 175.

60 Kaminski, 'Neo-serfdom in Poland', pp. 262–3. For the increase in week-work, see Davies, *God's Playground*, I, p. 284.

61 Hagen, 'Village life', pp. 175–6; Frost, 'The nobility of Poland-Lithuania', p. 200.
62 Hagen, 'Village life', p. 176.
63 Miller, *Nobility in Polish Renaissance Society*, p. 173.
64 For tax, see Lukowski, *Liberty's Folly*, p. 49. For impact of Partition, see B. Lesnodorski, 'Le Processus de l'abolition du régime féodale dans les territoires polonais aux XVIIIe et XIXe siècles', *L'Abolition de la féodalité*, I, p. 463; P. S. Wandycz, *The Lands of Partitioned Poland, 1795–1918* (London, 1974), pp. 18–19.
65 Kaminski, 'Neo-serfdom in Poland', pp. 257–8; Kieniewicz, *Emancipation*, pp. 9–12; Miller, *Nobility in Polish Renaissance Society*, p. 228; Frost, 'Nobility of Poland-Lithuania', p. 200.
66 Madariaga, 'Catherine II and the serfs', p. 36.
67 Bush, *Rich Noble, Poor Noble*, pp. 112–14.
68 Davies, *God's Playground*, II, p. 206.
69 Lukowski, *Liberty's Folly*, pp. 48–9.
70 Hagen, 'Village life', p. 176; Lukowski, *Liberty's Folly*, p. 49; Blum, *End of the Old Order*, p. 32.
71 Lukowski, *Liberty's Folly*, pp. 46–8, 49; Kieniewicz, *Emancipation*, p. 16; M. M. Siekierski, *Landed Wealth in the Grand Duchy of Lithuania: the Economic Affairs of Prince Nicholas Christopher Radziwill (1549–1616)* (Ph.D., Berkeley, Calif., 1984), pp. 165–6; Miller, *Nobility in Polish Renaissance Society*, pp. 191–2.
72 For reliance on waged labour, see A. Wyczanski, 'En Pologne: l'économie du domaine nobiliaire moyen', *Annales*, 18 (1963), p. 84; Kaminski, 'Neo-serfdom in Poland', p. 268; Lukowski, *Liberty's Folly*, p. 49; Frost, 'Nobility of Poland-Lithuania', p. 200. For enserfing effect of yearly residence, see ibid., p. 49.
73 French, 'Three-field system', p. 124; Kieniewicz, *Emancipation*, pp. 25–6, 49, 138; Lesnodorski, 'Processus', pp. 463, 465, 469–70.
74 For effects of population, see Blum, *End of the Old Order*, pp. 106–7; Davies, *God's Playground*, II, p. 180. To be properly appreciated as creating a demographic problem, the Davies figures for population density have to be placed in the context of the agrarian and predominantly peasant society that comprised most of Poland at that time. In other words, nothing is to be gained by comparing the Polish figures with those of an industrial society. For emigration, see Davies, *God's Playground*, II, pp. 276–7; O. Handlin, *The Uprooted* (Boston, 1951), pp. 25–8, 35–6.
75 Herman Rebel, 'Peasantries under the Austrian Empire, 1300–1800' in Scott (ed.), *The Peasantries of Europe*, pp. 212–14.
76 For landlord problems and solutions, see Bush, 'Tenant right', pp. 136ff.
77 For taxation, see C. A. Macartney, *The Habsburg Empire, 1790–1918* (London, 1968), pp. 28–32; P. G. M. Dickson, *Finance and Government under Maria Theresia, 1740–1780* (Oxford, 1987), II, chs. 6–8. For conscription, see Macartney, *Habsburg Empire*, pp. 15–18.
78 W. E. Wright, 'Neo-serfdom in Bohemia', *Slavic Review*, 34 (1975), p. 240.
79 Jerome Blum, 'The rise of serfdom in eastern Europe', *American Historical Review*, 62 (1957), pp. 812–13.
80 Bush, 'Serfdom', p. 205.
81 Wright, 'Neo-serfdom in Bohemia', pp. 240–1.
82 Bush, 'Tenant right', pp. 140–1.
83 Richard C. Hoffmann, *Land, Liberties and Lordship in a Late Medieval Countryside* (Philadelphia, 1989), pp. 135, 274, 286, 322.
84 Bush, *Noble Privilege*, pp. 11, 108.
85 Ibid., pp. 95, 115.
86 Frederick G. Heymann, *George of Bohemia, King of Heretics* (Princeton, 1965), p. 589.
87 William E. Wright, *Serfdom, Seigneur and Sovereign* (Minneapolis, 1966), p. 13.

88 Wright, 'Neo-serfdom in Bohemia', p. 240; Wright, *Serf, Seigneur*, p. 14.
89 R. J. W. Evans, *The Making of the Habsburg Monarchy, 1550–1700* (Oxford, 1979), pp. 197, 200–1; R. J. Kerner, *Bohemia in the Eighteenth Century* (New York, 1932), pp. 66–7; Macartney, *The Habsburg Empire*, pp. 53, 88–9; O. Odlozilik, 'The nobility of Bohemia, 1620–1740', *East European Quarterly*, 7 (1973).
90 Wright, *Serf, Seigneur*, pp. 14, 22–3, 48–9; Kerner, *Bohemia*, pp. 24–5, 276–7; A. Klima, 'Agrarian class structure and economic development in pre-industrial Bohemia', *Past and Present*, 85 (1979), p. 51; K. Mejdricka, 'L'État du régime féodal à la veille de son abolition et les conditions de sa suppression en Bohème', *L'Abolition de la féodalité*, I, p. 397.
91 Derek Beales, *Joseph II* (Cambridge 1987), I, pp. 342, 346ff; Kerner, *Bohemia*, p. 39; Wright, *Serf, Seigneur*, pp. 53, 60.
92 For government policy, see Kerner, *Bohemia*, pp. 27, 239. For demesne expansion, see Klima, 'Agrarian class structure', pp. 50–3; Wright, 'Neo-serfdom in Bohemia', p. 248.
93 Wright, *Serf, Seigneur*, pp. 22–3.
94 K. Bosl (ed.), *Handbuch der Geschichte der böhmischen Länder* (Stuttgart, 1967), II, pp. 211–12, 216–18; Wright, 'Neo-serfdom in Bohemia', p. 243.
95 Wright, 'Neo-serfdom in Bohemia', pp. 246–7.
96 Ibid., p. 243; Klima, 'Agrarian class structure', pp. 50–3; Mejdricka, 'L'État du régime féodal', pp. 393–7.
97 Ibid., pp. 393–6; Wright, 'Neo-serfdom in Bohemia', pp. 246–7.
98 Kerner, *Bohemia*, pp. 276–7; Mejdricka, 'L'État du régime féodal', p. 397.
99 Ibid., p. 396; Wright, *Serf, Seigneur*, p. 51.
100 Klima, 'Agrarian class structure', pp. 50–4.
101 Ibid., pp. 54–5, 62; Wright, 'Neo-serfdom in Bohemia', p. 250.
102 Klima, 'Agrarian class structure', p. 64; Bush, *Rich Noble, Poor Noble*, pp. 134–5.
103 Mejdricka, 'L'État du régime féodal', p. 403.
104 Macartney, *Habsburg Empire*, p. 72; Bush, *Noble Privilege*, p. 72; Wright, *Serf, Seigneur*, pp. 15–16; Mejdricka, 'L'État du régime féodal', p. 398.
105 Klima, 'Agrarian class structure', p. 54.
106 Wright, *Serf, Seigneur*, pp. 14, 17, 141; Wright, 'Neo-serfdom in Bohemia', p. 247; Macartney, *Habsburg Empire*, pp. 21–2; Kerner, *Bohemia*, p. 274.
107 Beales, *Joseph II*, p. 339.
108 Ibid., pp. 342, 347, 349.
109 Kerner, *Bohemia*, pp. 276–7; Wright, *Serf, Seigneur*, pp. 23–4.
110 Beales, *Joseph II*, pp. 339, 342, 346.
111 Mejdricka, 'L'État du régime féodal', p. 397.
112 Klima, 'Agrarian class structure', p. 59.
113 K. J. Dillon, *Kings and Estates in the Bohemian Lands, 1526–1564*, Studies Presented to the International Commission for the History of Representative and Parliamentary Institutions, 57 (Brussels, 1976), p. 13.
114 Wright, 'Neo-serfdom in Bohemia', p. 247.
115 Kerner, *Bohemia*, p. 278; Mejdricka, 'L'État du régime féodal', p. 402.
116 Blum, 'Rise of serfdom', pp. 812–13.
117 H. Marczali, *Hungary in the Eighteenth Century* (Cambridge, 1916), p. 171.
118 B. K. Kiraly, *Hungary in the late Eighteenth Century* (London, 1969), p. 51, n. 1.
119 Z. P. Pach, *Die ungarische Agrarentwicklung im 16–17. Jahrhundert* (Budapest, 1964), p. 27; Marczali, *Hungary in the Eighteenth Century*, p. 172.
120 B. K. Kiraly, 'Neo-serfdom in Hungary', *Slavic Review*, 34 (1975), p. 269; Evans, *Making of the Habsburg Monarchy*, p. 88; Kiraly, *Hungary*, p. 56.
121 Peter Schimert, 'The Hungarian nobility in the seventeenth and eighteenth centuries' in H. M. Scott (ed.), *The European Nobilities*, II, p. 172.
122 Kiraly, *Hungary*, p. 5.
123 Ibid., p. 10.

124 Orest Subtelny, *Domination of Eastern Europe: Native Nobilities and Foreign Absolutism, 1500–1715* (London, 1986), p. 10; Evans, *Making of the Habsburg Monarchy*, p. 87.

125 Kiraly, *Hungary*, pp. 52–3.

126 A. J. Janos, *The Politics of Backwardness in Hungary, 1825–1945* (Princeton, 1982), p. 27.

127 Bush, *Rich Noble, Poor Noble*, p. 139.

128 E. Niederhauser, 'L'Émancipation des serfs en Hongrie et en Europe orientale', *L'Abolition de la féodalité*, I, p. 420.

129 Janos, *Politics of Backwardness*, p. 30.

130 Kiraly, 'Neo-serfdom in Hungary', pp. 274–7.

131 Hungary was converted partially in 1687, when the monarchy was made hereditary in the male line of the Habsburgs, and completely in 1723, when it became transmissible in the female line as well. See Marczali, *Hungary in the Eighteenth Century*, p. 308.

132 N. von Preradovich, 'Der Adel in den Herrschaftsgebieten der deutschen Linie des Hauses Habsburg', *Deutscher Adel, 1555–1740*, ed. H. Rossler (Darmstadt, 1965), pp. 211–12.

133 Bush, *Rich Noble, Poor Noble*, pp. 49–50.

134 Kiraly, *Hungary*, p. 238. For the quote, see ibid., p. 8.

135 Janos, *Politics of Backwardness*, pp. 27–8; Kiraly, *Hungary*, p. 57.

136 Kiraly, *Hungary*, p. 52.

137 Marczali, *Hungary in the Eighteenth Century*, pp. 174–5.

138 See below, pp. 150–1.

139 Kiraly, *Hungary*, pp. 214–18.

140 Bush, *Rich Noble, Poor Noble*, p. 14; Janos, *Politics of Backwardness*, pp. 21–2.

141 J. Kovacsics, 'The population of Hungary in the eighteenth century', *Third International Conference of Economic History* (Munich, 1965), IV, p. 139. Besides the designated serfs, there were the cotters, many of whom must have been of serf status, comprising a further 12.9 per cent of taxpayers (see ibid.). Also see K. Benda, 'Le Régime féodal en Hongrie à la fin du XVIIIe siècle', *L'Abolition de la féodalité*, I, p. 414.

142 Kiraly, *Hungary*, pp. 43, 46.

143 Bush, *Rich Noble, Poor Noble*, pp. 10–11, 114–15.

144 See above, n. 140.

145 Janos, *Politics of Backwardness*, p. 21.

146 Kiraly, *Hungary*, p. 51, n. 1.

147 Kiraly, 'Neo-serfdom in Hungary', p. 273; Benda, 'Le Régime féodal', p. 417; Kiraly, *Hungary*, pp. 59–60, 69.

148 Kiraly, *Hungary*, p. 60.

149 Marczali, *Hungary in the Eighteenth Century*, p. 175; Janos, *Politics of Backwardness*, p. 27.

150 Marczali, *Hungary in the Eighteenth Century*, p. 173; Benda, 'Le Régime féodal', p. 415; Kiraly, *Hungary*, pp. 64–5.

151 Kiraly, *Hungary*, pp. 65–6; Blum, *End of the Old Order*, p. 64.

152 Kiraly, *Hungary*, 65–7; Marczali, *Hungary in the Eighteenth Century*, p. 173; Benda, 'Le Régime féodal', p. 415.

153 Marczali, *Hungary in the Eighteenth Century*, p. 193; Janos, *Politics of Backwardness*, p. 28. For extent, see Pach, *Die ungarische Agrarentwicklung*, p. 27.

154 Kiraly, *Hungary*, p. 63.

155 Ibid., p. 62.

156 Ibid.

157 Ibid., p. 61.

158 Janos, *Politics of Backwardness*, p. 27.

159 Ibid., p. 27; Kiraly, *Hungary*, pp. 57–8.

160 Kiraly, *Hungary*, pp. 63–4.
161 Bush, *Rich Noble, Poor Noble*, p. 139.
162 Kiraly, *Hungary*, pp. 65–6; Pach, *Die ungarische Agrarentwicklung*, pp. 18–23.
163 Schimert, 'Hungarian nobility', pp. 172–3; Marczali, *Hungary in the Eighteenth Century*, p. 47; Macartney, *Habsburg Empire*, pp. 72–3; Bush, *Noble Privilege*, p. 148.
164 Kiraly, *Hungary*, p. 55, n. 21.
165 For carrying services, see ibid., p. 67. For castle maintenance, see Marczali, *Hungary in the Eighteenth Century*, p. 173.
166 Macartney, *Habsburg Empire*, pp. 32, 130–1, 172, 175–6, 184–5; Kiraly, *Hungary*, p. 106.
167 For 1767, see Marczali, *Hungary in the Eighteenth Century*, pp. 192–3. For 1785, see Macartney, *Habsburg Empire*, pp. 127–8.
168 Marczali, *Hungary in the Eighteenth Century*, pp. 192–3; Kiraly, *Hungary*, p. 65.
169 T. C. W. Blanning, *Joseph II* (London, 1994), pp. 115–16.
170 Ibid., p. 116.
171 Kiraly, *Hungary*, p. 233.
172 Ibid., p. 60; Jerome Blum, *Noble Landowners and Agriculture in Austria, 1815–1848*, John Hopkins University Studies in Historical and Political Science, 65 (1948), p. 81.
173 Kiraly, 'Neo-serfdom in Hungary', p. 272.
174 Niederhauser, 'L'Émancipation des serfs', pp. 421–3; Blum, *End of the Old Order*, pp. 387–8.
175 Richard Hellie, *Enserfment and Military Change in Moscovy* (Chicago, 1971), pt II.
176 Ibid., p. 78; Edgar Melton, 'The Russian peasantries, 1450–1860' in Scott (ed.), *The Peasantries of Europe*, pp. 234–6; Peter Kolchin, *Unfree Labour* (Cambridge, Mass., 1987), pp. 6–9.
177 Melton, 'Russian peasantries', pp. 236, 238–9, 246–8, 254; David Moon, *Russian Peasants and Tsarist Legislation on the Eve of Reform, 1825–1855* (London, 1992), pp. 24–5, 55.
178 Steven L. Hoch, *Serfdom and Social Control in Russia* (Chicago, 1986), p. 15; Kolchin, *Unfree Labour*, p. 10; Melton, 'Russian peasantries', p. 238.
179 Madariaga, 'Catherine II and the serfs', p. 38.
180 Quoted by David Moon in his 'Reassessing Russian serfdom', *European History Quarterly*, 26 (1996), p. 502.
181 Melton, 'Russian peasantries', p. 233; Hellie, *Enserfment and Military Change*, p. 33ff.
182 Melton, 'Russian peasantries', p. 238.
183 Hoch, *Serfdom and Social Control*, pp. 15, 21.
184 For serf sales, see Kolchin, *Unfree Labour*, p. 41. For industrial serfs, see below, p. 157.
185 Kolchin, *Unfree Labour*, p. 117; Melton, 'Russian peasantries', p. 231.
186 Jerome Blum in *Lord and Peasant in Russia* (Princeton, 1961), p. 422, made the point that, by the late eighteenth century, 'the Russian serf was scarcely distinguishable from a chattel slave'. Kolchin agreed: see his *Unfree Labour*, p. 43.
187 Melton, 'Russian peasantries', pp. 233, 239; A. Kahan, *The Plow, The Hammer and the Knout* (Chicago, 1985), p. 78; Blum, *Lord and Peasant*, p. 225; Herman E. Melton, *Serfdom and the Peasant Economy in Russia, 1780–1861* (Ph.D., Columbia University, 1984), pp. 66, 69–72, 189.
188 Melton, 'Russian peasantries', pp. 254, 256–7.
189 Ibid., pp. 231, 262–3.
190 Blum, *Lord and Peasant*, p. 281.
191 Melton, 'Russian peasantries', pp. 230, 254.
192 Kolchin, *Unfree Labour*, p. 39.

193 For freedom through flight, see Melton, 'Russian peasantries', pp. 248–9. For freedom through conscription, see Moon, *Russian Peasants*, p. 114.
194 Moon, *Russian Peasants*, pp. 170–2.
195 Madariaga, 'Catherine II and the serfs', pp. 35–6, 57.
196 Melton, 'Russian peasantries', p. 253; Madariaga, 'Catherine II and the serfs', p. 37; Melton, *Serfdom and the Peasant Economy*, p. 64; Blum, *Lord and Peasant*, p. 49.
197 Madariaga, 'Catherine II and the serfs', pp. 36–7.
198 Moon, 'Reassessing Russian serfdom', pp. 512–13; Hoch, *Serfdom and Social Control*, p. 2.
199 Daniel Field, *The End of Serfdom* (Cambridge, Mass., 1976), pp. 13–15.
200 Kolchin, *Unfree Labour*, pp. 52, 58–9.
201 Hoch, *Serfdom and Social Control*, pp. 10–11, 134; Moon, 'Reassessing Russian serfdom', pp. 490–1, 497; Kolchin, *Unfree Labour*, p. 236.
202 Hoch, *Serfdom and Social Control*, pp. 10, 165.
203 Ibid., pp. 134–5, 149–50.
204 Melton, 'Russian peasantries', pp. 263–4; Kolchin, *Unfree Labour*, pp. 201–3; Hoch, *Serfdom and Social Control*, p. 134.
205 For flogging, see Hoch, *Serfdom and Social Control*, p. 162. For arrears of rent, see Kolchin, *Unfree Labour*, p. 153.
206 R. Portal, 'Le Régime féodal en Russie à la veille de son abolition', *L'Abolition de la féodalité*, I, p. 442; Madariaga, 'Catherine II and the serfs', pp. 42, 49–50; Kolchin, *Unfree Labour*, pp. 2, 41–2.
207 Kolchin, *Unfree Labour*, pp. 142–7; David Saunders, *Russia in the Age of Reaction and Reform, 1807–1881* (London, 1992), pp. 133–5; Moon, 'Reassessing Russian serfdom', p. 505; Blum, *Lord and Peasant*, pp. 428–9, 446; Field, *End of Serfdom*, pp. 14–15.
208 Kahan, *Plow, Hammer and Knout*, p. 68; Melton, *Serfdom and the Peasant Economy*, pp. 72–3.
209 Melton, *Serfdom and the Peasant Economy*, pp. 73–4.
210 Hoch, *Serfdom and Social Control*, ch. 4.
211 Melton, 'Russian peasantries', p. 258; Hoch, *Serfdom and Social Control*, pp. 26–8.
212 H. E. Melton, 'Proto-industrialization, serf agriculture and agrarian social structure: two estates in nineteenth-century Russia', *Past and Present*, 115 (1987), pp. 74–5, 81; Melton, 'Russian peasantries', pp. 260–1; Melton, *Serfdom and the Peasant Economy*, pp. 187, 189.
213 T. Esper, 'The condition of the serf workers in Russia's metallurgical industry, 1800–1861', *Journal of Modern History*, 50 (1978), pp. 669–70, 672. Esper calculates that by the mid-nineteenth century in Perma province, the centre of the Urals' metallurgical industry, 500,000 (a quarter of the population) 'lived from industrial labour'. See his 'The income of Russian serf ironworkers in the nineteenth century', *Past and Present*, 93 (1981), pp. 137–8.
214 Esper, 'Condition of the serf workers', pp. 664, 666–9, 674–7.
215 Hoch, *Serfdom and Social Control*, pp. 51–2, 56; Kolchin, *Unfree Labour*, p. 152.
216 Moon, 'Reassessing Russian serfdom', pp. 504–5.
217 For population growth and effect, see Blum, *Lord and Peasant*, pp. 280, 530–1; Kolchin, *Unfree Labour*, pp. 150–2.
218 Melton, *Serfdom and the Peasant Economy*, pp. 91–2.
219 Ibid., p. 90.
220 For state peasants, see Melton, 'Russian peasantries', p. 255; Moon, *Russian Peasants*, p. 25. For serfs, see Melton, 'Russian peasantries', p. 262; Kolchin, *Unfree Labour*, pp. 70–1; Moon 'Reassessing Russian serfdom', p. 510.
221 Melton, 'Russian peasantries', pp. 255, 265.

Notes to pp. 158–164

222 Moon, *Russian Peasants*, pp. 169–73.
223 Ibid., p. 137.
224 Blum, *End of the Old Order*, pp. 229–30.
225 Ibid., pp. 231–2.
226 Moon, *Russian Peasants*, ch. 3; Portal, 'Le Régime féodal en Russie', pp. 442–3; Blum, *Lord and Peasant*, p. 419; Saunders, *Russia in the Age of Reaction and Reform*, p. 139.
227 Moon, 'Reassessing Russian serfdom', p. 513.
228 Blum, *Lord and Peasant*, p. 408.
229 Terence Emmons, 'The peasant and the Emancipation', in *The Peasant in Nineteenth-century Russia*, ed. W. S. Vucinich (Stanford, 1968), ch. 2.
230 Moon, *Russian Peasants*, pp. 67–8.

Chapter 10   Islamic Slavery

1 See Allan G. B. Fisher and Humphrey J. Fisher, *Slavery and Muslim Society in Africa* (London, 1970), pp. 111–13, 116–18; Paul E. Lovejoy, *Transformations in Slavery: a History of Slavery in Africa* (Cambridge, 1983), pp. 31–4; Y. Hakan Erdem, *Slavery in the Ottoman Empire and its Demise, 1800–1909* (London, 1996), pp. 15–17.
2 Murray Gordon, *Slavery in the Arab World* (New York, 1989), p. 36.
3 Ibid., p. 64.
4 Ibid., p. 27.
5 Ibid., pp. 49–53, 185–9; Lovejoy, *Transformations*, pp. 31–2; Richard L. Roberts, *Warriors, Merchants and Slaves* (Stanford, 1987), pp. 47–50.
6 Erdem, *Slavery in the Ottoman Empire*, pp. 11–14; Halil Inalcik, *The Ottoman Empire in the Classical Age, 1300–1600* (London, 1994), pp. 112–13; Fisher and Fisher, *Slavery and Muslim Society*, pp. 111–13; Gordon, *Slavery in the Arab World*, pp. 41, 54–6.
7 Daniel Pipes, *Slave Soldiers and Islam* (New Haven, 1981), pp. 39–44.
8 Gordon, *Slavery in the Arab World*, ch. 4.
9 Ibid., pp. 57–8.
10 Ibid., pp. 95–6. On the other hand, slave soldiers presumably suffered a high death-rate as a result of war, and slave eunuchs suffered a very high death-rate from the act of castration, with only one in ten surviving.
11 Fisher and Fisher, *Slavery and Muslim Society*, pp. 43–52; Inalcik, *Ottoman Empire*, p. 87; Gordon, *Slavery in the Arab World*, pp. 42–4.
12 Gordon, *Slavery in the Arab World*, p. 62.
13 Ibid., pp. 161–7.
14 Ibid., p. 56; Fisher and Fisher, *Slavery and Muslim Society*, p. 82.
15 Gordon, *Slavery in the Arab World*, pp. 19, 37.
16 Ibid., p. 14.
17 Ibid., pp. 44–6, 223–9.
18 Pipes, *Slave Soldiers*, pp. xix, 45–6, 52.
19 I. M. Kunt, *The Sultan's Servants: the Transformation of Ottoman Provincial Government, 1550–1650* (New York, 1983), p. 32.
20 Pipes, *Slave Soldiers*, pp. xix, 8–9.
21 Patricia Crone, *Slaves on Horseback* (Cambridge, 1980), pp. 78–80.
22 Pipes, *Slave Soldiers*, p. 7.
23 For Mughals, see J. F. Richards, *The Mughal Empire* (Cambridge, 1993), pp. 59–64; William Irvine, *The Army of the Indian Moghuls* (New Delhi, 1962), pp. 3–4, 11. For Bornu, see Fisher and Fisher, *Slavery and Muslim Society*, p. 133.

24 Pipes, *Slave Soldiers*, pp. 44–50.
25 Ibid., p. 52; Gordon, *Slavery in the Arab World*, pp. 73–4; Fisher and Fisher, *Slavery and Muslim Society*, pp. 128–33, 140–1.
26 Pipes, *Slave Soldiers*, pp. 45, 53; Crone, *Slaves on Horseback*, p. 80.
27 Crone, *Slaves on Horseback*, pp. 75, 79, 87, 89; Pipes, *Slave Soldiers*, pp. 86–92.
28 Crone, *Slaves on Horseback*, pp. 79–80, 84.
29 *Cambridge History of Iran* (Cambridge, 1986), VI, pp. 262, 264–7, 344, 352–5, 357–67; *Encyclopedia of Islam* (London, 1965) [under Ghulam], p. 1083.
30 *Encyclopedia of Islam* [under Ghulam], pp. 1084–5; and see above, n. 23.
31 R. S. O'Fahey and J. L. Spaulding, *Kingdoms of the Sudan* (London, 1974), pp. 44–5, 47–50, 53–4, 56.
32 Ibid., pp. 151–8, 161.
33 Ibid., pp. 133–4.
34 Louis Brenner, *The Shehus of Kukawa* (Oxford, 1973), chs 5, 6.
35 Pipes, *Slave Soldiers*, p. 97; Crone, *Slaves on Horseback*, p. 84.
36 H. A. R. Gibb and Harold Bowen, *Islamic Society and the West* (Oxford, 1950), pt I, p. 62.
37 Barnette Miller, *The Palace School of Muhammad the Conqueror* (Cambridge, Mass., 1941), p. 4.
38 N. Itzkowitz, *The Ottoman Empire and Islamic Tradition* (New York, 1972), pp. 53, 78.
39 Ibid., p. 42; Inalcik, *Ottoman Empire*, p. 80; Miller, *Palace School*, p. 6.
40 Itzkowitz, *Ottoman Empire and Islamic Tradition*, pp. 49–51; A. H. Lybyer, *The Government of the Ottoman Empire in the Time of Suleiman the Magnificent* (Cambridge, Mass., 1913), p. 79.
41 Erdem, *Slavery in the Ottoman Empire*, pp. 8–9; Inalcik, *Ottoman Empire*, p. 118.
42 Miller, *Palace School*, ch. 5; Itzkowitz, *Ottoman Empire and Islamic Tradition*, pp. 52–3; Kunt, *Sultan's Servants*, pp. 6–7.
43 Itzkowitz, *Ottoman Empire and Islamic Tradition*, pp. 40–1, 44, 53; Inalcik, *Ottoman Empire*, ch. 13.
44 Gibb and Bowen, *Islamic Society*, pp. 146–7. For suggesting that *alay beyis* could also be slaves, see Lybyer, *Government of the Ottoman Empire*, p. 103.
45 Ibid., ch. 7; Itzkowitz, *Ottoman Empire and Islamic Tradition*, pp. 55–7.
46 Itzkowitz, *Ottoman Empire and Islamic Tradition*, pp. 55, 60.
47 Lybyer, *Government of the Ottoman Empire*, p. 186.
48 Kunt, *Sultan's Servants*, p. 52; Miller, *Palace School*, pp. 70–1.
49 Gibb and Bowen, *Islamic Society*, p. 158; Suraiya Foroqli, 'Politics and socio-economic change in the Ottoman Empire of the late sixteenth century', *Suleyman the Magnificent and his Age*, ed. I. M. Kunt and Christine Woodhead (London, 1995), p. 105; Itzkowitz, *Ottoman Empire and Islamic Tradition*, pp. 31–4, 39–41.
50 Cornell H. Fleischer, *Bureaucrat and Intellectual in the Ottoman Empire* (Princeton, 1986), pp. 5, 19, 212.
51 Gibb and Bowen, *Islamic Society*, pp. 159–71. Also see Lybyer, *Government of the Ottoman Empire*, pp. 28–32.
52 Itzkowitz, *Ottoman Empire and Islamic Tradition*, p. 91; Lybyer, *Government of the Ottoman Empire*, p. 69.
53 Gibb and Bowen, *Islamic Society*, p. 180; Miller, *Palace School*, p. 172; Lybyer, *Government of the Ottoman Empire*, p. 69, n. 3.
54 Kunt, *Sultan's Servants*, p. 76; Gibb and Bowen, *Islamic Society*, p. 181.
55 Itzkowitz, *Ottoman Empire and Islamic Tradition*, pp. 89–91; Kunt, *Sultan's Servants*, p. 80; Gibb and Bowen, *Islamic Society*, pp. 181–2.
56 Gibb and Bowen, *Islamic Society*, pp. 182, 192.
57 Ibid., p. 196; Kunt, *Sultan's Servants*, p. 97; Miller, *Palace School*, p. 173; Lybyer, *Government of the Ottoman Empire*, pp. 49–50.

58 Ehad R. Toledano, 'Ottoman concepts of slavery in the period of reform, 1830s–1880s', *Breaking the Chains*, ed. Martin A. Klein (Madison, 1993), p. 39; Kunt, *Sultan's Servants*, pp. 40–1.
59 Lybyer, *Government of the Ottoman Empire*, pp. 49–50.
60 Toledano, 'Ottoman concepts', pp. 53–5.
61 Miller, *Palace School*, pp. 173, 182.
62 Lybyer, *Government of the Ottoman Empire*, pp. 57–8.
63 Erdem, *Slavery in the Ottoman Empire*, p. 43.
64 Kunt, *Sultan's Servants*, p. 32.
65 Gibb and Bowen, *Islamic Society*, pp. 179–80.
66 Lybyer, *Government in the Ottoman Empire*, pp. 92–3; Gibb and Bowen, *Islamic Society*, p. 179.
67 Itzkowitz, *Ottoman Empire and Islamic Tradition*, p. 92; Gibb and Bowen, *Islamic Society*, pp. 179–80; Erdem, *Slavery in the Ottoman Empire*, p. 11; Kunt, *Sultan's Servants*, p. 80.
68 Erdem, *Slavery in the Ottoman Empire*, p. 11.
69 Inalcik, *Ottoman Empire*, pp. 112–13; Erdem, *Slavery in the Ottoman Empire*, pp. 12–14.
70 Erdem, *Slavery in the Ottoman Empire*, p. 15.
71 Ibid., pp. 8, 15.
72 For manumission contracts, see ibid., p. 15.
73 Ibid., pp. 1, 186.
74 Toledano, 'Ottoman concepts', p. 42.
75 Erdem, *Slavery in the Ottoman Empire*, pp. 9, 12–13, 19.
76 Ibid., pp. 19, 52–3.
77 Ibid., pp. xvii, xix.
78 Ibid., pp. 44–5; Inalcik, *Ottoman Empire*, p. 78; Miller, *Palace School*, p. 76.
79 Erdem, *Slavery in the Ottoman Empire*, pp. 21, 29–30.
80 Ibid., pp. 15, 45, 47–8; Miller, *Palace School*, 75–6, 175.
81 Erdem, *Slavery in the Ottoman Empire*, pp. 54–5, 185; Miller, *Palace School*, p. 77.
82 Erdem, *Slavery in the Ottoman Empire*, p. 55. Toledano (see 'Ottoman concepts', pp. 42–3) proposes 11–13,000 in the 1830s; but then suggests the supply was choked off by the 1880s through British pressure.
83 Erdem, *Slavery in the Ottoman Empire*, pp. 186–7.
84 Ibid., pp. xix–xx, 35–7.
85 Ibid., pp. 52–3.

Part III   Emancipation and After

Chapter 11   Abolition in Europe and the Americas

1 See David Turley, 'Slave emancipations in modern history', *Serfdom and Slavery*, ed. M. L. Bush (Harlow, 1996), pp. 182–3; David Brion Davis, *The Problem of Slavery in Western Culture* (London, 1970), pp. 466–73; Jerome Blum, *The End of the Old Order in Rural Europe* (Princeton, 1978), pp. 305–10.
2 Turley, 'Slave emancipations', pp. 190–1.
3 For religious objections to slavery, see ibid., pp. 183–4. For Protestant objections to serfdom, see E. Belfort Bax, *The Peasants' War in Germany, 1525–6* (London, 1899), p. 68; Anthony Fletcher, *Tudor Rebellions* (London, 1983), p. 122. For Russian sects, see G. T. Robinson, *Rural Russia under the Old Regime* (New York, 1932), pp. 45–6.
4 For economic decline issue, see Stanley L. Engerman, 'Economic adjustments to emancipation in the U.S. and British West Indies', *Journal of Interdisciplinary*

History, 13 (1982), pp. 195–203, 208–9. For the peasantization issue, see Robin Blackburn, *The Overthrow of Colonial Slavery* (London, 1988), pp. 257, 463; Rebecca J. Scott, *Slave Emancipation in Cuba* (Princeton, 1985), pp. 244ff; Jay R. Mandle, *Not Slave, Not Free* (London, 1992), ch. 3; Sidney W. Mintz, 'Slavery and the rise of peasantries', *Roots and Branches*, ed. Michael Craton (Oxford, 1979), ch. 7; Engerman, 'Economic adjustments', pp. 199–200, 205, 212–17. For lack of material benefit, see Peter Kolchin, 'Some controversial questions concerning nine-teenth-century emancipation from slavery and serfdom' in Bush (ed.), *Serfdom and Slavery*, pp. 58ff.

5 Blum, *End of the Old Order*, ch. 16.
6 Ibid., p. 356. For Savoy, see ibid., pp. 216–18. For Baden, see ibid., p. 228. For Austria and Bohemia, see ibid., p. 224. For Denmark, see H. Arnold Barton, *Scandinavia in the Revolutionary Era, 1760–1815* (Minneapolis, 1986), ch. 7.
7 M. L. Bush, *Noble Privilege* (London, 1983), p. 166.
8 Ibid., pp. 173–4.
9 P. M. Jones, *The Peasantry in the French Revolution* (Cambridge, 1988), chs 3–4. For physiocrats, see J. Q. C. Mackrell, *The Attack on 'Feudalism' in Eighteenth-century France* (London, 1973), pp. 139ff.
10 Bush, *Noble Privilege*, p. 174; Blum, *End of the Old Order*, pp. 368–70.
11 Blum, *End of the Old Order*, pp. 229–30.
12 Bush, *Noble Privilege*, pp. 177–8.
13 Blum, *End of the Old Order*, pp. 370–1.
14 See above, p. ••.
15 Blum, *End of the Old Order*, p. 362.
16 This point arose from an unpublished paper delivered by C. E. B. Brancovan to a conference held at Manchester in 1994 on serfdom and slavery.
17 Blum, *End of the Old Order*, pp. 371, 375–6.
18 Ibid., pp. 305–10.
19 Bush, *Noble Privilege*, pp. 175–6; Blum, *End of the Old Order*, pp. 361–2.
20 Bush, *Noble Privilege*, p. 176.
21 For slave imports, see Paul E. Lovejoy, *Transformations in Slavery* (Cambridge, 1983), p. 19. For internal slave trades, see Michael Tadman, *Speculators and Slaves* (Wisconsin, 1989), pp. 6–7 (US); Robert Conrad, *World of Sorrow* (Baton Rouge, 1986), pp. 172–9 (Brazil). For flourishing nature of slave plantations, see Blackburn, *Overthrow of Colonial Slavery*, p. 544; Robert W. Fogel, *Without Consent or Contract* (London, 1989), ch. 3; Turley, 'Slave emancipations', pp. 185–6.
22 Blackburn, *Overthrow of Colonial Slavery*, pp. 47–54; Davis, *Problem of Slavery*, chs 13, 14; M. de Secondat, Baron de Montesquieu, *The Spirit of Laws* (Edinburgh, 1762), I, pp. 257, 261, 263, 265.
23 E.g., see John Millar, *The Origin of the Distinction of Ranks* (Edinburgh, 1806 edn), pp. 250–1, 255, 284.
24 For profits of slave plantation system, see above, n. 21. For awareness of Haiti/Jamaican emancipations, see Peter Kolchin, *American Slavery* (London, 1993), p. 191. For awareness of wage-slaves, see ibid., p. 194.
25 Davis, *Problem of Slavery*, chs 10, 12; Fogel, *Without Consent*, pp. 210–12; David Turley, *The Culture of English Antislavery, 1780–1860* (London, 1991), pp. 18–25, 28–9, 33–5.
26 *The Works of the Reverend John Wesley*, 3rd edn (London, 1830), XI, p. 73.
27 Ibid., pp. 70–1.
28 Ibid., p. 79.
29 Ibid., p. 78.
30 Ibid., pp. 60, 65.
31 Ibid., pp. 75, 77.

32 Moncure Conway (ed.), *The Writings of Thomas Paine* (New York, 1894–99), I, pp. 4–9.

33 John Keane, *Tom Paine* (London, 1996), pp. 99, 194. For preamble to 1780 Emancipation Act, see Conway (ed.), *Writings of Thomas Paine*, II, pp. 29–30.

34 Fogel, *Without Consent*, pp. 212, 217, 227, 231. For the number of petitions, see Turley, *Culture of English Antislavery*, pp. 63–7.

35 Turley, 'Slave emancipations', pp. 186–7; Fogel, *Without Consent*, pp. 247ff.

36 Blackburn, *Overthrow of Colonial Slavery*, ch. 7; Ira Berlin, *Many Thousands Gone* (Cambridge, Mass., 1998), ch. 9.

37 David Geggus, *Slavery, War and Revolution* (Oxford, 1982), ch. 2; Blackburn, *Overthrow of Colonial Slavery*, chs 5–6.

38 Fogel, *Without Consent*, p. 207. For significance, see Engerman, 'Economic adjustments', pp. 191–2.

39 Blackburn, *Overthrow of Colonial Slavery*, pp. 497–501, 507–8.

40 Ibid., pp. 322–3; Turley, *Culture of English Antislavery*, pp. 31–2.

41 Fogel, *Without Consent*, p. 217; Blackburn, *Overthrow of Colonial Slavery*, pp. 421–3; Turley, *Culture of English Antislavery*, pp. 40–3.

42 Fogel, *Without Consent*, pp. 227, 231.

43 Ibid., pp. 228, 230–1.

44 Blackburn, *Overthrow of Colonial Slavery*, pp. 428–33; Fogel, *Without Consent*, pp. 226–7.

45 Blackburn, *Overthrow of Colonial Slavery*, p. 428; Fogel, *Without Consent*, p. 226.

46 The slave population in the British West Indies declined by 14 per cent between 1807 and 1834. See Blackburn, *Overthrow of Colonial Slavery*, pp. 423–4. In Cuba it fell by 46 per cent between 1862 and 1877. See Scott, *Slave Emancipation in Cuba*, p. 86. In Brazil it fell by 40 per cent between 1851 and 1872, and by 53 per cent between 1872 and 1887. See Conrad, *World of Sorrow*, p. 22; Robert Conrad, *The Destruction of Brazilian Slavery, 1850–1888* (Berkeley, 1972), p. 26 and table 3 (p. 285).

47 For growth in Barbados, see Blackburn, *Overthrow of Colonial Slavery*, p. 424. For prospect of Jamaican growth, Ward, *British West Indian Slavery*, pp. 121–2, 185.

48 Fogel, *Without Consent*, p. 246.

49 Blackburn, *Overthrow of Colonial Slavery*, ch. 9.

50 Kolchin, *American Slavery*, ch. 6.

51 Fogel, *Without Consent*, pp. 302–9.

52 Ibid., p. 339.

53 Ibid., p. 381.

54 Ibid., p. 319.

55 Kolchin, *American Slavery*, p. 201; Fogel, *Without Consent*, pp. 386–7.

56 Fogel, *Without Consent*, pp. 326–8, 353.

57 Kolchin, *American Slavery*, pp. 203–7; Turley, 'Slave emancipations', p. 190.

58 For slave numbers, see Scott, *Slave Emancipation in Cuba*, p. 86; Robert Conrad, *The Destruction of Brazilian Slavery*, table 1 (p. 283). For nature of military conflict, see Scott, *Slave Emancipation in Cuba*, ch. 2.

59 Ibid., pp. 64–6, 68.

60 Ibid., pp. 45–8, 63.

61 Ibid., pp. 111–13.

62 Ibid., pp. 10, 89.

63 Ibid., pp. 73, 86, 96–7.

64 Ibid., pp. 6–7.

65 Ibid., pp. 29–35.

66 Ibid., pp. 114–18, 122.

67 Ibid., pp. 123–4. Also see Franklin W. Knight, *Slave Society in Cuba during the Nineteenth Century* (Madison, 1970), ch. 7.

68 Conrad, *Destruction of Brazilian Slavery*, pp. 27, 84–5, 140.

69 Ibid., ch. 2.
70 Ibid., pp. 72–80.
71 Ibid., pp. 87, 91.
72 Ibid., tables 1 (p. 283) and 3 (p. 285); Conrad, *World of Sorrow*, p. 22.
73 Conrad, *Destruction of Brazilian Slavery*, p. 122.
74 Ibid., p. 262.
75 Ibid., pp. 210, 219.
76 Ibid., pp. 156–9. For falling price of slaves, see ibid., pp. 189, 211.
77 Ibid., chs 11–12, especially pp. 186–7, 189.
78 Ibid., pp. 199–200, 204–5.
79 Ibid., pp. 228–9, 240–2, 247–56. For the attitude of the army towards runaways, see ibid., p. 251.
80 Ibid., pp. 261, 267.
81 For native free population, see ibid., table 1 (p. 283). For incoming Italians, see ibid., p. 257.
82 Ibid., pp. 262, 271.

Chapter 12   The Survival of Servitude

1 Stanley Engerman, 'Contract labour in sugar and technology in the nineteenth century', *Journal of Economic History*, 43 (1983), pp. 637–8.
2 David Northrup, *Indentured Labour in the Age of Imperialism, 1834–1922* (Cambridge, 1995), pp. 8–9; Engerman, 'Contract labour', pp. 635–7; David Eltis, 'Free and coerced transatlantic migrations: some comparisons', *American Historical Review*, 88 (1983), pp. 258, 270, 272. For general improvement of shipping, see Northrup, *Indentured Labour*, ch. 4.
3 Ibid., p. 9. The cost was not entirely borne by the planters but subsidized by about 25 per cent out of public revenue. For example of British Guiana, see Alan H. Adamson, 'The impact of indentured immigration on the political economy of British Guiana', *Indentured Labour in the British Empire, 1834–1920*, ed. Kay Saunders (London, 1984), p. 49.
4 For Pennsylvania, see Robin Blackburn, *The Overthrow of Colonial Slavery* (London, 1988), pp. 117–18. For Cuba, see Rebecca J. Scott, *Slave Emancipation in Cuba* (Princeton, 1985), p. 68. For Brazil, see Robert Conrad, *The Destruction of Brazilian Slavery* (Berkeley, 1972), pp. 90–1.
5 For British, see Northrup, *Indentured Labour*, p. 19. For Portuguese, see ibid., p. 50. For Dutch, see ibid., p. 28. For Spanish, see Scott, *Slave Emancipation*, pp. 123–4. For French, see Blackburn, *Overthrow of Colonial Slavery*, p. 505.
6 See above, p. 198.
7 Northrup, *Indentured Labour*, p. 19; Hugh Tinker, *A New System of Slavery* (Oxford, 1974), p. 2.
8 Tinker, *New System*, pp. 2, 10.
9 Northrup, *Indentured Labour*, pp. 19–20; W. A. Green, 'The West Indies and indentured labour migration in the Jamaican experience' in Saunders (ed.), *Indentured Labour*, p. 6; M. D. North-Coombes, 'From slavery to indenture: forced labour in the political economy of Mauritius, 1834–67' in Saunders (ed.), *Indentured Labour*, pp. 80, 84.
10 For numbers of exported workers, see Northrup, *Indentured Labour*, table A1 (pp. 156–7). To his 2 million total one needs to add the 80–100,000 workers sent from Angola to São Tomé (see below n. 18); the 200,000 Chinese recruited by the British and French in the First World War to work in France (Northrup, *Indentured Labour*, p. 59; Lynn Pan, *Sons of the Yellow Emperor* (London, 1990), pp. 78ff); the indentured Indians who worked on the plantations of Burma, Malaya and

Ceylon (see Northrup, *Indentured Labour*, table 5.3 p. 132); Tinker, *New System*, p. 264); the indentured Chinese and Malays brought to work on the plantations of German and British New Guinea (Pan, *Sons*, pp. 75–6).

11 For sugar plantations, see Northrup, *Indentured Labour*, pp. 106, 108–12. For railway construction, see Tinker, *New System*, pp. 277–8; Watt Stewart, *Chinese Bondage in Peru* (Durham, North Carolina, 1951), pp. 16–26. For mining, see Northrup, *Indentured Labour*, pp. 35, 59; Tinker, *New System*, p. 168; Doug Munro, 'The Pacific islands labour trade', *Slavery and Abolition*, 14 (1993), p. 97.

12 See Northrup, *Indentured Labour*, p. 59 and table A1 (p. 156), revised.

13 See ibid., table A1 (p. 156); ibid., p. 55; Pan, *Sons*, pp. 43–5, 51.

14 For Africans, see Monica Schuler, '*Alas, Alas, Kongo*' (Baltimore, 1980), p. 2; Northrup, *Indentured Labour*, p. 24. For Pacific islanders, see Northrup, *Indentured Labour*, table A2 (p. 160); Munro, 'Pacific islands', p. 87.

15 Northrup, *Indentured Labour*, p. 143, table A1 (p. 157).

16 Ibid., table A1 (p. 156) and p. 24.

17 Paul E. Lovejoy, *Transformations in Slavery: a History of Slavery in Africa* (Cambridge, 1983), p. 146; Northrup, *Indentured Labour*, table A1 (pp. 156–7) and p. 59.

18 Northrup, *Indentured Labour*, p. 50; Lovejoy, *Transformations*, p. 146.

19 Northrup, *Indentured Labour*, table A1 (pp. 156–7). Also see ibid., p. 28; Pan, *Sons*, pp. 75–6.

20 Northrup, *Indentured Labour*, p. 142.

21 Ibid., pp. 22–3, table A1 (p. 156); Engerman, 'Contract labour', p. 639.

22 Northrup, *Indentured Labour*, table A2 (pp. 159–60).

23 Ibid., pp. 5, 17, 26 29. For Cuba, see Scott, *Slave Emancipation*, pp. 29–35. For Peru, see Stewart, *Chinese Bondage*, pp. 12–16.

24 Ibid., pp. 30–41; Engerman, 'Contract labour', pp. 652–3.

25 Northrup, *Indentured Labour*, p. 111.

26 Engerman, 'Contract labour', p. 644.

27 Northrup, *Indentured Labour*, pp. 19–20, 39; North-Coombes, 'From slavery to indenture', pp. 80, 84; Tinker, *New System*, pp. 2, 219; Green, 'West Indies and indentured labour migration', pp. 2, 6, 11–12.

28 Northrup, *Indentured Labour*, pp. 35–6, 39; Tinker, *New System*, p. 96; Munro, 'Pacific islands', p. 87.

29 M. D. Ramesar, 'Indentured labour in Trinidad, 1880–1917', in Saunders (ed.), *Indentured Labour*, pp. 58, 67; Adamson, 'Impact of indentured immigration', pp. 46–7; Northrup, *Indentured Labour*, pp. 117, 119.

30 Northrup, *Indentured Labour*, table 5.3 (p. 132). For length of service required to qualify for free return, see ibid., pp. 4, 27–8, 63; Tinker, *New System*, pp. 64, 85, 99, 179.

31 For concessions to workers, see Northrup, *Indentured Labour*, pp. 131, 133–4; Ramesar, 'Indentured labour in Trinidad', p. 57. For desertion, see Northrup, *Indentured Labour*, p. 127. For high mortality, see ibid., pp. 121–2.

32 Engerman, 'Contract labour', pp. 636, 645–6; Northrup, *Indentured Labour*, pp. 5–6. For abductions in the coolie trade, see Northrup, *Indentured Labour*, pp. 57–8.

33 Ibid., ch. 3; David W. Galenson, *White Servitude in Colonial America* (Cambridge, 1981), pp. 180–1; Tinker, *New System*, p. 116; Northrup, *Indentured Labour*, pp. 64–6. For colonial taxation, see Munro, 'Pacific islands', p. 98. For abductions in the African and Pacific trades, see Northrup, *Indentured Labour*, pp. 50, 71. Not all were entitled to the return journey, notably the Chinese taken to Peru and Cuba.

34 Northrup, *Indentured Labour*, pp. 148–9. For ethnic discord, see Tinker, *New System*, pp. 217–19; Stewart, *Chinese Bondage*, p. 130.

35 Northrup, *Indentured Labour*, pp. 33–6, 39–41; Engerman, 'Contract labour', pp. 649–50.

36 Northrup, *Indentured Labour*, pp. 106, 112; Brij V. Lal, 'Labouring men and nothing more: some problems of Indian indenture in Fiji' in Saunders (ed.), *Indentured Labour*, pp. 133, 136.

37 Northrup, *Indentured Labour*, pp. 129–38; 154; Munro, 'Pacific islands', pp. 100–1.

38 Northrup, *Indentured Labour*, pp. 143–7.

39 For poor accommodation, see ibid., p. 104; Lal, 'Labouring men', p. 147. For wage penalties, see Tinker, *New System*, pp. 186–9. For severe punishment, see ibid., pp. 191–2; Munro, 'Pacific islands', p. 89; North-Coombes, 'From slavery to indenture', p. 114; Lal, 'Labouring men', p. 135. Also see Pan, *Sons*, pp. 49–50, 67–9; Stewart, *Chinese Bondage*, pp. 96–104; Kay Saunders, *Workers in Bondage* (St Lucia, 1982), ch. 4.

40 For USA, see Stewart, *Chinese Bondage*, p. 56. For Japanese, see Northrup, *Indentured Labour*, p. 109. For Chinese, see ibid., pp. 56, 109, 143; P. C. Campbell, *Chinese Coolie Emigration to Countries within the British Empire* (London, 1923), pp. 158–9; Stewart, *Chinese Bondage*, p. 53. For British, see Northrup, *Indentured Labour*, pp. 28, 56, 143–4. For commissions of inquiry and enacted regulations by British, see ibid., pp. 109, 111; Tinker, *New System*, ch. 7.

41 For Chinese, see Northrup, *Indentured Labour*, p. 112. For Japanese, see ibid., pp. 39–40.

42 Tinker, *New System*, chs 8 and 9; Northrup, *Indentured Labour*, pp. 113, 144–5; Pan, *Sons*, pp. 66–7.

43 Northrup, *Indentured Labour*, pp. 142, 147; Pan, *Sons*, pp. 93–8.

44 Northrup, *Indentured Labour*, p. 146.

45 Kay Saunders, 'Indentured labour in Queensland' in Saunders (ed.), *Indentured Labour*, p. 236. Also see her *Workers in Bondage*, ch. 7.

46 Northrup, *Indentured Labour*, p. 146.

47 For 1906, see Campbell, *Chinese Coolie Emigration*, pp. 214–16; Pan, *Sons*, pp. 165–7. For 1916, see Campbell, *Chinese Coolie Emigration*, p. xviii.

48 Tinker, *New System*, pp. 34, 235; Engerman, 'Contract labour', pp. 652–3; Adamson, 'Impact of indentured immigration', p. 50; Lal, 'Labouring men', p. 152; Saunders, 'Indentured labour in Queensland', p. 232; Northrup, *Indentured Labour*, p. 153; North-Coombes, 'From slavery to indenture', p. 116.

49 Northrup, *Indentured Labour*, pp. 64–7; Tinker, *New System*, p. 113; Engerman, 'Contract labour', p. 647; Pan, *Sons*, p. 43. The proportions are based on 1,400,000 Indian indentured emigrants against a total of 4,350,000 Indian emigrants; and on 400,000 Chinese indentured emigrants against a total of 2 million Chinese emigrants.

50 For Indian methods of debt bondage, see Ravindra K. Jain, *Indian Communities Abroad* (New Delhi, 1993), p. 11. For credit-ticket, see Patricia Cloud and David W. Galenson, 'Chinese immigration and contract labour in the late nineteenth century', *Explorations in Economic History*, 24 (1987), pp. 26–9.

51 Northrup, *Indentured Labour*, pp. 11–12; Tinker, *New System*, pp. 179–80; Bruno Lasker, *Human Bondage in Southeast Asia* (Chapel Hill, 1950), p. 147; Ravindra K. Jain, 'South Indian labour in Malaya, 1840–1920' in Saunders (ed.), *Indentured Labour*, p. 171.

52 Cloud and Galenson, 'Chinese immigration', p. 24; Northrup, *Indentured Labour*, p. 12; Gunther Barth, *Bitter Strength: a History of the Chinese in the United States* (Cambridge, Mass., 1964), ch. 4.

53 For India, see Northrup, *Indentured Labour*, p. 142. For Malaya, see Lasker, *Human Bondage*, p. 148. Also see below, pp. 216–17.

54 For 1860s legislation, see Stewart, *Chinese Bondage*, p. 56. For 1880s legislation, see Pan, *Sons*, p. 96.

55 For Chinese, see Northrup, *Indentured Labour*, p. 56. For Japanese, see ibid., pp. 12, 74.

56 Andrew Pearse, *The Latin American Peasant* (London, 1975), ch. 1; Colin A. Palmer, *Slaves of the White God* (Cambridge, Mass., 1976), pp. 65–6; F. P. Bowser, *The African Slave in Colonial Peru* (Stanford, 1974), pp. 324–5. For use of convict labour, see Alan Knight, 'Debt bondage in Latin America', *Slavery and Other Forms of Unfree Labour*, ed. Leonie Archer (London, 1988), p. 102.

57 Pearse, *Latin American Peasant*, pp. 32–4.

58 John Tutino, *From Insurrection to Revolution in Mexico* (Princeton, 1986), pp. 223, 230, 234.

59 W. Kloosterboer, *Involuntary Labour since the Abolition of Slavery* (Leiden, 1960), pp. 108–9; William Glade, *The Latin American Economy* (New York, 1969), p. 126; Knight, 'Debt bondage', pp. 108–9.

60 Knight, 'Debt bondage', p. 109–10.

61 Kloosterboer, *Involuntary Labour*, p. 107; Arnold J. Bauer, 'Rural workers in Spanish America', *Hispanic American Historical Review*, 59 (1979), pp. 37–9; Knight, 'Debt bondage', pp. 106–7.

62 Bauer, 'Rural workers', p. 37; Knight, 'Debt bondage', pp. 103, 107; Eric Wolf, *Peasant Wars in the Twentieth Century* (London, 1973), p. 41.

63 Knight, 'Debt bondage', p. 111.

64 Ibid. For the economic and social impact of the Porfirian regime, see Wolf, *Peasant Wars*, ch. 1; Alan Knight, *The Mexican Revolution* (Cambridge, 1986), I, chs 1, 3. For the natural phasing out of debt bondage, see Bauer, 'Rural workers', pp. 39, 57; Pearse, *Latin American Peasant*, p. 37.

65 Pearse, *Latin American Peasant*, pp. 96–7; Kloosterboer, *Involuntary Labour*, pp. 104–5.

66 Northrup, *Indentured Labour*, p. 142; Lasker, *Human Bondage*, pp. 163–4, 167.

67 Paul E. Lovejoy, *Transformations in Slavery: a History of Slavery in Africa* (Cambridge, 1983), p. 137.

68 For impact on transatlantic trade, see ibid., p. 140. For impact on Mediterranean and Indian Ocean trades, see Murray Gordon, *Slavery in the Arab World* (New York, 1989), pp. 161–9.

69 Gordon, *Slavery in the Arab World*, p. 221.

70 Lovejoy, *Transformations*, pp. 9–11, 21–2, 142, 161, 171, 184–5, 224, 246; Martin A. Klein (ed.), *Breaking the Chains* (Madison, 1993), pp. 10–11; Klein, 'Slavery and emancipation in French West Africa' in Klein (ed.), *Breaking the Chains*, p. 171; John Grace, *Domestic Slavery in West Africa* (New York, 1975), pp. 32–3, 169–71; Richard L. Roberts, *Warriors, Merchants and Slaves* (Stanford, 1987), p. 119.

71 For African plantations, see Lovejoy, *Transformations*, pp. 148–9, 171–4, 223–4. For factors affecting the supply of slaves, see Grace, *Domestic Slavery*, pp. 12, 32–3; Roberts, *Warriors*, pp. 118–19; Lovejoy, *Transformations*, pp. 256–7.

72 Lovejoy, *Transformations*, pp. 72–3, 124; Claude Meillassoux, *The Anthropology of Slavery* (London, 1991), pt II, ch. 2 (2).

73 See below, p. 220.

74 Grace, *Domestic Slavery*, pp. 2–4; Lovejoy, *Transformations*, pp. 116, 122, 180, 236; Meillassoux, *Anthropology*, pp. 220–1, 245.

75 Grace, *Domestic Slavery*, pp. 2, 7, 13.

76 Ibid., pp. 6–8; Meillassoux, *Anthropology*, pp. 317–20.

77 Toyin Falola and Paul E. Lovejoy (eds), *Pawnship in Africa* (Boulder, Colorado), ch. 1.

78 Lionel Caplan, 'Power and status in South Asian Slavery', *Asian and African Systems of Slavery*, ed. James L. Watson (Oxford, 1980), p. 181.

79 Ibid., pp. 172, 181–2; Tanika Sarkar, 'Bondage in the colonial context', *Chains of Servitude: Bondage and Slavery in India*, ed. Utsa Patnaik and Manjari Dingwaney (London, 1985), pp. 99–103; Klein (ed.), *Breaking the Chains*, p. 6.

80 Caplan, 'Power and status', pp. 178–9; Manjari Dingwaney, 'Unredeemed promises: the law and servitude' in Patnaik and Dingwaney (eds.), *Chains of Servitude*, pp. 285–6.

81 Sarkar, 'Bondage', pp. 103–6; D. Kumar, 'Colonialism, bondage and cash in British India' in Klein (ed.), *Breaking the Chains*, p. 112.

82 Sarkar, 'Bondage', p. 108.

83 Ibid., pp. 108–9; N. D. Kamble, *Bonded Labour in India* (New Delhi, 1982), pp. 5–6, 8; Sarma Marla, *Bonded Labour in India* (New Delhi, 1981), p. 7.

84 Gyan Prakash, *Bonded Histories: Genealogies of Labor Servitude in Colonial India* (Cambridge, 1990), pp. 222–3; Dingwaney, 'Unredeemed promises', pp. 312–13; Sarkar, 'Bondage', pp. 110–13.

85 Kumar, 'Colonialism', p. 121; Kamble, *Bonded Labour*, p. 9.

86 Sarkar, 'Bondage', pp. 115–16.

87 Kamble, *Bonded Labour*, pp. 9–11, 135; Marla, *Bonded Labour*, p. 17, table 1 (p. 154).

88 Anthony Reid (ed.), *Bondage and Dependency in Southeast Asia* (St Lucia, Queensland, 1983), introduction and ch. 7. For indigenous attitude towards wage labour, see ibid., pp. 34–5; Reid, 'The decline of slavery in nineteenth-century Indonesia' in Klein (ed.), *Breaking the Chains*, p. 67.

89 Lovejoy, *Transformations*, pp. 155–6; Gordon, *Slavery in the Arab World*, p. 214.

90 Lovejoy, *Transformations*, p. 261.

91 Grace, *Domestic Slavery*, pp. 51, 99.

92 Lovejoy, *Transformations*, pp. 247–8.

93 Roberts, *Warriors*, p. 175.

94 Ibid., p. 176.

95 For colonial attitude, see ibid., pp. 181–2. For public opinion, see ibid., pp. 176–7.

96 Lovejoy, *Transformations*, p. 247.

97 Grace, *Domestic Slavery*, pp. 99, 179–80.

98 Lovejoy, *Transformations*, pp. 253–4, 258.

99 Grace, *Domestic Slavery*, p. 36.

100 Gordon, *Slavery in the Arab World*, pp. 216–18.

101 Grace, *Domestic Slavery*, pp. 98–9.

102 Lovejoy, *Transformations*, pp. 264–5.

103 Grace, *Domestic Slavery*, pp. 100, 251.

104 Ibid., pp. 251–2.

105 Gordon, *Slavery in the Arab World*, pp. 218, 224.

106 Lovejoy, *Transformations*, pp. 247, 252–3, 260, 266–8; Roberts, *Warriors*, pp. 184–97.

107 Lovejoy, *Transformations*, pp. 247, 266; Roberts, *Warriors*, p. 179; Grace, *Domestic Slavery*, pp. 184–5.

108 Grace, *Domestic Slavery*, p. 72; Lovejoy, *Transformations*, p. 262.

109 Lovejoy, *Transformations*, pp. 252, 263; Grace, *Domestic Slavery*, pp. 72–8.

110 Gordon, *Slavery in the Arab World*, pp. 210–12, 220–3, 235–6.

111 Ibid., p. 47.

112 Ibid., pp. 225–34.

113 Daniel Goldhagen, *Hitler's Willing Executioners* (London, 1996), pp. 290–2.

114 For conscripted labour, See Edward L. Homze, *Foreign Labour in Nazi Germany* (Princeton, 1967) and Ulrich Herbert, *Hitler's Foreign Workers* (Cambridge, 1997). For wages issue, see Herbert, *Hitler's Foreign Workers*, p. 90. For lawlessness in concentration camps, see Goldhagen, *Hitler's Willing Executioners*, pp. 170, 174; Edwin Bacon, *The Gulag at War* (London, 1994), p. 66.

115 For Nazi Germany, see Herbert, *Hitler's Foreign Workers*, pp. 1, 181; Albert Speer, *The Slave State: Heinrich Himmler's Master-Plan for SS Supremacy*

(London, 1981), p. 47. For Soviet Union, see Bacon, *Gulag at War*, tables 2.1 (p. 24) and 2.3 (p. 30). There must also have been prisoners of war taken by the Russians and put to labour who need to be added. See ibid., pp. 119–20.
116 Herbert, *Hitler's Foreign Workers*, pp. 16–17.
117 Ibid., pp. 18–19.
118 Ibid., pp. 21–6.
119 Ibid., pp. 16–17, 19–22.
120 Goldhagen, *Hitler's Willing Executioners*, p. 170.
121 Ibid., p. 171.
122 Herbert, *Hitler's Foreign Workers*, p. 1.
123 Ibid., p. 45.
124 Speer, *Slave State*, p. 301.
125 Herbert, *Hitler's Foreign Workers*, p. 3.
126 Ibid., p. 28.
127 Ibid., pp. 1, 133.
128 See below, p. 225.
129 For German women, see Herbert, *Hitler's Foreign Workers*, pp. 39–42. For German men mobilized, see Homze, *Foreign Labour*, p. 231.
130 Herbert, *Hitler's Foreign Workers*, p. 58.
131 Gitta Sereny, *Albert Speer: His Battle with Truth* (London, 1995), p. 332; Homze, *Foreign Labour*, pp. 100–1, 214.
132 Goldhagen, *Hitler's Willing Executioners*, pp. 291–2.
133 For Poles, see Homze, *Foreign Labour*, p. 23. For west, see Herbert, *Hitler's Foreign Workers*, p. 95. For Russians, see Homze, *Foreign Labour*, pp. 80, 83.
134 Ibid., pp. 75–6.
135 Ibid., pp. 23–4, 46.
136 Ibid., pp. 80–1, 83.
137 For east, see ibid., pp. 154–5. For west, see ibid., p. 186.
138 Herbert, *Hitler's Foreign Workers*, p. 1.
139 Ibid., pp. 72–3.
140 Ibid., pp. 163–6 (for Feb.); pp. 189–90 (for Aug.).
141 Homze, *Foreign Labour*, p. 264; Herbert, *Hitler's Foreign Workers*, p. 190.
142 Herbert, *Hitler's Foreign Workers*, pp. 82–3; ibid., pp. 200–1.
143 For Poles, see ibid., pp. 85–7. For Russia, see ibid., pp. 169–70. See ibid., pp. 279–81 for the deportations of 1943–4. For France, see Homze, *Foreign Labour*, pp. 186–8, 193–4; Herbert, *Hitler's Foreign Workers*, p. 274. See Homze, *Foreign Labour*, pp. 195–6 for deportations of 1944.
144 Ibid., pp. 107, 152–3.
145 For shop-floor brutality, see Herbert, *Hitler's Foreign Workers*, pp. 237–8. For effect of bombing raids, see ibid., pp. 205, 217–18.
146 Ibid., p. 95; Homze, *Foreign Labour*, pp. 47–8.
147 Homze, *Foreign Labour*, pp. 119, 264, 267; Herbert, *Hitler's Foreign Workers*, pp. 163–4, 210.
148 For labour education camps, see Herbert, *Hitler's Foreign Workers*, pp. 119–20, 123.
149 For punishing worker disobedience, see ibid., pp. 74, 190; Homze, *Foreign Labour*, pp. 122–3. For developing concentration camps as industrial plants, see Speer, *Slave State*, pp. 16–17, 49; Herbert, *Hitler's Foreign Workers*, p. 11; Homze, *Foreign Labour*, pp. 254–6.
150 Speer, *Slave State*, p. 47.
151 Ibid., ch. 15 (esp. pp. 210, 212).
152 Homze, *Foreign Labour*, pp. 123–4, 172; Herbert, *Hitler's Foreign Workers*, p. 324.
153 Herbert, *Hitler's Foreign Workers*, pp. 313–15; Homze, *Foreign Labour*, pp. 278–9, 284.

154 Herbert, *Hitler's Foreign Workers*, pp. 214–15, 315.
155 Ibid., pp. 322–3; Homze, *Foreign Labour*, pp. 267–8, 271.
156 Herbert, *Hitler's Foreign Workers*, pp. 237, 326, 329; Homze, *Foreign Labour*, pp. 253–4. For low productivity, see Homze, *Foreign Labour*, pp. 259–60; Herbert, *Hitler's Foreign Workers*, table 21 (p. 224).
157 Herbert, *Hitler's Foreign Workers*, pp. 331, 335, 338.
158 Ibid., pp. 340–4.
159 Ibid., pp. 358, 370–6.
160 S. G. Wheatcroft and R. W. Davies, 'Agriculture', *The Economic Transformation of the Soviet Union, 1913–1945*, ed. R. W. Davies, Mark Harrison and S. G. Wheatcroft (Cambridge, 1994), p. 117.
161 Bacon, *Gulag at War*, table 2.1 (p. 24).
162 Ibid., pp. 60–2, 73, 83. For the Gulag system, see ibid., ch. 4.
163 Ibid., table 2.1 (p. 24); John Barber and Mark Harrison, *The Soviet Home Front, 1941–1945* (London, 1991), pp. 169–70.
164 Stephen Nicholas and Peter R. Shergold, 'Transportation as global migration', *Convict Workers*, ed. Stephen Nicholas (Cambridge, 1988), pp. 36–7. Also see ibid., table 3.1 (p. 30).
165 Bacon, *Gulag at War*, p. 43.
166 Ibid., pp. 44–5.
167 Ibid., pp. 46–7.
168 Ibid., pp. 39, 49, 73–6; Robert Conquest, *The Great Terror: a Reassessment* (London, 1990), pp. 330–3.
169 For profitability, see David J. Dalin and Boris I. Nicolaevsky, *Forced Labour in Soviet Russia* (1947; repr. New York, 1974), pp. 88–9. For quotas, see Bacon, *Gulag at War*, pp. 50, 52; Dalin and Nicolaevksy, *Forced Labour*, p. 104.
170 For article 58, see Alexander Solzhenitsyn, *The Gulag Archipelago* (London, 1974), pp. 60–8.
171 Bacon, *Gulag at War*, p. 51.
172 Ibid., pp. 51–2.
173 Barber and Harrison, *Soviet Home Front*, p. 12; Bacon, *Gulag at War*, pp. 49, 62; S. G. Wheatcroft and R. W. Davies, 'Population' in Davies, Harrison and Wheatcroft (eds), *Economic Transformation*, pp. 68, 70.
174 Barber and Harrison, *Soviet Home Front*, p. 12; Wheatcroft and Davies, 'Population', pp. 69–70.
175 Dalin and Nicolaevsky, *Forced Labour*, p. 104.
176 Ibid., pp. 88–9.
177 Ibid., pp. 89–92.
178 Bacon, *Gulag at War*, p. 67; Conquest, *The Great Terror*, p. 323.
179 Bacon, *Gulag at War*, pp. 67–8; Dalin and Nicolaevsky, *Forced Labour*, pp. 102–3.
180 Bacon, *Gulag at War*, p. 69.
181 Dalin and Nicolaevsky, *Forced Labour*, pp. 100–1; Conquest, *The Great Terror*, pp. 333–9.
182 Bacon, *Gulag at War*, p. 126.
183 Dalin and Nicolaevsky, *Forced Labour*, pp. 100–1; Bacon, *Gulag at War*, p. 78; Conquest, *The Great Terror*, p. 322.
184 For troop call-up and falling population, see Barber and Harrison, *Soviet Home Front*, table 3 (p. 130). For war work of convicts, see Bacon, *Gulag at War*, pp. 134ff.
185 Ibid., p. 148.
186 Dalin and Nicolaevsky, *Forced Labour*, p. 105; Barber and Harrison, *Soviet Home Front*, pp. 117–19; Bacon, *Gulag at War*, ch. 7.
187 Bacon, *Gulag at War*, pp. 101, 103; Barber and Harrison, *Soviet Home Front*, pp. 116–17.

188 Barber and Harrison, *Soviet Home Front*, p. 118.
189 Bacon, *Gulag at War*, tables 2.1 (p. 24) and 2.3 (p. 30).
190 Ibid., table 2.1 (p. 24), p. 61; Barber and Harrison, *Soviet Home Front*, p. 118.
191 Bacon, *Gulag at War*, table 2.3 (p. 30).
192 Ibid., tables 2.1 (p. 24) and 2.3 (p. 30).
193 Jean Pierre Vaudon, 'Last days of the Gulag', *National Geographic*, 177 (March, 1990), pp. 40–9.

Index